D1561401

TILL THE
**DARK
ANGEL**
COMES

TILL THE DARK ANGEL COMES

COMES

Abolitionism and the Road to the
Second American Revolution

William S. King

WESTHOLME
Yardley

Westholme Publishing, LLC
904 Edgewood Road
Yardley, Pennsylvania 19067
Visit our Web site at www.westholmepublishing.com

First Printing December 2015
10 9 8 7 6 5 4 3 2 1
ISBN: 978-1-59416-238-1
Also available as an eBook.

Printed in the United States of America.

How cautiously most men sink into nameless graves, while now and then one forgets himself into immortality.

—Wendell Phillips

CONTENTS

1

The Mystic Spell of Africa

On the night of November 7, 1837, Elijah Parish Lovejoy, editor of the *Observer*, was shot and killed in Alton, Illinois, as he and other armed sympathizers guarded his printing press from threatened destruction at the hands of proslavery vigilantes. With Lovejoy's murder, the well-known abolitionist William Lloyd Garrison was to write in the *Liberator* that same month, the nation had been stirred in such a way as to "cause the foundation of the republic to tremble."

Originally from Maine, Elijah Lovejoy was a Presbyterian-trained minister who had settled in St. Louis, Missouri, and begun publishing a paper with an antipapist and antislavery editorial policy. Given the city's position in the upper South as a shipping center on the Mississippi River, vigorous opposition soon arose in St. Louis demanding the paper's abatement. When a black man was removed from jail and lynched, the editor responded with an article under the caption "Awful Murder and Savage Barbarity." A grand jury, convening to

investigate the lynching, was instructed by the judge to bring indictments against only a few of the individuals involved and blamed the
Observer, by the tenor of its articles, for inciting the mob. As Lovejoy
was in the process of moving across the river to a more amenable community in Alton, Illinois, proslavery men from St. Louis followed him
and destroyed his press.

Beginning publication again with a new press in September 1836, the
Observer continued for some months, gathering growing subscriptions.
In January of the following year an Illinois legislative committee,
responding to Southern demands that antislavery publications be suppressed, called upon the public to "firmly and powerfully rebuke" all
antislavery activity. With Lovejoy's activity continuing, a committee of
protest was formed headed by prominent citizens, and on August 27,
1837, Lovejoy's press was again destroyed. As a new press was brought
in from Cincinnati, it too was seized and tossed into the river. Obtaining
another, the editor armed himself, and with other armed sympathizers
guarded it in a warehouse through the night before it was to be installed.
With a proslavery mob surrounding the building threatening to set fire
to it, Lovejoy came out and was shot in the chest and killed.

The event shocked many in the North, and meetings of indignation
and protest were held in many places. In Boston, Garrison published an
account of Lovejoy's martyrdom edged in black, and editorialized that
the country seemed to be "diseased beyond the powers of recovery" by
slavery; while the Cincinnati *Journal Extra*'s headline shouted, "HORRID
TRAGEDY! BLOOD CRIETH!" The Reverend Dr. William Ellery Channing
applied to Boston's Board of Aldermen for the use of Faneuil Hall to
denounce the murder as an injury to free press and free speech, but the
request was rejected on the grounds that a meeting might become "a
scene of confusion which would be disreputable to the city and injurious to the glory of the consecrated Hall."[1]

It was evident city officials had bowed to pressure; as the *Liberator*
remonstrated, a crowd assembled protesting the action. When another
application was made it was announced the hall would open to memo-
rialize the martyr of Alton; and on the morning of December 8 five
thousand people packed into the public room. With a divided public,
but with only a handful of abolitionists present, all were poised to make
their response during the proceedings. Jonathan Phillips took the chair,
while Channing began a brief address; then resolutions were offered,
followed by another speaker.

As the last concluded, James Tricothic Austin, attorney general of
Massachusetts, thrust himself through the crowd with the intention of

disrupting the framework being proposed. There was a conflict in law between Missouri and Illinois, he maintained when reaching the platform, and he likened Lovejoy to one who would break the bars of slavery to let loose a menagerie of beasts to prowl the streets. Those who put him down, he said, were like the patriots who "threw the tea into Boston Harbor in 1776." Lovejoy had "died as the fool dieth"; he'd been "presumptuous and imprudent."

In the audience was the young kinsman of the chair, Harvard-trained lawyer Wendell Phillips, who had accompanied his wife and her cousin, Maria Weston Chapman. Phillips had come to the meeting prepared to take his place in the line of speakers, and as a roar of approval arose as Austin closed he seized the moment. Fashionably attired in a long surtout with a short cape, he was removing his outer garment as he started for the platform when his wife drew his arm back: "Wendell, what are you going to do?" "I am going to speak," he replied, "if I can make myself heard."[2]

Striding to the platform, he began: "Mr. Chairman—We have met for the freest discussion of these resolutions, and the events which gave rise to them." With calls filling the hall both encouraging him and to gag him, he continued: "I hope I shall be permitted to express my surprise at the sentiments of the last speaker—surprise not only at such sentiments from such a man, but at the applause they have received within these walls. A comparison has been drawn between the events of the Revolution and the tragedy at Alton. We have heard it asserted here, in Faneuil Hall, that Great Britain had a right to tax the Colonies, and we have heard the mob at Alton, the drunken murderers of Lovejoy, compared to those patriot fathers who threw the tea overboard! (Great applause.) Fellow-citizens, is this Faneuil Hall doctrine? ('No, no!')"[3]

Frederick Douglass forty-five years on would note the occasion and the Hall in his autobiography *Life and Times of Frederick Douglass*: It was in Faneuil Hall, he wrote, "that Mr. Phillips made his famous speech in denunciation of the murder of Elijah P. Lovejoy in 1837, which changed the whole current of his life, and made him pre-eminently the leader of antislavery thought in New England." This spontaneous utterance was to make Wendell Phillips famous and sound the keynote for his subsequent career.

After this coming out, Maria Chapman, eminent in Boston society and a principal in the Garrisonian antislavery school inaugurated earlier that decade, met with Phillips and persuaded him to stand full-time on the platform of the New England Anti-Slavery Society.

Elsewhere, too, meetings had been held in memorial and protest, like one in Franklin Mills (now Kent), Ohio, where a man in the audience—gaunt, tall, clean shaven, with piercing eyes, as he was described—seeing that the crisis he anticipated had come, now offered his vow: "Here, before God, in the presence of these witnesses, from this time, I consecrate my life to the destruction of slavery." That man was John Brown.

John Brown was born in Torrington in Litchfield County, Connecticut; when his father, Owen, was in his seventy-seventh year, he was asked by his daughter, Marian, to write a brief account of his life. Owen wrote in his narration, "In 1800, May 9 John was born one hundred years after his Great Grandfather, nothing else very uncommon."

After a treaty with Indians opened Ohio to settlement for Europeans, Owen Brown migrated with his family to the Western Reserve in the northeastern district, held especially for emigrants from Connecticut. It was a seven-week trek by ox-cart through primeval forests without roads; he wrote, "We had some hardships to undergo but they appear to be greater in history than are in reality."[4]

Years later in the pages of an autobiographical sketch John Brown wrote at the behest of twelve-year-old Henry Stearns, son of George Luther Stearns, the Boston merchant who became his most important supporter and confidant, he told of his days in the Ohio wilderness. In 1812, during the war with England when his father sold beef cattle to General William Hull's army on its retreat from Dayton to Detroit, "John," then himself twelve, drove these cattle one hundred miles. Telling what he saw of camp life and narrating his story in the third person, he wrote: "During this war he had some chance to form his own boyish judgment of *men & measures*: & to become somewhat familiarly acquainted with some who have figured before the country since that time. The effect of what he saw during the war was to so far disgust him with Military affairs that he would neither train, *or drill*; but paid fines; & got along like a Quaker until his age has finally cleared him of Military duty."[5]

As Brown stayed in the inn of a landlord one of the formative incidents of his life occurred at this time "that in the end made him a most *determined Abolitionist*: & led him to declare, or *Swear: Eternal war* with slavery." John Brown continues:

> He was staying for short time with a very gentlemanly landlord since a United States Marshall who held a slave boy near his own age very active, intelligent, & good feeling; & to whom John was under considerable obli-

gation for numerous little acts of kindness. *The Master* made a great pet of John: brought him to the table with his first company; & friends; called their attention to every little smart thing he *said or did*: & to the fact of his being more than a hundred miles from home with a company of cattle alone; while the *negro boy* (who was fully if not more than his equal) was badly clothed, poorly fed; & *lodged in cold weather*: & beaten before his eyes with Iron Shovels or any other thing that came first to hand. This brought John to reflect on the wretched, hopeless condition, of *Fatherless & Motherless* slave children: for such children have neither Fathers or Mothers to protect, & provide for them. He sometimes would raise the question: *is God their Father?*[6]

This is an unusual story in that slavery had been outlawed in Ohio at the time by the Northwest Ordinance of 1787, but shows it still existed, and as Frederick Douglass would point out, John Brown's story had obvious parallels to the biblical story of Moses, with which he of course was very familiar. Brown concluded his narrative with this advice for Henry:

> Now some of the things I have been *telling of*; were just such as I would recommend to you: & I would like to know what you had selected those out; & adopted them as part of your own plan of life; & I wish you to have some *definite plan*. Many seem to have none: & others never stick to any that do they form. This was not the case with John. He followed up with *tenacity* whatever he set about so long as it answered his general purpose: & hence he rarely failed in some good degree to effect the things he undertook. This was so much the case that he *habitually expected* to succeed in his undertakings. With this feeling *should be coupled*; the consciousness that our plans are right in themselves.[7]

James Russell Lowell, poet and educator, who would serve as editor of the *Atlantic Monthly* before serving as a diplomat, would call Brown's the finest piece of autobiography extant. After his early education at a school in Plainfield, Massachusetts, run by Rev. Moses Halleck, to prepare for Amherst and the ministry, would be curtailed because of chronic "eye inflammation," by his late teens Brown was foreman and cook in his father's tannery, keeping a bachelor apartment with his cousin. Mastering arithmetic, he became a surveyor, as well as learning animal husbandry; the rudiments of grammar and spelling he taught himself, acquiring his peculiar, albeit effective, punctuation and spelling. He married at twenty, and fathered seven children with Dianthe Lusk. As Brown wrote in his sketch, she was "*a remarkably plain*; but neat industrious & economical girl; of excellent character;

earnest piety; & good practical common sence [*sic*]; about one year younger than himself." By 1825, with his growing family, he made the first of many migrations, to Randolph, later called New Richmond, in Crawford County in northwestern Pennsylvania. Brown began a tannery on twenty-five acres he'd cleared with an abundance of oak and hemlock whose bark could be used in tanning. The tannery building measured 26 by 50 feet, built of native stone two feet thick. Receiving hides from the Western Reserve, he employed up to fifteen men, working twelve vats. He also built a log house and large barn with a secret compartment for fugitive slaves, and established a United States post office where he served as postmaster from 1828 to 1832.

John Brown would never be called "a man of books," but the reading he did do was closely held and he had a love of it. He had "Rollins' *Ancient History*, Josephus and Plutarch and lives of Napoleon and Cromwell," DuBois tells us in his *John Brown*, and he also had Baxter's *Saint's Rest*, Henry *On Meekness*, and *Pilgrim's Progress*. "But above all others," his daughter Ruth would relate in Franklin Sanborn's *Life and Letters of John Brown*, "the Bible was his favorite volume and he had such a perfect knowledge of it that when any person was reading he would correct the least mistake."[8]

Dianthe, suffering torments that deranged her mind, died in childbirth in 1832, while in the previous year the couple had lost a four-year-old son. In 1833 Brown was again married, to Mary Ann Day, a girl of seventeen while he was then thirty-three. In 1843 four of their children would be swept away; and in 1846 and 1859 two infant girls were lost, and a boy in 1852. Five of Brown's children survived from his first marriage—John Jr., Jason, Owen, Salmon, Frederick, and Ruth—and Mary would bear thirteen, seven of whom died young; of these, two sons and four daughters would grow to maturity. Three of Brown's sons would predecease their father; Frederick killed in Kansas, and Oliver and Watson at Harpers Ferry.

His daughter Ruth would relate in Sanborn's volume:

> Father used to hold all his children while they were little at night and sing his favorite songs. The first recollection I have of father was being carried through a piece of woods on Sunday to attend a meeting held at a neighbor's house. After we had been at the house a little while, father and mother stood up and held us, while the minister put water on our faces. After we sat down father wiped my face with a brown silk handkerchief with yellow spots on it in diamond shape. It seemed beautiful to me and I thought how good he was to wipe my face with that pretty handkerchief. He showed a great deal of tenderness in that and other ways. He some-

times seemed very stern and strict with me, yet his tenderness made me forget he was stern. . . . When he would come home at night tired out with labor, he would before going to bed, ask some of the family to read chapters (as was his usual course night and morning); and would almost always say: "Read one of David's Psalms."9

To an onlooker these are ceaseless changing years for John Brown, both in youth and maturity; he lived in Hudson, Franklin Mills, and Richfield in Ohio, and then in Pennsylvania, and later in Massachusetts and New York. Many have seen the mark of adversity and failure settling on his affairs, but also, it must be said, that of a man struggling to master the adversity of a frontier with an uncertain economy. A man who worked for him in Pennsylvania said, "It became almost a proverb that Speaking of an enterprising man, 'He was as enterprising and as honest as John Brown.'"10 But the supply of hides for the tannery was too far away, his markets too distant for economical transport, and the business collapsed. Returning to Ohio with the prospect of a new tannery in Portage County, instead he became contractor for the Ohio and Pennsylvania Canal from Franklin Mills to Akron. Engaging in land development in the Franklin Mills area with $20,000, he was caught in the Panic of 1837, as financial crises were then called, and his properties assigned to creditors. Brown would never really recover his footing after this episode; canals soon were to be bypassed in their economic importance by railroads. His next enterprise was in wool, but he would take before that a brief turn at breeding race horses. His son, John Jr., argued him out of the business, pointing out it was an enterprise for "slaveholders and gamblers."11

John Brown's eldest son, only twenty-one years his junior, set out as a schoolteacher in his earliest endeavor. The father wrote about its challenges in a letter in 1841 that again became an item in Sanborn's volume:

I think the situation in which you have been placed by Providence at this early period of your life will afford to yourself and others some little test of the sway you may be expected to exert over minds in after life, and I am glad on the whole to have you brought in some measure to the test in your youth. If you cannot now go into a disorderly country school and gain its confidence and esteem, and reduce it to good order and waken up the energies and the very soul of every rational being in it—yes, of every mean, ill-behaved, ill-governed boy and girl that compose it, and secure the good-will of the parents,—then how are you to stimulate asses to attempt a passage of the Alps? If you run with footmen and they should weary you, how should you contend with horses? If in the land of peace they have wearied you, then how will you do in the swelling of Jordan? Shall I answer the question myself? "If any man lack wisdom, let him ask of God, who giveth liberally and upbraideth not."[12]

W. E. B. DuBois, at the opening of his biography *John Brown*, published in 1909, wrote: "The mystic spell of Africa is and ever was over all America." A spell it was whose influence was binding, not only on the republic created from the former colonies of Great Britain, but on the fated life of this protagonist as well. In the same year he was born, several writers have pointed out, in Southampton County, Virginia, another child was born who would grow up to give him much to ponder and contemplate: the man known as Nat Turner. That year also saw the formidable plot near Richmond of the slave Gabriel; a year, too, in which Toussaint L'Ouverture, at the head of the Black Revolution in St. Domingue in the eastern part of the island of Hispaniola, later named Hayti, held sway. Until 1802, when Napoleon sent twenty thousand troops, who would capture L'Ouverture and bring him to France, where he would die in a dungeon while the First Counsel of the republic crowned himself emperor.

In the following year, 1803, surprisingly Napoleon would relinquish France's holdings on the North American continent, the Louisiana Territory, after the American president, Thomas Jefferson made overtures about acquiring the city of New Orleans. These events unleashed for the coming years—aided by the invention in the previous decade of the cotton engine, or the so-called cotton gin—a newly burgeoning cotton culture in the Atlantic states of the Old South; to begin its westward expansion into the newly opened Gulf States, with an equally burgeoning black slave population.

In 1808 the chronicle continued as the U.S. Congress prohibited the Atlantic slave trade, banning the importation of new slaves into the country after that year. This would, however, only become effective when enforcement legislation was passed in 1820, when the Missouri Compromise allowed slavery into Missouri, while prohibiting it in the remaining territory of the Louisiana Purchase north of its border. This enactment the aging founder and former president Thomas Jefferson heard as a "fire bell in the night."

In 1822, Charleston, South Carolina, would experience the aftereffects of the crushing of an attempted insurrection of slaves and freemen working as carters, draymen, sawyers, porters, laborers, stevedores, mechanics, and those working in lumber yards and waterfront rice mills, together with slaves from rice and cotton plantations, led by Denmark Vesey. In the year prior to this formidable but aborted plot, John Brown had married his first wife and started a family. This wife would die the year following the slave rebellion that is still confounding to many today—Nat Turner's Rebellion. While struggling to support and raise his growing family, John Brown could but have noted these events, as they certainly will be seen later stirring his mind, as they were stirring the minds of other men, black as well as white. "Something was forcing the issue," DuBois would write, "—call it what you will, the Spirit of God or the spell of Africa." This issue was becoming strongly woven into the fabric and into the vitality of the new nation, and into the frame of this man and of his family, as indicated here.

In 1776 the father of John Brown's father had been called into service with the Continental army in New York, as John Brown's father, Owen, told it. His fields hadn't yet been plowed, and there was scarcely a man left in their part of Connecticut who could be called upon to do the work undone. "When I was a child four or five years old," wrote Owen Brown in 1850, "one of the nearest neighbors had a slave that was brought from Guinea." He continues:

> In August, our good neighbor, Captain John Fast, of West Simsbury, let my mother have the labor of his slave to plough a few days. I used to go out into the field with this slave,—called Sam,—and he used to carry me on his back, and I fell in love with him. He worked but a few days, and went home sick with the pleurisy, and died very suddenly. When told that he would die, he said he should go to Guinea, and wanted victuals put up for the journey. As I recollect, this was the first funeral I ever attended in the days of my youth.[13]

As old Africa waned in the midst of the United States as the century grew, its children faced a future without parallel in recorded annals: a life of unremitting bondage that would rule from Maryland's Eastern Shore clear through Virginia into the Carolinas and Georgia, from Florida to the Mississippi River and beyond, from the Gulf of Mexico to the northern border of Missouri. From the first day African bondage was introduced at Jamestown in Virginia in 1619, together with one hundred pauper children intended as indentured servants, one might presume there were those, and not just the enslaved, who looked upon it with horror. In the Revolutionary period many thought its existence might be interned in the new republic being founded, but to assure union and to knit the colonies into states, compromises would be struck which entered the Constitution of 1787: notably the three-fifths clause, which would apportion political power on the basis of the slave population counting as less than full persons; the provision to recover absconding fugitives, who were fleeing into Spanish Florida and existing as maroons in remote swamps and backcountry; as it pledged the military power of the United States to put down an insurrection of slaves. On this basis in succeeding decades, with the development of the cotton crop and the conquest of new land in the west, slavery became a world-determining force: whatever compunctions there may have been were now to be sidestepped.

Still under the humanitarian influence of the Revolutionary era, Vermont became the first of the states to abolish slavery at the end of eighteenth century. This would follow in all states of the so-called North, and conclude by the second decade of the nineteenth century. This manumission was gradual and began to be coupled with schemes for the colonization of the freed people. By 1816 the American Colonization Society would be in operation, leading to the founding of Liberia on the Atlantic coast of Africa, and would, for several decades, attract leading and powerful political support, including the venerable Henry Clay of Kentucky, who became one of the presidents of the society.

As the growing political and economic power vested in slavery became evident, a new response began to be configured in the North where slavery had been eradicated. The *Genius of Universal Emancipation*, published by Benjamin Lundy, had struggled through a number of iterations with only a few subscribers, first established in Ohio, then relocating in Tennessee and finally in Maryland, in Baltimore. Joining Lundy in Baltimore as editorial partner was a twenty-two-year-old zealot and printer from Newburyport, Massachusetts, named William Lloyd Garrison. The two had met in Boston when Lundy was visiting, and the younger man had been immensely impressed by his Quaker simplicity and his devotion to a cause that was assuming great importance for him. Before joining Lundy, like predominant opinion at that time, Garrison espoused a gradualist emancipation reform, along with support for colonization. But with the evangelism that had swept the country in the 1820s the idea of *immediatism* based on repentance came to the fore, and in the coming decades would become the central tenet of Garrisonian abolitionism. In Baltimore, too, Garrison would associate with many of the city's free blacks, and out of this experience and their discussions he would come to repudiate colonization.

Forthright advocacy of these positions in the pages of *Genius* soon brought Garrison into court as he was sued for libel by a slaveholder and was jailed when he could not pay the fine. After forty-nine days the fine would be paid by the New York philanthropist Arthur Tappan, and Garrison returned to Boston, his sojourn in Baltimore seemingly yielding failure. In retrospect, however, that now seems to be anything but the case, as on January 1, 1831, Garrison began publication of the *Liberator*, espousing immediate emancipation without compensation to slaveholders, and without colonization of the freed blacks.

Again his initial subscriptions were few, and his prospects apparently obscure. But in August of that year Nat Turner struck to obtain freedom for blacks, as whites had done against the British to get theirs, and the *Liberator* garnered new significance as officials in Virginia and editorialists throughout the South clamored to have Garrison's print suppressed. These fulminations also brought forth an obscure book published in 1829, also in Boston, by a free black named David Walker. This book bore the title *Appeal to the Coloured Citizens of the World*, and its author wrote that if the abomination of slavery were rightly understood, "one continual cry would be raised in all parts of the confederacy and would cease only with the complete overthrow of the system of slavery, in every part of the country." Avenues were now explored to bring these to account, and suppress the publications, while they were banned in the South. Walker had died in obscurity, it is conjectured in a murder, prior to this; while Boston's mayor, Harrison Otis, was frantically implored to silence the nuisance editor, whom he'd scarcely been aware of.

Faced with these exigencies and seeing the necessity for a more thorough organization of their activities, fifteen men met in a lawyer's office in Boston in November 1831. It was essential, they agreed, that a society be formed to further their ideas with a public. Out of this meeting the New England Anti-Slavery Society was formed on the program of immediatism. Seventy-two names were affixed to the constitution of the new society, a few coming from the city's prominent lists, but most from more ordinary ranks, while nearly twenty were from among Boston's free blacks.

Garrison and his coadjutors, particularly those in New York and Philadelphia, began preparing to take national action. When the First Annual Convention of People of Colour met in Philadelphia on June 1, 1831, Garrison and Lundy and Arthur Tappan were among the invited guests. In its sessions, joined by a number of Philadelphia Quakers, they discussed plans that included a national antislavery society.

Concerted effort for such, however, would be deferred for a time due to the eruption of the Turner revolt in Southampton, which many abolitionists found disconcerting, and by disagreements arising among whites about admitting blacks on equal terms. While the Garrison branch of the society did admit blacks, some of the conversant wondered if that might mean the society would demand equal voting rights for them as well. Only the signal change coming with Britain's West Indian Emancipation would compel these groups to call for a convention in Philadelphia to organize an American Anti-Slavery Society.

That gathering in Philadelphia in December 1833 would draw sixty-two persons; of them twenty-one were Quakers, including two women, and three of the signers of the society's constitution were black: James Barbadoes, Robert Purvis, and James McCrummell. Garrison, Samuel May, and John Greenleaf Whittier drew up a "Declaration of Sentiments," a document stating they were uniting to complete the unfinished work of the American Revolution. The patriots who had spilled their blood "like water in order to be free" had grievances that "were trifling in comparison to those of the slaves." But the abolitionists declared they would renounce "all carnal weapons for deliverance from bondage" and seek "the destruction of error by the potency of truth—the overthrow of prejudice by the power of love—and the abolition of slavery by the spirit of repentance." They would, too, demand the immediate, uncompensated abolition of slavery without colonization; seeking "to secure to the colored population of the United States, all the rights and privileges which belong to them as men and as Americans."[14]

The declaration went on to announce that all laws supporting slavery were "before God utterly null and void," but conceded that Congress "under the present compact" had no power to interfere with slavery in any state. It did, however, have the power to legislate on the domestic slave trade and to abolish slavery in the territories and in the District of Columbia.

How does John Brown stand when viewed against this background of the modern antislavery movement in the antebellum period? Many writers have asserted he had no relation to it, never joined an antislavery society, and was scarcely known to its meetings. The truth can be met by referring to his words as cited from his autobiographical sketch, and in his letters, and letters of members of his family, from which a portrait can be drawn. John Brown's eldest son wrote:

> When I was four or five years old, and probably no later than 1825, there came one night a fugitive slave and his wife to father's door—sent,

perhaps, by some townsman who knew John Brown's compassion for such wayfarers, then but few. They were the first colored people I had seen; and when the woman took me upon her knee and kissed me, I ran away as quick as I could, and rubbed my face "to get the black off"; for I thought she would "crock" me, like mother's kettle. Mother gave the poor creatures some supper; but they thought themselves pursued and were uneasy. Presently father heard the trampling of horses crossing a bridge on one of the main roads, half a mile off; so he took his guests out the back door and down into the swamp near the brook to hide, giving them arms to defend themselves, but returning to the house to await the event. It proved a false alarm; the horse men were people of the neighborhood going to Hudson village. Father then went out into the dark wood,—for it was night,—and had some difficulty in finding his fugitives; finally he was guided to the spot by the sound of the man's heart throbbing for fear of capture. He brought them into the house again, sheltered them a while, and sent them on their way.[15]

In 1833, the year Prudence Crandall's school was shut in Connecticut and the building burned because she had admitted black girls, Brown wrote his brother Frederick:

Since you have left me, I have been trying to devise some means whereby I might do something in a practical way for my poor fellow men who are in bondage; and having fully consulted the feelings of my wife and my three boys, we have agreed to get at least one Negro boy or youth, and bring him up as we do our own,—viz., give him a good English education, learn him what we can about the history of the world, about business, about general subjects, and above all, try to teach him the fear of God.... I have for years been trying to devise some way to get a school a-going here for blacks, and I think that on many accounts it would be a most favorable location. Children here would have no intercourse with vicious people of their own kind, nor with openly vicious persons of any kind.[16]

John Jr. also tells of an incident happening about 1837 when the Brown family joined the Congregational Church in Franklin Mills. A revival was being held and the church was selected, it being the largest, where a general meeting would be convened. Invitations were sent to adjoining towns, and soon the church was crowded and every pew occupied. A number of free blacks and fugitives slaves came and were given seats by themselves by the door. Noticing this, his son related, in the evening when the next meeting began John Brown arose "and called attention to the fact that, in seating the colored portion of the audience, a discrimination had been made, and said that he did not believe God 'is a respecter of persons.'" He then invited the blacks to occupy his family's pew, which they accepted, and the Brown family took their vacated seats.

Soon after this the family moved to Hudson, only three miles away, becoming regular attendants at another congregational church. A letter then arrived informing Mr. Brown that "any member being absent a year without reporting him or herself to that church should be cut off." John Jr. wrote: "This was the first intimation we had of the existence of the rule. Father, on reading the letter, became white with anger. This was my first taste of the pro-slavery diabolism that had intrenched [sic] itself in the church, and I shed a few uncalled for tears over the matter, for instead I should have rejoiced in my emancipation. From that day my theological shackles were a good deal broken, and I have not worn them since (to speak of),—not even for ornament."[17]

The year 1837 was also that of Lovejoy's murder, when, as related, John Brown arose at a public memorial to "declare or *Swear: Eternal war* with slavery," as he wrote. Nominally at this time he was a nonresistor, having a "disgust with Military affairs" and getting "along like a Quaker." But he and Garrison each have come to personify the antithesis of the other, and Brown would soon begin to evince his characteristic contempt for the moral-suasion school of abolitionism, and as DuBois remarks, would never visit the offices of the *Liberator* when he was in Boston. There is evidence that Brown began a study of the historical precedents for carrying out a war on slavery at this time. These included the slave revolts, particularly in the United States and in Haiti and Jamaica. There was no better example for the efficacy of armed resistance to be found than that of the maroons on the island of Jamaica. Oratorical philanthropy had played an important part in Britain's recent West Indian emancipation, but as Brown and others had seen, it had occurred largely too because it had been concluded the maroons were militarily unconquerable. Closer to home, Brown naturally began to assess the strategic importance of the Allegheny range. To his cousin Rev. Edward Brown, near whom he lived in Hudson, Ohio, he "often remarked that, with a good leader, the slaves escaping to those fastnesses and fortifying themselves, could compel emancipation."[18]

In the South so abundant was land it could be purchased for a "pepper-corn," it was said, or as the saying goes, "for a song." In Maryland and Virginia the crop best suited to its soil and conditions was tobacco; on the South Carolina and Georgia coasts, rice and later indigo were grown; and all three were planted in various parts of North Carolina.

None of these, however, could be cultivated and marketed to benefit except at considerable scale. While all over the South "short staple" or "upland" cotton was grown in small quantities, the prime difficulty for a successful planter lay in the shortage of labor.

"It is supposed," wrote Frederic Bancroft in *Slave Trading in the Old South*, "that in all the continental colonies there were about 75,000 slaves in 1725, a little more than 250,000 in 1750 and about 500,000 in 1776."[19] Down to the Revolutionary period most slave trading was in persons of African origin, and in those brought in from the West Indies. Shipments came directly into Charleston and Savannah, but Northern ports were also used for transshipment to regions where the Africans were expected to work. This trade enabled the building up of large estates, particularly in Virginia and South Carolina; the richest man in all the colonies, Gabriel Manigault, died in 1781 leaving an estate in South Carolina of 43,532 acres and 490 slaves. By 1861, Charleston was the richest city per capita in the United States. In the few years prior to the banning of the international trade, 40,000 enslaved individuals were rushed into Charleston in anticipation of prohibition. Bancroft estimates despite the closing of the foreign trade upward of 250,000 persons were imported into the United States from Africa and the West Indian islands between 1808 and 1861.

At the turn of the century Maryland and Virginia held the balance of slaves. As further importation was cut off, planters in the Carolinas and Georgia were eager to obtain these; while their owners were eager to maintain the value of their property. Thus an interstate trade came into existence, one that had already been demonstrated in the pioneer territory opening in Kentucky and Tennessee. This would continue into territory that would become Alabama and Mississippi. Still, all this would have been negligible but for an invention.

A bale of cotton, about 375-400 pounds, took a single hand one year's labor to prepare, making it far too expensive for making fabric for common use. Because of its lower expense in seeding, and because it had shown superiority for making fabric, the "long-staple" or "sea-island" cotton grown in South Carolina and Georgia began to attract attention. Eli Whitney, a New Englander with a natural propensity for solving mechanical problems, was in South Carolina to teach school when the conundrum came to his attention. His "saw-gin," patented in 1793, was a revolving cylinder with sawteeth which drew cotton through a fine screen, separating the seeds from the lint. Now a single person turning a hand-gin could accomplish as much as one hundred times the work as previously, and a machine harnessed to a horse could handle up to a thousand pounds in a day. As the obstacles to the economic exploitation of cotton vanished, in the decade after Whitney's invention came into use, the crop was to increase thirty-five-fold. By 1820 it had been demonstrated that the plant could flourish in "the alluvial belt of Alabama, Mississippi and Louisiana."[20] But as miraculous as the machine appeared, it did not increase the amount of cotton a single person could cultivate. For that the heavy hoe, and the horse-drawn, or ox- or mule-drawn plow, were still necessary. To prosper a planter needed to continually add to the lands under cultivation, make extensive clearings, and add new hands. The invention contributed immeasurably to the South's economy, but it would not have become what it did, unless it drew on an interstate trade in slaves.

By 1840 a yield of more than two million bales was produced. The area under intensive cultivation—ranging through South Carolina and Georgia, the agricultural parts of Florida, through the fertile parts of Alabama, Mississippi, and northern Louisiana, and from western Tennessee into parts of Arkansas—produced 2,867,000 cotton bales in 1849. With the acquisition of Texas the crop would rise to 4,861,000 bales in 1860. Concomitantly, James D. B. De Bow, editor of the influential *Commercial Review of the South and West* published in New Orleans, popularly known as De Bow's Review, estimated there were 800,000 slaves and 100,000 white laborers raising cotton in 1840; by 1850 the number committed to the crop's cultivation—clearing, plowing, seeding, hoeing, picking and ginning, and bringing it to market—was over 1,800,000. By 1860 the number was 2,225,000, and the price of slaves doubled, and then trebled.

In 1860 a slave trader from Virginia, W. A. J. Finney, was able to mark-up the following table for slaves (figures now part of the display in the Old Slave Mart Museum in Charleston):

Extra men	$1,500–1,600
Number one men	$1,400–1,500
Second rate	$1,100–1,250
Extra women	$1,325–1,400
Number one girls	$1,275–1,325
Second rate girls	$800–1,100

Men sold by traders were commonly referred to as "bucks" and women were "wenches." So-called "fancy girls," or prospective concubines, were openly sold, but more than any other places, Lexington, Kentucky, and New Orleans specialized in these, giving both an air of licentiousness. Still Bancroft notes, "There was hardly anything more obvious about slave trading than the fact that slaves, no two being alike, could not be standardized and quoted in market reports like stocks, bonds, hogs, poultry, potatoes, hides or sugar. Personal and physical elements, ever-varying but hardly perceptible to strangers, were often very important, and chance entered into nearly every purchase."[21]

Slaves were held in jails or pens until sold, so-called "nigger jails," and "slave pens," where they would be "groomed" and examined for sale, often being fed better to fatten them while held, while "boys" were urged to step lively, hair colored to remove the gray, bodies oiled to show luster and let the musculature stand out, perspective "fancy girls" bidden to turn their backsides, while scars from whippings were seen as a sign of a slave's intransigence.

Persons for sale would commonly stand on an auction block before bidders—traders, agents, slaveholders themselves; many would be presented in ordinary clothing, while others wore better, the difference between field hands and servants, while some were partially stripped of clothing and some wholly naked. There was ever the possibility of families being broken; husbands sold away from wives, wives from husbands, mothers and fathers from their children; while "single" adult age slaves were considered as devoid of family as a mule or a steer. To recognize marriage rights would have "gravely interfered with property rights."[22] Many families were sold as a unit intact, as many slaveholders desired to appear humane. Slaves sold in the upper South faced the dreaded prospect of being sold into the Deep South and the lasting separation of sister from brother, sister from sister, brother from brother. While apologists for the trade claim the South was often sentimental in this regard, there was ever the certainty an owner's gain would take priority.

When slaves were sold they would be transported in coffles over the road, or on barges or flatboats, on steamboats, on trains and sailing vessels, from centers of sale, in Baltimore, Richmond, Charleston, Savannah, New Orleans, Memphis, Lexington, or Galveston, and scores of lesser towns like Natchez, to the places where they would be utilized. The trade in the east would see slaves transported down the coast to Florida and over to the gulf to reach New Orleans; from Richmond they might be sold into Kentucky and Tennessee; from Charleston and Savannah they moved through Georgia and into Alabama, filling Mississippi and the entire river valley with slaves, while they were transported up and down the river and all its tributaries, as the city of St. Louis became a center for the trade in Missouri and Arkansas.

Evidence of this trade includes the following in the *Gazette and Virginia Advertiser*, September 30, 1860, from Alexandria, Virginia:

WANTED TO PURCHASE FIFTEEN OR TWENTY YOUNG NEGROES, of both sexes, for my own use, to take to Arkansas, for which the highest cash prices will be paid. Any communication addressed to me, at Warrenton, Va., will receive prompt attention.—D.B. Fisher.

And this in the *National Intelligencer*, August 19, 1833:

NEGROES WANTED.—A GENTLEMAN from the South wishes to purchase 40 or 50 effective Slaves, of good character, for his own service, and among them it is desirable to have a blacksmith, carpenter, coachman, and a man cook. His address is with the Editor of the Alexandria Gazette.—Wash., D.C.

While in the North, in Lowell and Lawrence, Massachusetts, in Pawtucket and Woonsocket, Rhode Island, large mills had been set up for the manufacture of wool cloth. This wool was passed through sets of rollers, revolving at different speeds, and was drawn out before it passed to a spindle which gave the fabric a twist, and from this "spinning jenny" it went to a "water-frame," or later the hybrid of the machine called a mule, when yarn was woven into fabric. Developed in the previous century in Great Britain, roller spinning of yarn, be it wool, flax, or cotton, was able to transform the methods for producing cloth, and associated with new forms of power—water and then steam—large-scale economy, with large concerns and integrated processes could be introduced employing thousands of "hands," the mechanics and millwrights, the supervisory staff and the management, and all the ancillary businesses and workers to support these. With them came new machinery, and new processes, and the roads and bridges, the canals and railways to transport products and bring them to market.

It was on the basis of cheap calicoes made of cotton that the first stage of this new industrialism was built.[23] And this vast new industry in textiles stood squarely on African slavery in the American South as its pedestal: on it a world market depended. "Cotton is king," it was proclaimed; as there developed complex relations of finance between Southern slaveholders and Northern bankers, with banks and insurance companies holding mortgages on slaves, and merchants invested in all aspects of the emerging "peculiar institution," as it was called. "Direct slavery," the economist Karl Marx wrote in 1847, "is just as much the pivot of bourgeois industry as machinery, credits, etc."[24]

What kind of labor is it that creates the value sought by capitalist and slaveholder alike? asked Marx. His answer appears paradoxical; it is not the labor of a particular person in a given manner—be it a blacksmith, a weaver, a dock worker, or a slave turning a saw-gin—but labor in the *abstract* that creates value. Value is created, he writes, "by abstract universal labor that belongs to a certain organization of society."[25] This reification is brought about because labor must be "socially necessary" to create value, it must be performed at a given time and in given conditions—a slave, for example, operating a saw-gin and not separating cotton seed from fiber by hand—and that work is measured by a clock, and thus is standardized and comparable to all other commodities produced in the same mode, regardless of their nature. It is this act that transforms *concrete labor* into *abstract labor* to make it quantitative for comparison. It is this that allows human labor to be transmuted into gold.

The difference between slave labor and free wage labor, Marx pointed out, essentially is that in the latter case all the workers' labor-time appears compensated, while in the former all labor-time appears as unpaid. In the one instance the money relation conceals the labor of the worker for the capitalist; in the other the property relation conceals the labor of the slave for himself. Both, however, produce surplus labor or surplus value or profit: the one for the owner of the means of production, and the other for the owner of the slave's very existence. It is the worker, in the free-labor system as it was called, that is affected by the advantage or disadvantage as compared to the average (the socially necessary time), while it was the owner in the slave-labor system who was affected by this comparison to the average. The price put on a slave was the expected profit "to be ground out of him."[26] Nonetheless, wrote Marx, "It is characteristic in the determination of the minimum wage or the natural price of labor, that it is lower for the free wage-laborer than for the slave."[27]

It was this difference within labor and its product that allowed gold, or money, to assume the position as universal equivalent for all things. Hence value is not a thing, but a social relationship. Marx could not have developed this critique of the "labor theory of value" as articulated by classical political economy without the contemporaneous display of free as against slave labor. The concept of labor in the abstract, "as average socially necessary time," was entirely a product of history. Marx wrote, "This example of labor shows strikingly how even the most abstract categories, despite their validity—precisely because of their abstractness—for all epochs, are nevertheless, in the specific character of this abstraction, themselves likewise a product of historic relations, and possess their full validity only for and within these relations."[28] This was the keystone for the development of all other categories in

Marx's inquiry and its presentation. And these are derived from the actual movement of the method.[29] This was the presupposition of Marx's critique developed in these crucial decades. But despite its importance to the world market and to the parturition of industrial capitalism, without which they would not exist—slavery, Marx held, was an anomaly.

With the African slave trade excised in the United States and with the demand for fresh hands created by an expanding cotton economy in the Southwest, it became obvious that this supply could only be maintained by the rearing of slaves in the older and now unprofitable sections, for sale into those where the demand was high.[30] In the extended debate in the Virginia legislature on the gradual abolition of slavery in the winter of 1831–32 in the aftermath of the Nat Turner rebellion, one of the disputants, Jesse Burton Harrison, said the following, even as he was supporting the proposition:[31]

> The only form in which it can safely be said that slaves on a plantation are profitable in Virginia, is in the multiplication of their number by births. If the proprietor, beginning with a certain number of negroes, can but keep them for a few years from the hands of the sheriff or the slave trader, though their labour may have yielded him not a farthing of net revenue, he finds that gradually but surely, his capital stock of negroes multiplies itself, and yields, if nothing else, a palpable interest of young negroes.... The process of multiplication will not in this way advance the master towards the point of a nett revenue; he is not the richer in income with the fifty slaves than with twenty. Yet these young negroes have their value: and what value? The value of the slaves so added to his number is the certain price for which they will at any time sell to the southern trade. ... An account, on which we may rely, sets down the annual number of slaves sold to go out of the State at six thousand, or more than half the number of births! ... And will "the aspiring blood of Lancaster" endure it to be said that a Guinea is still to be found in America, and that Guinea is Virginia?

In his letter to his brother Frederick of November 21, 1834, detailing his proposal to his family "to get a Negro boy or youth, and bring him up as our own," John Brown wrote further, "This has been with me a favorite theme for reflection for years." At first his ideas for affecting slavery had a broad philanthropic and educational thrust. "If the young blacks of our country," he wrote, "could once become enlightened, it would most assuredly operate on slavery like firing powder confined in rock, and all slaveholders know it well." But Brown was moving beyond these strictures. There had been a constant series of attacks on abolitionist meetings throughout the North that had not gone unobserved by him, accompanied by a virulent anti-Negro sentiment. Then in 1836, after being flooded for years with petitions for emancipation in the District of Columbia, James Hammond, a representative from South Carolina, moved that the House refuse to receive these petitions, while John C. Calhoun, representing the same state in the Senate, introduced a similar resolution. They reasoned that if Congress barred anti-slavery petitions, abolitionist voices would be stilled in the national forum, severely handicapping them and securing the future of slavery. But these motions stirred as much controversy as slavery itself, and Martin Van Buren, Jackson's heir apparent, and Henry L. Pinckney, a prominent Southern Democrat, worked out an alternative measure. Known as the "gag rule," the Pinckney resolution provided that all petitions relating to slavery would be laid on the table without being referred to committee or printed. This resolution was to be readopted by Congress in each subsequent session until its repeal on December 2, 1844.

Contending the rule was a direct violation of the Constitution, John Quincy Adams, then a representative from Massachusetts, was imperiled with expulsion to silence him for his "impudence." In his first anti-slavery speech in a meeting of the Massachusetts Anti-Slavery Society, Wendell Phillips rose to Adams's defense: "I have said, Mr. President, that we owe gratitude to Mr. Adams for his defense of the right of petition. A little while ago it would have been absurd to talk of gratitude being due to any man for such a service…. But it is true that, now, even for this we ought to be grateful. And this fact is another, a melancholy proof of the stride which the influence of slavery has made within a few years. It throws such dimness over the minds of freemen that what would once have been thought the alphabet of civil right, they hail as a discovery."[32]

So accustomed had the North become to the standing reality of slavery, that the region was becoming numb to its influence. John Brown's wife was to remark that her husband never took an active part nor cared about politics or parties after the presidency of Andrew Jackson, seeing that the essential component on the national scene was in the actual collisions between slavery and freedom. In the following year his sensibility had been further shocked by the outrage of Lovejoy's murder, and the issue began to turn in new ways in his mind. Then Pennsylvania Hall in Philadelphia was burned, days after the wedding of Theodore Weld and Angelina Grimké, and soon after Marlborough Chapel in Boston was sacked, where DuBois surmises John Brown had been present and had taken part in battling the mob. That there could be peaceful emancipation in the United States was plainly being shown to be a fallacy; slaveholders must be compelled to emancipate, or it would not happen in the lifetime of those currently engaged in the project. What is more, slavery had become so powerful it now threatened constitutional liberty and republican government. John Brown had reached a turning point in his life; he would become the bane of slavery. DuBois wrote:

> It was in 1839, when a Negro preacher named Fayette was visiting Brown, and bringing his story of persecution and injustice, that this great promise was made. Solemnly John Brown arose; he was then a man of nearly forty years, tall, dark and clean-shaven; by him sat his young wife of twenty-two and his oldest boys of eighteen, sixteen and fifteen. Six other children slept in the room back of the preacher. John Brown told them of his purpose to make active war on slavery, and bound his family in solemn and secret compact to labor for emancipation. And then, instead of remaining standing to pray, as was his wont, he fell upon his knees and implored God's blessing on his enterprise.[33]

John Brown acquired his abhorrence of slavery from his father, as he had his religious faith, as we have seen. Of Calvinist lineage, he was, as he wrote in his autobiographical sketch, "a firm believer in the divine authenticity of the Bible," holding to divine sovereignty and human depravity. Brown's God was that of the Old Testament, many have remarked: righteous and wrathful, a God moreover who bestowed providential direction on the chosen. As he brooded and prayed for guidance as he approached his fortieth year he came to believe he was God's chosen instrument by which slavery would be destroyed in America. Many who would hear him voice this in subsequent decades were astonished, but were deeply impressed by his earnestness and conviction. Thomas Wentworth Higginson would remark nearly two decades later that he would never forget "the quaint way" Brown told him, too, that the Allegheny mountain ranges had been created out of the foundation of the world, thrusting as they did into the heart of slavery, so that they might become a refuge for fugitive slaves. All of this, John Brown believed, had been determined in eternity.

Such was the faith that girded this man. But John Brown, too, was of the lineage of the War of the Revolution, as it was then often called. Both his grandfathers fought in it, and he imbibed the faith of his father's fathers as imparted by the Spirit of 1776; esteeming alike the Declaration of Independence and the Sermon on the Mount. He referred to Christ as his master, calling him "the captain of liberty." A faith and a man that reached in the profoundest way into the benighted people cast through the southern states of the republic: a dark brooding humanity that also responded out of its depths to this same Hebraic faith.

Before Garrison, leading abolitionists were mostly orthodox in their religion, indeed many were clergy; among the Quakers they were overtly devout. But other than their antislavery views there often wasn't much to distinguish them from others of the community. The total membership of the various state and regional abolition societies throughout the North at the end of the decade of the 1830s was slightly above 100,000. The great center of Garrisonian abolitionism was in Boston, with strong influence on local societies throughout Massachusetts, Rhode Island, Maine, New Hampshire, Vermont, and Connecticut, with some adherents in New York and Pennsylvania. There were three centers of non-Garrisonian abolition. In New England there was the strong influence of Dr. William Ellery Channing; in New York in the east there was the leadership of the Tappan brothers, Lewis and Arthur, and in Peterboro the significant influence of Gerrit Smith emanated. The Tappans were wealthy merchants, supported several antislavery newspapers, and were issuers of opinion in the form of tracts. Gerrit Smith was the largest holder of land in America at that time, about 750,000 acres. Over the years he would give $50,000 in cash to support antislavery societies, in addition to bestowing 120,000 acres to black men and their families. Among the first "political" abolitionists, Smith helped found the Liberty Party. Finally in the West, principally in Ohio, were Salmon P. Chase, Gamaliel Bailey, editor in Cincinnati of the *Philanthropist*, the lawyer James Birney, who would stand in the presidential canvas in numerous elections as the Liberty Party candidate, and clergyman Theodore Weld, a graduate of Lane Seminary whose influential *American Slavery as It Is* became a classic of abolition literature.

William Lloyd Garrison, besides being the advocate of "immediatism," preached nonresistance, abstinence, anti-Sabbatarianism, black equality, and women's rights, with a variety of other reforms. His signature slogan was to become "No Union with slaveholders!" Despairing of the efficacy of extending political action before consummating the moral struggle, he denounced the U.S. Constitution as "a covenant with death, and an agreement with Hell." Wearing steel-rimmed glasses, he was prematurely bald, and wore a black coat with a black cravat about his neck. Indeed he had an austere, sectarian appearance; from the working class, he had an egalitarian ethos, admitting blacks and women, to the scandal of many, into the Massachusetts Anti-Slavery Society. When he started the *Liberator*, among his first important financial contributors was John B. Vashon, the black abolitionist of Pittsburgh; maintaining a barber shop there, he was a veteran of the War of 1812. It was Vashon who brought Garrison a hat, after he was mobbed in Boston in broad daylight on October 21, 1835, and dragged with a rope around his waist. While his only injuries were his torn clothes, he was lodged in jail for his protection; as Vashon extended the new hat, he remarked he brought it "at a venture as to the precise size required."[34]

The "up standing" of society and their clergy looked upon Garrison and his crowd with indignation and contempt; he was "a low-lived" and "insignificant mechanic," "connected with no church" and "responsible to nobody." Garrison explained his mission on the initial page of the convening number of the *Liberator*. He was determined "to lift up the standard of emancipation in the eyes of the nation, within sight of Bunker Hill and in the birth place of liberty." And he wrote: "I will be as harsh as truth, and as uncompromising as justice. On this subject I do not wish to think, or speak, or write, with moderation. No! no! . . . I am in earnest—I will not equivocate—I will not excuse—I will not retreat a single inch—AND I WILL BE HEARD."[35]

Better than anyone Wendell Phillips understood Garrison and his mission. That cause, said Phillips, owed its ultimate success to Garrison's forgetting that he was white; and in fact many people without any personal knowledge of him assumed he was black. In a second instance, the success of the movement hinged on Garrison's espousal of nonresistance. Although not holding to that view himself, Phillips did believe that the tenets of pacifism and peaceful emancipation accomplished through moral suasion prevented even more dangerous and vociferous attacks being hurled at abolitionists than they were then experiencing. But there was dissension too in the abolition society: to curb Garrison's perceived incendiary rhetoric in the *Liberator* it was suggested by "a few gentlemen" that all articles published would be reviewed and edited by them, and nothing was to see print without meeting their approval. Garrison would have none of it. Phillips hastened to his defense, and wrote in an open letter to the paper published February 15, 1839, "I regard the success of the *Liberator* as identical with that of the Abolition cause itself. . . . The spirit of the *Liberator* is the touchstone of true hearts. Success to it!"

In his column titled "Watchman, What of the Night?" next to Phillips's letter, Garrison cautioned, "Strong foes are without, insidious plotters are within the camp." The showdown would come at the tenth anniversary meeting of the American Anti-Slavery Society in New York in May 1840. Those opposed to Garrison's track in the national society, which included among many others Dr. Channing, the Tappan brothers, and James Birney, would try to wrest the organization from his dominating influence. Phillips was absent in Europe, having sailed on the packet *Wellington* on June 6, 1839, with his ailing wife, whose physicians had prescribed the trip with hopeful visits to spas. Lamenting the departure after the last meeting of the society, the board addressed a letter of commendation to their departing colleague: "You buckled on the Abolition armour when there were blows to take as well as to give, and from that hour to the present we have ever found you in the front rank of the conflict. . . . We shall regard your absence as a real loss to the board, to the society we represent, and to the great anti-slavery organization in the land."[36]

Dismayed that Garrison's prominence had allowed the movement to be portrayed as "Jacobin" and "fanatical," the dissenters now would curb his radicalism. The issue would come on the question of women's rights. The employment of women as lecturers— most prominently Sarah and Angelina Grimké, two sisters from a Charleston, South Carolina, slaveholding family, who had denounced slavery and come north—particularly was regarded as an affront to standard mores by clergy. Theodore Weld, following the building controversy in the West through the columns of the *Liberator*, wrote Gerrit Smith, October 23, 1839, that he'd hoped to find in Garrison's paper "the heart of Jesus," but only found "the vibrations of serpents' tongues and the darting of envenomed stings." This after the editor reproached his clerical critics, calling them "blind leaders of the blind, dumb dogs that cannot bark, spiritual popes—that . . . love the fleece better than the flock." The test came in a maneuver demonstrating parliamentary flourish when Abby Kelly, a young Quaker woman from Lynn, Massachusetts, was nominated to the Society's Business Committee. When the vote came it was 557 votes for and 451 against. Garrison had won, and now Lucretia Mott, Lydia Maria Child, and Maria Chapman ascended to the executive committee. So exasperated were many of the dissenters that they left the meeting.

To pack the meeting with his supporters and the promise of victory Garrison had chartered a steamer from Providence to New York, after putting out a rallying cry in the pages of the *Liberator*. Four hundred and fifty adherents had promptly responded—every member would have a vote—prepared to "preserve the integrity of the anti-slavery movement." "There never has been such a mass of '*ultraism*' afloat," Garrison wrote in his letter to the editor dated May 12. Garrison's analysis of his success in thwarting this attempt at his overthrow he attributed to mass organization. On June 21, he wrote in the *Liberator*, "A Farce in One Act":

> The true secret of the wonderful progress of our cause, aside from its intrinsic excellence, has been the entrusting of its management to the people—the bone and muscle of the community—the unambitious, unaspiring, courageous, disinterested, true-hearted friends of bleeding humanity. It has thus fought its way to public respect and popular favor, and under the same auspices would still continue to advance in a geometrical ratio. But an example of this kind, it is clearly foreseen by the Doctors and Rabbis, if tolerated much longer, must prove fatal to their monopoly of power, and to the supremacy of a religious aristocracy. No marvel, now that abolition is a prize worth seizing, that these proud men are eager to get possession of it.[37]

The defeated faction, under the leadership of the Tappan brothers, now withdrew and formed a rival organization, the American and Foreign Anti-Slavery Society. The new society urged political action as a duty on each citizen and pronounced the admission of women "repugnant of the constitution of the society," deploring it as "a firebrand in anti-slavery meetings." This group would continue in existence only til 1853, when it expired. The American Society would now see its annual income drop precipitously from $47,000 to $7,000, and its membership decline just as appreciably.

Following this split a group of black abolitionists, meeting in Hartford, recommended a national convention of blacks be held in New Haven in September 1840, such being necessary, as the Reverend J. W. C. Pennington phrased it, because "of the division among our friends . . . we must act ourselves."[38] *The Anti-Slavery Standard*, the paper of the American Anti-Slavery Society after the division, cautioned against a separate meeting, while Whipper and Robert Purvis sent word to David Ruggles, organizer of the convention, that they would not attend a meeting "exclusive in character," a controversy that would continue to roil in the ranks of African Americans throughout the antebellum period and beyond.

In April 1839 Gerrit Smith donated two thousand acres of land along with a cash gift of $2,000 to the newly founded Oberlin College, in

the Western Reserve, near Cleveland, a school made possible principally by the financing of Arthur Tappan. Most of this donated land was in
western Virginia in Tyler County, just across the border from Ohio. The
lands, Oberlin College decreed, although in a slave state, were to be
made available "to Christian tenants and free laborers." Owen Brown
was a trustee of Oberlin, and his son soon learned of these. Writing the
Prudential Committee of the college, John Brown said he would like to
obtain part of these for settlement of himself and his family, and his
three eldest sons, "all resolute, energetic, intelligent boys & as I trust of
very decided religious character." Since Smith's titles were in dispute,
Brown offered to survey the parcels on an inspection tour, and would
perform the work for a $1 a day plus expenses. The college accepted
Brown's offer and voted him $50 for the task.

Brown left Franklin Mills on April 14, 1840, and returned on May
14. On April 27 he wrote his family from Ripley, Virginia:

> I like the country as well as I expected, & its inhabitants rather better;
> and I think we can find a place in it that will answer all the purposes for
> which we kneed (sic) this world, & have seen the spot where if it be the
> will of Providence, I hope one day to live with my family. . . . Were the
> inhabitants as resolute and industrious, as the northern people, & did
> they understand how to manage as well, they would become rich, but they
> are not generally so. They seem to have no Idea of improvement in their
> Cattle, Sheep, or Hogs nor to know the use of enclosed pasture fields for
> their stock, but spend a large portion of their time in hunting for the
> Cattle, Sheep & Horses, & the same habit continues from Father to Son.
> They have so little idea of moving off any thing they have to sell, or of
> going away for anything they kneed [sic] to buy, that their Merchants
> extort upon them prodigiously. By comparing them with the people of
> other parts of the Country, & world, I can see new and abundant proof
> that knowledge is power.[39]

It was not to be "the will of Providence" that Brown and his family
would occupy these lands. Although Oberlin had promised him a
thousand acres, with the turmoil of his pending bankruptcy in Ohio
and his hesitancy in coming to resolution, and the uncertainty of the
finances of the college itself, the offer was withdrawn. Brown was
informed of this in a letter from the college secretary, Levi Burnell, on
January 20, 1840. In his letter of inquiry in the previous year he'd written concerning "provision for religious and school privileges," but there
was no mention in this regard of his proposal for educating black
youth. Nor is it likely he had projected this site as a base for the warfare
in the Virginia mountains, as he would later conceive it, as some writ-

ers have maintained. That was all still in the future; he had however made an indirect introduction to a man who would be a figure in that endeavor: Gerrit Smith.

At its founding Oberlin would receive many of the students of Lane Seminary in Cincinnati, who had overtly embraced abolition and had withdrawn from Lane under pressure. These "Lane Rebels," as they were called, were the seminarians from whose core Theodore Weld had drawn "The Seventy," as evangelists under commission of the American Anti-Slavery Society were called. They had toured the North preaching the new doctrine of immediatism in the mid-1830s.

After the rupture in New York in May, Garrison sailed for London where a "World's Convention" of anti-slavery societies was to convene in June. First proposed in the *Emancipator*, then the official organ of the American Anti-Slavery Society, and promptly endorsed by the societies in England, the meeting was sponsored by the London Anti-Slavery Committee, which oversaw the preparations. The convention opened at Freemasons Hall on June 12 at eleven o'clock with nearly five hundred delegates present, many Americans among them. With Garrison still at sea in rough weather, Phillips's wife Anne, Maria Chapman, Lucretia Mott, and Elizabeth Cady Stanton entered the hall, as Wendell Phillips was asked to present their credentials. Doing so, he was informed by the Executive Committee of the British and Foreign Society that they would not admit women. As the venerable president of the convention, Thomas Clarkson, withdrew, Phillips made a motion "That a committee of five be appointed to prepare a correct list of the members of this convention, with instruction to include in such list all persons bearing credentials from an anti-slavery body."

This "woman-intruding" event shocked the convention, and angry debate ensued. It was contrary to British usage and custom, the house maintained; the clergy present were particularly incensed at the idea being asserted. It brought their severe rebuke, but the "rhapsodists of the United States," as the women were called, were there to contest the issue.[40] As Phillips was requested to withdraw his motion, he rose again, saying—

> We cannot yield this question if we would, for it is a matter of conscience. But we would not yield it on the ground of expediency. In doing so, we should feel that we were striking off the right arm of our enterprise. . . . We have argued it over and over again, and decided it time after time, in every society in the land, in favor of the women. We have not changed by crossing the water. We stand here the advocates of the same principle that we contend for in America. . . . Massachusetts cannot turn aside to

succumb to any prejudices or customs, even in the land she looks upon with so much reverence as the land of Wilberforce, of Clarkson, and of O'Connell. It is a matter of conscience, and British virtue ought not to ask us to yield.[41]

As Phillips conducted the case before the committee, he and the women delegates met with rebuff. They were denied admission to the floor and relegated to the spectators' gallery. The men, among them Phillips and Charles Lenox Remond, a thin-visaged, dark-skinned man of whom it was said he felt the proscriptions against his race with an almost neurological acuteness, took seats in the gallery; while others, James Birney among them, took seats with the "gentlemen" delegates. When Garrison arrived he sat with the delegates denied admittance, where, it was reported, he conversed "calmly with Lady Byron." Lucretia Mott and Elizabeth Cady Stanton, walking arm in arm down Great Queen Street on the night of their rejection by the "World's Convention," resolved to make arrangements to hold a woman's rights convention on their homecoming.

When back in Boston, a reception was given for Garrison with nearly twenty-five hundred in attendance, hosted by the black members of the society. The *Liberator* reported some of the testimony about the convention given by one of the delegates, Nathaniel P. Rodgers, in the issue published August 28, 1840. Referencing Haman and Mordecai from the Book of Esther, he recalled:

I took myself up into the gallery, in company with Garrison and Remond, to overlook what remained of the proceedings. That act was decisive in its effect. Haman never looked more blank on seeing Mordecai sitting in the king's gate with his hat on, than did this "committee in conference" on seeing us take the position we did. Garrison was besought to come down. They tried by every means in their power to seduce him down. Every time he was mentioned, that whole conference would applaud, as if they thought they could clap him down.

2

The North Star

A s with murder, in the state of Maryland, the supreme penalty was often meted out to persons "aiding and abetting the escape of a slave"; so wrote Frederick Douglass in an article for *The Century* magazine in November 1881. Forty years after writing his first narrative of his experiences in slavery, in this article he explained the reasons he had withheld the details of his escape for so long. The penalty was very severe for those implicated, and he did not want to give out information that could preclude others from using the very means he'd employed. In all of his autobiographical writings, *Narrative of the Life of Frederick Douglass*, *My Bondage and My Freedom*, and *Life and Times of Frederick Douglass*, he'd never revealed the details until that time.

Douglass wrote: "My means of escape were provided for me by the very men who were making laws to hold and bind me more securely in slavery."[1] Among his circle of friends in Baltimore where Douglass worked in its shipyards—his master living on the Eastern Shore,

Thomas Auld, had allowed him to hire his labor out in exchange for receiving his wages—was a black sailor. This sailor was in fact "a free American sailor," and had papers for his protection certifying his status and describing his person. Douglass would use them for his escape and see that the papers were returned by mail when free. Giving these the appearance of an authorized document, at their head was the American eagle; the description of the two men, however, did not at all correspond, calling for a much darker man than himself, and if examined would have caused his arrest.

To avoid scrutiny by railroad officials, Douglass arranged for a Baltimore hackman to bring his baggage to the Philadelphia-bound cars just at the moment they were in motion, as he himself jumped upon the train. "In choosing this plan," he wrote, "I considered the jostle of the train, and the natural haste of the conductor, in a train crowded with passengers, and relied upon my skill and address in playing the sailor, as described in my protection, to do the rest."

Rigged out in "sailor style," he wore a red shirt and tarpaulin hat, with a cravat tied loosely around his neck; elements to play upon the feeling then prevailing of "Free trade and sailors rights," in Baltimore and other seaports. The train was well on the way to Havre de Grace, Douglass writes, before the conductor came into the "Negro car" and began examining in a brusque manner the "free papers" of the black passengers in it. Douglass was surprised to see the conductor's manner change as he came to him, asking, "I suppose you have your free papers?" "No, sir," Douglass answered, "I never carry my free papers to sea with me." "But you have something to show that you are a freeman, haven't you?" Drawing out the borrowed protection papers from his deep sailor's pocket, Douglass answered, "Yes, sir, I have a paper with the American eagle on it, and that will carry me around the world." Giving these only a cursory glance, the conductor returned them, collected his fare, and went about his duties.

But Douglass was not yet out of danger. There were several people he had seen on the train who knew him in Baltimore, and if not for his dress they would likely have identified him and reported him to the conductor, who would arrest him and return him to Baltimore at the next station. But it was not in the interior of a slave state where the danger lay for an escaping fugitive, but at its borders where the "human slave hounds" were active and vigilant. Douglass wrote: "The train was moving at a very high rate of speed for that epoch of railroad travel, but to my anxious mind it was moving far too slowly. Minutes were hours, and hours were days during this part of my flight." On reaching the

Susquehanna River, train passage was exchanged for ferryboat, among
whose "hands," Douglass found, was a young black who knew him.
Getting away from him and his prying questioning as soon as conven-
ient, Douglass went to another part of the boat to complete the passage. But a new danger soon was presented. Days before, Douglass had
been working on a revenue cutter in a Baltimore shipyard under the
care of Captain McGowan. At this point the northbound train, which
he had boarded, and the southbound train were stopped on the tracks
opposite, and McGowan was positioned at the window; if he had
looked directly at Douglass he would not have failed in identifying him.
Also on the train with Douglass was a German blacksmith who knew
him well, who Douglass supposes saw him but "held his peace." Danger
of arrest still lurked in Wilmington, where passengers would again disembark to board a ferry for Philadelphia.

Reaching the Quaker City, Douglass enquired to the nearest friendly
face he came upon, a black man, how he could reach New York.
Directed to the William Street Depot, he waited for the train, and
boarding that night, he reached his destination less than twenty-four
hours from starting out. The date was September 4, 1838; one more
free man "added to the mighty throng which, like the confused waves
of a troubled sea, surged to and fro between the lofty walls of
Broadway," wrote Frederick Douglass forty-three years later.

In the experience of many slaves contemplating escape, few had
known of examples of success, but many knew failure. Aware that if
apprehended they awaited cruel treatment and flogging and the near
certainty of being sold into the Deep South. With no knowledge of distance and direction, how could a slave know where one state ended and
another began? Indeed was there safety where they were going; would
they meet judicious friends whom they could trust, and could charge
with their liberty, with their life? With escape also came the thought of
the human bloodhounds who would be set upon their track, of weari-
ness and hunger, on a course that often lay through thick and heavy
woods and back lands, where one could venture forth only under cover
of night. A solitary wanderer from home and friend, whose only guide
was the North Star; melancholy travelers whose course northward
must be rapid, cheered only by the wild hope that someday they would
be free. Yet with each advancing step, came the prospect of utter destitution; thoughts of captors lurking, waiting to waylay "runaway niggers," where it would be demanded, by the law of slavery, who they
"belonged to," and "where they had come from?" Where in all the providence of God would they find a friend?[2]

One sees in the growth of the Cotton Kingdom the foundation of a new slavery corresponding to the modern factory system in its worst form. Field hands were compelled to labor in a mechanical task system, with its interposing layer of overseers and drivers. Pushing through the South and into the West, the system "marked the aggressive world-conquering visions of the slave barons."[3] But outside this expansive dynamic, Southern society was static. The slave gestated in a folk society, with a multiplicity of folkways and notions, songs and stories, sayings and pastimes, superstitious beliefs and practices, all inflected by African origins; having too their own code of behavior as a complement to the slave code.[4] Antebellum Southern society was also distinctly regional: upper and lower South, Sea Islands, Tidewater, Deep South and Southwest; as was its produce: tobacco, cotton, and sugarcane.

In the aftermath of Nat Turner, a harsher regime for blacks that the economic revolution was mandating in practice began to crystallize into law. DuBois wrote:

> A wave of legislation passed over the South, prohibiting the slaves from learning to read and write, forbidding Negroes to preach, and interfering with Negro religious meetings. Virginia declared in 1831 that neither slaves nor free Negroes might preach, nor could they attend religious service at night without permission. In North Carolina slaves and free Negroes were forbidden to preach, exhort, or teach "in any prayer meeting or other association for worship where slaves of different families are collected together" on penalty of not more than thirty-nine lashes. Maryland and Georgia and other states had similar laws.[5]

The truly effective revolt against slavery after the failure of Nat's War was in the flight of the fugitive slaves. The network of stations and safe houses, of persons, black and white, called the Underground Railroad, who were prepared to assist these fugitives, and left its most indelible and enduring imprint, not in the pathways and routes chosen, or the names of places and of its agents, but on the political will of the North.

The first organized assistance began among the Quakers, with fugitives often traveling from Quaker family to Quaker family.[6] Among those who began to participate were farmers, preachers, and physicians, and finally every class of society, including many prominent citizens in many communities. Women's antislavery societies were organized to provide clothing, money, and food; agents were prepared to receive fugitives at any time, and vigilance committees were organized to warn of new arrivals. At first most of the fugitives were men, and they would often be sent along singly to the next station on the underground. But as women and children began to be numbered among them they were taken on horseback, in wagons, or on boats to the next stop, never more than a day's journey. Fugitives traveling north would often settle in the communities along these pathways, always ready to resume their flight if their existence became insecure.

These paths to freedom fell largely within four regions. On the eastern Atlantic coast, seaports were used, and coastal waterways and tributaries, swamps, and wetlands. Flight routes originating from Baltimore might use the Chesapeake Bay; sometimes too the lower ports were the starting point. Fugitives would begin at Wilmington, Georgetown, Charleston, and travel up to Philadelphia, New York, Providence, New Bedford and Boston, and points north.

A second network was active in the hill country west of Baltimore to Frederick and Hagerstown in Maryland, up into central Pennsylvania to Lancaster County, and in the west into Chambersburg, Bedford, and Pittsburgh. Fugitives running in this region might be moved on to Philadelphia, to New York and to Albany, across the northern tier, to Utica, Syracuse, Auburn, Rochester, and Buffalo, or into Canada, to Hamilton, St. Catharines, Toronto, and Chatham. It is estimated perhaps nine thousand fugitives were helped to freedom through these branches of the Underground Railroad north of Philadelphia before 1860.[7]

A third, and the most active network, extended along the longest frontier between the free and the slave states, the Ohio River, nearly four hundred rolling miles. Beginning at the confluence of the Allegheny and Monongahela rivers between whose triangle the city of Pittsburgh is built, it ranged from western Virginia across the entire irregular northern frontier of Kentucky, terminating in the Mississippi and the state of Missouri. Touching upon Ohio, Indiana, and Illinois, the river was a wide and brisk flowing stream known to slave folklore as the Jordan. It was on its ice floes that Eliza escaped with her baby in Harriet Beecher Stowe's fictional account in *Uncle Tom's Cabin*, serialized in the *National Era* in 1852.

Another important branch of the "railroad" operated on the Mississippi River running up to Iowa and into Wisconsin; and finally the last outlet would be opened with the settlement of the Kansas Territory, running fugitive slaves up from Missouri into the same.

Cincinnati, where Levi Coffin resided—often called the "President of the Underground Railroad"—was its active center in the west. In the east another prominent figure was Thomas Garret, a Quaker in Wilmington, Delaware; another was William Still in Philadelphia, who would chronicle his activities in 1872, publishing *Underground Railroad*. In New York there was David Ruggles; and in Columbia, Pennsylvania, at the end of the bridge across the Susquehanna, was the home of William Whipper, another station on the Underground Railroad. Other important figures were John Jones in Chicago, a tailor and abolitionist and friend of John Brown; in Detroit was William Lambert, also to become an important ally of John Brown; and another was Lewis Hayden, of Boston's Beacon Hill. Many prominent figures of the "railroad" were themselves fugitive slaves, like John Brown's friends the Rev. Henry Highland Garnet, escaped from New Market, Maryland, together with his entire family, and the Rev. Jermain Wesley Loguen of Syracuse, New York, a fugitive from slavery in Tennessee.

Douglass soon found, though exhilarated by the novel condition of a free man, and "dazzled with the wonders" which he met on every hand, New York was not as safe a refuge as he supposed. He learned from a chance encounter with another fugitive from Baltimore, whom he'd known, that many Southerners were in the city returning from spas in the north, and that many of their own kith and kin would betray them for a few dollars, that there were hired men on the lookout for fugitives. Don't be seen around "colored" rooming houses, nor go to the wharves, he was told, for these places were closely watched. Now every door seemed closed to him, and a sense of loneliness and insecurity dimmed his enthusiasm.

Standing near "the Tombs" on Center Street, Douglass ventured a conversation with a black sailor as he approached. Soon he was introduced to David Ruggles, secretary of the New York Vigilance Committee, and was hidden for several days. During this time, Douglass's intended wife, Anna, a free woman who had supplied the money for his escape, came at his call. They were married by the Rev. J. W. C. Pennington, a Presbyterian minister. Learning that Douglass's trade was "caulker," Ruggles decided the best place for him would be New Bedford, in Massachusetts. It would not do for Douglass to seek employment in New York's shipyards, for surely his master, Thomas Auld, might come looking for him there. So on the day of the marriage ceremony the newlywed couple, carrying what little luggage they had, boarded a steamer for Newport, Rhode Island. Douglass related details of their arrival forty years later:

> We arrived at Newport the next morning, and soon after an old-fashioned stagecoach with "New Bedford" in large, yellow letters on its side, came down the wharf. I had not money enough to pay our fare and stood hesitating to know what to do. Fortunately for us, there were two Quaker

gentlemen who were about to take passage on the stage—Friends William
C. Taber and Joseph Ricketson—who at once discerned our true situation, and in a peculiarly quiet way, addressing me, Mr. Taber said, "Thee
get in." I never obeyed an order with more alacrity, and we were soon on
our way to our new home.[8]

As he approached his seventieth year, asked where he had gotten his
education, Douglass replied unequivocally, "from Massachusetts
abolition University: Mr. Garrison, president."[9] Douglass's first months
in New Bedford were tough, but he'd learned to grapple with difficulties and was quick to grasp new opportunities. Unable to be employed
as a caulker in the shipyards because white working men would not
work alongside him, he found his first job loading caskets of oil on a
sloop bound for New York. Other jobs open to him were sawing wood,
sweeping chimneys, driving coach, and operating a bellows in a copper
foundry. The first child of Frederick and Anna was Rosetta, born in
1839. In 1840, Lewis was to follow, Frederick junior in 1842, Charles,
1844, and finally, in the early 1850's, Annie. Douglass was able to earn
as much as a dollar a day and it was not long too before he became
aware of the abolitionist movement. Six months after settling in New
Bedford, he was a subscriber to the *Liberator* and began to master the
principles and philosophy springing from its columns. On August 9,
1841, three years a free man, Douglass attended the annual meeting of
the Bristol Anti-Slavery Society, and Garrison was there. Both mutual-
ly impressing the other, two days later Douglass joined the eminent
abolitionist and forty of his colleagues as they journeyed to an antislavery meeting on Nantucket Island. It was at that meeting Douglass was
asked to speak from the stand, and his halting, stammering words were
received to great effect. He was immediately followed by Garrison, who
made the fugitive slave "his text."

Before the meeting adjourned, Douglass was approached by the general agent of the Massachusetts Anti-Slavery Society, John A. Collins, a
disciple of Fourier, and asked to join it as a lecturer. Initially hesitant,
not having recovered from the embarrassment of his first effort, he
would be induced to try it for three months. A week later, appearing
with Wendell Phillips and Garrison at a meeting in Millbury, he began
his new vocation.[10]

By 1840 many antislavery campaigners were ready to consolidate
their prospective influence in the agency of a new party. Advanced
opinion of the day held that the Constitution of the United States was

an antislavery document and that slavery was utterly at variance with the Declaration of Independence. Article IV, section 4 of the Constitution said, "The United States shall guarantee to every State in this Union a Republican Form of Government." This covenant, sanctioned by the Fifth Amendment, was the means by which a "person's" natural right to life, liberty, and the pursuit of happiness were to be protected and guaranteed.

Garrison had gained control of the American Anti-Slavery Society as a no-government man, dismissing political action. But the majority of antislavery advocates rejected or ignored his plea, holding that effective opposition to the political ascendency of the Slave Power could only be done by those engaged in "direct, open and determined efforts" to abolish slavery. All the national bodies at that time—be they the Democratic and Whig parties, or the institutionalized religious denominations, Presbyterian, Baptist, and Methodist churches—were institutions in which slaveholders wielded power. None could be turned against slaveholder interests, except by splitting them along sectional lines; the friends of liberty must counteract political power with political action.[11]

Holding conventions in Cleveland, Ohio, and in Warsaw, New York, in the fall of 1839, advocates of political action, although not yet organizing the new party, nominated James Birney and Francis J. LeMoyne for president and vice president of the United States. Both declined their nominations, reasoning that this would only split abolitionists further, as had the woman question, and the peace and no-government positions. In January 1840 the movement would be decisively propelled by a new convention in western New York, in Arcade, making Myron Holley, William L. Chaplin, and Gerrit Smith the leaders; also in the forefront of the movement were the New York abolitionists Alvan Stewart, Joshua Leavitt, William Goodell, and of Ohio, Salmon P. Chase and Joshua Giddings. The convention condemned both William Henry Harrison and Martin Van Buren, the candidates of the Democrat and Whig parties, as unacceptable and criticized the denominational ministers who refused to preach against slavery.

Now another convention was called in Albany for April 1, known as the National Convention of Friends of Immediate Emancipation, although the party in formation was already being spoken of as the Liberty Party. In a close vote, delegates again chose Birney as their presidential candidate, and Thomas Earle for vice president. The platform pledged to oppose "slavery to the full extent of legislative power under the Constitution, with particular emphasis upon abolition of slavery in

the district of Columbia and of the interstate slave trade."[12] Never gar-
nering a significant number of votes, the party would field few local
candidates, and Birney would be in England from May to November
attending the World Anti-Slavery Convention. But the creation of the
party has been called "the most important event after the founding of
the American Anti-Slavery Society in 1833";[13] the movement, as the
Republican Party, would attain power in the national government and
in many states of the North by 1860.

In October 1842, a fugitive slave from Norfolk, Virginia, owned by
James B. Gray made his escape, reaching Boston where he was arrested
on charges of theft and lodged in jail. Abolitionists demanded he
receive a jury trial. The judge, however, refused, citing the United States
Constitution, Article IV, section 2, which states: "No Person held to
service or Labour in one State, under the Laws thereof, escaping into
another, shall, in Consequence of any Law or Regulation therein, be
discharged from such Service or Labour, but shall be delivered up on
Claim of the Party to whom such service or Labour may be due." The
runaway's name was George Latimer, and the controversy around his
capture was to culminate in one of the largest petitions ever to reach
the Congress.

An open meeting was called for in Faneuil Hall "For the Rescue of
Liberty," and as placards and handbills were distributed, Boston was in
the throes of tumult. When the meeting began the chairman, Samuel E.
Sewall, was interrupted: "We'd like to see you with darkies for a
week"—"Get o' dat Nigger's heel," were some of the comments hurled.
As Joshua Leavitt tried to read the resolutions, he could scarcely be
heard. When he finished, Edmund Quincy moved for the adoption of
the resolutions. Then Charles Lenox Remond rose to speak amid
shouts and hisses. When he could not proceed, Wendell Phillips stood
up:

> Fellow citizens, I will ask your attention but for a single moment.... No
> generous man will drown my voice, when I plead the cause of one not
> allowed to speak for himself.... This old hall cannot rock, as it used to,
> with the spirit of liberty. It is chained down by the iron links of the United
> States Constitution. (Great noise, hisses, and uproar.) Many of you, I
> doubt not, regret to have this man given up—but you cannot help it.
> There stands the bloody clause in the Constitution—you cannot fret the
> seal off the bond. The fault is in allowing such a Constitution to live an
> hour.... When I look upon these crowded thousands, and see them tram-
> ple on their consciences and the rights of their fellow men, at the bidding
> of a piece of parchment, I say, my CURSE be on the Constitution of these

United States! (Hisses and shouts.) Those who cannot bear free speech had better go home. Faneuil Hall is no place for slavish hearts. (Hisses.)[14]

Following the Faneuil Hall meeting on October 30, other "Latimer meetings" were held across the state. The result was seen in the "Great Petition to Congress" sent to Washington, an immense roll of paper bearing 51,862 signatures, headed by George Latimer, asking for an amendment to separate the people of Massachusetts from all Constitutional provisions upholding slavery. A Latimer Committee was appointed after the Boston meeting to co-ordinate the protests, bringing out a periodical, the *Latimer Weekly and North Star*.[15] Another huge petition circulated for the state legislature, the "Great Massachusetts Petition," bringing 62,791 signatures. This demanded a state law barring the use of public property or public officials from assisting in the arrest and detention of fugitive slaves. This became the basis of the Personal Liberty Act passed March 24, 1843.[16]

James Russell Lowell was to write, "We Americans are very fond of this glue of compromise. Like so many quack cements, it is advertised to make the mended parts of the vessel stronger than those which have never been broken, but like them it will not stand hot water."[17] Consistent abolitionism was anathema to that revered American parchment called the Constitution, declared the "come-outers," a band of abolitionists that included Phillips, Garrison, and Quincy. In May 1842 Garrison hoisted the doctrine to the head of the editorial columns of the *Liberator*—"A REPEAL OF THE UNION BETWEEN NORTHERN LIBERTY AND SOUTHERN SLAVERY IS ESSENTIAL TO THE ABOLITION OF THE ONE AND THE PRESERVATION OF THE OTHER." This banner was to remain in place for the rest of the year, and the Massachusetts Anti-Slavery Society would adopt the "Come-Outer" resolutions in January 1843. Garrison was the shaper of their Hebraic words: "*Resolved* That the compact which exists between the North and South is a covenant with death and an agreement with hell—involving both parties in atrocious criminality and should be immediately annulled."

James B. Gray, the owner of Latimer, surprised by the depth of indignation aroused throughout New England and subject to counter charges brought by Latimer's defenders, decided to relinquish his title to the man in exchange for $400. The Latimer protest had seen black abolitionists in its forefront; men like the Rev. Pennington who delivered a sermon at the Fifth Congregational Church at Hartford, November 17, 1842, titled "Covenants Involving Moral Wrong Not Obligatory Upon Man." Charles Dickens must not hear of the Latimer case, Pennington prayed, lest he write an addendum to his *Notes on*

America.[18] The past half dozen years had seen active efforts by blacks to secure their civil rights in the northern states, with efforts to gain the franchise, secure attendance in public schools for their children, and ban discriminatory practices in public transportation. These efforts were led by men like Pennington in Hartford, Robert Purvis in Philadelphia, John B. Vashon in Pittsburgh, William Whipper in Columbia, Theodore S. Wright in New York, and Lewis Woodson in Ohio. All of whom and scores of others were among the participants on record in these same years in the "Colored Convention" movement, as well as being core contributors to the formation of the modern anti-slavery movement. An important moment of that ongoing debate was the efficacy of forming societies with exclusively black contingency and orientation. A milestone in the movement was reached in 1843, in the convention scheduled for the end of August in Buffalo, New York, which would bring important new contributors to the fore.

Delegates attending a preliminary meeting in New York under the chairmanship of Theodore Wright signed a proclamation declaring it the duty of the oppressed to conduct their own struggle; that organization was the paramount requisite, and that there was no better way to promote this than by meetings conducted on a regular basis.[19] One of the signers was the Rev. Henry Highland Garnet, who had begun a Presbyterian ministry in Troy, New York, and been a founding member of the Liberty Party.

When the Buffalo meeting convened, Frederick Douglass was in attendance, his first appearance in such gatherings, along with seventy other delegates. Garnet was elected chairman of the committee of correspondence, and he read the convention the call. Upon his motion Samuel Davis took the seat as temporary chairman and addressed the delegates, urging them to secure their rights by direct action instead of relying on petitions, urging that blacks develop their own resources and organizations.[20]

Chairing the business committee, Garnet used his mandate to offer resolutions endorsing the Liberty Party, to urge blacks to acquire land and work in agricultural pursuits, and create a national press controlled by them. As important as these resolutions were, Garnet's overwhelming and enduring contribution to this convention was to be in his speech titled "An Address to the Slaves of the United States of America." His opening sentences clearly stated his words were intended as a break from past practices: "Your brethren of the North, East, and West have been accustomed to meet together in National Conventions, to sympathize with each other, and to weep over your unhappy condition. In these meetings we have addressed all classes of the free, but we have never, until this time, sent a word of consolation and advice to you." Blacks could plead their own cause, "and do the work of emancipation better than any others," he said. The pith of his statement came with this: "You had far better all die—*die immediately*, than live slaves, and entail your wretchedness upon your posterity. If you would be free in this generation, here is your only hope. However much you and all of us may desire it, there is not much hope of redemption without the shedding of blood. If you must bleed, let it all come at once—rather *die freemen, than live to be the slaves.*"

The convention had some discussion of this incendiary address, and after seeking to have it modified (as it would certainly appear in print), failed to endorse it by one vote. Douglass and Remond, both Garrisonians, as well as William Wells Brown, belittled Garnet's statement and declined to endorse the resolution on the Liberty Party; Douglass suggesting there was "too much physical force in both the address and the speaker."[21] But the excoriation to come at the hands of the editors of the *Liberator*, which covered the convention, was much greater than by the delegates themselves. The address was "inflammatory," "provocative," and a "flight of fancy." During the debate, the *Liberator* reported, "Wm. L. Garrison was brought for his share of abuse;" while the "Massachusetts delegates" had been "true to the interests of the slave."[22]

Two weeks later the *Liberator* published a long article by Maria Weston Chapman stating that Garnet had fallen under "bad counsel." In a letter dated November 17, 1843, Garnet made his reply: "Respected Madam: Some time ago you wrote an article in the *Liberator*, condemnatory of the National Convention of colored people, which was held in the city of Buffalo, in the month of August last. I should have sent a reply, ere this time, had I not been engaged so much in the cause of freedom, since the appearance of your article. I must confess that I was exceedingly amazed to find that I was doomed to share so much of your severity, to call it nothing else."

And to leave no doubt that he intended to rebuke the "paternalism" of her tone, also heard in the attitude of other whites, Garnet answered her with this retort: "You are not the only person who has told your humble servant that his humble productions have been produced by the '*counsel*' of some anglo-saxon. I have expected no more from ignorant slaveholders and their apologists, but I really looked for better things from Mrs. Maria W. Chapman, an anti-slavery poetess, and editor *pro tem.* of the Boston *Liberator*. I can think on the subject of human rights without 'counsel,' either from men of the West, or the women of the East."

On September 28, 1842, John Brown's bankruptcy was finalized, an affair stemming from overextended credit and the consequence of the 1837 panic; the national financial crisis brought over six hundred bank failures in its wake, with ten thousand employees thrown out of work. Brown had already conceived "his vision of vast service," as DuBois phrased it, formally dedicating his life to its consummation. Mary Brown, his wife, said in later years, "My husband always believed that he was to be an instrument in the hands of Providence, and I believed it too. . . . Many a night he had lain awake and prayed concerning it."[23] By 1841, turning his attention to sheep farming, he leased a farm in Richfield, Summit County, Ohio, of one hundred seventy acres; while continuing to operate a tannery on the property. He had a natural liking for the work, and because of the growing prosperity of the wool trade, he chose this employment. But the chief idea behind it, Franklin Sanborn would write, was "it bid fair to afford him the means of carrying out his greater or principal object." As his affairs appeared to be on the mend, on September 25, 1843, he wrote his eldest son from Richfield of the poignant death of four of his children:

> God has seen fit to visit us with the pestilence since you left us, and Four of us that are still living have been more or less unwell but appear to be nearly recovered. On the 4th Sept Charles was taken with the Dysentery and died on the 11th, about the time that Charles died Sarah, Peter, & Austin were taken with the same complaint. Austin died on the 21st, Peter on the 22nd & Sarah on the 23d and were all buried together in one grave. This has been to us all a bitter cup indeed, and we have drunk deeply, but still the Lord reigneth and blessed be his great and holy name forever.[24]

By January 1844, the family was again prospering. John Brown had entered into a business partnership with Simon Perkins. That agreement stipulated that both men would join their flocks and "share equally the gain or loss yearly." Perkins was to provision the sheep, while Brown would tend them, wash, shear, sack, and ship the wool to market. Both were to pasture, and improve and increase the flock as the business justified. While Perkins would let Brown "the frame dwelling-house on his farm (near Akron) . . . door-yards, garden grounds, and the privilege of getting wood for fuel" all for thirty dollars per year.

On the 11th of that month, Brown again wrote John Jr. about this turn in his fortune:

Your Letter dated 21st Dec was received some days ago but I have purposely delayed till now in order to comply the better with your request that I should write you about every thing. We are all in health; amongst the number is a new sister (Anne) about three weeks old. I know of no one of our friends that is not comfortably well. I have just met with Father he was with us a few days since & all were then well in that quarter. Our flock is well and we seem to be overtakeing [sic] our business in the tannery. Divine Providence seems to smile on our works at this time, I hope we shall not prove unthankful for any favour, nor forget the giver. I have gone to sleep a great many times while writing the above.... I have lately entered into a copartnership with Simon Perkins Jr of Akron with a view to carry on the Sheep business extensively.[25]

By mid-summer 1844, with industry John Brown and his family were prospering, as he reported 560 lambs birthed, the flock yielding 2,700 pounds of wool. For the fleeces he'd received an offer of fifty-six cents per pound, marking it high grade. The *Ohio Cultivator*, a publication for Ohio farmers, was to remark in the following year of his efforts—"too much cannot be said in praise of these sheep, and especially in praise of the care displayed by Mr. Brown."[26] Brown had seen, though, one of the shortcomings of the industry had been the poor quality of the wool for which farmers could only realize the lowest prices, and he began to introduce a superior breed. His daughter Ruth recounted:

As a shepherd, he showed...watchful care over his sheep.... One Monday morning I had just got my white clothes in a nice warm suds in the wash-tub, when he came in bringing a little dead-looking lamb. There seemed to be no sign of life about it. Said he, "Take out your clothes quick, and let me put this lamb in the water." I felt a little vexed to be hindered with my washing, and told him I didn't believe he could make it live; but in an hour or two he had it running around the room, and calling loudly for its mother. The next year he came from the barn and said to me, "Ruth, that lamb I hindered you with when you were washing, I have just sold for one hundred dollars." It was a pure-blooded Saxony lamb.[27]

Brown was soon working to improve the situation of growers, who, unorganized and untrained, had difficulty in realizing fair prices. Wool was sold in bulk ungraded to agents of manufacturers in the East, with the lowest grade setting the price. Delivering lectures on proper methods of shearing, Brown traveled extensively in Pennsylvania and Ohio, educating farmers in the proper care of their sheep and the washing of

fleece, and the firm of Perkins and Brown instituted a prize for growers showing the best results. To overcome the disadvantage of growers
in the market they proposed establishing a permanent selling agent for
western growers, selecting Springfield, Massachusetts, for that site. The
wool would be graded and warehoused there for one cent per pound
and sold at another cent per pound to manufacturers, with the profits
distributed equably according to the quality of the fleece. In a letter to
John Jr. dated March 24, 1846, John Brown wrote: "I am out among the
wool-growers, with a view to next summer's operations. Our plan
seems to meet with general favor." The firm would send out a circular
to woolgrowers dated March 17, 1847: "The undersigned, commission
wool-merchants, wool-graders, and exporters, have completed
arrangements for receiving wool of growers and holders, and for grading and selling the same for cash as its real value, when quality and condition are considered."[28] John Brown would manage the business trans-
acted in Springfield while his son ran the farm in Ohio. Moving his
family to Springfield, he wrote to his father, Owen: "We are getting
along with our business slowly, but prudently, I trust, and as well as we
could reasonably expect under all the circumstances; and so far as we
can discover, we are in favor with this people, and also with the many
we have had to do business with."[29] But the manufacturers were uneasy
about the firm's operations, the tariff of 1846 had cut into their profits,
and they were looking to recoup on the backs of others. The firm
organized a woolgrowers' convention in Steubenville, Ohio, where
Brown instructed farmers on preparing wool for market; "We have at
last found out," he said, "that some of the principal manufacturers are
leagued together to break us down."[30] Although weeks later he reported to his son of marked progress in the business, saying he had "turned
about four thousand dollars' worth of wool into cash since I returned;
shall probably make it up to seven thousand by the 16th."[31]

It has often been a point if inquiry as to when John Brown began to
take the active steps that would lead him ultimately onto the path culminating at Harpers Ferry. In 1858 in Kansas, a year before that event,
in an extended talk with Richard J. Hinton, John Brown said for twenty years he had never made any business arrangement which would
prevent him "at any time answering the call of the Lord. I have kept my
affairs in such a condition that in two weeks I could wind them up and
obey that call, permitting nothing to stand in the way of that call, neither wife, children or worldly goods." The letter cited above to his son
was to conclude: "Our unexampled success in minor affairs might be a
lesson to us of what unity and perseverance might do in things of some

importance." This would indicate such planning was then an ongoing concern between his eldest son and himself.[32] It is likely, following Brown's timeline, that he had begun his study of the historical antecedents for carrying out an insurgent war as early as 1838. One of the young men later joining with him, an Englishman named Richard Realf, would be called to testify before the Senate committee of the 36th Congress impaneled to investigate Harpers Ferry:

> He stated that he had read all the books upon insurrectionary warfare, that he could lay his hands on: the Roman warfare, the successful opposition of the Spanish chieftains during the period when Spain was a Roman province,—how, with ten thousand men, divided and subdivided into small companies, acting simultaneously, yet separately, they withstood the whole consolidated power of the Roman Empire through a number of years. In addition to this he had become very familiar with the successful warfare waged by Schamyl, the Circassian chief, against the Russians; he had become thoroughly acquainted with the wars in Hayti and the islands round about.[33]

Brown began this reading no later than sometime in 1840, if not before, but he would have more time to devote himself to it assuredly from the middle of the decade on. His residence in Springfield was to bring him, too, into extensive contact with the people for whom his vision of emancipation was intended, as there were about three hundred blacks in the western Massachusetts town at the time, most of them fugitive slaves. Brown was to thoroughly immerse himself in their affairs, visiting and confiding with them, hiring them in his business, and worshiping together with them at the Sanford Street Church, where the Rev. John Mars was pastor. Situated at the top of the valley of the Connecticut River, Springfield was a center of the Underground Railroad in the region, and Brown would appear in a well-known photograph taken at this time standing next to a flag decorated with the initials S. P. W., for "Subterranean Passage Way," the name of the route to which he was connected.

One of Brown's first acquaintances was a fugitive from Maryland's Eastern Shore, Thomas Thomas, whom he hired as a porter at his warehouse. "How early shall I come to-morrow?" Thomas asked. "We start at seven. But I wish you would come around earlier so that I can talk with you." The next morning Brown "disclosed a plan for increasing and systematizing the work of the Underground Railroad by running off larger bodies of slaves" to his new employee.[34] Evidently the Appalachian range was already an object of Brown's theorizing, and this is the first time he expressed it in confidence to a black person. Soon after this it would gain other important auditors. DuBois remarks of Frederick Douglass that, returning from his sojourn in the British Isles, Douglass heard whisperings of a "strange determined man of Springfield who flitted silently here and there among the groups of black folk."[35] This referred to meetings and confidences Brown had sought with the Rev. Henry Highland Garnet in Troy, and with the Rev. J. W. Loguen in Syracuse, both individuals with important and rising profiles as leaders. While in Springfield, Brown contributed a revealing essay titled "Sambo's Mistakes" to a New York paper edited by blacks called the *Ram's Horn*, which appeared from January 1847 to June 1848. Written in the first person as if he himself were black, Brown offered readers the benefit of his hard-won experience, viz. his "mistakes," where Sambo recites his characteristic habits with the refrain, that by his "peculiar quick sightedness … [he] can see in one second where [he] missed it." A copy of the essay in Brown's handwriting was found among his papers in a search of the Kennedy farm, from which he had set up his headquarters for the attack on Harpers Ferry, and would likely otherwise have been lost. In one of its passages he counseled resistance:

> Another trifling error of my life has been that I have always expected to secure the favour of the whites by tamely submitting to every species of indignity contempt & wrongs instead of nobly resisting their brutal [sic] aggressions from principle & taking my place as a man & assuming the responsibilities of a man, a citizen, a husband, a father, a brother, a neighbor, a friend as God requires of every one (if his neighbor will allow him to do it): but I find that I get for all my submission about the same reward that the Southern Slaveocrats render to the Dough faced Statesmen of the North for being bribed & browbeat, & fooled & cheated, as the Whigs & Democrats love to be, & think themselves highly honored if they may be allowed to lick up the spittle of a Southerner. I say I get the same reward. But I am uncommon[ly] quick sighted I can see in a minute where I missed it.[36]

Following the Latimer case, Douglass had been employed in a series of Sunday discourses for three months in Rhode Island. Then in May 1843, at the tenth annual meeting of the American Society convening in New York City, Douglass was appointed to the business committee whose principal work was the consideration of an antislavery campaign to unfold in "One Hundred Conventions." Douglass wrote:

I had the honor to be chosen one of the agents to assist in these proposed conventions, and I never entered upon my work with more heart
and hope. All the American people needed, I thought, was light. Could
they know slavery as I knew it, they would hasten the work of extinction.
The corps of speakers who were to be associated with me in carrying on
these conventions ... were all masters of the subject, and some of them
able and eloquent orators. It was a piece of good fortune to me, only a few
years from slavery as I was, to be brought into contact with such men. It
was a real campaign, and required nearly six months for its accomplish-
ment.[37]

The agents for this campaign, conducted in New Hampshire,
Vermont, New York, Ohio, Indiana, and Pennsylvania, were to go out
singly or in pairs to comb a designated state county by county. After
each had made appearances holding meetings anywhere where they
found a venue and an audience, they were to unite in a large meeting
or convention; and go on like this throughout a state. Douglass and
Remond set out first in Vermont to a disappointing response. In their
tour of New York, not being able to obtain any meeting hall, they
stirred a crowd of five hundred in a public park in Syracuse, and were
joined by John Collins, who was inclined rather to espouse the gospel
of "no-propertyism," the utopian socialism of Fourier. Collins had
arranged for a discussion on "communism" to succeed the one on abolitionism, and was preparing to introduce a group of speakers when
Douglass objected. He argued it would impose an additional burden
on an already unpopular cause, and was an act of bad faith to the "hundred conventions." Douglass was to remark on this: "Strange to say, my
course in this matter did not meet the approval of Mrs. M. W.
Chapman ... and called out a sharp reprimand from her, for insubordination to my superiors. This was a strange and distressing revelation
to me, and one of which I was not soon relieved. I thought I had only
done my duty, and I think so still. The chief reason for the reprimand
was the use which the Liberty party-papers would make of my seeming
rebellion against the commanders of our antislavery army."[38]
Going on to Rochester from there, on obtaining a church, the
Garrisonians did engage Liberty Party supporters in respectful debate;
one opposing carrying the antislavery cause to the ballot box, while the
other believed in carrying it there: one regarding slavery as a creature
of public opinion, the other looking at it as a creature of law. Douglass
wrote: "It is surprising how small the difference appears as I look back
to it, over the space of forty years; yet at the time of it this difference
was immense." The *Liberator*, August 25, 1843, reported that Douglass

gave the crowd in a park a rendition of an abolition solo. When in Buffalo, "a rising city of steamboats, bustle, and business," he single-handedly proclaimed his message in an abandoned post office. With those attending the meetings growing daily, this location became too small and a Baptist church was offered, where Douglass addressed five hundred.

Douglass's activity during the "hundred conventions" was to bring him into association with two former fugitive slaves who were also beginning to make significant contributions. These were William Wells Brown and Henry Highland Garnet. Brown, from Lexington, Kentucky, had been a cook and barber before becoming a lecturer for the Western New York Anti-Slavery Society; in addition, he would author books, among them a novel, *Clotel, Or the President's Daughter*, and write an important chronicle of the war of 1861–1865, titled *The Negro in the American Rebellion*. His history went to press January 1, 1867, only two years from the war's close; he wrote: "I waited patiently, before beginning this work, with the hope that some one more competent would take the subject in hand; but up to the present, it has not been done, although many books have been written upon the Rebellion." Before leaving Buffalo, the black men taking part in the campaign, with others joining them, convened a convention for consultation previously scheduled and explicated above, including Douglass, Remond, Garnet, Brown, Theodore S. Wright, Amos G. Beaman, and Charles M. Ray.

Moving on to Ohio and then Indiana, Douglass as well as others were to be roughly handled. In Pendleton, Indiana, settled by immigrants from Virginia and North Carolina not amenable to abolitionism, they were unable to obtain a meeting hall. Dr. Fussell, a physician, extending his hospitality, saw to it that a speaker's platform was constructed in some woods, where a large audience began to assemble. Forty years later Douglass wrote:

> As soon as we began to speak a mob of about sixty of the roughest characters I ever looked upon ordered us, through its leaders, to be silent, threatening us, if we were not, with violence. We attempted to dissuade them, but they had not come to parley but to fight, and were well armed. They tore down the platform on which we stood, assaulted Mr. White and knocked out several of his teeth, dealt a heavy blow on William A. White, striking him on the back part of the head, badly cutting his scalp and felling him to the ground. Undertaking to fight my way through the crowd with a stick which I caught up in the melee, I attracted the fury of the mob, which laid me prostrate on the ground under a torrent of blows.

Leaving me thus, with my right hand broken, and in a state of uncon-sciousness.[39]

But the "hundred conventions" had drawn good audiences, and been encouraging to abolitionists. Douglass was now recognized as the lead-ing orator among black men and was a prominent participant in their convention movement—an almost mercurial rise, a phenomenon. First taught his ABCs by the wife of his master in Baltimore so that he might read the Bible, he saw this tutelage come to an end due to the dis-approval of his master. However Douglass continued to learn using various stratagems with his white boyhood playmates, deducing new letters and new words. On the lecture circuit he would soon exceed the expectations of his mentors, displaying genuine talent for public speak-ing. He had a melodious, commanding voice, and as an editor at the *New York Tribune* reported on May 28, 1842, his speech was already dis-tinguished by "the appropriateness of his elocution and gesticulation, and the grammatical accuracy of his sentences." With a bent for self-assertion and independent minded, Douglass was truly unique in that he was now able, forthrightly, to step into his own shoes once he'd emancipated himself. In the previous year on one of his first speaking occasions, appearing before Massachusetts society, he said: "I appear before the immense assembly this evening as a thief and robber. I stole this head, these limbs, this body from my master, and ran off with them."

Returning to the East Douglass would preside over a meeting in Lynn, Massachusetts, now his place of residence, in April. There was a meeting of the New England Society in May, and in the summer months Douglass and Remond toured in Chester County, Pennsylvania, visiting West Chester, Oxford, Kennett Square, and London Grove. In a letter to J. Miller McKim, dated August 22, 1844, Douglass wrote he was now enabled to form a favorable opinion about Pennsylvania antislavery people. They had not "quite rid themselves of what seems to me to be prejudice against color," he noted, "but they are advancing and I trust will soon free themselves from its last vestige."[40]

Douglass sat out the winter months of 1844–45 writing his *Narrative of the Life of Frederick Douglass*, the first of its kind in American letters. A slim one hundred and twenty-five-page volume, it told the story of his life as a slave on Maryland's Eastern Shore and in Baltimore, nam-ing his master and his family. Douglass had been urged to make these disclosures because many of his auditors had begun to question the authenticity of his story—could a man of such eloquence and bearing have been so recently a slave, it was asked. The book was immediately

popular, both in the North and in England, but because of its publication Douglass was now in peril. Advertising himself thus, he became
"painfully alive to the liability" surrounding him—his master could
come and claim him under United States law. To both Douglass and his
supporters, this dictated that he must seek refuge in England.

"A rude, uncultivated fugitive slave," he wrote forty years later in *Life
and Times*, "I was driven to that country which American young gentlemen go to increase their stock of knowledge, to seek pleasure, and to
have their rough democratic manners softened by contact with English
aristocratic refinement." Departing on the steamer *Cambria* of the
Cunard Line, he was accompanied by James N. Buffum of Lynn, a carpenter of some means and vice president of the American society. In a
bow to "American prejudice," he was compelled to berth in the forecas-
tle deck; among his fellow travelers were the Hutchinson Family singers
who often came to his quarters during the passage "and sang their
sweetest songs, making the place eloquent with music and alive with
spirited conversation." On his departure well-wishers had provided
Douglass with a purse covering his expenses—the proceeds of his book
were to go to his wife and family—and introductory letters had been
written for those he'd meet abroad. "Be yourself," advised Phillips, "and
you will succeed."[41]

It was in spring 1843 a small coterie of Germans in Paris welcomed a
young Dr. Karl Marx and his wife, Jenny, arriving from Cologne in
Germany's Rhineland. Freshly laureled among them for his three-year
editorship of the periodical *Rheinische Zeitung*, which had been suppressed by the Prussian government, he had come to join his friend
Arnold Ruge as co-editor of the *Deutsch-Franzosische Jahrbucher*. The
city radiated as the center of enlightened and progressive thought in
Europe in the 1830s and 1840s and beyond. Educated in Bonn and in
Berlin, Marx had just turned his back on an academic position. He had
been a fledgling—he was then twenty-three—but promising member of
the so-called Young Hegelians, including Ruge, Bruno Bauer, David
Strauss, Max Stirner, and Ludwig Feuerbach. Having thoroughly mas-
tered Hegelian philosophy and the dialectical method, Marx would now
embark on his first exhaustive studies of the political economy of the
emergent capitalist system, the theoretical elaborations of Adam Smith
and David Ricardo, of Jean-Baptiste Say and James Mills. In Paris Marx
would also become conversant in the doctrines being advanced in
utopian schemes for social improvement by Saint-Simon, Robert Owen,

and Charles Fourier. It was Owen, a wealthy English factory owner, who had coined the words "communist" and "socialist" in 1827.

These three areas of Marx's radical critique—Hegelian dialectics, political economy, and utopian socialism—were first presented in the so-called Paris or *Economic-Philosophic Manuscripts of 1844*, where he would work out his conception of historical materialism. Not published until 1932, they nevertheless are seen as marking his new departure in thought, Marx typifying his new outlook in these writings in this way: "We see how thoroughgoing Naturalism or Humanism distinguishes itself both from Idealism and Materialism, and is, at the same time, the truth uniting both. We see, at the same time, how only Naturalism is capable of grasping the act of world history." He'd written Arnold Ruge before joining him, "The world has long had the dream of something and must only possess the consciousness of it in order to possess it actually."[42]

There had been three estates much discussed after the French Revolution—the nobility, the clergy, and the bourgeoisie—the last a French word, whereas the English termed it "the middle class." To describe the growing schism within modern society, to this schema the erudite would add the proletariat. The masses of impoverished factory hands, named after the most miserable social formation in ancient Rome whose only function was to produce children— *proles*. It was in June 1844 that the intellectual elites, as well as the ruling structures of Europe, were startled by an uprising of weavers in Silesia in eastern Prussia. The weavers, responding to a sharp cut in wages, burned their own dwellings—landlord's rents were onerous on them—and attacked enterprises, singling out first the manufacturer Zwanzinger, who was particularly hated. The revolt was suppressed by the Prussian army, with eleven weavers killed, and the other participants flogged and imprisoned.

The first addition of the Marx-Ruge collaboration was to be its last, when it could not pass the German border for distribution, and its editors were financially insolvent. But further collaboration between the two would be ended with Ruge's response to the Silesian weavers whom he deprecated in an article written as "a Prussian." Marx responded in the periodical *Vorwarts!* with what was to become his customary polemical vehemence, titled *Critical Notes on "The King of Prussia and Social Reform."* Heinrich Heine, too, had written of *The Silesian Weavers*, first translated into English by Frederick Engels:

> The shuttle is flying, the weaving looms roar.
> Day and night we weave with you at the door.

Old Germany, we weave the cloth of the dead.
Threefold be the curse we weave 'round your head.
We're weaving, we're weaving.

In his criticism of Ruge, Marx contended, as he had in his criticism of Hegel and in an essay *On the Jewish Question*, that the state was ineffectual against the debasement and slavery characteristic in modern economic relations—what was needed was a social revolution. Marx's entire inquiry and presentation is presaged in these years, not in a system as many have taken it, but as a method: historical materialism. He would now engage in long discussions with Pierre Proudhon, the leading theoretician of "socialism," who came to him that he might learn something of the "Hegelian dialectic." And Marx began to attend meetings of the League of the Just, watchmaker Wilhelm Weitling's group, soon to become the Communist League. And he again met Frederick Engels, after encountering him for the first time in Cologne, who was to become his life-long collaborator, whose wealthy family owned and ran a factory in Manchester, England. Engels, undoubtedly a man of talent, as he would remark, having already written and published his *History of the English Working Class*, was to sit in long discussions with Marx, with the two quickly coming to complete agreement. Engels was to find that his friend's entire conception of historical materialism had already been worked out. Their self-sacrificing collaboration and friendship over four decades was to become a paragon in history; but of the two, Marx was the genius.

Now Marx would unleash his unsparing "ruthless" criticism on former collaborators, now his opponents, the withering sarcasm of whose tone still strikes the ear of readers: the Young Hegelians with *The Holy Family* (1844); Proudhon with *The Poverty of Philosophy* (1847); and all with *The German Ideology* (1845–47). This last is his first mature statement, authored jointly with Engels, of his new treatment of philosophy, economics, and history. Marx worked toward its completion at a furious pace, smoking like a chimney and staying up whole nights. After he read the manuscript to his wife, she pointed out that no one had ever denied that economic factors were important in human affairs. But he had struck a determined and convincing chord; it would now only take time and hard work to present its verification. This text, too, would not be published until 1932, subject, Marx would write, "to the gnawing criticism of Mice." Only twenty-seven, this man had already grown the full beard by which posterity would recognize him—and a legacy that may now be his method rather than his perceived system building.

There is a letter to his friend Ludwig Kugelmann in Hanover, June 27, 1870, where Marx stresses his debt to Hegel:

> The German professorial gentlemen have recently found themselves obliged to take notice of me here and there, even if in a stupid fashion.... Herr Lange sings my praises loudly, but with the object of making himself important. Herr Lange, you see, has made a great discovery. The whole of history can be subsumed under a single great natural law. The natural law is the *phrase* (in this application Darwin's expression becomes merely a phrase) "the struggle for life," and the content of this phrase is the Malthusian law of population, or, rather over-population. Thus, instead of analyzing the struggle for life as represented historically in varying and definite forms of society, all that has to be done is to translate every concrete struggle into the phrase, "the struggle for life," and this phrase itself into the Malthusian "population fantasy." One must admit that this is a very impressive method—for bombastic, sham-scientific, pompous ignorance and intellectual laziness.
>
> What this same Lange has to say about the Hegelian method and my application of it is truly childish. First, he understands rien [nothing] of Hegel's method, and thus, secondly, even much less of the critical way I applied it. . . . Herr Lange wonders why Engels, I, etc., take the dead dog Hegel seriously, long after Buchner, Lange, Dr. Duhring, Fechner, etc., had agreed that they had buried him.... Lange is naïve enough to say that in the empirical material I "move with rare freedom." He has not the least idea that this "free movement in material" is altogether nothing but a paraphrase of the *method* of treating the material—namely, the *dialectical method*.[43]

Beginning with *On the Jewish Question*, it is clear that at this early point in his theoretical/practical thinking Marx already had the American scene in view. He pointed out that in the northern states, in particular as codified in state constitutions, a separation of church from state was the only basis upon which Jews could become emancipated in Europe—a future prospect that would also entail their assimilation. Marx would continue to give attention to the continent across the Atlantic, and would write as the European correspondent for Horace Greeley's *New York Tribune*, on sale for two cents—the first mass distribution newspaper in the world. The portentous struggle against slavery, of which the paper was a partisan, and the coming war, would likewise loom large in his thought, and had an impact and gave direction to the very form of his protracted studies.

Douglass was to remain abroad for twenty months, dividing his time among England, Scotland, Wales, and Ireland. He arrived in the midst of the agitation for the repeal of the Corn Laws (in Britain corn meaning grain, and therefore bread), sharing counsel with and coming to know its chief leaders. He also was to play a controversial part in the temperance movement; this happened when an American clergyman objected to his participation for interjecting abolitionism into the discussion, and there was to be an exchange of letters between them, airing their differences. In Scotland he also engaged in the dispute aroused when the Evangelical churches, seeking to build a world alliance, accepted slaveholder-donated money from America, and there was a protracted but unsuccessful campaign demanding they "send the money back." He was not, however, to have any contact with the Chartist labor movement, that being an insular affair that wasn't looking beyond its immediate concerns.

But undoubtedly the greatest impact on him—after, of course, that of hearing many of the best orators of the day, and listening to them with unquenchable adoration, including a hearing and a meeting with Ireland's Daniel O'Connell—was the unchallenged acceptance of his manhood. In "monarchial England" unlike "republican America," nowhere was he barred entry for his color; he could dine in its public restaurants and taverns with other patrons, travel on public conveyances, and be welcomed as a guest into some of the best homes. No reader will miss the stinging injury Douglass felt, nor his indignation at that American refrain—"*We don't allow niggers here*"—as he repeats it seven times in the space of a single page as he remarks on this aspect of American practice in *Life and Times*.

In Edinburgh, in company with the Scottish abolitionist George Thompson, James Buffum, and Garrison—who had come to England the year after Douglass arrived—they all had breakfast at the home of George Combe, the philosopher and author of *Constitution of Man*. "Of course, in the presence of such men," Douglass wrote, "my part was a very subordinate one. I was a listener. Mr. Combe did the most of the talking, and did it so well that nobody felt like interposing. . . . He discussed the corn laws, and the proposal to reduce the hours of labor."[44] Garrison and Thompson would also accompany Douglass to a meeting with Thomas Clarkson, one of the inaugurators of the British antislavery movement. Douglass writes the elderly man took one of his hands in both of his, saying, "God bless you, Frederick Douglass! I have given sixty years of my life to the emancipation of your people, and if I had sixty years more they should all be given to the same cause." And he would also meet other old-line leaders of the movement, William Wilberforce, Thomas Buxton, and Granville Sharpe.

The most intense controversy was to be raised when Douglass's English friends raised money and contacted his master in Maryland to buy his freedom. It was a tacit acknowledgment of the legality of ownership of a human being, it was objected, while the *Liberator* was compelled to devote many columns over a three-month period defending the manner of Douglass's manumission.[45] In the transaction by a document dated November 14, 1846, his person was transferred from the ownership of Thomas Auld to his brother Hugh Auld; and thence, as the document below attests, possession of Frederick Douglass was transferred from Hugh Auld to himself:

> To all whom it may concern: Be it known that I, Hugh Auld of the City of Baltimore, in Baltimore County in the State of Maryland, for divers good causes and considerations me thereunto moving, have released from slavery, liberated, manumitted, and set free, and by these presents do hereby release from slavery, liberate, manumit, and set free, MY NEGRO MAN named Frederick Bailey, otherwise named Douglass, being of the age of twenty-eight years or thereabouts, and able to work and gain a sufficient livelihood and maintenance; and him, the said negro man named Frederick Douglass, I do declare to be henceforth free, manumitted, and discharged from all manner of servitude to me, my executors and administrators forever.
>
> In witness whereof, I the said Hugh Auld, have hereunto set my hand and seal the fifth of December, in the year one thousand eight hundred and forty-six.
> Hugh Auld
> Sealed and delivered in presence of t. Hanson belt, James N.S.T. Wright.

With this "ransom" paid, Douglass was no longer subject to arrest as a fugitive slave in accordance with the Fugitive Slave Act of 1793—the price, one hundred and fifty pounds sterling, or $700. Shortly after this, as Douglass contemplated returning to his home and family, Garrison convinced him to remain in England for another six months. The British antislavery societies were in need of modernization, and Douglass could be an important influence and have bearing on that. His *Narrative* had been popular and sales brisk as a second edition was issued, and it had been translated into French and would be published in France. Douglass was to leave England for Boston in April 1847.

As he prepared to depart, his many prominent friends in the antislavery ranks had intimated that they were preparing a testimonial that he might return to the United States, not only a free man, but relieved of the responsibility of providing for himself and his family—and so labor full-time in the cause of emancipation. The amount raised would come to something over $2,000. But Douglass immediately had other ideas for its use, writing in *Life and Times*:

> How such a project would have succeeded I do not know, but many reasons led me to prefer that my friends should simply give me the means of obtaining a printing press and materials to enable me to start a paper advocating the interests of my enslaved and oppressed people. I told them that perhaps the greatest hindrance to the adoption of the abolition principles by the people of the United States was the low estimate everywhere placed upon the Negro as a man. . . . The grand thing to be done, therefore, was to change this estimate by . . . demonstrating his capacity for a more exalted civilization than slavery and prejudice had assigned him. In my judgment, a tolerably well-conducted press . . . by calling out and making them acquainted with their own latent powers, by enkindling their hope of a future and developing their moral force, prove a most powerful means of removing prejudice and awakening an interest in them. At that time there was not a single newspaper in the country regularly published by the colored people, though many attempts had been made to establish such, and had from one cause or another failed.[46]

On his return Douglass was feted, offering graphic descriptions of his time abroad, in numerous meetings and parties. Telling his Boston cohorts of his plan for publishing a paper, they had many arguments against it: It would cut into his usefulness as a speaker, besides he was better fitted to speak than to write. The landscape, too, was littered with other failed attempts, and there was no way he could make it self-sustaining. "My American friends," Douglass wrote, "looked at me with astonishment. 'A wood-sawyer' offering himself to the public as an editor! A slave, brought up in the depths of ignorance, assuming to instruct the highly civilized people of the North…. The thing looked absurd."[47] To dissuade him Douglass was offered two columns weekly in the *Anti-Slavery Standard*, salaried at $150 a year. Soldiering on despite his disappointment, Douglass would resume his work on the lecture platform and accompany Garrison on a western tour.

Invited to address the annual convention of the Western Anti-Slavery Society at New Lyme, Ohio, scheduled for August 18, 1847, Garrison had also been extended invitations to visit, on their way and on the return trip, various societies in Pennsylvania and New York. He had never been west of the Alleghenies, as in the West abolitionism was largely under the influence of Theodore Weld and the Tappans. Douglass would join him early in the tour, and they would also include in the entourage Stephen S. Foster, an ex-preacher whose fiery language often succeeded in provoking his audiences. Foster's tract *Brotherhood of Thieves*, with reference to the clergy, was for a time one of the most widely circulated pamphlets.

The circuit began in Norristown August 4 at the annual meeting of the Eastern Pennsylvania Anti-Slavery Society, among whose leaders were Robert Purvis and Lucretia Mott. When Douglass arrived, fresh from an August 1 celebration of West Indian emancipation, the *Standard* reported he was "the lion of the occasion." By now a Douglass appearance on the platform was an anticipated event—his was a dramatic presence, with a strong physical stance and a mass of hair, with a well-formed nose, his visage emitting a critical yet sensitive air. He was ever quick to engage at a moment's bidding. His rich baritone pulsing with emotional sensitivity, he could address audiences in powerful tones ready to defy the most erring acoustics. Given the proximity of Philadelphia, a public reception by the "colored" societies and churches of that city was arranged for Garrison and Douglass, with Purvis presiding. In Harrisburg, however, the other side of the ledger was seen as their appearance was marred by "rotten eggs" and the sting of firecrackers and curses. Pelted with stones and brickbats from the audience, Douglass was saved from injury when a group of black men stepped in to act as his bodyguard. It was on the mail coach from Chambersburg, and two long days of travel over the mountains to Pittsburgh, when Douglass was refused the right to eat with other passengers, that he resolved he must persevere in his plan to edit and publish a newspaper. He wrote soon afterward that such a paper "would do a most indispensable work, which it would be wholly impossible for our white friends to do for us.... We must be our own representatives and advocates."[48] It was up to those who suffered wrong to demand redress.

With Garrison and Douglass expected for two days of meetings in Pittsburgh, a reception was planned where they would be met by the Duquesne Brass Band. When the mail coach pulled in and the passengers got off, introductions were performed on the corner in the gaslight. When these formalities were over a dark-hued man with a bald pate strode forward to grasp Douglass's hand. "Martin Delany," Douglass exclaimed. "You're the man I want to talk to." Delany had been born in Charles Town, Virginia, to a free mother and a slave father. Moving across the Mason-Dixon Line with his family, Delany had grown up in Chambersburg. Coming to Pittsburgh at nineteen, he began grappling with abolitionism and the political and social condition of his people under the guidance of John Vashon. Beginning the study of medicine, he became competent in the practice of "cupping and leaching," still prominent in treatment at that time. In spring 1843, as a rough and ready editor, he had launched *The Mystery*, a four-page antislavery weekly. In it Delany was the scourge of the American Colonization Society and of slave catchers alike, for the city at the juncture of the Ohio, Allegheny, and Monongahela rivers was a destination for slaves escaping from Virginia, and the state's proximity meant fugitives must ever be on the alert. In one case in that winter of 1847 *The Mystery* reported that a black weaver, Thomas Johnson, had helped slave catchers and authorities locate a fugitive from Virginia, Daniel Lockhart. Held in the Monongahela House, Delany led a crowd of blacks who wrestled the man free, spiriting him off to Canada. Johnson sued Delany for libel and won. The old English rule prevailed in Pennsylvania; the case hinging on the single point: was it libelous to call a black a "slave catcher"?[49] A jury of twelve white men found it "slanderous and disgraceful," and Delany was fined $150. Finding the outcome scandalous, newspapers all over the state contributed to a fund to pay the fine, and Pittsburgh's *Daily Dispatch* set up a collection box.

Douglass and Garrison, now joined by Foster, held five spirited meetings in Pittsburgh. Garrison wrote his wife August 18 that he'd "seen nothing like it this side of the Atlantic." Delany gave a close hearing of Douglass's plan as it was confided to him, but Douglass wanted more— he wanted Delany to join him in it. Delany answered in the affirmative on the spot. The two would continue their discussions aboard a steamboat, ending at Beaver, Pennsylvania, when the abolitionists continued on omnibus to New Brighton. The meeting there, held in the upper room of a general store, was described by Garrison in the letter to his wife: "Over our heads were piled up across the beams many barrels of flour; and while we were speaking, the mice were busy nibbling at them, causing their contents to whiten some of our dresses, and thinking perchance, that our speeches needed to be a little more *floury*.... The meetings were addressed at considerable length by Douglass and myself, and also by Dr. Delany, who spoke on the subject of prejudice against color in a very witty and energetic manner.... Black as jet (he is) a fine fellow of great energy and spirit."[50]

The abolition triumvirate, now taking the canal boat to Youngstown, reached New Lyme August 15, three days before the convention, which was held in a huge tent with seating for four thousand. Garrison was to give an exposition of his theory of disunionism. He was challenged in this by Joshua R. Giddings, elected to the U.S. House of Representatives in 1838 from the Western Reserve, who had notably carried the anti-slavery fight into the Congress. But Garrison was not without authority in Ohio, and the influential *Anti-Slavery Bugle* of Salem took its cue from the *Liberator* and the *Standard*, proclaiming from its masthead—"No Union with Slaveholders." Garrison was to report to his wife that he was gratified when Giddings "alluded to me in very handsome terms, as also to Douglass."[51]

After the Western Anti-Slavery Society meeting the trio was in Oberlin, where, Garrison was to report to his wife, they met the graduating Lucy Stone. From Oberlin, Douglass and Garrison proceeded without Foster through Richfield, Medina, Massillon, Leesburg, and then Salem. The *Bugle* would report a gathering of five thousand representing "the largest anti-slavery gathering ever convened in the country." A week later meetings convened in Cleveland, the last held in the open air in drizzling rain. Garrison was overcome with exhaustion and fever; their travel through the country had been rigorous and full of hardship, riding in horse-drawn wagons to towns thirty and forty miles apart. Confined to bed under a doctor's care, Garrison urged Douglass to continue the tour.

Reaching Buffalo, then Rochester, then Syracuse, a week after leaving his friend and mentor, Douglass learned his condition had become critical. He thought of returning to Cleveland but did not; instead he expressed his concern for Garrison to Samuel J. May, who would write him. As five weeks passed, and as Garrison recovered, in a letter to his wife he would convey his astonishment that so far as he knew Douglass had neither written nor made inquiry about his health. His reproach of Douglass's seeming lack of solicitude indeed had an underlying cause, as near the end of September Douglass announced his intention to launch a newspaper. On November 1, 1847, Douglass moved his family to Rochester, New York.

The two had never had a moment's discussion about the newspaper during their tour, and Garrison wrote his wife October 20 that Douglass's conduct in regard to the paper "has been impulsive, inconsiderate and highly inconsistent with his decision in Boston." The former colleagues would remain outwardly on cordial terms, but a personal breach had arisen between them. In only a few years Douglass would begin to repudiate one after another of his former positions—the first to go would be reliance on "moral suasion," then the efficacy of abstaining from political engagement, then the charge that the U.S. Constitution was pro-slavery. When Douglass repudiated this last tenet in 1851, Garrison exclaimed suddenly from the platform "there is roguery somewhere." After 1853 the two would never communicate personally again, and there would be years of rancor between them.

Douglass would call the paper the *North Star*, and its prospectus read as follows: "The object of the NORTH STAR will be to attack *Slavery* in all its forms and aspects; advocate *Universal Emancipation*; exalt the standard of *Public Morality*; promote the Moral and Intellectual Improvement of the COLORED PEOPLE; and hasten the day of FREEDOM to the Three Millions of our *Enslaved Fellow countrymen*."

William C. Nell, a black Garrisonian, was to be the publisher, and Martin Delany would join Douglass as co-editor. Douglass would remain in Rochester while Delany would travel, lining up agents, correspondents, and subscriptions. When Garrison dissuaded Douglass from seeking to publish his own paper earlier that year, no doubt he was speaking from hard experience, cautioning that trying to edit a paper while meeting the demands of the speaking circuit was more than a daunting undertaking. Douglass undoubtedly was not wholly naïve in regard to the prospect before him, and his stand must be seen as both courageous and principled; but he might also have thought if Garrison could surmount the difficulties, then perhaps he might too. As important as Garrison and the *Liberator* are, both on the contemporary scene and in retrospect, Frederick Douglass and the *North Star* and its successors were to loom equally large.

In his *Life and Times* Douglass begins his chapter "John Brown and Mrs. Stowe" this way: "About the time I began my enterprise in Rochester I chanced to spend a night and a day under the roof of a man whose character and conversation, and whose objects and aims in life, made a very deep impression upon my mind and heart. His name had been mentioned to me by several prominent colored men, among whom were the Rev. Henry Highland Garnet and J. W. Loguen. In speaking of him their voices would drop to a whisper and what they said of him made me very eager to see and to know him. Fortunately, I was invited to see him in his own house."

Douglass gives two accounts of this initial meeting with John Brown, in *Life and Times* and in a speech he delivered at Harpers Ferry, West Virginia, on May 30, 1881, at the fourteenth anniversary of the founding of Storer College. The first edition of the autobiography was completed and published that year and substantial parts of the account in both are identical, with the speech containing several interesting remarks not figuring in the book. When that volume appeared John

Brown Jr. and Richard Hinton noticed an intriguing discrepancy, and in the following decade Hinton would publish his biography of Brown, noting that Douglass clearly conflated details of the first meeting with another happening in 1858 in Douglass's own house. Details that could only have come with the experience of the subsequent decade—elements, specifically, that would be added after the Kansas warfare—are omitted in this account, and will be discussed in a later chapter.

Douglass indicates it was in 1847 that he first met John Brown, without stating the exact date; in fact; it was only weeks after his return from his tour in Great Britain. Garnet and Loguen, as indicated, informed Douglass about an unusual white man flittering among the blacks in Springfield, Massachusetts. Whether one or both personally conveyed an invitation from him to Douglass cannot be known, but Douglass received such and lost no time in traveling to that city, arriving on May 15. Brown wrote to his eldest son on that date saying he was "in hourly expectation of a visit from [Douglass]."[52] Douglass would again be in Springfield on February 1 in the next year when he spoke at the town hall, with Brown undoubtedly in his audience. And Douglass would speak a second time on October 29, 1848, in Springfield, and make another personal visit to Brown on November 18, alluded to in the *North Star* on December 8 as a "recent interview with Mr. John Brown." Of the October appearance, Douglass reported in his paper: "Since leaving Rochester on the 27th . . . I have spoken once in Springfield, once in Lynn, three times in New Bedford."

Arriving at the establishment of Perkins and Brown, Douglass found it a substantial brick building on a prominent and busy street, giving him the impression the man he'd come to see must have considerable wealth. After a cordial welcome, as the hours of business were ending Brown conveyed his guest to his home. Now an entirely changed perception was before him—the house in which his host resided with his family was a small wooden structure on a back street, in a neighborhood chiefly occupied by laboring men and mechanics. Plain as the outside was, the inside of the house, Douglass observed, was even plainer; "its furniture would have satisfied a Spartan." But his "welcome," he wrote, "was all that I could have asked. Every member of the family, young and old, seemed glad to see me, and I was made much at home in a very little while." The meal prepared for him was a hearty beef soup with cabbage and potatoes, served by all the members of Brown's large family on a table of the plainest workmanship, "passed," Douglass remarked, "under the misnomer of tea."

The man whose name Douglass heard spoken in whispers, he found, was manifestly the directing spirit of this house and for his family, "and was likely to become (his) too if (he) stayed long enough with him." Douglass depicted him in a striking paragraph:

> In person he was lean, strong, and sinewy, of the best New England mold, built for times of trouble and fitted to grapple with the flintiest hardships. Clad in plain American woolen, shod in boots of cowhide leather, and wearing a cravat of the same substantial material, under six feet high, less than 150 pounds in weight, aged about fifty, he presented a figure straight and symmetrical as a mountain pine. His bearing was singularly impressive. His head was not large, but compact and high. His hair was coarse, strong, slightly gray, and closely trimmed, and grew low on his forehead. His face was smoothly shaved, and revealed a strong, square mouth, supported by a broad and prominent chin. His eyes were bluish-gray, and in conversation they were full of light and fire.

After the meal, Brown and Douglass withdrew into the family parlor where they would engage in discussion from eight in the evening till three the next morning. Brown began cautiously, apprehending opposition to his views, knowing Douglass's position as a notable "Garrisonian." Douglass's evocative account continues:

> He denounced slavery in look and language fierce and bitter, thought that slaveholders had forfeited their right to live, that the slaves had the right to gain their liberty in any way they could, did not believe that moral suasion would ever liberate the slave, or that political action would abolish the system. He said that he had long had a plan which could accomplish this end, and he had invited me to his house to lay that plan before me. He said he had been for some time looking for colored men to whom he could safely reveal his secret, and at times he had almost despaired of finding such men, but that now he was encouraged, for he saw heads of such rising up in all directions. He had observed my course at home and abroad, and he wanted my cooperation.

"He was not averse to the shedding of blood," Douglass wrote, and "thought the practice of carrying arms would be a good one for the colored people to adopt." "It would give them a sense of their manhood," for "no people, he said, could have self-respect, or be respected, who would not fight for their freedom." DuBois was to write this "earlier scheme probably looked toward the use of Negro allies almost exclusively outside his own family. This was eminently fitting but impractical, as Douglass and his fellows must have urged. White men could move where they would in the United States, but to introduce an armed band exclusively or mainly of Negroes from the North into the South was difficult if not impossible. Nevertheless, some Negroes of the right type were needed and to John Brown's mind the Underground Railroad was bringing North the very material he required."[53]

Drawing Douglass's attention to a map of the United States, pointing out the route of the Allegheny range stretching away from the borders of New York into the southern states, Brown began: "These mountains are the basis of my plan. God has given the strength of the hills to freedom; they were placed here for the emancipation of the Negro race; they are full of natural forts, where one man for defense will be equal to a hundred for attack; they are full also of good hiding-places, where large numbers of brave men could be concealed, and baffle and elude pursuit for a long time." Brown's proposal was to create an armed force to act in the very heart of the South. The plan was "to take at first about twenty-five picked men, and begin on a small scale—supply them with arms and ammunition and post them in squads of fives on a line of twenty-five miles. The most persuasive and judicious of these shall go down to the fields from time to time, as opportunity offers, and induce the slaves to join them, seeking and selecting the most restless and daring." These mountains, he told Douglass, afford an excellent "pathway for a grand stampede from the Slave States, a grand exodus into the Free States, and, through the latter, into Canada."[54]

As they began running slaves off, retaining the strong and brave in the mountains, and sending others north via the Underground Railroad, operations would be enlarged and wouldn't be confined to one locality. In some cases slaveholders would be approached at midnight and induced to give up their slaves, and take their best horses to ride away upon. "But," Douglass interjected, "suppose you succeed in running off a few slaves, and thus impress the Virginia slaveholders with a sense of insecurity in their slaves, the effect will be only to make them sell their slaves further south." "That," said Brown, "will be what I want first to do; then I would follow them up. If we could drive slavery out of *one county*, it would be a great gain—it would weaken the system throughout the state."

"But they would employ bloodhounds to hunt you out of the mountains," Douglass proposed. "That they might attempt," Brown said, "but chances are, we should whip them, and when we should have whipped one squad, they would be careful how they pursued." "But you might be surrounded and cut off from your provisions or means of subsistence." This could not be done, Brown thought, so that they could not cut their way out.

Bringing up a cardinal trope of Garrison's, Douglass suggested that slaveholders might be converted. Brown became much excited; "that could never be," he said, "I know their proud hearts. They can never be induced to give up their slaves, until they have felt a big stick about their heads."[55] In Brown's view, slavery was a state of war "to which the slaves were unwilling parties and consequently they had a right to anything necessary to their peace and freedom." He would shed no blood and avoid a fight except in self-defense, Douglass wrote, "when he would of course do his best." In his Storer College speech Douglass was to give this summation of the objectives sought by Brown: "He believed this movement would weaken slavery in two ways—first by making slave property insecure, it would become undesirable; and secondly it would keep the anti-slavery agitation alive and public attention fixed upon it, and thus lead to the adoption of measures to abolish the evil altogether. He held that there was need of something startling to prevent the agitation of the question from dying out; that slavery had come near being abolished in Virginia by the Nat Turner insurrection, and he thought his method would speedily put an end to it, both in Maryland and Virginia."

"He often said to me," Douglass informed his audience, "though life was sweet to him, he would willingly lay it down for the freedom of my people; and on one occasion he added, that he had already lived about as long as most men, since he had slept less, and if he should now lay down his life the loss would not be great, for in fact he knew no better use for it." In *Life and Times*, Douglass remarks, "I might have noticed the simple manner in which he lived," observing "that he had adopted this method in order to save money to carry out his purposes…. Had some men made such display of rigid virtue, I should have rejected it, as affected, false, and hypocritical, but in John Brown, I felt it to be real as iron or granite."[56]

The basis for Douglass's accounts would appear then to be a composite of conferences in succession, the commencement of a sustained and substantial relationship spanning twelve crucial years—1847 to 1859. Significantly, "From this night," Douglass concluded his account in *Life and Times*, "while I continued to write and speak against slavery, I became all the same less hopeful of its peaceful abolition. My utterances became more and more tinged by the color of this man's strong impressions."

For the Sake of the Union

On September 14, 1847, as U.S. envoy to Mexico Nicholas Trist signed the treaty ending the war between the two nations at Guadalupe Hidalgo, the nation to the north enlarged its territory by nearly one quarter while the nation to the south reduced its by nearly half—thus concluding sixteen months of war. In return for payment of fifteen million dollars and assumption of all Mexican debts owed to American citizens, that treaty stipulated Mexico recognized the Rio Grande boundary of Texas and ceded New Mexico and Upper California to the United States. On August 8 of the previous year during a debate in Congress on an appropriations bill for the Mexican War, Pennsylvania representative David Wilmot proposed an amendment "that, as an express and fundamental condition to the acquisition of any territory from the Republic of Mexico . . . neither slavery nor involuntary servitude shall ever exist in any part of said territory." Reflecting on what that war darkly presaged, Ralph Waldo Emerson wrote, "The

United States will conquer Mexico, but it will be as the man swallows the arsenic, which brings him down in turn. Mexico will poison us all."[1]

In the cotton belt and across the South by the decade of the 1840s—from steamboat landing to dusty crossroad village, from railroad depot to hotel lounge, and from front parlors and front porches as well as counting houses and lawyers' offices, but especially along with the clink and libation flowing in countless tavern bars, the subject of all conversation was ever cotton and slaves; or in an epigrammatic judgment constantly repeated: "Niggers and cotton—cotton and niggers."[2] Southerners confidently believed these were now among the strongest players in the world, responsible for a burgeoning international system joining industrial factory with bank finance through the mighty strand of a plant fiber harvested by black-skinned labor. A proper view of Southern political economy is attainable then only through simultaneous appraisal of these twin commodities, as paradoxical as that may be in its implications.

Cotton planting began on an extensive scale, we have seen, in South Carolina and Georgia. By the 1820s these states were growing half the cotton in the United States. Thence it continued its fateful journey through an extensive region, holding Alabama, Mississippi, and Louisiana in turn; reaching northward into large districts of Tennessee and Arkansas, while carrying its expansion into the eastern counties of Texas. Concomitantly a black slave population ranged throughout these areas of intensive cultivation, whose numbers, on a contiguous county by county basis, exceeded the white population. They were closely regulated in a separate sphere as chattels and under the control of superintending whites. The profitability of this system depended on it being applied on an extensive scale on large landed estates, which necessitated a substantial outlay of capital and goods; on this the South, as this section came to call itself, would rise in all its portentous meaning. Other commodities produced on an extensive scale using slave labor in the South were tobacco in Maryland, Virginia, and Kentucky, rice along the South Carolina and Georgia coasts, sugarcane in Louisiana's Mississippi Delta and along the Gulf Coast south of Galveston in Texas, and a mixed crop of hemp and tobacco in Missouri. While this system was expansionist of necessity in its quest for profit—the *raison d'être* of any capitalist concern—it was also of necessity expansionist in the political sphere.

By the census of 1860, of a population of five million whites and four million slaves there were only 300,000 slaveholders; of these only about 50,000 could be ranked as significant planters with twenty slaves or more, capable of assuming a commanding social and political role on established estates. With the growth of their cotton kingdom, they accrued both political power and rising prestige, becoming a class with an outsized ambition that was secure in its dominance and influence in the national government for many decades. The basis of representation in the national government was, of course, derived from the numbers of population and their component as states. While the northern free states were gaining over the southern slave states in Congress, the basis of southern power could and was maintained by control in the Senate and of the presidency. This necessitated equilibrium, and while the Northwest Ordinance enacted by the first Congress had prohibited slavery in those territories, by 1820 a new balance was sought as Maine was admitted as a free State, with the addition of Missouri as a slave state despite its location in the prohibited territory. The Missouri Compromise engineered by Kentucky's venerable senator Henry Clay, himself a slaveholder, became the model on which the much vaunted Union had its foundation.

But this basis on which Southern "civilization" rested was problematic. A man's wealth and importance were assessed only by the number of slaves he owned; a reckoning of considerable consequence—having, as it did, its substance neither in things nor in capital. And while it appeared that slaves by and large were docile and contented—when not contaminated by extraneous influences—the proportion of black to white itself epitomized the South's dilemma. Congregated in numbers, slaveholders themselves observed, their slaves often became insolent, with the planter always mindful of the experience of St. Domingo. While assuaged by "the innate patience," the "docility," the "child-like simplicity" of servile blacks, slaveholders and other onlookers were ever aware and impressed by the portent that these "children in imagination" were bearers of a fully human nature. This was a reckoning that had to be deferred at all cost—nothing would be allowed to get in the way of the alchemy of procuring wealth from cotton fiber and black skins. It has also been observed there was a periodicity to the major slave risings in the United States—Gabriel in 1800, followed by Vesey in 1822, followed by Nat Turner in 1831; with each too, although not often noted, having their antecedents, portending latent forces of revolt. After the Vesey conspiracy a South Carolina publicist wrote: "We regard our negroes as the 'Jacobins' of the country, against whom we should always be upon our guard, and who, although we fear no permanent affects from any insurrectionary movement on their part, should be watched with an eye of steady and unremitting observation."[3] Another of the discerning observers and a key participant in this system, Robert Toombs, who was quoted by Marx in an article he wrote for Vienna's *Die Press* on the American Civil War in 1862, commented on the significance of this aforementioned proportionality: "In fifteen years more, without a great increase in slave territory either the slaves must be permitted to flee the whites, or the whites must flee the slaves."[4]

That a black could break this bondage by running away was obvious, as many did from countless motives, and not only toward free states. Notices were constantly appearing in southern papers, often providing a motive for runaways—that said individual was thought to be lurking near another plantation where his wife and children were held, and so on. Throughout the South many slaves sought to maintain themselves as maroons in swamps and remote areas, and there were constant intimations in letters and newspapers of incidents of insubordination and outright insurrection. For order in the "quarters" a thorough system of patrol was maintained that became the responsibility of every white man, particularly those in the militia, and searches and ferretings for contraband and weapons were constant. But this system of control inevitably depended on brute force and punishment—there was no deterrent, after all, to be had in lengthening the term of service, for slaves were already slaves for life unless manumitted by the beneficence of an owner. The whip must be relied upon.

But, then as ever, each decade of the American chronicle has been a "reopening of a never-long interrupted drama" of a subjugated people's struggle "to throw off their yoke."[5] And the decade of the 1840s was not exceptional. The *New Orleans Picayune* reported on November 17, 1842: "Some excitement prevailed in the parishes of Concordia, Madison, and Carroll, in consequence of the discovery of a contemplated rising of the negroes. There are now in the swamps of that region about 300 runaway negroes belonging to said parishes, all armed, it is presumed. Some fifteen or twenty negroes have been arrested and examined, and from the facts elicited, it is believed that an insurrection was contemplated about Christmas. The plot seems to have been extensive, embracing negroes from nearly every plantation in the three parishes."

The *Liberator* carried a report on January 31, 1845, describing "an apparently spontaneous outbreak [that] occurred in Tennessee when several patrols broke into a meeting of about one hundred Negroes. The slaves, some of whom were crudely armed, resisted, and a general melee resulted, the precise outcome of which is not clear." That July the *Baltimore Patriot* carried an interesting account of an unusual formation of slaves said to be from St. Mary's, Charles, and Prince George's counties. Marching six abreast "headed by a powerful negro fellow, sword in hand," they were intent on reaching Pennsylvania—a free state. Intercepted near Rockville, in Montgomery County, about twenty miles north of Washington and fifty miles south of their declared destination, they were surrounded from several directions. These walkers, armed also with a pistol, with others carrying scythes and clubs, were again reported on in the *Liberator*, this dated October 10, 1845: "Several of the Negroes were shot, thirty-one were captured and lodged in Rockville jail, five of them were wounded, one severely."

In 1834 James K. Polk, an important southern politician and slaveholder in Tennessee prior to his election as president ten years later, decided to buy land near Coffeeville, Mississippi, to establish a plantation and ship his slaves. Polk wrote his wife September 26: "The negroes have no idea they are going to be sent to the South, and I do not wish them to know it, and therefore it would be best to say nothing about it at home, for it might be carreyed [sic] back to them." This relocation from Tennessee to north-central Mississippi was part of a spectacular emigration in the decade, with slaves representing well over half the increase. Settlement beyond this region—in Texas—first occurred as early as 1812, however, with an expedition for "republicanization" and conquest by McGee and Gutierrez from the Red River. With these annihilated in the following year; by 1816 Galveston Island was occupied, and Louis-Michel Aury declared governor. This again failing, occupation of Galveston was achieved by the brigand Jean Lafitte. By 1820, with a treaty signed between the United States and Spain making the Sabine River the boundary, Moses Austin, an investor in Virginia and Missouri mines and father of Stephen Austin, conceived an idea for American settlement, applying to colonize the Brazos region with three hundred families. His application was granted, providing the settlers were Louisianans of good character and Roman Catholics. After little more than a decade, in 1836 with the Mexican General Santa Anna as their prisoner, and the martyrs of the Alamo revenged, the Americans sent commissioners to Washington with instructions to propose annexation. Now commenced a Republic of Texas with the recognition of slavery, which had been prohibited by Mexico. The question of annexation was to occupy the presidential office for the next two election cycles, and have a determining impact down to 1860 and the election of Abraham Lincoln.

An aging war hero, William Henry Harrison, was elected president in 1840, with John Tyler as his vice president. Tyler, an aristocratic slaveholder from Williamsburg, Virginia, became the first vice president succeeding a deceased president, for Harrison was dead one month after his inauguration. The pending Texas annexation, deferred because of its deleterious effect on the sectional balance struck after the Missouri Compromise, was now to become the primary mission of Tyler's presidency. "Texas was the great scheme that occupied me," he later admitted.[6] Expelled for taking this position from the Whig Party to which he'd been an adherent, Tyler announced his expansionist agenda in his first address to Congress, June 1, 1841. He argued that annexation would preserve the balance between the states, thus avoiding a sectional conflict, and thereby protect an important American institution—slavery. Down the road, he could foresee too, it might secure his reelection.

This priority of his administration was delayed, however, while Secretary of State Daniel Webster (held over from Harrison's administration) completed the Webster-Ashburton Treaty, finalizing the eastern boundary between the United States and Canada. Webster, an opponent of annexation, would make way for Abel P. Upshur, also a Virginia slaveholder, who would begin secret negotiations when assuming office with the Texas government. Promised military protection from Mexico in exchange for a commitment to annexation, Tyler faced a constitutional quandary, since congressional approval of such commitments was required. It also would require a two-thirds majority, which clearly would not be forthcoming in the present balance in Congress. Thus the matter stood in abeyance, as, on February 28, 1844, the presidential party and cabinet and governmental officials and officers gathered aboard the USS *Princeton* in anchorage in the Potomac to witness a demonstration of the longest naval gun in the world. After several successful firings, the presidential party went below for refreshment and conviviality. Hearing that another firing was being prepared, Tyler began returning to deck when he paused to hear his son's rendition of a ditty for the guests. Meanwhile on deck the gun had misfired, killing the secretaries of state and of the navy, along with other persons standing by—a tragedy greater than any yet confronting the nation or the presidency, until the assassination at Ford's Theatre in April 1865. Of equal portent, John Cadwell Calhoun would now succeed Upshur as secretary of state.

Calhoun was, along with Henry Clay and Daniel Webster, part of a triumvirate of powerful statesmen who would be on the American scene as much as four decades. Clay had played a determining role in the United States war with Britain in 1812, as he had in the formation of the American Colonization Society and in the Compromise of 1820. He was regarded as the preeminent politician of the West, with an up-

and-coming Whig Party member from Illinois looking to him as his model—Abraham Lincoln. Also a Whig, Clay was a plantation owner and slaveholder in Lexington, Kentucky, who appeared at various levels in state and national government, as representative and senator and as secretary of state, running on a presidential ticket three times. By the time he reached Congress in 1812, he had positioned himself as an important and determining figure. Calhoun, representing South Carolina and thus articulating the Southern sectional position in general, was of equal renown. His convictions about the "positive good" of slavery and "state's rights" have been aptly described as having "cast iron rigidity." High strung with a serious demeanor, he is portrayed as stately and reserved, but had a severe countenance not noted for charisma. Publishing his views in an essay, *South Carolina Exposition and Protest*, he proposed a theory of a "concurrent majority," where through the doctrine of nullification a state had a right "to interpose, in the last resort, in order to arrest an unconstitutional act of the General Government, within its limits." He contested these views during the famous "nullification crisis" in the presidency of Andrew Jackson, where war with South Carolina was averted by the "Great Pacificator," Henry Clay.

An equally admired member of this set was Daniel Webster, a Dartmouth-trained lawyer originally from New Hampshire who relocated to Boston. A gifted orator, also a Whig, he had become closely identified with the families with cotton-spinning interests in Lowell and Lawrence, himself enamored of wealth and ostentation. Theodore Parker would say of him after the Compromise of 1850, in which he played a key part, "No man living has done so much to debauch the conscience of the nation."[7]

In June 1844, a Tyler-Calhoun annexation treaty with Texas was rejected in the Senate. With a new president, James K. Polk, elected that November—the lame duck Tyler in his annual message to Congress announced that "a controlling majority of the people and a large majority of the states have declared in favor of immediate annexation," with the new president's election. The issue, it was decided, could now decisively and with finality be dealt with. Tyler called for a joint resolution of Congress requiring a simple majority vote; in late February 1845, a resolution on Texas annexation was approved by Congress and signed by the Tyler on March 1. On his last day in office, too, Florida was admitted to the Union as the twenty-seventh state, making it the fifteenth slave state. Elected on a platform demanding the addition of the territory of Oregon north to 54 degrees 40 minutes latitude and of Texas to the Rio Grande, Polk would compromise with Britain at the 49th latitude, but demand New Mexico and Upper California be granted to the United States from Mexico. Later that year, on December 29, 1845, Texas accepted the terms and entered the Union as the twenty-eighth state, making the sixteenth slave state. With General Zachary Taylor dispatched to the disputed Rio Grande, Polk would address the Congress May 11, 1846, when he declared that a state of war existed between Mexico and the United States over the ceded territory. Santa Fe would be occupied by Missouri volunteers and a regiment of regulars led by Stephan Watts Kearny, while in California, where San Francisco Bay was principally coveted, a group of settlers hoisted the banner of the "bear flag republic" assisted by the son-in-law of Missouri's powerful Senator Thomas Hart Benton, John C. Frémont, captain in the United States army and famous as the "pathfinder" of the West.

These, it was conjectured, might make for territories where slavery could be profitably utilized, as many in the South foresaw a line might be drawn demarking Missouri's southern boundary straight across the southwest, 36 degrees 30 minutes north latitude. Advocates foresaw a region, with the annexation of Cuba, whereby slavery might be "diffused" into Mexico and Central America, and a mighty empire reign. This diffusion, it was proposed, from the states of the Old South into lands westward, coupled with deportation of freedmen, might resolve the political and social antagonism threatening the American republic down the road. In the meantime, it was said, ownership of slaves in a thriving economy represented the acme of the "American dream."

Differing explanations are given for the motives inducing John Brown to locate at Springfield, Massachusetts. "The best authenticated records, thus far produced," James Redpath wrote, "go to show that it was the result of the same spirit of resistance to organized wrong that had distinguished itself in his own history and the history of his ancestry."[8] In the year following that move Brown wrote his father about the condition of his affairs in a letter dated January 16, 1848: "The country in this direction has been suffering one of the severest money pressures known for many years. The consequence to us has been, that some of those who have contracted for wool from us are as yet unable to pay for and take the wool as they agreed, and we are on that account unable to close our business. This, with some trouble and perplexity, is the greatest injury we have suffered by it."[9]

The panorama, so broadly atmospheric, Brown offers in accounting for economic phenomena are clearly provided by a world affected with telegraph and railroad, mass circulation newspapers, and the rapidly extending reach of industrial and finance capital, not at all surprising for a man of his acumen. The planters of the South were no less attuned to these pressures, arising in seemingly obscure places that could turn mere eddies into gales, sweeping beyond horizons on a globalizing extent. It was also during this month, in far-away California, gold was discovered near San Francisco at Sutter's Mill. The initial reaction of the owner of the land on which the metal was found, with plans for a growing fruit and vegetable concern, was to suppress the finding. But as rumor spread, it was finally published in newspapers; the *New York Herald* reported the discovery August 19, 1848. By December 5 in his address to the Congress President James K. Polk confirmed it. San Francisco would explode from a hamlet of two hundred persons before the discovery, to over a thousand early in 1849, and into a burgeoning city with twenty-five thousand residents by 1850. Prospectors and jobbers, contractors and merchants, sailing ships and deserting sailors, with all their accoutrements, poured in from nearly every continent in the world.

Meanwhile after the New Year in 1848 one of the grandest revolutionary tempests ever witnessed moved across Europe. In broad summary, starting from Paris, it took over fifty separate cities and localities in its throes; moving on to Berlin and Frankfurt and Cologne, to Vienna and Buda and Pest and to Prague; sweeping across nation states and empires, principalities, provinces, and cantons; from France to Belgium to Denmark, through Germany and Switzerland into Poland, from Austro-Hungary to Italy. With antecedents in poor grain harvests in 1846 and strife in Galicia, as the price of bread shot up along with other staples, profits began to plummet, as workers and their families found wages could barely sustain them. In France's urban centers the bourgeoisie—doctors, lawyers, merchants, with some leading industrialists—began an active campaign for greater suffrage through a *champagne des banquets*, so named because its leaders sought to raise money at dinners featuring prominent speakers. When a scheduled banquet on February 22 was cancelled by officials, fearing an organized protest would include the working classes, factory workers and skilled artisans, middle-class liberals, and bohemians alike poured into the streets erecting barricades. Suppressed by an army garrison stationed in Paris, King Louis Philippe, nevertheless, bowed before reforms. Rejected by the masses, the king fled on February 24, and a Second Republic was proclaimed.

These tidings sent revolt cascading east: Kaiser Friedrich Wilhelm IV yielded, promising a Prussian Assembly. Then Germany's desperate provinces joined in a Frankfurt Assembly to form a national constitution. In Vienna insurgent forces, joined by students, framed a constituent assembly, while Lajos Kossuth led a movement of Magyars for national autonomy in Hungary. Prague was similarly in rebellion; while new constitutions were proclaimed in Tuscany and Piedmont in Italy to overthrow their Austrian masters. By August, though, Austrian legions crushed democratic movements piecemeal in Vienna, in Buda and Pest, and in Prague. In Paris, in June a revolt of the urban proletariat was sparked when the national workshops, deemed ineffectual and pointless by the bourgeoisie of the Second Republic, were closed. Demanding "bread or lead," protesters poured out of workshops and from the hovels of the poor. The resulting battles on the barricades of June 23–26 told of the death of over 10,000 insurgents, and the deportation of 4,000 to Algeria.

The contest began at the barricade erected at the Porte Saint Denis on June 23, as the First and Second Legions of the National Guard marched in from the boulevards. When within range, the massed insurgents fired their volley, scattering the cobblestone streets with the corpses of soldiers. This served to irritate the guards rather than to intimidate them, Victor Hugo wrote of that emblematic tableau on the ramparts in his memoirs titled "The June Days."

> At this juncture a woman appeared upon its crest, a woman young, handsome, disheveled, terrible. This woman, who was a prostitute, pulled up her clothes to her waist and screamed to the guards in that frightful language of the lupanar that one is always compelled to translate: "Cowards! fire, if you dare, at the belly of a woman!" Here the affair became appalling. The National Guard did not hesitate. A volley brought the wretched creature down, and with a piercing shriek she toppled off the barricade. A silence of horror fell alike upon besiegers and besieged. . . . It was then that the war commenced. . . . On one side the despair of the people, on the other the despair of society.[10]

In November of the previous year, at the congress of the Communist League, Karl Marx and Frederick Engels had been commissioned to write its manifesto. Completed in German by January 1848, it was hurried to the publisher a few weeks before February 24 and brought out in French translation shortly before the June insurrection; all across Europe prior to 1848 both ruled and rulers held their breath in expectation of revolution, as if waiting for a deluge. Heinrich Heine, in Paris,

projected the fall of Louis Philippe as the taking down of the conspicuous elephant of the Bastille: letting loose a thousand rats. But the
Manifesto of the Communist Party, like the revolution it heralded,
seemed destined, as quickly as it sprang into existence, for oblivion.
Concluding his account, Hugo wrote: "For four months we have been
living in a furnace. What consoles me is that the statue of the future will
issue from it. It required such a brazier to melt such a bronze."

There is no doubt that John Brown as well as others knew of these
events, and had been moved by them—although Brown probably was
only somewhat aware of a nascent communist movement, he notably
has been described by more than a few observers as a "red republican."
Victor Hugo in *Les Miserables* would model his hero after him.

The prospect for realizing a fair price for wool growers in the west,
Brown saw, was onerous on the farmers and their families alike, keeping them at a subsistence income. To maintain their monopoly, buyers
for the mills brought wool ungraded, paying the lowest prices, grading
it afterward to gather their profits. To counter this, Perkins and Brown
started a campaign to educate farmers in raising higher quality fleeces,
and in the proper sorting and cleaning of the wool. The firm also established a warehouse in Springfield to receive, sort, grade, and ship the
product—all on the initiative of John Brown.

He was noted among wool dealers, his early biographers emphasize,
for the deftness of his touch in sorting the different qualities of wool
and for his skill in testing them. To pack the wool he brought new bags,
making sure each bag was firm, hard, and true—"almost as if they had
been turned out in a lathe."[11] DuBois was to remark of Brown, "business was a philanthropy. We have not even to-day reached this idea."[12]
Yet at the end of three years a combination of manufacturers was able
to force him out of business. Franklin Sanborn suggests this was done
by bribing one of his clerks, who changed the marks on the bags so that
all the wool would be sold at the lowest prices. But given his orientation perhaps Brown too was ill suited to conduct business on the
expected terms; he never had the intention of making himself rich. On
May 20, 1851, he wrote son John offering advice on the proper
approach to buyers, including this assessment of them: "Wool buyers
generally accuse each other of being unscrupulous liars; and in that *one*
thing *perhaps* they are not so."[13]

On August 1, 1846, on the twelfth anniversary of Britain's West India
emancipation, Gerrit Smith had taken the occasion to offer 100,000
acres on lands he owned in the Adirondack region in Franklin and
Essex counties to free blacks on easy terms. Smith's intention was to

give them an opportunity to become self-sustaining farmers, but also so that they could meet New York's $250 property threshold to become voters. "It was not a well thought-out scheme," DuBois wrote, "the climate was bleak for Negroes, the methods of culture then suitable, were unknown to them; while the surveyor who laid out these farms cheated them as cheerily as though philanthropy had no concern with the project."[14] Most of those accepting Smith's offer, moreover, were city dwellers accustomed to working as waiters and barbers, maids and laborers, and as coachmen. The colony soon began to fail. Hearing of this, Brown visited the Smith estate in Peterboro in the Finger Lakes district of New York: the date, April 8, 1848. Proposing to Smith that he was disposed to put the colony on a better footing, Sanborn relates Brown saying: "I am something of a pioneer; I grew up among the woods and wild Indians of Ohio, and am used to the climate and the way of life that your colony find so trying. I will take one of your farms myself, clear it up and plant it, and show my colored neighbors how such work should be done, will give them work as I have occasion, look after them in all needful ways and be a kind of father to them."[15]

Seeing this as "an opening through which he thought he might carry out his cherished scheme," Brown also thought this would be a secure location for his wife and younger children after he'd turned his attention fully to it.[16] The remote area was expeditiously reached by taking a train to Rutland, Vermont, then taking conveyance to Vergennes and crossing Lake Champlain by boat; arriving at Westport, New York, then taking conveyance to Keene, traveling the steep wooded road across Keene Mountain into North Elba. Brown would sign a deed November 9, 1849, for 244 acres at a dollar an acre with Smith. His family had moved there in the previous year, to begin on a leased farm with a small one-story frame house.

Leaving John Jr. to run the warehouse in Springfield, Brown brought his family north, his daughter Ruth relates: "The day we crossed the mountains from Keene was rainy and dreary and father wanted us to notice how fragrant the air was with the perfume of the pines, hemlocks and balsams." It was a daunting move, no doubt, and the daughter wondered how nine people could be accommodated in the tiny abode. After a first night's sleep in the new home, she related: "Before noon a bright, pleasant colored boy came to our gate (or rather, our bars) and inquired if John Brown lived there. 'Here is where he stays,' was father's reply. The boy had been a slave in Virginia, and was sold and sent to St. Augustine, Fla. From there he ran away, and came to Springfield, where by his industry and good habits he had acquired some property. Father hired him to help carry on the farm, so there were ten of us in the little house; but Cyrus did not take more than his share of room, and was always good natured."17

That Brown and his family skimped and saved almost to the appearance of destitution was well remarked upon by Douglass in his *Life and Times*, describing his first visit with them in Springfield. Writing in Sanborn's volume after the publication of the former, Ruth wrote: "Frederick Douglass has said in his last book, that John Brown economized so closely in order to carry out his plans, that we did not have a cloth on the table at meal-time. I think our good friend is mistaken; for I never sat down to a meal at my father's table without a cloth."18

Garrisonian abolitionism, framing itself as a moral crusade, abjured violence as it likewise spurned political action. Douglass was still largely under this influence in his first years in Rochester, and his relations with his Boston and Massachusetts colleagues continued cordially. But the warmth of feeling displayed formerly between him and Garrison had now markedly cooled. Garrison had not forgotten Douglass's apparent lack of solicitude when he was ill, nor had he forgiven him for disregarding his advice in starting a paper. But living beyond Boston's ambit Douglass was also coming under other influences, most demonstrably and on his own account that of John Brown, and of political abolitionists in central New York like William Goodell and Gerrit Smith. The key to Garrison's anti-political stance was the interpretation of the Constitution; as Douglass said it was a "bloody conspiracy" against the rights of the millions of enslaved. Slaveholders themselves upheld the view in line with Garrison's interpretation: American institutions were a covenant for "white supremacy." But Douglass, too, would begin to think beyond these strictures.

The words "Wilmot Proviso" were flaunted like a banner in 1848, and voiced on lips throughout the North and the West. David Wilmot had struck Goliath as surely as did David of old, it was said. The House of Representatives passed his bill twice, while it twice failed in the Senate. The storm presaged by the "proviso" and the response to it was perhaps a watershed in Douglass's evolution toward beginning to advocate "political action." On June 10, 1848, he would hail it in the *North Star*, in a column titled the "Great Uprising of the North:" "We look upon the Wilmot Proviso and its supporters as indications of the presence of a great principle in the national heart, which by patient cultivation will one day abolish forever our system of human bondage."

Out of this fervor would come the Free Soil Party, as the old parties in the election, Democrat and Whig, would split in nearly every Northern state. Confronting this schism in June 1847, in an attempt to broaden the appeal of the Liberty Party, a group of some forty members met in Wayne County, New York, taking the name Liberty League, and adopting a platform espousing positions beyond the single issue of slavery—on tariffs and banks, on distribution of public lands and the annexation of Texas. The league nominated Gerrit Smith and Elihu Burritt for the paramount national offices. In October that year, the Liberty Party, holding its convention at Buffalo, would ignore the league and nominate John P. Hale of New Hampshire and Leicester King of Ohio to the same, on a "one idea" platform.

Now Smith called for another convention to meet the following summer, again at Buffalo. One hundred and four delegates responded on June 14, 1848, Frederick Douglass and Henry Highland Garnet among them. This convention called itself the National Liberty Party to distinguish it from the "one idea" party, and heard *An Address to the Colored People of the Northern States* by Smith, urging temperance, economy, industry, and education on blacks "in order to disprove the frequently repeated charge that Negroes were only fit for slavery," and advising they withdraw "from pro-slavery political parties and churches."[19] Smith included in his address a demand for "universal suffrage in its broadest sense, females as well as males being entitled to vote," also calling for a ten-hour working day and rights for workers. When Douglass was prevailed upon to speak, he did so briefly (he was suffering a throat inflammation), still defending Garrison's position on the Constitution. He informed readers of the *North Star*: "Our attendance at this Convention, while it has done much to remove prejudices from our mind respecting some of the prominent men engaged in it, has also deepened our conviction that the only true ground for an American Abolitionist is, *No Union with Slaveholders*."

The women's rights meeting promised by Elizabeth Cady Stanton and Lucretia Mott as they walked arm in arm down London's streets at the beginning of the decade had been in abeyance until July 1848. Living in Philadelphia, Mott was scheduled to tour in central New York that summer and the opportunity could now be taken to inaugurate the movement in Seneca Falls. To plan the projected event, Stanton, Mott, her sister Martha Wright, Mary M'Clinton, and June Hunt, met at the Hunt home in Waterloo over tea, drawing up an announcement to run in the *Seneca County Courier* of a "WOMAN'S RIGHTS CONVENTION . . . to discuss the social, civil, and religious condition and rights of woman." Douglass's *North Star* also carried the notice. Taking place over two days, July 19–20, at the Wesleyan Methodist Chapel, this initial meeting was followed two weeks later by another in Rochester, and then by the first in a series of annual National Women's Rights Conventions, in 1850 in Worcester, Massachusetts.

Assembling outside the chapel before ten on a hot July morning, the delegates—up to 300 would attend over the two days, women as well as men—found the doors barred. Stanton's young nephew Daniel was hoisted through an open window, the doors were unbolted, and the first of two sessions began promptly at eleven. Although about forty men were present on the first day, none was to be permitted to speak until the sessions on day two. That first day heard exhortations from Stanton and Mott and a reading and discussion of the Declaration of Sentiments, with a list of grievances and resolutions, modeled on the Declaration of Independence authored in 1776 by Jefferson. Among the resolutions being advanced for the first time publicly was a demand for the elective franchise for women, controversial even among these delegates. It read: "Resolved, that it is the duty of the women of this country to secure to themselves their sacred right to the elective franchise." Those opposing the resolution felt it would raise too great an opposition, losing for the Declaration the support it would otherwise garner; it was social, civil, and religious rights for women that needed to be given precedence, not political rights. Lucretia Mott herself and her husband, James, opposed it, Mott exclaiming, "Why Lizzie, thee will make us ridiculous." Elizabeth Cady Stanton defended the concept, as did Frederick Douglass. Invited by Stanton to attend the convention, Douglass remarked in an eloquent appeal, "In this denial of the right to participate in government, not merely the degradation of women and the perpetuation of a great injustice happens, but the maiming and repudiation of one-half of the moral and intellectual power of the government of the world."[20] The document was adapted unanimously and had one hundred signatories, sixty-eight women and thirty-two men.

The Democratic National Convention held that May had nominated Lewis Cass of Michigan for president on a platform framed to please the South, while Zachary Taylor, freshly laureled in the Mexican conflict, was nominated in June on the Whig ticket, without a platform but, like the Democrats, repudiating the "Proviso." Now Liberty Party supporters, "conscience" Whigs, "free-soil" Democrats, and New York "barnburners"—so-called because of a Dutch farmer who burnt his barn to rid it of rats—landed together at Buffalo to form the Free Soil Party, nominating Martin Van Buren and Charles Francis Adams on a rousing platform: "We declare that Congress has no more power to make a slave than to make a king. . . . We inscribe on our banner: 'FREE SOIL, FREE SPEECH, FREE LABOR, AND FREE MEN,' and under it will fight on, and fight ever, until a triumphant victory shall reward our exertions." Douglass wrote in *Life and Times* that heretofore antislavery agitation "had only been sheet-lighting," and "the Buffalo convention sought to make it a thunderbolt."[21] The convention represented a significant uprising; with 465 delegates representing eighteen states, as many as ten thousand people attended some of its mass meetings. Douglass was at the convention as were Samuel Ringgold Ward, Garnet, Charles Remond, and Henry Bibb. Ward and Douglass were called upon to speak, although Douglass, still suffering from his throat ailment, again only spoke briefly; he remarking later that Ward especially attracted the attention of the convention. Gaining about a tenth of 2,882,120 votes cast in an election won by Zachary Taylor and Millard Fillmore, the Free Soil Party, although short-lived, was an advance, electing five men to Congress. The organizers of the movement, however, assumed a low profile after the election, and Douglass would write in the *North Star*, March 23, 1849, that it had proved to be "a dull and indolent concern, gone to sleep and refusing to wake, until roused by the thunders of another political campaign."

This year can also be regarded as propitious in the antebellum calendar for the National Negro Convention convening in Cleveland, Ohio, for three days during the second week in September. Drawing from sixty to seventy delegates from across the North, with men coming from a representative sampling of trades and professions, they were welcomed as guests in some of Cleveland's best hotels, as Douglass would report in his *North Star*, September 15. He also reported the state "law administrators [threw] open the doors of ... public buildings for our accommodation" so the convention could meet at the courthouse and the Tabernacle.

The convention promptly chose Douglass as president, and he found himself at once at the head of a community of which he'd only been tangentially a part in the preceding years. Coming on the heels of the Free Soil convention and that summer's initial women's rights meeting, it likewise reflected and dealt with the issues they raised. In a similar meeting the previous year a plan had been proposed to establish a "Negro press," which had been opposed by Douglass on grounds that it was impractical and could only devolve into a "clique." The current meeting now endorsed the *North Star* and urged blacks to support it as their representative organ, while, as reported September 19 in the

North Star, appointing a committee to organize vigilant groups in the various states "so as to enable them to measure arms with assailants without and invaders within." At its various gatherings a series of resolutions were drafted—endorsing the Free Soil Party, reprobating the churches as pro-slavery, and urging "a change in the conduct of colored barbers who refused to treat colored men on a basis of equality with whites." Another of the notable resolutions, with direct bearing on Seneca Falls and Douglass's participation there, was one stating, "Hereby invite females hereafter to take part in our deliberations." Douglass was on record as having opposed the preamble to the 17th resolution "in as much as it intimated that slavery could not be abolished by moral means alone"; and moved to amend the 33rd resolution declaring the word "persons" designating delegates be understood "to include women."[22] The last of the resolutions considered attempted to address the underlying weakness of these "national conventions"—that they were called at irregular intervals and by diverse individuals acting on their own initiative; that after adjournment there was a failure to implement the consensus, with the indefinite dispersal of the delegates.

In concluding his assessment of the convention Douglass was optimistic that its influence would justify its existence, expressing hope that "The delegates in attendance from Illinois, Michigan, Ohio, and New York, will return to the various circles who sent them, and carry to them new zeal and increased knowledge, a firm determination to dedicate their energies to higher and holier objects than those to which we, as a people, have been too long and too deeply devoted." Receiving reports on the convention and on Douglass's conduct in it, Gerrit Smith was elated, writing Charles B. Ray, Congregationalist pastor and former editor of the *Colored American*, November 11, 1848, that Douglass "has the talents and dignity that would adorn the Presidency of the nation."

Douglass would devote a good deal of his time in the interim to securing an enduring organizational structure for the national convention movement. Projecting the idea of a National League of Colored People, in the *North Star*, August 10, 1849, he published an outline of a constitution for the organization in an editorial column under the heading "The Union of the oppressed for the Sake of Freedom." Its preamble read:

Whereas, the voice of reason, and the admonitions of experience, in all ages alike, impress us with the wisdom and necessity of combination; and that union and concert of action are highly essential to the speedy success of any good cause; that as in division there is weakness, so in union there

is strength; and whereas, we have long deplored the distracted and divided state of the oppressed, and the manifold evils resulting therefrom, and
desiring as we do to see an union formed which shall enable us to better
grapple with the various systems of injustice and wrong by which we are
environed, and to regain our plundered rights, we solemnly agree to unite
in accordance with the following.

The League, it was proposed, would be constituted as a council with
nine members, headed by a president, and have a secretary and treasurer. Its object was the abolition of slavery, and the elevation and
improvement of the "Colored people." Douglass called for a convention
to convene on September 21, 1849, in Philadelphia. But his appeal
raised little attention that year and he was forced to abandon the project, to his disappointment.

Engaged in a rancorous argument with Henry Highland Garnet just
as he published his plan, he was also having a bitter feud with Henry
Bibb; moreover, those he sought to unite were scattered across the
northern states. Martin Delany, who was seldom in Rochester and
whose fund-raising for the *North Star* had been largely fruitless, ended
his relationship with the paper in June 1849. In the ongoing debate
among black abolitionists Delany would increasingly be seen as
Douglass's foil; while in his disagreements with Garnet, it will be seen,
Douglass began to adopt Garnet's positions. He would now go on as
sole editor and proprietor of his paper, flirting briefly with the idea of
merging it with the Liberty Party paper, before bringing it out under
his own name in 1851 as *Frederick Douglass' Paper*. His plan for a
"National League" had been premature, but such was inevitable he
concluded, and Douglass wrote in the *North Star* on October 26, 1849:
"It is impossible to keep a people asunder for any long time, who are so
strongly and peculiarly identified together, when there is a vigorous
effort made to unite them. We shall never despair of our people—an
union shall yet be effected—the contempt in which we are held—the
wrongs which we endure, together with a sense of our own dignity as
men, *must* eventually lead us to combine."

The *Liberator* reported on a Frederick Douglass speech at Boston's
Faneuil Hall, June 8, 1849, where he astonished many in the audience
when he declared: "I should welcome the intelligence tomorrow,
should it come, that the slaves had risen in the South, and that the sable
arms which had been engaged in beautifying and adorning the South,
were engaged in spreading death and devastation." This was pure apos-
tasy to Garrisonian doctrine, and the reaction of the audience was
audible as Douglass redoubled his avowal; holding before them the

stinging contrariety of recent history: "Why, you welcome the intelligence from France, that Louis Philippe had been barricaded in Paris—you threw up your caps in honor of the victory achieved by Republicanism over royalty—you shouted aloud—'Long live the republic!'—and joined heartily in the watchword of 'Liberty, Equality, Fraternity'—and should you not hail with equal pleasure the tidings from the South that the slaves had risen, and achieved for themselves, against the iron-hearted slaveholder, what the republicans of France achieved against the royalists of France."

This was a startling reversal, and coming so soon after his meeting with John Brown, it suggests the importance of their relationship, and undoubtedly is an indication of their developing alliance. In his three years in Springfield, Brown had begun to seek blacks in whom to confide, those who might become his collaborators. He had gone up to the Adirondack region to survey the lands Gerrit Smith made available to black families and from which many had been cheated, while selecting a farm for himself to secure his family. "But he had another object," Thomas Wentworth Higginson wrote: "he thought that among these men he should find coadjutors in his cherished plan. He was not wholly wrong, and yet he afterwards learned something more. Such men as he needed are not to be *found* ordinarily; they must be *reared*. John Brown did not merely look for men, therefore; he reared them in his sons."[23]

Sanborn tells of an interview he had after Brown's death with Thomas, who disclosed Brown had sent him during his time in Springfield to "look up Madison Washington." That was the fugitive slave who had returned from Canada, to which he'd made his way, to Virginia attempting to rescue his wife. But he was captured and reenslaved. Sold to traders for the New Orleans market, he led the revolt aboard a coast-wise slaver, the *Creole*, in November 1841. One hundred and thirty-four slaves were freed, with but one of these killed along with one white man. Making their way to the nearest British port at Nassau, Daniel Webster, then secretary of state, demanded their surrender as pirates and murderers. The British, though, could not see the point. Brown thought, Thomas reported, Madison Washington would be a potential "leader among his colored recruits." But when found he "proved to be an unfit person for such a responsible place."[24]

Redpath quotes Brown's eldest daughter, Ruth, in his book: "How often have I heard him speak in admiration of Cinques' [Joseph Cinque, the leader of the successful revolt aboard the Spanish slave ship *La Amistad*] character and management in carrying his points with so little bloodshed."[25] It was Brown's contention that to obtain equality

where slavery existed, it was necessary for blacks to fight the whites and
defeat them; forcible separation between master and slave was necessary, too, to educate the blacks for self-government. If this was not
done, Brown held, then the only alternative would be for the blacks to
seek an independent area of their own to inhabit. Nat Turner and
Cinque stood first in his esteem because of their fight for freedom,
reported Redpath.

Brown now emerges as a man totally preoccupied with his idea; even
in his business it begins to predominate. In his struggle with New
England wool dealers, he played what can be seen as an extremely risky
card. While they tried to break him, he would seek a market for his
stock in England. Sanborn writes, he "transversed a considerable part
of England and the continent on business connected with his merchan-
dise, but also, with an eye to his future campaigns against slavery."[26]
With 200,000 pounds of his finest, expertly packaged and graded wool,
Brown sailed for England, arriving on August 26, 1849.

Brown, however, was on unfamiliar terrain with English traders, who
had no regard for American wool. Here was a clean-faced Yankee New
England farmer, and they would test him. Approached by several
traders with samples of differing grades of wool, Brown inspected
them, grading the wool, while telling what each was good for in manufacture. Introduced to another sample, he was asked, "what he would
do with such wool as that?" Feeling it between his fingers, and finding
the fiber had none of the hooks wool must have to make yarn, Brown
replied: "Gentlemen, if you have any machinery that will work up dog's
hair, I would advise you to put this into it."[27] The facetious Englishman
had sheared a poodle and brought the hair in his pocket.

In the interim before the sale of his product, Brown took a swift
excursion on the Continent. In Paris on the 29th and 30th, he passed
through Germany and Austria by rail, visiting some of the battlefields
of Napoleon and taking notes on the fortifications he saw. Witnessing
the evolution of Austrian troops, Sanborn writes that he declared they
could always be defeated by soldiers who should maneuver more rapidly. "The French soldiers he thought well drilled, but lacking individual prowess; for that he gave the palm to our own countrymen."[28]
Hinton, while largely relying on Sanborn who interviewed Brown
about his trip "while driving from Concord to Medford, to visit Mr.
Stearns, one Sunday in April, 1857," writes: "Above all he inquired into
moral, social, and economic conditions or results."[29] Making keen
observations on European agricultural practices; he paid especial interest to a kind of earthen redoubt he'd seen, while criticizing Napoleon

on a point of strategy. The stronger ground, Brown maintained, should be a ravine rather than a hill-top—an appeal to his developing conception of mountain warfare as applied to the United States; obviously his interest being not in the deployment of a regular army, but a defensive war of his projected bands in the mountains of Virginia. Redpath states, evidently on evidence of his own interview with him: "When in England at this time, John Brown divulged his plan of liberation to several prominent anti-slavery men; but there, as elsewhere, while they felt and professed an unbounded sympathy for the slave, they neither countenanced nor approved of this very earnest scheme of this dreadfully-in-earnest abolitionist."[30] Sanborn notes, finally, that Brown "may have visited the Continent again in October, for he did not disembark in New York until the last week in October."[31]

When Brown returned to London, his venture met disaster, as he was forced to sell at half-price. The wool, moreover, would be reshipped to the United States to be bought by the very dealer whose offer Brown had originally refused. When the wool arrived again in Springfield, the dealer sought out "Uncle John" in his counting room, telling him he must come down to the depot to see the wool he'd purchased. As Brown saw the wool, he turned, walking briskly away with his long springy steps, his coat tails trailing behind him.

Brown always maintained he'd been swindled, a potent part of business practices. He would be involved in lawsuits for several years, occupying him up to 1854, in trials conducted in Boston, and in Troy, New York. He lost a judgment urged by his lawyers in Boston presided over by Caleb Cushing, before the judge went on to become Franklin Pierce's attorney general; but he won in Troy. By 1850, Brown's wife and younger children were back in Akron, to return to the farm in North Elba as he turned his attention to the West in 1855—to Kansas. As he got back to New York in the last week of October 1849, unknown to him, in Dorchester County on Maryland's Eastern Shore, an obscure slave woman of about twenty-seven years, whose family and friends called her Minty, slowly made her way via the Underground Railroad the ninety miles to the Pennsylvania border and up to Philadelphia. Crossing the Mason-Dixon Line from Delaware into a free state, she later related: "When I found I had crossed the line, I looked at my hands to see if I was the same person. There was such a glory over everything; the sun came like gold through the trees, and over the fields, and I felt like I was in heaven."[32]

A petite five-feet in height, she had a tough muscularity gained from doing the roughest fieldwork and driving oxen. With a religious disposition tinged with stories from the Old Testament not uncommon among slaves, she was induced too by strong visionary experiences. Hit in the head in her early years by a two-pound metal object hurled by an overseer with the intent to maim another, she was disabled by her injury and suffered epileptic-like seizures and often seemed to fall into fitful unconscious states or semi-sleep. Besides these episodes, she had potent dreams she saw as divine premonitions. Withal she was possessed by a fiery quest for freedom, for herself and for her people, saying to her chronicler: "There was one of two things I had a right to, liberty or death; if I could not have one, I would have the other."[33] But in Philadelphia, despite the help of William Still and the Vigilance Committee, and of her ability to find work for wages, she felt she was "a stranger in a strange land." Her father, her mother, her brothers and her sisters, and all her friends were in Maryland. "I was free," she said, "and they should be free."[34]

In the course of the next decade, through her daring activity on their behalf in the Underground Railroad, she would rise to unprecedented recognition as one of the most remarkable persons of the age. She also came to know John Brown, and become intimate with his remarkable plan, and become a fervent supporter of it. This woman was Harriet Tubman.

Of the routes available for travel to California, overland or by sea, for the first emigrants drawn by gold fever, none was easy. But the discovery of gold in California's northern mountains was to bring over 300,000 persons in its wake. Argonauts, as sea voyagers were called, could take five to seven months from the East Coast around the tip of South America. An alternate was to sail to the Isthmus of Panama, cross by canoe and mule, then sail on the Pacific side for San Francisco. Some wayfarers, starting at Veracruz, cut across Mexico; while thousands trekked the continental United States—all hazarding shipwreck, cholera and typhoid, or privation. By the beginning of 1849, gold fever had spread around the world.

Among the first arriving—after an initial rush of native Californians, often whole families scouring and panning together—were several thousand Oregonians. Next came people from the Sandwich Islands, followed by Mexicans, Peruvians, and Chileans. The overland route from the United States drew only five hundred in the first year; then an inundation began, with many crossing the Appalachian Mountains from the East, traveling on riverboats in Pennsylvania and Ohio, poling keelboats to the Missouri's assembly ports, and then joining wagon trains for the trek on the California Trail. Australians and New Zealanders picked up the news, as the Chinese too soon began arriving. Then the fallen from Europe's revolutions of '48 started to appear, particularly the French, but Germans, Italians, and Britons as well. Ships arriving in San Francisco were deserted by their crews for the gold fields, where ordinary prospectors might find ten to fifteen times the daily wage of a laborer in the East. Six months prospecting could exceed six year's wages.

Earlier that year, February 5, 1849, John Brown had written his son Owen from Springfield: "We have been selling wool middling fast of late, on contract, at 1847 prices. We have in this part of the country the strongest proofs that the great majority have made gold their *hope*, their only hope."[35] Sensing a rare opportunity not for riches but for conservation and consolidation, Brown foresaw a moment, due to scarcity of labor, when wages would rise. He counseled his sons and their families to sell unneeded assets thus utilizing the trice as others frittered it away. Brown's reasoning was strongly based, as has been seen, on his and his sons' projected war on slavery, which in these years had taken a decisive step forward. "His book-keeper tells me," James Redpath wrote, "that he and his eldest son used to discuss slavery by the hour in his counting room." A local journalist wrote, he then added, "his mission was to make the institution insecure, and thus to act upon the fear and prudence of the slaveholder."[36] The presidential contest that year had embroiled all in its issues, bringing Zachary Taylor to office. Born into a Virginia slaveholding family who joined the early emigration to Kentucky, by the time of his presidency, Taylor made his home in Baton Rouge, Louisiana, and he owned a Mississippi plantation, along with a hundred slaves. First seeing war in 1812, he had gained distinction in Florida in the Semolina Wars in 1837. As brigadier general Polk sent him to command troops near the disputed Rio Grande boundary with Mexico; and as war began, Taylor was ordered to hold northern Mexico while Gen. Winfield Scott was sent to capture Mexico City. Spurning his orders, Taylor won the heralded Battle of Buena Vista, opening "the road to the city of Mexico and the halls of Montezuma, that others might revel in them." "Old Rough and Ready" was, by his presidency, thoroughly an American nationalist, although his preferred topic of conversation, it's said, was cotton. As president, though, he would not be a defender of Southern sectional interests. With controversy raging over the Wilmot Proviso, Taylor invited settlers in New Mexico and California to draft constitutions, bypassing the territorial stage. Southern congressional leaders were furious, accusing the president of usurping their policy-making prerogatives; the president's plan, said Jefferson Davis, was one "of concealing the Wilmot Proviso under a so-called state constitution."[37] While opponents on each side clamored to end slavery and the slave trade in Washington, D.C., or for a more effective fugitive slave law, Southern leaders met in conference with the president in February 1850, threatening secession. The president responded by declaring he would personally lead the army against them, hanging persons in rebellion against the Union with less reluctance, he vowed, than he had hung deserters and spies in Mexico.

As the famous Compromise of 1850 began its fitful passage to its denouement in September, Henry Clay, Daniel Webster, and John C. Calhoun were competing in their final national exhibit. Days before, on January 29, Henry Clay stepped into the well of an expectant Senate to present a series of eight resolutions intended to "adjust amicably all existing questions of controversy . . . arising out of the institution of slavery." Paired to appeal to majorities contending on both sides, Clay's resolutions were merely a prelude in a seven-month drama that sought ostensibly to safeguard the national union, but would prove to be only temporary. The first set admitted California as a free state, with the remainder of the Mexican cession to enter the territorial stage without "any restriction or condition on the subject of slavery." The next settled the boundary dispute between Texas and New Mexico in favor of the latter, while compensating Texas by assuming its debts during its period as an independent republic. A third would abolish the slave trade in the capital city, while guaranteeing slavery there. The final pairing resolved that Congress had no power over the interstate slave trade, while providing slaveholders with a more stringent fugitive slave law.

Called upon to draft an "address" setting forth the South's position on Clay's resolutions, Calhoun's death would come at the end of the first act. Too ill to deliver the valedictory himself, he would have it read by Virginia's senator James Mason, as he sat silently by. Assisted to his desk a few minutes past noon, March 4, his speech was a carefully prepared manuscript of forty-two pages, dictated over the course of two days to his secretary. Then sixty-eight, Calhoun was suffering from tuberculosis; he was emaciated and spectral in appearance. In his better years Calhoun was tall with a lank frame, with fine dark blue eyes and overhanging brow; his features angular with a broad square forehead. His visage was striking, even stark; his hair standing "frowningly," as Mathew Brady said, around his shoulders. The last daguerreotype of Calhoun was made in Brady's studio at Broadway and Tenth Street in New York just before his death. Now the gaunt Carolinian sat in his chair wrapped in black flannels, his piercing eyes staring from deep sockets as from within the shroud. His speech asserted that the equilibrium that existed between the sections was destroyed; the admission of California as a free state and the abolition of the slave trade in the District of Columbia were not negotiable; the sovereignty of states was at issue. The speech rehearsed a long litany of northern "aggressions"—the Northwest Ordinance, the Missouri Compromise, the personal liberty laws enacted in the northern states, the Wilmot Proviso. He reiterated it was the South's constitutional right to take slaves into all territories; it was their "property, prosperity, equality, liberty, and safety" that was at stake. If these could not be secured then the South had the right to secede; two nations, in reality, now existed, and if their differences could not be settled, they should part in peace. A total of 46 of 73 southern Democrats in Congress signed the address, but only 2 of 48 Whigs. Calhoun's presence, many could see, had only demonstrated that his power in the Senate was broken, as Douglass observed: "The mighty man of slavery, [had been] found to be mightier in his silence than in his eloquence."[38]

Three days later Calhoun was again in the Senate, a brooding presence, as Daniel Webster prepared to deliver his famous March 7 speech. Enduring for three and a half hours, as the final words of the text were read, Calhoun, wrote one of his biographers, "sat motionless in his chair, sweeping the chamber now and again with his deeply luminous eyes."[39] His political future at stake, Webster had begun:

> It is not to be denied that we live in the midst of strong agitations, and are surrounded by very considerable dangers to our institutions and our government. The imprisoned winds are let loose. The East, the North, and the stormy South combine to throw the whole sea into commotion, to toss its billows to the skies and disclose its profoundest depths. I do not affect to regard myself, Mr. President, as holding, or as fit to hold, the helm in this combat with the political elements; but I have a duty to perform, and I mean to perform it with fidelity, not without a sense of existing dangers, but not without hope. I have a part to act, not for my own security or safety, for I am looking out for no fragment upon which to float away from the wreck, if wreck there must be, but for the good of the whole, and the preservation of all. . . . I speak to-day for the preservation of the Union. "Hear me for my cause."

Webster, having opposed the Mexican War and been a supporter of the Wilmot Proviso, now dealt at length in his speech that the northern states needed to break with the past and deliver up the fugitive slaves to the South. Traduced, particularly in Massachusetts, Webster knew his star had fallen; he could not now be reelected. John Greenleaf Whittier assessed all Webster had abandoned: "When faith is lost, when honor dies, the man is dead!"

Generations of schoolchildren would recite Webster's speech, and perhaps Calhoun's and others from the compromise debate. One in particular was to sound the clarion that a new dispensation in party allegiances was offering. On March 11, New York senator William Seward, who was a confidant of the president, delivered his "Higher Law" speech. The crisis being addressed, said Seward, "embraces the fearful issue whether the Union shall stand, and slavery, under the steady, peaceful action of moral, social, and political causes, be removed by gradual voluntary effort, and with compensation; or whether the Union shall be dissolved and civil war ensue, bringing on violent but complete and immediate emancipation."[40] With the matter in abeyance on April 19 a committee of thirteen was selected with Clay as chairman. Three were northern Democrats, Lewis Cass of Michigan, Daniel Dickinson of New York, and Jesse Bright of Indiana; and three were northern Whigs, Daniel Webster of Massachusetts, Samuel Phelps of Vermont, and James Cooper of Pennsylvania. Southern Democrats were William Rufus de Vane King of Alabama, James Mason of Virginia, and Solomon Downs of Louisiana; and southern Whigs were represented by Willie Mangum of North Carolina, John Bell of Tennessee, and John Berrien of Georgia.

Calhoun died March 31, and unexpectedly Zachary Taylor would die on July 9, to be succeeded by Millard Fillmore. Webster would resign his Senate seat to become the new president's Secretary of State. Henry Clay, himself ill with consumption, would withdraw for his health to Newport, Rhode Island, at the end of July. Clay died in Washington on June 29, 1852, another of those, Frederick Douglass would write, who died "without attaining the aim of their ambition."[41] Webster would be injured falling from his horse at the end of October 1852, after his last failed presidential bid, severely lacerating his head; he would be dead, due to this injury and from cirrhosis of the liver, before that year's election was held.

The new president was sympathetic to the Compromise and would bend to the South as much as his predecessor had tipped toward the North. With Clay's "omnibus" bill defeated, Stephen A. Douglas would occupy center stage for the final act. Nicknamed the "Little Giant" because of his short stature, he was a tireless worker, noted in his party as an adroit tactician. Chairman of the Committee on Territories, he became a dominant figure in the Senate in the 1850s with the passing of the triumvir. Severed into its parts so each could gain majority support, the Compromise would pass as four separate acts in September. California was admitted as a free state on the 9th; also on that day bills organizing the territories of New Mexico and Utah were enacted. On the 18th the Fugitive Slave Law was enacted, and on the 20th the slave trade in the District prohibited. As those who brought the perilous debate to its fateful conclusion retired or went on to other work, Frederick Douglass surveyed the American scene in a speech titled "Lecture on Slavery" at Corinthian Hall on December 1, 1850, his first public address in Rochester, saying:

> Slavery forms an important part of the entire history of the American people. Its presence may be seen in all American affairs. It has become interwoven with all American institutions, and has anchored itself in the very soil of the American Constitution. It has thrown its paralyzing arm over freedom of speech, and the liberty of the press; and has created for itself morals and manners favorable to its own continuance. It has seduced the church, corrupted the pulpit, and brought the powers of both into degrading bondage; and now, in the pride of its power, it even threatens to bring down that grand political edifice, the American Union.
>
> *That* must be a powerful influence which can truly be said to govern a nation; and that slavery governs the American people, is indisputably true . . . that to which such men as Cass, Dickinson, Webster, Clay and other distinguished men of this country, are devoting their energies, is nothing more nor less than American slavery.[42]

On January 3, 1850, standing on the floor of the Senate, Virginia's James Mason had given notice he would introduce a bill for a "more effectual execution" of the Fugitive Slave Law enacted in 1793. The following day the bill was read, printed, and referred to the Judiciary Committee. The committee chairman, Andrew P. Butler of South Carolina, reported on January 16, that the debate on the bill was scheduled to begin January 24. That bill had four sections. The first provided that the owner or his agent, after arresting a fugitive slave, could take him "before any judge of the circuit or district courts of the United States, or before any commissioner, or clerk of such courts, or marshal thereof, or any postmaster . . . or collector of customs" within the state where the arrest was made. If satisfied as to the claim on the proof of the claimant, the officers were required to issue a certificate

which would be "sufficient warrant for taking and removing such fugitive . . . to the State or Territory from which he or she had fled." The second section stipulated that upon proper application a warrant would
be issued to a federal marshal for the arrest of the fugitive. A third section provided that anyone attempting to harbor, conceal, or rescue a
fugitive would be liable to a fine of one thousand dollars. The final section required that the officials enumerated in the first section would
proceed as if the slave had been arrested by the owner or his agent in
the same manner.[43]

Butler opened the debate with a dour reflection: "I have no very great
confidence that this bill will subserve the ends which seem to be contemplated by it. The Federal Legislature . . . has too limited means to
carry out the article of the Constitution to which this bill applies. . . .
And that the cardinal articles of the Constitution are not to be preserved by statutory enactments upon parchment. They must live and
be preserved in the willing minds and good faith of those who incurred
the obligation to maintain them."[44]

In the ensuing debate Mason offered two amendments: anyone guilty
of obstructing the act's execution would be liable to a fine of one thousand dollars, and that the testimony of a fugitive could not be admitted
in evidence. In his remarks on the bill on February 5, Henry Clay added
another stipulation: as he saw it not only was the clause in the
Constitution mandated upon Congress, but it extended to every state
in the Union. "And I go one step further," he added. "It extends to every
man in the Union, and devolves upon him the obligation to assist in the
recovery of a fugitive slave from labor, who takes refuge in or escapes
into one of the free States."[45]

Frederick Douglass gave two years of intensive study and discussion
to the issue of whether or not the Constitution was proslavery. The first
indication of this evaluation was given in the *North Star*, on February
9, 1849, when he wrote: "On close examination of the Constitution, I
am satisfied that if strictly 'construed according to its reading,' it is not
a pro-slavery instrument." Six weeks later he noted that if he could be
convinced the Constitution was antislavery in its origins and purpose,
he would be quick to use the ballot box, but he still harbored doubt.[46]
In a careful and systematic way Douglass arrived at the view espoused
by Gerrit Smith and William Goodell, to wit that in its preamble the
Constitution was antislavery; its object being to establish "a more perfect union," "promote the general welfare, and secure the blessings of
liberty." He repudiated Garrison's notion of dissolution of the Union
on the grounds that a northern secession would deny the slaves their

most important allies and isolate them, leaving them at the mercy of their masters. Instead of "No Union with Slaveholders," Douglass would say "No Union with Slaveholding," reasoning that slavery could never be more than what it was: a lawless system of violence.

This change in creed did not become public until 1851. Informing Stephen S. Foster and Samuel J. May, Douglass then informed Gerrit Smith in a letter dated May 21, 1851. On May 23 under the title "Change of Opinion Announced," reprinted in the *Liberator*, the following appeared in the *North Star*:

> The change in our opinion on the subject has not been hastily arrived at. A careful study of the writings of Lysander Spooner, of Gerrit Smith, and of William Goodell, has brought us to our present conclusion.... Of course, this avowal did not pass without animadversion, and it would have been strange if it has passed without some crimination; for it is hard for any combination or party to attribute good motives to anyone who differs from them in what they deem a vital point. Brother Garrison at once exclaimed, "There is roguery somewhere!" but we easily forgive this hastily expressed imputation falling, as it did, from the lips of one to whom we shall never cease to be grateful.[47]

Douglass began this journey of conversion to a radical abolitionist as a result of his own identifiable and significant outreaching of thought and activity, but under extraneous guidance. In the *North Star* of February 11, 1848, he noted his "private interview" with John Brown of Springfield, Massachusetts. "Though a white gentleman," he wrote, Brown was "in sympathy a black man, and as deeply interested in our cause, as though his own soul had been pierced with the iron of slavery." Douglass would never deviate for this view throughout his twelve-year alliance with Brown, and reported significantly of his first meeting with him that Brown had expressed joy at the appearance of men "possessing the energy of head and heart to demand freedom for their whole people." The result "must be the downfall of slavery."[48]

In April 1848, after obtaining permission from David Walker's widow to republish her husband's *Appeal*, Henry Highland Garnet brought that issue of 1829 together with his own "Address to the Slaves of the United States of America," delivered at the National Colored Convention in Buffalo in 1843. In his preface Garnet wrote of the *Appeal*: "The work is valuable because it was among the first, and was actually the boldest and most direct appeal in behalf of freedom which was made in the early part of the anti-slavery reformation." Along with this production, an article would appear by the hand of Garnet in the

North Star, May 19, 1848: "This age is a revolutionizing age; the time has been when we did not expect to see revolutions; but now we expect them, and they are daily passing before our eyes; and change after change, and revolution after revolution will undoubtedly take place, until all men are placed upon equality. Then, and not till then, will all enjoy that liberty and equality that God has destined us to participate in." Garnet's publication of his *Address to the Slaves* together with Walker's *Appeal*, perhaps little noticed, had been paid in part by John Brown.

By way of addendum, another individual's influence on the maturation of Frederick Douglass should not pass unmentioned. Julia Griffiths was an educated young Englishwoman and daughter of a close friend of Wilberforce. Douglass and Griffiths met in London during Douglass's tour in 1845–47 and at once became more than congenial friends, although within the bounds of decorum, and real colleagues. She helped to raise the funds for the testimonial that would be presented to him on his departure, and he confided in her that it was his intention to use the money to begin a paper in America for "colored people." Coming to the United States shortly after Douglass's homecoming, Griffiths went to Rochester, and there resided in the Douglass household as the *North Star* was being initiated. Douglass had been warned, by Garrison and others, of the difficulties he would face, and such he would find was the case. Starting the paper, he informed Martin Delany, his expenses were $55 per week. Four months on and the situation was critical; subscriptions were far from robust, and in the first issue for the week of May the *North Star* printed an urgent appeal for "pecuniary aid." To remain viable Douglass was compelled to mortgage his home.

Julia Griffiths now took charge of the finances and would devote almost all of her time for nearly eight years to the interests of the paper. A skilled editor with a flair for journalism, she was Douglass's closest associate and intimate in these years, as he was in every sense her eager apprentice and ready confidant. Returning to England in the fall of 1849, she was back in March 1850 with her sister, Eliza. Douglass met them in New York, escorting the two to numerous meetings, where they were also eager apprentices to the American "flavor" of the antislavery debates. On May 7 the annual meeting of the American Society was held in the Tabernacle at the corner of Broadway and Anthony (now Worth) Street in New York City, an auditorium with a large square room sloping down to the platform. James Gordon Bennett's *New York Herald* ran howling headlines on that day—"The Annual congress of Fanatics—The Disunionists, Socialists, Fourierists,

Communists, and other abolitionists. May the seventh has come, and
with it a host of fanatics worse than the locusts of Egypt."[49] The *New
York Globe* pointed out the nature of the pestilence in the list of speakers, reported in the *Liberator*, May 17, 1850: "Wendell Phillips, of
Boston, white man merely from blood. . . . Frederick Douglass: If this
Douglass shall proclaim his treason here, and any man shall arrest his
diabolical career . . . thousands will exclaim, 'Did he not strike the vil-
lain dead?'" The meeting was held on schedule, but could only proceed
fitfully, the joke going around that it used to be hard for abolitionists
to find a hall to get into; now it was hard to get into the hall.[50] The dis-
rupters did pummel in, mostly a motley crew under the handling of
Captain Isaiah Rynders, an unsavory New York political operative,
intent on causing pandemonium. The second day of the meeting was
canceled, while another venue was sought out at Henry Ward Beecher's
Plymouth Church in Brooklyn. Douglass introduced the Griffiths sisters to Garrison and Samuel May, and Lucretia Mott; strolling arm in
arm with Julia and Eliza on New York's Battery, Douglass was assaulted by a mob of "low and vicious people." The *Times* of London took
notice, denouncing the incident in a column. Douglass wrote the editor on June 29, 1850, his letter appearing July 18:

> Sir, you were perfectly right in taking that outrage, as a fair illustration
> of the bitter antipathy which is entertained here, even by the better class
> of white people, against colored persons. Polished American gentlemen
> would applaud a deed of ruffianism like the one in question, although
> they might shrink from the performance of the deed itself. My offence is
> alleged to be that of walking down Broadway in company of "two white
> women." This, however, is not a fair statement of that offence. My offence
> was that I walked down Broadway, in company with white persons, on
> terms of equality. Had I been with those persons simply as a servant, and
> not as a friend, I should have been regarded with complacency by the
> refined and with respect by the vulgar class of white persons who throng
> that great thoroughfare. The clamour here about human equality is
> meaningless. We have here an aristocracy of skin.

"Think what editing a paper was to me before Miss Griffiths came!"
Douglass would say in her tribute.[51] She set a high standard for the
paper, helping to put it on a sound financial footing, as well as modify-
ing Douglass's views, while influencing those that were emerging. In a
letter of May 1, 1851, Douglass was to report to Gerrit Smith: "The
North Star sustains itself, and partly sustains my large family. Hitherto
the struggle of its life has been to live. Now it more than lives, and was
just as your letter came to hand about to make some little improvement

in the quality of the paper upon which it is printed." With the issues resolved between them on the nature of the U.S. Constitution and the necessity for political action, Douglass and Smith were contemplating merging the Liberty Party paper with his own. Douglass wrote of this in his letter, remarking of his confrere:

> The money matters of the paper might well be left to the care of my industrious and vigilant friend and co-worker Julia Griffiths. With her eye on the subscription list, I think very little would go wrong in that quarter. Had she had the management of my books at the commencement, I feel sure that I should have had double the number of subscribers I now have. To her the credit belongs that the Star is now out of debt. . . . She ought to have this credit for you need not be told that she has had much to annoy and at times to weigh down her spirit. I shall count much upon her assistance in any event.

The merger would not take place, and Douglass renamed the *North Star*, henceforward called *Frederick Douglass' Paper*. Among the rancor beginning to surface between Garrison and himself at this time, Douglass was ridiculed for placing his own name on the masthead. In retort Douglass said that he had once heard the illustrious editor refer to himself as a "Garrisonian."

In layout and typography the *North Star* had been modeled after the other antislavery papers—the *Liberator*, the *Bugle*, the *Freeman*, and the *Standard*. Although it was Frederick Douglass's imprint, Julia Griffiths was his equal in all of its affairs. Consisting of four pages of six columns each, each issue featured on the front page antislavery speeches of Congress. Henry Wilson, Charles Sumner, and Joshua Giddings were all given special notice, as was Gerrit Smith. Douglass's contributions were featured prominently. The sermons of Henry Ward Beecher and Theodore Parker were welcomed, and the debates on the nature of the Constitution and on the efficacy of political action filled numerous columns. Reports from abolition societies in the form of letters from corresponding secretaries could always be found, and it was a common practice to reprint items from the other antislavery papers. There were also regular contributors and local correspondents, like J. McCune Smith, who wrote under the pseudonym "Communipaw"; Samuel Ringgold Ward sent letters from Canada; and from Brooklyn came reports from William J. Wilson signed "Ethiope." William Wells Brown often sent well-written contributions from the antislavery lecture circuit, and other frequent contributors were Martin Delany, George T. Downing, and J. W. Loguen, along with Henry Highland Garnet. Julia Griffiths handled "literary notices" and had her own column.

Julia Griffiths was a founding member and the permanent secretary of the Rochester Ladies Anti-Slavery Society, doing effective work in organizing bazaars to raise money for the paper, and to ensure Douglass would have a forum at Rochester's Corinthian Hall, where he delivered several of his noted speeches, including his enduring Fourth of July oration in 1852. Among Griffiths's successes was a volume she edited entitled *Autographs for Freedom*, appearing in 1853 and reprinted in 1854. Gathering a plethora of writers between its covers—there were contributions from Charles Reason, a black mathematician, J. McCune Smith, Charles Mercer Langston, Joshua Giddings, William H. Seward, and William Jay; Beecher and Parker; and the writers Antoinette Brown, Jane Swisshelm, and Harriet Beecher Stowe. Facsimiles of the author's signatures were emblazoned before each of their offerings, giving the book its title.

4

At the Point of a Bayonet

On October 4, 1850, five hundred persons filed into City Hall in Syracuse, New York, to protest the just enacted Fugitive Slave Law. With the mayor presiding, the Rev. Samuel Ringgold Ward led off from the rostrum; next up, the Rev. J. W. Loguen proposed Syracuse be made an "open city" for fugitive slaves. Thundering his defiance, Loguen said:

> Whatever may be your decision, my ground is taken. I have declared it everywhere. It is known over the state and out of the state—over the line in the North, and over the line in the South. I don't respect this law—I don't fear it—I won't obey it! It outlaws me, and I outlaw it, and the men who attempt to enforce it on me. . . . I say if you will stand with us in resistance to the measure, you will be the saviors of your country. Your decision tonight in favor of resistance will give vent to the spirit of liberty, and it will break the bands of party, and shout for joy all over the North. Your example only is needed to be the type of popular action in

Auburn, and Rochester, and Utica, and Buffalo, and all the West, and eventually in the Atlantic cities. Heaven knows that this act of noble daring will break out somewhere—and may God grant that Syracuse be the honored spot.[1]

The meeting voted 395 in favor of his proposal, with 96 against.

On October 14 in a similar meeting, hundreds assembled to protest the draconian law at Faneuil Hall in Boston. Charles Francis Adams presided, and Wendell Phillips and Theodore Parker spoke, as did Frederick Douglass. Parker said he would do all in his power "to rescue any fugitive slave from the hands of any officer who attempts to return him to bondage. . . . What is a fine of a thousand dollars and gaoling for six months to the liberty of a man."[2] Meetings of indignation and protest also convened in Worcester, Massachusetts, and in Ohio's Western Reserve; in the West, in Chicago the Common Council voted ten to three to condemn the law as "revolting to our moral sense, and an outrage upon our feelings of justice and humanity," and pledged not "to aid or assist in the arrest of Fugitives from oppression." Stephen Douglas took the immediate action of persuading the council to rescind the vote, but this did nothing to allay the sentiment against the law.[3]

A few years before, abolitionists had begun to counsel the efficacy of harboring fugitives in the northern states rather than continuing their flight into Canada. On April 9, 1846, Theodore Weld wrote to Lewis Tappan that although fugitives would be subject to recapture, their presence in the North would "make home the battle ground . . . and do more to abolitionize the free states than all other instrumentalities afoot."[4] A little less than two months after the law came into effect, John Brown wrote his wife from Springfield where he was then wrapping up the affairs of Perkins and Brown: "It now seems that the Fugitive Slave Law was to be the means of making more Abolitionists than all the lectures we have had for years. It really looks as if God had His hand on this wickedness also. I of course keep encouraging my colored friends to 'trust in God and keep their powder dry.' I did so to-day at Thanksgiving meeting publicly."[5]

As consternation and fear spread among those whom the law was intended to apprehend, in the aftermath of the legislation associations and committees would be formed in Springfield and in a number of other cities and towns across the north to aid runaway slaves and protect them from arrest. Now was to begin a "refugee march," particularly among fugitive slaves residing along the routes where they had been deposited by the Underground Railroad.[6] Many blacks went over ground on the actual railways too, as in many places abolition societies and vigilance committees contributed toward their fare. Whole families, as well as individuals, determined not to be taken, bundled meager belongings, as large groups armed with pistols and Bowie knifes trekked through the country northward. It has been estimated that nearly three thousand fugitive slaves fled to Canada within three months of the law's signing, making Canada definitively the last depot on the Underground Railroad.[7] Nearly all black waiters in the Pittsburgh hotels fled to Canada, with an estimated three hundred taking flight from the city only ten days after the president signed the bill.[8] Black churches in Rochester and Buffalo, and in other towns near the border, saw the preponderance of their members flee, reducing pews in some instances from hundreds to a handful of parishioners.

No more than a week after the law's enactment a fugitive slave named James Hamlet was taken in New York City, to be remanded at government expense to slavery. At Harrisburg in Pennsylvania, days later two more fugitives were taken and remanded to slavery; while blacks were seized in Detroit and in Philadelphia as fugitives, but were released. Then three fugitives were seized to be remanded in Quincy, Illinois, followed by three more in New Albany, Indiana. Before another week was out another fugitive would be arrested in Marion, Illinois; then another in Philadelphia. By the end of the year a fugitive was caught in Springfield, Massachusetts; followed at the year's turning by another in Shawneetown, Illinois.[9]

In reverse of the spectacle being enacted across the North, in December Harriet Tubman appeared in Baltimore on a covert mission. Familiarizing herself with the people and influences willing to become abettors to escaping slaves; she had determined to become an agent of this work. Hearing, via the sources available to her, that her sister, living on the Eastern Shore in Cambridge, was about to be sold along with her two children, Tubman arranged to have them cross the Chesapeake Bay to Baltimore, where she would meet them.

Harkness Bowley, the son of Tubman's sister, later related how his mother's escape occurred. During the course of the sale, taking place in the Cambridge Court House, the auctioneer broke for dinner. Bowley's mother, meanwhile, was hidden in a house only a few blocks away. "When the auctioneer returned," he reported, "mother was gone. My father . . . took mother and two children in a small boat to Baltimore. Aunt Harriet had a hiding place there for her. In a few days she took her and the children and several others aboard the Underground Railroad."[10]

Baltimore was no easy place for slaves to escape from; any black going by rail or boat was prohibited from leaving without being weighed and measured, and was required to have a bond signed by a well-known local white person; and there were many nefarious individuals and gangs eager to waylay anybody resembling a fugitive.[11] Demonstrating exceptional bravery and daring, only a few months later Tubman brought away her brother and two other men, piloting them all the way to St. Catharines, Ontario, where she would reside herself till some time in 1857. Tubman's activity on Maryland's Eastern Shore and in Delaware would continue late into 1860, and by some accounts would amount to nineteen "trips of mercy," but surely more than a dozen. Unable to read or write, she relied on the cooperation of many, one of whom was a free black on the Eastern Shore, Jacob Jackson. In one letter mid-point in the decade, as she prepared to rescue her own parents, in a significant passage to Jackson she dictated: "Read my letter to the old folks, and give my love to them, and tell my brothers to be always *watching unto prayer*, and when the *good old ship of Zion comes along, to be ready to step aboard.*"[12]

In New York City early in January 1851, Henry Long was arrested and taken to a federal commissioner for a hearing. His case was moving along when the American Anti-Slavery Society came to his defense. With the expenses of his claimant rising, members of the Union Safety Committee, formed by the city's important merchants to suppress dissent to the compromise measures, then came to rescue the slaveholder's interests. George Wood, chairman of the committee and a prominent lawyer, appeared in court on behalf of the claimant; failure to do so would be seen as an act of bad faith, committee members argued. With Long's identity ascertained, the fugitive was remanded to the custody of a federal marshal, who delivered the slave to Alexandria, Virginia. Long would be sold in the Richmond slave market for $750, to a trader from Atlanta, Georgia, who had to post a $3,000 bond stipulating he would move the slave farther south. The expenses for recovering Long for his claimant were in excess of $2,000, toward which the Union Safety Committee paid $800.[13]

On January 17, 1851, still in Springfield, John Brown sent the following to his wife:

Since the sending off to slavery of Long from New York, I have improved my leisure hours quite busily with colored people here, in advising them how to act, and in giving them all the encouragement in my power. They very much need encouragement and advice; and some of them are so alarmed that they tell me they cannot sleep on account of either themselves or their wives and children. I can only say I think I have been enabled to do something to revive their broken spirits. I want all my family to imagine themselves in the same dreadful condition. My only spare time being taken up (often till late hours at night) in the way I speak of, has prevented me from the gloomy homesick feelings which had before so much oppressed me: not that I forget my family at all.[14]

The meetings Brown wrote of culminated in the formation of the "League of Gileadites," a name drawn from the biblical injunction, "Whosoever is fearful or afraid, let him return and depart early from Mount Gilead." It was the most thorough and systematic arrangement of any known at that time to provide for the security and protection of fugitive slaves, and is a decisive manifestation of how far his "special" activity had evolved. The League's agreement and resolutions, with a letter of instructions, were all of Brown's hand, but were produced after a series of meetings over several weeks, to which forty-four persons, all of them black except Brown, affixed their names. Constituting a practical manual, these considered all the exigencies on the conditionality of black resistance in the United States; two of its characteristic features, indicative of Brown's views—members were pledged under the emblem of the "stars and stripes," and they sought no removal to "a Queen's colony." All members were to be armed, and were instructed on how to act in a unified and concerted way in the event of an emergency. Members were, moreover, urged to compel their white neighbors to take part in their defense, "for you may safely calculate on a division of the whites, and may by that means get to an honorable parley." All were urged to stand by their weapons and never part with them, and to stand by one another "while a drop of blood remains; and be hanged if you must, but tell no tales out of school."[15]

In his *Words of Advice* Brown wrote:

Nothing so charms the American people as personal bravery. Witness the case of Cinques, of everlasting memory, on board the "Amistad." The trial for life of one bold and to some extent successful man, for defending his rights in good earnest, would arouse more sympathy throughout the nation than the accumulated wrongs and sufferings of more than three millions of our submissive colored population. We need not mention the Greeks struggling against the oppressive Turks, the Poles against Russia, nor the Hungarians against Austria and Russia combined, to prove this. *No jury can be found in the Northern States that would convict a man for defending his rights to the last extremity. This is well understood by Southern Congressmen, who insisted that the right of trial by jury should not be granted to the fugitive.*[16]

Finally Brown counseled: "Union is strength. Without some well digested arrangements, nothing to any good purpose is likely to be done, let the demand be never so great. Witness the case of Hamlet and Long in New York, when there was no well defined plan of operations or suitable preparation beforehand. The desired end may be effectually secured by the means proposed; namely, the enjoyment of our inalienable rights."[17]

On February 15 the Boston papers noted a fugitive had been arrested and was being held for arraignment. The "Shadrach" case, as the fugitive Frederick Minkins was called, was the first of a series of challenges to the Fugitive Slave Law, and the federal administration's attempt to enforce it: followed by the attempted rescue of Thomas Sims, also in Boston, and the resistance of William Parker and others at Christiana in Pennsylvania, and the rescue at Syracuse, New York, of "Jerry," as the fugitive slave William Henry was known. With a retrospective glance afforded by decades of activity, Frederick Douglass would write in his *Life and Times*, after these signal instances of resistance the fugitive slave law became "almost a dead letter"; it not only failed to put slaveholders in possession of their slaves, but the attempt at enforcement "brought odium upon themselves and weakened the slave system."[18]

Shadrach escaped in May 1850 from the "service" of John Debree of Norfolk, a purser in the United States Navy; arriving in Boston he found employment as a waiter at the Cornhill Coffee House. Hearing of his whereabouts, his "owner" made out an affidavit in a Virginia court and sent an agent to secure the rendition of his slave. A warrant was issued and the fugitive arrested. In court, his defense appealed for a delay to have more time to prepare. A delay was granted. Seated between two marshals, Shadrach waited as the court was cleared. Thomas Wentworth Higginson, decades later, recalled the scene in his *Cheerful Yesterdays*. "The fact was noted in a newspaper by a colored man of great energy and character," he wrote. Asking for leave from his employer, the man hurried to the Court House, where many black men were standing at the door. As he was known to those working in the court, assuming an air of frivolity, he strolled into the courtroom, with others joining spontaneously behind him. "There were but constables on duty," Higginson continued, "and it suddenly struck this leader, as he and his followers passed near the man under arrest, that they might as well keep on and pass out at the opposite door, taking among them the man under arrest, who was not handcuffed. After a moments beckoning the prisoner saw his opportunity, fell in with the jubilant procession, and amid continued uproar was got outside the Court House when the crowd scattered in all directions."[19]

This shucking and jiving, as undoubtedly it can be called, was treated in Washington as if it were a political earthquake. President Millard Fillmore issued a proclamation calling upon all citizens and officials "in the vicinity of this outrage, to aid and assist in quelling this and other such combinations."[20] Professing consternation because the rescue had been carried out by a "band who are not of our people," Henry Clay introduced a resolution in the Senate requesting the president disclose full information about the affair. Secretary of State Daniel Webster, in a letter to the Union Safety Committee of New York, offered his opinion that the incident constituted "strictly speaking a case of treason."[21] Eight persons were indicted in the Shadrach case. There were no convictions, however, due to hung juries.

In spring, Webster, accompanied by the president, embarked on a campaign across the North to carry the message of the administration. In a swing across central New York, starting at Albany, Webster said that resolutions passed in conventions in Ohio, New York, and Massachusetts castigating the law were "distinctly treasonable," and the rescue of Minkins "was an act of clear treason . . . [it was] levying war against the Union."[22] In Syracuse, standing on a balcony across from City Hall, in a signal toward coming events and exposing the administration's desire for high level prosecutions, Webster vowed the Fugitive Slave Law would be enforced "here in Syracuse in the midst of the next anti-slavery convention, if the occasion shall arise."[23]

The next case up concerned the fugitive Thomas Sims, and was staged so as to show that the despised law would be enforced even in Boston. Sims, "a spruce-looking" seventeen-year-old, had escaped from Chatham County, Georgia. Arriving in March 1851, and finding work as a waiter, he was to be followed closely by his master, after learning his slave had stowed away on a vessel bound for Boston. He was arrested on April 4, his hearing was scheduled for the 11th in a court house now cordoned in heavy chain and rope, and as the *Boston Courier* reported, guarded by "a large posse of police officers," as a detachment of soldiers, too, stood without.

Summoned from his home in Newburyport to join in the consultations of the Vigilance Committee at the *Liberator*'s office, Higginson later wrote: "It is impossible to conceive of a set of men, personably admirable, yet less fitted on the whole than this committee to undertake any positive action in the direction of forcible resistance to authorities. In the first place, half of them were non-resistants." Others on the committee, being political abolitionists or "free-soilers," had insuperable reasons not to wish to appear unfit as citizens. Remarking on the state of indecision at the meeting, Higginson observed that at least the blacks had just proved their mettle, and doubtless would do so again. To which Lewis Hayden nodded cordially, "Of course they will."

Without resolving on a plan, as the meeting adjourned Hayden drew Higginson aside, startling him as he remarked, "I said that for bluff, you know. We do not wish anyone to know how really weak we are. Practically there are no colored men in Boston; the Shadrach prosecutions have scattered them all. What is to be done must be done without them."24

Presented with all the precautions, and the overwhelming force of authorities, resistance was futile. Sims was remanded to slavery. Escorted by three hundred deputized policemen and United States Army soldiers to the wharf before dawn to board the brig *Acorn* for Savannah, Georgia; soon Sims would stand on an auction block in Charleston's Slave Mart—a sale transporting him thence to New Orleans, and afterward to Vicksburg, Mississippi. Sims would survive and again be free in summer 1863, when General Grant would write out a pass authorizing his use of government transportation back to Boston.

On April 16 President Fillmore would write his Secretary of State: "I congratulate you and the country upon a triumph of law in Boston. She has done nobly. She has wiped out the stain of the former rescue and freed herself from the reproach of nullification."25

In the pre-dawn hours of September 11, 1851, a slaveholding farmer from Maryland, Edward Gorsuch, arrived outside the home of William Parker near Christiana, Pennsylvania—together with a marshal and his deputy, with two other men, and with two of his sons, a doctor neighbor, and four other men making up the posse. They carried warrants for the arrest of four fugitive slaves. A fugitive from Baltimore himself, Parker had come to the central Pennsylvania district in 1839 to make a life and raise a family, and had risen into leadership of blacks in the area, forming an "organization for mutual protection." Forewarned of the pending arrival of the posse by a messenger sent by William Still, Parker reported the warning "spread through the vicinity like a fire in the prairies."26 Inside the home were his wife, Eliza, his brother-in-law and his wife, with another man, and two of Gorsuch's fugitives—all anxious, but determined to resist arrest. The slaveholder and the marshal invaded the house, demanding the fugitives, Gorsuch calling to his slaves in the upper rooms to surrender peacefully. Standing on the stairs, with the sound of guns being loaded behind him, Parker demanded, "Who are you?"

"I am the United States Marshal," was the reply.

"Take another step, and I'll break your neck," Parker warned.

"Yes," answered the marshal, "I have heard a negro talk as big as you, and then have taken him; and I'll take you."

"You have not taken me yet," Parker responded, "and if you undertake it you will have your name recorded in history for this day's work."

So there would be no misunderstanding the marshal read the warrants; but since there was no possibility of such, the reading produced no effect. As the marshal threatened to burn the house unless the fugitives came down, from a garret window Eliza Parker blew a horn. "It was a custom with us, when a horn was blown at an unusual hour," Parker related in his *Story*, "to proceed to the spot promptly to see what was the matter." Sounding the horn again, Parker's wife was fired upon by those outside the building. Now beside himself, Gorsuch remonstrated: "I want my property, and I will have it." Instigated by the slaveholder, the marshal fired a shot at Parker through a window, shattering the glass. Parker returned fire, grazing Gorsuch's shoulder.

After this a curious parley resumed, both sides maneuvering and looking for advantage and to gain the upper hand for their position. With everyone waiting for the fracas' renewal, an exasperated Gorsuch called out, as if soliloquizing, "I want my property and I will have it." Now the marshal, playing at writing out a note to the sheriff in Lancaster, bluffed in a loud voice to his intended courier, calling for one hundred reinforcements. At this time, Parker related, a large number of white men began arriving, apparently those having extraneously followed the posse, and the marshal began enrolling them as special constables. With those inside the house becoming alarmed, there was talk of giving up. Grabbing a corn-cutter, Eliza swore she would "cut off the head of the first one who should attempt to give up."

With the sun well up, news that Parker's house was surrounded by kidnappers was spreading through the countryside. Men, many of them Quakers, dropped their work in fields, hurriedly finished breakfast, or closed stores, hastening to the site. Leavening the spirits of those in the house, an even more salutary influence began showing up, as blacks summoned by Eliza's horn were coming out of the woods and across the fields, among them the two remaining Gorsuch fugitives— and those not carrying firearms were carrying anything they'd found at hand: stones, scythes, corn-cutters, rails, pitchforks. Later estimates put their number at between fifteen and twenty-five.[27] With Gorsuch threatening Parker, who now stood in his door with the others behind him, and the variously armed black men arriving, the marshal saw the wisdom of discretion. As he "hallooed" his men to move off, the fighting began. Gorsuch, struck with a club, fell to his hands and knees; raising a pistol, one of Gorsuch's sons was clubbed and shot in the side. As Gorsuch rose to his feet, he was suddenly seized by his old notion, declaring with a "calm and stern" look, as it was described—"My property is here, and I will have it or perish in the attempt."28

The two sides now engaged in a pitched battle. Gorsuch was knocked down twice by one of his slaves, the antagonists clubbing their weapons as soon as they were discharged. Holding his pistols to the last, Gorsuch was beaten down by his own man, who "bent his gun" in subduing him. Edward Gorsuch lay in his own blood, flies buzzing around his corpse, as the marshal and his posse retreated.29

Parker and two of the fugitives fled to the nearby village of Gap, where they were put on a train. "Almost in advance of the lightning, and much in advance of probable pursuit," Frederick Douglass wrote in his autobiography *Life and Times*, they arrived at his home in Rochester. Douglass described the occasion: "The hours they spent at my house were . . . hours of anxiety as well as activity. I dispatched my friend Miss Julia Griffiths to the landing three miles away on the Genesee River to ascertain if a steamer would leave that night for any port in Canada, and remained at home myself to guard my tired, dust-covered, and sleeping guests, for they had been harassed and traveling for two days and nights, and needed rest. Happily for us the suspense was not long, for it turned out that that night a steamer was to leave for Toronto, Canada."30

When the hour came, Douglass put the men in his carriage and started for the landing. Arriving fifteen minutes before the time of departure, they remained on board with Douglass until the order to haul in the gangplank was given. Shaking hands with Parker and the others, Douglass "received from Parker the revolver that fell from the hand of Gorsuch when he died, presented now as a token of gratitude and a memento of the battle for liberty at Christiana."31

In Baltimore a meeting of indignation was called for Monument Square on September 15, drawing as many as ten thousand, hearing speakers denouncing the abuse of the "constitutional rights of every Southern man." On the 17th a mass meeting with an even more strident tone assembled in Philadelphia's Independence Square, merchants being especially upset because of the "probable effect upon the business of the city" of the "riots."32 Pennsylvania's governor issued a proclamation offering a $1,000 reward for the capture and conviction of the guilty parties; while Maryland's governor wrote an open letter to

President Fillmore calling for action in the case, with "the fullest retribution upon the criminals." As news of the incident had been flashed to Washington, the U.S. Attorney in Philadelphia was summoned to a meeting with the president, Secretary of State Webster, and Attorney General John Crittenden, where it was decided defendants prosecuted in the case would be charged with treason to the United States. On November 13 indictments were brought against forty-one men, thirty-six black and five white.

In the last week of September, just as the city was crowded with visitors to the Onondaga County Fair, the New York Liberty Party convention convened in a church in Syracuse. Living in the city was a fugitive slave who had escaped from the "service" of John McReynolds of Marion County, Missouri, named William Henry, popularly known as Jerry. A barrel maker and cooper by trade, he was arrested, ostensibly for theft, but when brought to the commissioner, he learned he'd been arrested as a fugitive slave. Hearing this he put up considerable fight, and was heavily manacled. As the inquiry began, a large crowd gathered outside the commissioner's office as church bells tolled. With the hearing going on, several lawyers entered offering themselves as Jerry's council and objecting that the alleged fugitive was sitting in irons; the commissioner consented they be removed. When the court was about to adjourn for lunch, a group of men, led by a thick-set black man who worked as an iron-maker, rushed the commissioner's office. The fugitive was hustled onto the street and across a bridge over the Erie Canal. Overtaken by police, Jerry, now heavily manacled, was driven in a wagon to the city jail.

That afternoon when the hearing resumed, as a large crowd was milling, the proceeding was adjourned till the following morning. The marshal called for assistance from the marshals in Auburn, Canandaigua, and Rochester, to help exert control. By this point the crowd in the streets was enormous, the Rev. Samuel May among them. Two weeks later in a speech he would say, as he saw it there had been no pre-determined plan, only "indignation flashed from every eye." The fugitive was forcibly removed from jail and hidden away for several days in Syracuse, before being driven to Lake Ontario to sail on a vessel to Kingston, Ontario. The next day, as the Liberty Party convention reconvened, Gerrit Smith introducing the following resolution, which passed:

> Whereas, Daniel Webster, that base and infamous enemy of the human race, did in a speech of which he delivered himself in Syracuse last Spring, exultingly and insultingly predict that fugitive slaves would yet be taken

away from Syracuse and even from anti-slavery conventions in Syracuse, and whereas the attempt to fulfill this prediction was delayed until the first day of October, 1851, when the Liberty party of the State of New York were holding their annual convention in Syracuse; and whereas the attempt was defeated by the mighty uprising of 2,500 brave men, before whom the half-dozen kidnappers were "as tow," therefore,

RESOLVED, That we rejoice that the city of Syracuse—the anti-slavery city of Syracuse—the city of anti-slavery conventions, our beloved and glorious city of Syracuse—still remains undisgraced by the fulfillment of the satanic Daniel Webster.[33]

Many notables were in the crowd that freed William Henry, among them the Reverends Loguen, Samuel Ringgold Ward, and Samuel May, as well as Gerrit Smith and Charles Wheaton, and others. The district attorney would try to make a case of constructive treason against Smith, May, Wheaton, and five other defendants, and hoped to add sixteen others to the list for aiding and abetting the escape of a fugitive slave. But, given the lack of evidence, the district court refused. A federal grand jury in Buffalo did bring charges against twenty-six individuals, not for treason, but for being "engaged in the Syracuse riots." Loguen fled to Canada for a time; the Rev. Samuel Ringgold Ward would leave the United States permanently. Another of the notables present at the "Jerry rescue," but who rarely is credited as being there, was John Brown.[34]

Writing many years later about the effect of the fugitive slave law, in his *Life and Times* Frederick Douglass observed:

Living, as I then did, in Rochester, on the border of Canada, I was compelled to see the terribly distressing effect of this cruel enactment. Fugitive slaves who had lived for many years safely and securely in western New York and elsewhere, some of whom had by industry and economy saved money and bought little homes for themselves and their children, were suddenly alarmed and compelled to flee to Canada for safety as from an enemy's land—a doomed city. . . . My old friend Ward . . . found it necessary to give up the contest and flee to Canada, and thousands followed his example. Bishop Daniel A. Payne of the African Methodist Episcopal Church came to me about this time to consult me as to whether it was best to stand our ground or flee to Canada. When I told him I could not desert my post until I saw I could not hold it, adding that I did not wish to leave while Garnet and Ward remained, "Why," said he, "Ward? Ward, he is already gone. I saw him crossing from Detroit to Windsor." I asked him if he were going to stay, and he answered. "Yes; we are whipped, we are whipped, and we might as well retreat in order."[35]

For Douglass this was a stunning blow; Ward was a man whose abilities were without parallel among his peers, no other could replace him. Wendell Phillips said of him that Ward was a man of exceedingly dark complexion—so dark if he closed his eyes, you could not see him.[36] "Mr. Phillips," Ward once returned, was "a man who I always loved, a man who taught me my hornbook on this subject of slavery."[37]

To his wife, Mary, John Brown wrote in a letter dated December 22, 1851, from Boston:

> I shall take a few moments to write as prompted by my inclination rather than from feeling that I have any other sufficient reasons. My prospects about getting back soon are rather poor at this moment, but still it may be I shall be on my way within a day or two. . . . I wrote to Fred'k Douglas[s] a few days since to send on his paper, which I suppose he has done before this, as he very promptly acknowledged the receipt of my letter. There is an unusual amount of very interesting things happening in this and other countries at present, and no one can foresee what is yet to follow. The great excitement produced by the coming of Kossuth, and the last news of a new revolution in France, with the prospect that all Europe will soon again be in blaze seem to have taken all by surprise. I have only to say in regard to these things that I rejoice in them from the full belief that God is carrying out his eternal purpose in them all. . . . I know of nothing unfavorable in our prospects except the slow progress we make and the great expense attending it.[38]

The Hungarian Revolution in 1848 was one of many closely linked throughout Europe. When news of the events in France reached Hungary, a province of the Habsburg Empire, Louis Kossuth in a stirring speech in German demanded parliamentary government for his nation. The speech became an item in the agitation of students in Vienna, helping bring the fall of Metternich. Establishing a government, Kossuth was to be defeated in the following year, and fled into exile where he was imprisoned in Turkey. In March 1850 in a resolution the Congress asked President Taylor to intercede and bring Kossuth to the United States. The intercession successfully done, disembarking the United States frigate *Mississippi* at Gibraltar, Kossuth would tour England before arriving at New York on December 4, 1851.

Kossuth was to receive a tremendous reception, particularly among newly emigrated Germans, as "Magyar-mania" spread like a contagion across the country in the winter of 1851–52. Here was a liberator and worker in the cause of universal emancipation! On December 6 he was given a great reception in New York City; President Fillmore would receive him at the executive mansion on January 5, and he would address a joint session of the United States Congress.

On December 9, five days after his arrival, Kossuth met with a reception committee on behalf of the "Negro people," and was addressed by George T. Downing. Downing's speech was reported on in the *Liberator*, December 19, where he said: "Respected sir, your mission is too high to be allied with party or sect; it is the common cause of crushed, outraged humanity. . . . May you, when you leave our shores in furtherance of your heaven-high mission, carry with you the sympathy of *all*, the active countenance of *all*."[39]

Notwithstanding this appeal, Kossuth would refrain from uttering a word against slavery during his entire visit, saying he wished to avoid "entanglements." His aim was to get the United States to abandon its nonintervention policy, and recognize Hungary's independence, something which President Fillmore refused. But given the preceding months, Kossuth's stance, while himself a fugitive, seemed base hypocrisy.

Feted at banquets and receptions in New York, Philadelphia, and Baltimore, Kossuth toured throughout New England, the South, and the Midwest giving six hundred speeches—a tour which was, Edmund Quincy wrote, "one continual Festival." Newspapers praised his eloquence and heroism, with many in his audience donning "Kossuth hats" in his honor, his reception paralleling that given the Marquis de Lafayette decades earlier. Garrison and the American Anti-Slavery Society produced a stirring *Letter to Louis Kossuth*, published as a 112-page pamphlet. Frederick Douglass gave notice to its issue in his *Monthly* on February 26, 1852, calling it "a most searching production":

> He who comes to this country, hoping to escape "entanglements" on the slavery question . . . must not only keep his mouth shut and his ears closed, but must actually put his eyes out, or cover them with bandages too thick to allow him to catch the lineaments of our national face; and in choosing one to lead him, must be sure to select an individual as blind as himself; for so sure as these conditions are not complied with, he will find his fond hopes blasted—The line between Freedom and Slavery, in this country, is tightly drawn.

On December 2, 1851, before dawn Paris was beginning to awaken to a capital plastered round with placards announcing the dissolution of the National Assembly; at dawn the president of the Second Republic and Louis-Napoleon Bonaparte's most implacable political and military foes were arrested and imprisoned. In planning since August, the coup d'état had been fixed by the anniversary of the coronation of Napoleon in 1804, and the victory of Austerlitz in 1805. "The little Napoleon" declared that a new constitution was being framed, and that he intended to restore a "system established by the First Consul." Later that day deputies not under arrest from across the city gathered to defend the principles of the Republic, declaring that Bonaparte was stripped of his functions as president, and also declaring that "citizens are ordered to refuse to obey him," that "by right, executive power is passed to the National Assembly."

Soldiers loyal to Louis-Napoleon made an attempt to arrest the deputies, but withdrew after being read the decrees and ordered to disperse. The decrees were then proclaimed to the streets, announcing the removal and indictment of the president. A Parisian insurrection erupted, but was crushed in only a few days, with two hundred people killed. Karl Marx was to write shortly thereafter in his study of the events leading to the coup d'état:

> On December 2 the February Revolution is conjured away by a card-sharper's trick, and what seems overthrown is no longer the monarchy but the liberal concessions that were wrung from it by centuries of struggle. Instead of *society* having conquered a new content for itself, it seems that the *state* only returned to its oldest form, to the shamelessly simple domination of the sabre and the cowl. This is the answer to the *coup de main* of February 1848, given by the *coup de tete* of December 1851.[40]

On January 23, 1852, Brown addressed a letter to Akron for his "Dear Children," from Troy, New York—"If you find it difficult for you to pay for Douglass' paper, I wish you would let me know, as I know I took liberty in ordering it continued."[41] With this remark and the foregoing letter it seems clear that Brown valued his ongoing bond with Frederick Douglass. The tenor of the letter too reveals an unusual understanding between wife and husband; they are completely familiar in confiding about world affairs, and their bearing on Brown's sanctioned mission. Although few have discerned it, even with all his preoccupations, that is his overarching interest. "I know of nothing unfavorable in our prospects except the slow progress we make and the great expense attending it." Now his goal would be one he and his family, he understood, would henceforth embrace out of poverty.

By this time Douglass had aligned his views with those of Gerrit Smith; a continual correspondence between them was maintained, as

Douglass was as well a grateful recipient of the philanthropist's largess, receiving pecuniary support for his paper. After announcing his change of opinion on the Constitution and on the efficacy of political action, Douglass wrote to Smith asking his advice on how best to answer the attacks that were sure to come in regard to his present outlook. He knew too well the temper of his old companions "to hope to escape the penalty which all others have paid who have ventured to differ from them."[42]

The crux of the attack would fall not directly on the offender, however, but on his most trusted coadjutor. This began to be seen in January 1852 as Douglass tersely answered his friend S. D. Porter, a Rochester abolitionist of some wealth, about the perceived impropriety of Julia Griffiths's continuing presence in his home. Douglass informed him that she had moved two months before, and was then living with a "nobler" family. As objections were raised too in far-away Boston, and as they continued to fester well into the next year, Garrison blustered in the pages of the *Liberator*, November 18, 1853: "For several years past, he has had one of the worst advisers in his printing-office, whose influence over him has not only caused much unhappiness in his own household, but perniciously biased his own judgment . . . and whose sectarianism is manifestly paramount to any regard for the integrity of the anti-slavery movement." On September 24, stooping into the same slough, the *Anti-Slavery Standard* had cited Griffiths as "a Jezebel whose capacity for making mischief between friends would be difficult to match." With denunciatory articles continuing in the *Pennsylvania Freeman*, Douglass devoted twelve columns of his paper on December 9, 1853, to his rejoinder.

Furious at Garrison for the bitterness of his attack, he refused to discuss his family in the press, but hit back with a salient retort. Charging that the illustrious editor harbored contempt for the very people whose benefactor he purported to be, Douglass quoted Garrison's observation that "the anti-slavery cause, both religiously and politically, has transcended the ability of the sufferers from American Slavery and prejudice, *as a class*, to keep pace with it, or to perceive what are its demands, or to understand the philosophy of its operations." Douglass astringently observed: "The colored people ought to feel profoundly grateful for this magnificent compliment (which does not emanate from a Colonizationist) to their high, moral worth, and breadth of comprehension so generously bestowed by William Lloyd Garrison!—Who will doubt, hereafter, the natural inferiority of the *Negro*, when the great champion of the Negroes' rights, thus broadly concedes all that is claimed respecting the Negro's inferiority by the bitterest despisers of the Negro race."[43]

Assessing the Compromise of 1850 in all its ramifications, "and judging from the events and indications of the past years, the black man must see that a crisis had arrived in his relations with the American people." Such was Douglass's charge in a speech at the annual meeting of the American and Foreign Anti-Slavery Society in May 1853, "The Present Condition and Future Prospects of the Negro People." It was evident, said Douglass, that under the keystone of this grand arch of the Compromise, there was in the country a coalescing of a purely proslavery party. This had five cardinal objectives: The first being the complete suppression of all antislavery discussion; second, the expatriation of the entire free people of color from the United States; third, the perpetuation of slavery in the republic; fourth, the naturalization of slavery to the extent of making slavery respected in every state in the Union; and fifth, the extension of slavery over Mexico and all the South American states.[44]

One of the distressing signs of this debilitating tendency was in the Black Law considered and enacted in Illinois that spring. The first section of the law declared that no "Negro or mulatto slave" could be brought into the state from any of the southern states, for the purpose of emancipating said slave. It shall not be done on Illinois soil, the law stated, and anyone attempting it shall be liable to a fine of from one hundred to five hundred dollars, and imprisonment in the county jail. The bill's second section provided for the extradition of any person indicted under the law, who may have escaped into another state or territory. Illinois "means not only to get rid of Negro residents in a state of freedom," Douglass gave notice in his paper, March 18, 1853, "but in imitation of . . . the Fugitive Slave Law . . . means to hunt them and fetch them back for punishment." This "harassing legislation" prompted a letter from H. O. Wagoner, a resident of Illinois, published as a column of *Frederick Douglass' Paper* calling on the free colored people of the northern states to assemble in convention to consider their present status and condition. We must come together, Wagoner wrote, in no "flourishing" mood, but in a sober and determined manner, or, as Douglass commented, it would "fail to comprehend . . . the gravity of the crisis which is rapidly approaching and for which we are admonished to prepare, or be overwhelmed." "Let us meet, then, in Convention," he concluded, "and let us appeal to *our country* and to *the world*, in behalf of those principles of justice and humanity which have been struck down in our persons."[45]

It was during this period Douglass gave notice of the appearance of what he called "the master book of the nineteenth century,"[46] *Uncle Tom's Cabin.* "In the midst of these fugitive slave troubles came . . . a work of marvelous depth and power. Nothing could have better suited the moral and humane requirements of the hour. Its effect was amazing, instantaneous, and universal. No book on the subject of slavery had so generally and favorably touched the American heart. It combined all the power and pathos of preceding publications of the kind, and was hailed by many as an inspired production."[47]

Gamaliel Bailey, editor of the weekly journal *National Era*, had acknowledged a letter dated March 9, 1850, from a woman then living in Brunswick, Maine, who wrote, "I feel now that the time is come when even a woman or a child can speak a word for freedom and humanity. . . . I hope every woman who can write will not be silent."[48]

In June 1851 the first installment of Harriet Beecher Stowe's *Life Among the Lowly* was published in the *National Era.* Appearing weekly as a serial from June 5, 1851, to April 1, 1852, *Uncle Tom's Cabin* was published in book form on March 20, 1852, with an initial print run of 5,000 copies. In less than a year the book had sold an unprecedented 300,000 copies, followed in December 1853 by an edition priced at 37 1/2 cents to encourage further sales. The author became the object of wide attention, which brought her in turn growing celebrity; the book too won for her affluence. Eminent persons whose antislavery enthusiasm had been roused by the book had invited her to visit England, where she had been promised a testimonial. Before her departure she bid Frederick Douglass come to her home, now in the collegiate town of Andover, Massachusetts.

Delighted by the unexpected opportunity, Douglass wrote, he lost no time in making his way to Andover, where he was received "with genuine cordiality," when she detailed her purpose for summoning him:

> I have invited you here because I wish to confer with you as to what can be done for the free colored people of the country. I am going to England and expect to have a considerable sum of money placed in my hands, and I intend to use it in some way for the permanent improvement of the free colored people, and especially for that class which has become free by their own exertions. In what way I can do this most successfully is the subject about which I wish to talk with you. In any event I desire to have some monument rise after *Uncle Tom's Cabin*, which shall show that it produced more than a transient influence.[49]

In considering the matter the two quickly came to agreement on an industrial school, set up as a series of workshops where black youth

could be trained in trades—in iron and wood, in clay and leather—
where they had heretofore been barred in the apprentice system, as no
white tradesmen would take them. Stowe asked Douglass to put his
views in the form of a letter, which she could then show those she would
meet in England, and he did so, publishing it as a lengthy column in his
paper. His proposal caught the eye of Martin Delany, and soon Delany's
letter together with Douglass's remarks on it, appeared in a subsequent
addition of *Frederick Douglass' Paper*. Delany's letter, dated March 23,
1853, contended querulously: "Now I simply wish to say, that we have
always fallen into great errors in efforts of this kind, going to others than
the *intelligent* and *experienced* among *ourselves*; and in all due respect
and deference to Mrs. Stowe, I beg leave to say, that she *knows nothing
about us*, 'the Free Colored people of the United States,' neither does any
other white person—and consequently can contrive no successful
scheme for our elevation; it must be done by ourselves."[50]

Delany was in accord with the suggestion of H. O. Wagoner for a
National Council for consultation provided the "*intelligence, maturity,
and experience* . . . could be gathered together." If it turned into a mockery like the Convention of 1848, he wrote, as "a coming together of
rivals to test their success for the "'biggest offices,'" he would not lend
aid to the work. "But something must be done, and that speedily."
Delany's letter concluded: "The so-called free states, by their acts, are
now virtually saying to the South, "you *shall not* emancipate; your
blacks *must be slaves*; and should they come North, there is no refuge
for them." I shall not be surprised to see, at no distant day, a solemn
Convention called by the whites in the North, to deliberate on the propriety of changing the whole policy to that of slave states. This will be
the remedy to prevent dissolution."[51]

Martin Delany and Frederick Douglass had been closely linked prior
to this; now this clash of views would mark each as the foil of the other,
coming to represent divergent tendencies within the African
Americans' struggle in the United States. In the previous year, at age
thirty-seven, Delany had sought to further his medical training by
enrolling at Harvard Medical School. But after he began his studies, the
white medical students resolved they could not share their educational
platform with blacks, and he and two other black students enrolled
under the auspices of the Colonization Society were dismissed. Waiting
in vain to see if a protest would be lodged in the *Liberator*, Delany
began writing a summation of his experiences, together with his evolving thinking on how Africans could break the impasse presented by
their position in the country.

Published in May 1852, *The Condition, Elevation, Emigration and Destiny of the Colored People of the United States Politically Considered*, was a polemical tour de force, where Delany proposed selective immigration to Central and South America, and the West Indian Islands, and even to the east coast of Africa, where blacks would form the ruling element. "We must ... ESTABLISH a NATIONAL POSITION for OURSELVES," Delany wrote, "and never may expect to be respected as men and women, until we have undertaken, some fearless, bold, and adventurous deeds of daring."52

In his response to Delany's reproach that blacks lead in any scheme designed to permanently aid themselves, Douglass agreed that was "a consummation devoutly to be wished," but until then, why throw cold water on plans proposed by others? Wasn't the field open? Delany had looked in vain for notice of his exposition in *Frederick Douglass' Paper* in the previous year; now, in his remarks on his letter about Stowe, Douglass conceded that notice:

> The assertion that Stowe "knows nothing about us," shows that Bro. Delany knows nothing about Mrs. Stowe; for he certainly would not so violate his moral, or common sense if he did. When Brother Delany will submit any plan for benefitting the colored people, or will candidly criticize any plan already submitted, he will be heard with pleasure. But we expect no plan from him. He has written a book—and we may say that it is in many respects, an excellent book ... but it leaves us just where it finds us, without a chart or compass, in more doubt and perplexity than before we read it.53

Four years before a proposition had been made in the columns of the *North Star* for a "National League," said Douglass; that proposal had been met with indifference, and the plan failed. Stowe had sought for and wished to consult with such a body—but there was no such body to answer. "The fact is," Douglass wrote in his recant of *The Letter of M. R. Delany*, May 6, 1853, "brother Delany, we are a disunited and scattered people, and very much of the responsibility of this disunion must fall upon such colored men as yourself and the writer of this. We want more confidence in each other, as a race—more self-forgetfulness." Would "not friend Delany draw up a call for such a convention, and send it to us for publication?"54

A hundred and forty delegates from nine states answered the call to assemble in Rochester, New York, in July 1853. That call had pronounced that all the vicissitudes facing blacks in America beckoned as if "trumpet-tongued for our union, co-operation, and action." J. W. C.

Pennington was elected president, with Douglass, Nell, and Vashon as vice-presidents. As chairman of the committee on Declaration of Sentiments, Douglass drew up the "address of the colored convention to the people of the United States," asserting all the historical evidence that established the ground that blacks were American citizens, titled "The Claims of Our Common Cause." Yet Douglass lamented:

> As a people, we feel ourselves to be not only deeply injured, but grossly misunderstood. Our white fellow-countrymen do not know us. They are strangers to our character, ignorant of our capacity, oblivious of our history and progress, and are misinformed as to the principles and ideas that control and guide us as a people. The great mass of American citizens estimate us as being a characterless and purposeless people; and hence we hold up our heads, if at all, against the withering influence of a nation's scorn and contempt.[55]

The most important issue before the convention was the founding of a manual labor school for black youth, and Douglass read the delegates his letter to Stowe. With a number of the delegates hostile to the proposal, Douglass, Pennington, and James McCune Smith led the argument in its favor. With the proposal winning, a council was instituted to provide for its operation before the next national convention. With four such committees organized the deliberations were concluded.

The *Rochester Democrat*, in an article reprinted in the *Liberator*, July 22, 1853, observed: "There can be no doubt that these people have the ability to devise and carry out measures for their own social advancement, and for the general improvement of their condition. . . . Let them have the sympathy and pecuniary aid of others, but let their plans be devised and executed by themselves." But as the convention received positive notice, the very sign of its achievement was to bring disappointment, as upon returning from her sojourn in England, Harriet Beecher Stowe informed Douglass she'd reconsidered her offer. Douglass wrote: "I have never been able to see any force in the reasons for this change. It is enough, however, to say that they were sufficient for her, and that she no doubt acted conscientiously, though her change of purpose was a great disappointment, and placed me in an awkward position before the colored people of this country, as well as to friends abroad, to whom I had given assurances that the money would be appropriated in the manner I have described."[56]

The next scheduled meeting did not produce a quorum, and the national convention movement collapsed. There would not be a comparable assemblage again until 1864.

Delany and others who had not attended the Rochester convention now announced a National Emigration Convention to convene the following August in Cleveland, Ohio, "then and there, to consider and decide upon the great and important subject of emigration from the United States." Douglass hastened to head it off in the columns of his paper, July 17, 1853, "Arguments on the Call for a National Emigration Convention": "Our enemies will see in this movement, a cause of rejoicing, such as they could hardly have anticipated so soon, after the manly position assumed by the colored National Convention held in this city. They will discover in this movement a division of opinion amongst us upon a vital point, and will look upon this Cleveland Convention as opposed in spirit and purpose to the Rochester Convention."[57]

J. M. Whitfield, a twenty-three-year-old poet noted for his panegyric on Britain's August 1 Emancipation, replied to Douglass, published in his monthly, November 25, 1853. In his briskly reasoned repartee, Whitfield wrote:

> So far from rejoicing, I believe that our enemies will see as much greater cause for dreading the holding of the Cleveland than the Rochester Convention, as a master would have greater reason for fearing the loss of the slave, who arms himself and leaves his premises with the determination to be free or die, than he would the one who, after a few vain supplications, submits to the lash, and devotes the energies which should be employed in improving himself and his children, to building up the fortune of a tyrant. . . . I suppose the purpose of the Cleveland Convention to be as much superior to that of the Rochester Convention, as deeds are superior to words.[58]

As far as it went the Rochester Convention was a step in the right direction, "to give efficiency, by forming a kind of national organization here, under the overshadowing influence of our oppressors." But "colored men can never be fully and fairly respected as the equals of the whites, in this country," Whitfield wrote, "until they are able to show in some part of the world, men of their own race occupying a primary and independent position."

Douglass seems to have appreciated fully the novitiate's jousts, as he retorted: "If they believe with us, that by remaining *here*, and battling for the right we shall evidently stand out in the sunlight on the broad platform of equality, why turn their backs upon the contest, and flee from the country under the pretext of 'shaping the policy of the American continent'?" There were more than a hundred delegates in Cleveland on August 24, 1854, arriving, amidst the taunts and jeers of the white public outside, from ten states and Canada, with a handful of them women. As president pro tem, chairman of the business committee, and keynote speaker, Delany pointed out that this was "not merely a talking and theoretical, but an acting and practically doing Convention." Sessions began on time and ran efficiently, causing the *Cleveland Morning Leader* to observe: "Few conventions of whites behave themselves more orderly or observe parliamentary rule more exactly, or discuss important topics with more ability and self-possession."[59]

On the second day of the proceedings, sixteen hundred people, black and white, crowded into the church where the convention was held, to hear Delany's address, "The Political Destiny of the Colored Race." That speech thoroughly imbibed the principle that "A people, to be free, must necessarily be their own rulers; that is, each individual must, in himself, embody the essential ingredient . . . of the sovereign principle which composes the true basis of his liberty."[60] After a discussion of the report, it was unanimously adopted.

Now one of the younger delegates, a free black from New Orleans then residing in Chicago, held the house for an hour. H. Ford Douglass cautioned his auditors against basing their hopes "upon the ideal sands of a sickly sentimentality":

> The mingled tones of sorrow and woe which come up upon every breeze from the deep and damning hell of Negro slavery speaks a common language to each and every individual, no matter how humble he may be. . . . A truth told by a patrician would be no less the truth when told by a plebian. Because Mr. Douglass, Mr. Smith or Mr. Langston tell me that the principles of emigration are destructive to the best interests of the colored people in this country, am I to act the part of a "young robin." . . . Is not the history of the world, the history of emigration? . . . The coming and going out of nations. . . . Let us then be up and doing. To stand still is to stagnate and die.[61]

With the speeches concluded, on the third day of the convention the design of a national organization, a National Board of Commissioners, was proposed. These offices included provision for a Foreign Secretary and a Committee on Foreign Relations to collect information on the geography, economy, and politics of countries that might be welcoming to "Africo-American" emigration. After conducting inquiries the commissioners were to travel to these countries to assess conditions first-hand. Envisioning a prolonged research and investigation, the constitution of the National Board stipulated monthly meetings, with annual reports, and conventions every two years. But the Cleveland

Convention was to stir no more interest or comment than had Delany's polemic when issued two years before. Yet it is still pertinent, even as it was in its day significant amidst the dubious perturbations of an evolving American scene, as it would also have bearing on the roads John Brown traveled to Harpers Ferry.

I n a lengthy letter addressed to Frederick Douglass sent from Akron, dated January 9, 1854, the longest extant between them, John Brown began by confiding he had "thought much of late of the extreme wickedness of persons who use their influence to bring law and order and good government, and courts of justice into disrespect and contempt of mankind." His only reassurance for sending the letter was as a suggestion, he wrote, that Douglass might "take it up and clothe it in the suitable language to be noticed and felt."

Who are these malignant spirits, Brown began, who "would break down all that opposes the passions of fallen men . . . and . . . would give to the world a constant succession of murder, revenge, fire and famine . . . of anarchy in all its horrid forms."

The first of these were office electioneers, who attaining office "pass unjust and wicked enactments"; then came those who filled "the offices of Chief Magistrate of the United States and of different states, and affix the official signature to such enactments." These were followed by "another set from the same horde"— judges, justices, and commissioners; next came "a set of Capt. Rynders men—marshals, sheriffs, constables and policemen." Another were those "as sometimes succeed in getting *nominated* for some office," who could be loudly heard "at hotels, in cars, on steam-boats, and in stages" urging upon all the duty of upholding these enactments. "*Last, but not least*," came the fellows in "*black cloth*."

Drawing his enumeration to a close, Brown then added:

> There is one other set of the same throngers of the "broad way" which I have not mentioned. . . . I mean Editors of, and writers in the pro-slavery newspapers and periodicals. These seem to vie with each other in urging men on to greater and still greater lengths in stifling conscience, and insulting God. . . . But I have done. I am too destitute of words to express the tithe of what I feel, and utterly incapable of doing the subject any possible degree of justice, in my own estimation. . . . I want to have the enquiry everywhere raised—Who are the men that are undermining our truly republican and democratic institution at their very foundations?[62]

The answer to Brown's question came on a dual track. On January 4 a bill purporting to repeal the Missouri Compromise by dividing the Nebraska Territory in two had been reported in the Senate. The idea of a transcontinental railroad had gained traction in the previous year, and as many would-be settlers and land speculators cast covetous eyes on the Nebraska Territory, Illinois senator Stephen Douglas, an adroit and hard-edged political infighter, would rest his presidential aspirations on a bill designed to garner southern congressional support for opening the territories to settlement. The presidential contest in 1852, where Millard Fillmore won the support of southern Whigs and the northern members of the party threw their support behind Winfield Scott—was the last for the party. On the fifty-third ballot Scott became the party's nominee. Pledging fidelity to the Compromise of 1850, Franklin Pierce became the Democratic nominee. With the Free-Soil Party moribund, Pierce and the Democrats won in a landslide; but the bill of their leading politician in the Senate bid an entirely new political faction into existence, the Republican Party.

Following the precedent of the Mexican cession, the Kansas-Nebraska Bill stipulated whether or not slavery was admitted to a territory would be determined by the eligible voters who became settlers there. Joining the Illinois senator in driving it through was David Rice Atchison of Missouri, president pro tempore of the Senate. Ostensibly proposed to strengthen the compromise already framed yet derisively called the "Squatter Sovereign" bill, the legislation was passed in the Senate March 4, 1854, and would pass in the House May 22.

Less than a week after a fugitive slave Anthony Burns had been arrested in Boston, President Pierce signed the bill and it became law May 30. As Burns stood before a judge in Boston, Massachusetts' Charles Sumner stood in the Senate to announce that the law "annuls all past compromises with slavery, and makes all future compromises impossible. Thus it puts Freedom and Slavery face to face, and bids them grapple."[63]

Emigrants continued the trek to California in the years following the gold rush, outfitting in towns along the Missouri River—St. Joseph, Weston, and Independence. Even before the bill opening Kansas and Nebraska was enacted, many more emigrants began appearing. That April the Massachusetts legislature incorporated an emigrant aid society, which began operation promptly in July. Eli Thayer, at the head of the company, began proselytizing for immigration to Kansas, proposing land preempted with company funds in blocks, sending whole communities of settlers to begin farms—exporting schoolhouses, saw mills, and steam engines. Stumping for his project, he extolled: "The steam engine is a singer, and will sing nothing but freedom. Set it sawing pine logs into boards and it will sing at its work day and night, 'Home of the Free. Home of the Free.' Set it to sawing tough gnarled oak and its song will be, 'Never a slave state! Never a slave state!'"[64]

Anthony Burns reached Boston March 24, 1854, aboard a sailing vessel from Richmond, Virginia; then twenty-four years old he was the slave of a merchant living in Alexandria, Virginia, Colonel Charles Suttle. His owner had hired him out to work for William Brent, who had also employed Burns's brother for five or six years, loading ships docked at Richmond's wharfs. Arriving in Boston, Burns quickly obtained employment at a clothing store on Brattle Street owned by Coffin Pitts. It was not long before Burns wrote to his brother apprising him of his new circumstances, using the subterfuge of mailing the letter from Canada, but inadvertently dating it from Boston. Intercepting the letter, Brent notified Suttle of the whereabouts of "his property." Obtaining an affidavit from a Virginia court, Suttle sailed for Boston.

Appearing at the Boston courthouse, the Virginia slave owner presented his document to United States marshal Freeman, who issued a warrant, charging his deputy to arrest Burns and jail him at the courthouse. Knowing that an out-and-out arrest of a fugitive was sure to raise a strong protest and resistance, and to justify an arrest by city officials, the deputy decided on arresting Burns by charging him in a crime. The next year when Anthony Burns was free due to the intersession of the Rev. Leonard Grimes, who arranged to purchase him, the man recounted the night of his detention:

> When I was going home one night I heard someone running behind me; presently a hand was put on my shoulder, and somebody said: "Stop, stop; you are the fellow who broke into a silversmith's shop the other night." I assured the man that it was a mistake, but almost before I could speak, I was lifted from off my feet by six or seven others, and it was no use to resist. In the Court House I waited some time, and as the silversmith did not come, I told them I wanted to go home to supper. A man then came to the door; he didn't open it like an honest man would, but kind of slowly opened it, and looked in. He said, "How do you do, Mr. Burns?" and I called him, as we do in Virginia, "master!"[65]

The master asked why his man had run away; Burns replied, "I fell asleep on board the vessel where I worked and, before I woke up, she set sail and carried me off."

"Haven't I always treated you well, Tony? Haven't I always given you money when you needed?" Suttle asked. Burns stated, "You have always given me twelve and one-half cents once a year."[66] This provided all the evidence needed under law that Burns recognized Suttle as master and was enslaved to him in Virginia.

The next morning a little before nine o'clock, May 25, appearing before United States commissioner Edward Loring, Burns, confused and frightened from his ordeal—he'd not even eaten since being picked up and carried off—was not disposed to contest Suttle's claim. Hearing that a fugitive inquest was in progress, Richard H. Dana, Jr. and Charles Mayo Ellis hastened into the court offering their counsel; while passing on the street and hearing of the arrest, Theodore Parker likewise came into the court where he convinced a reluctant Burns that he might challenge the proceeding. Now Dana asked for postponement of the hearing of the case, which Loring granted until May 27, the following Saturday.

Boston's Vigilance Committee now swung into action, issuing hand-bills calling a public meeting to assemble in Faneuil Hall Friday evening. To assure a sizable gathering, abolitionists in towns and villages in the vicinity were also notified. So that Higginson might be there and bring a contingent with him, Samuel J. May wrote him in Worcester, May 25, 1854: "Give all the notice you can. The friends here are wide awake and unanimous. . . . The country must back the city, and, if necessary lead it. We shall summon all the country friends." That same day, with news of Burns's arrest reaching Troy, New York, John Brown was sitting in his counsel's office in Troy going over the testimony from a previous suit. He suddenly got up from his chair, walking rapidly across the room several times. Abruptly turning to his counsel, he said, "I'm going to Boston!" "Going to Boston? Why do you want to go to Boston?" asked the astonished lawyer. Continuing with his rapid turnabout, Brown replied, "Anthony Burns must be released, or I will die in the attempt." Dropping his pen in consternation, it took a long and earnest talk with his counsel to persuade Brown to remain.[67]

Higginson sent messages to several persons, and was especially eager to reach Martin Stowell who had taken part in the rescue of Jerry at Syracuse, New York—urging all to follow promptly. Arriving that morning on the train from Worcester, Higginson found himself, he wrote, "presently in a meeting of the Vigilance Committee not essentially different from those which had proved so disappointing three years before." Not only had the meeting failed to arrive at a plan, they had "no set purpose of united action." As the committee adjourned, Higginson remained behind with Lewis Hayden and others who were willing to act in a forcible resistance. With the ranks of the committee reduced from sixty to thirty, Higginson was chosen chairman; after listening to the spirited advice of Dr. Samuel Gridley Howe, a committee of six was chosen to give definite leadership to any proposed plan. This included Phillips, Parker, Howe, Higginson, and an energetic Irishman named Kemp who was a former sea captain from Newburyport, to which was added at Higginson's request, Stowell. The matter, however, still lacked resolution as the meeting ended.

Writing decades later in his *Cheerful Yesterdays*, Higginson wrote all hopes rested on Stowell, who was to arrive from Worcester at six P.M. Meeting him at the train, Higginson walked with Stowell as they discussed the state of affairs. Stowell at once "suggested a new plan as the only thing feasible," he wrote:

> The man must be taken from the Court-House. It could not be done in cold blood, but the effort must have behind it the momentum of a public meeting, such as was to be held at Faneuil Hall that night. An attack at the end of the meeting would be hopeless, for the United States marshal would undoubtedly be looking for just that attempt, and would be reinforced accordingly; this being, as we afterwards found, precisely what that official was planning. Could there not be an attack at the very height of the meeting, brought about in this way? Let all be in readiness; let a picked body be distributed near the Court House and Square; then let some loud-voiced speaker, who should appear in the gallery of Faneuil Hall and announce that there was a mob of negroes already attacking the Court-House; let a speaker, previously warned,—Phillips if possible,—accept the opportunity promptly, and send the whole meeting pell-mell to the Court Square, ready to fall in behind the leaders and bring out the slave. The project struck me as an inspiration. I accepted it heartily, and think now as I thought then, that it was one of the very best plots that ever— failed.[68]

At seven that evening the assembly was to commence, and there was an immense throng descending on the Hall, and filing through its doors, the largest ever seen at the historic meeting place. With shouting and agitation, Higginson tried to convey the plan just resolved to the other members of the committee on entering the Hall. Howe and Parker were reached, but due to the pandemonium Phillips could not be reached. The crowd was roused to a pitch of excitement as Wendell Phillips rose to speak:

> Mr. Chairman and Fellow Citizens—You have called me to this platform—for what? Do you wish to know what I want? I want that man set

free in the streets of Boston. . . . When law ceases, the sovereignty of the people begins. I am against squatter sovereignty in Nebraska, and I am against kidnapper sovereignty in the streets of Boston. . . . The question tomorrow is fellow citizens whether Virginia conquers Massachusetts. If that man leaves the city of Boston, Massachusetts is a conquered State.... Will you adhere to the precedent of Thomas Sims? Will you adhere to the case of Sims and see this man carried down State Street between two hundred men? . . . Nebraska, I call knocking a man down, and this spitting in his face after he is down.[69]

Hurriedly consulting with Lewis Hayden, Higginson had five men with which to begin the rescue to which the Underground leader had pledged ten. All went singly and without hurry to the courthouse so as not to attract attention. As luck would have it the building was open as there was a night meeting of the Supreme Court, and with the doors ajar Higginson positioned himself unobtrusively at the entrance awaiting the arrival of the others. Suddenly one of the many deputies inside ran up from the basement and, looking him directly in the face, barred the door. Some axes had been provided beforehand, and with Stowell retrieving them, as he arrived he said to Higginson, "Some of our men are bringing a beam up to the west door, the one that gives entrance to the upper stairway." As the joist was brought up, Higginson gripped the front end with one of Hayden's stout men opposite, with Hayden and Stowell and others grabbing hold behind. Hammering against the door, it wasn't long before it began to break, but was hastily secured again from inside. With another blow it was knocked off one of its hinges—enough space to a man to squeeze through. Higginson and his companion pushed through as a shot rang out. A half-dozen officers began pummeling the pair with their nightsticks, as they lustily countered with fists. In the melee Higginson was cut on the chin with a saber, and one of the deputy marshals, a twenty-four-year-old Boston truckman named Batchelder, was mortally wounded in the groin by a blade thrust. The attack had already been thwarted, as a lad with a stentorian voice made the announcement of its commencement from the gallery of Faneuil Hall. While many had understood the summons as an attempt to break up the meeting, it was not properly understood by others. With the leaders still on the platform as the first of the audience began exiting, there would only be a dilatory movement toward the courthouse. As several hundred persons milled outside the well-lighted building, the only further disturbance was in excoriation from the crowd and in throwing stones. With Higginson standing on the steps outside, assessing whether another attempt could be made, a man quietly came out of the throng and begin ascending the steps alone. Reaching Higginson, he asked, "Why are we not within?" "Because these people will not stand by us," was his disparaging reply. The individual was the Transcendental philosopher A. Bronson Alcott. Higginson wrote: "He said not a word, but calmly walked up the steps,—he and his familiar cane. He paused again at the top, the centre of all eyes, within and without; a revolver sounded from within, but hit nobody; and finding himself wholly unsupported, he turned and retreated, but without hastening a step. It seemed to me that, under the circumstances, neither Plato nor Pythagoras could have done the thing better."[70]

On hearing of the attack on the courthouse, Boston's mayor issued an immediate call for two companies of artillery. People still were milling up and down Washington Street, standing in shop doors, with knotted groups standing on sidewalks. With rumor running and panic among friends, it was said there was to be another attack on the courthouse; that the "kidnappers" were to be sought out in their lodging at the Revere House; that even the life of Wendell Phillips was to be sought. At twelve o'clock the Boston Artillery and the Columbia Artillery arrived—one stationed at City Hall and the other in front of the courthouse. At two o'clock a detachment of United States troops from Fort Independence and a company of marines from the Charlestown Navy Yard arrived. The marshal also organized a special guard, of which the jailer was to remark among whom he saw many of his regular customers.

That morning after he'd read the cable sent by Marshal Freeman concerning the incident and what he had done, President Pierce replied, "Your conduct is approved. The law must be executed." Later in the morning Pierce ordered the U.S. Attorney in Boston to "incur any expense deemed necessary . . . to insure the execution of the law."[71] The president and his secretary of war, Jefferson Davis, now saw that they could enforce the law as a political demonstration against further defiance in the North.

The examination of Burns began on May 29. The streets around the courthouse and the square were crowded as never before; nine hundred persons had come in from Worcester alone.[72] Rows of soldiers with fixed bayonets and police stood before the courthouse, with soldiers lining the halls and clogging the stairs. Colonel Suttle, who'd been feted by Harvard professors, appeared at court with a bodyguard of Harvard students, all southerners, but they were not admitted into court. With Commissioner Loring determined to execute the law in Suttle's favor, all arguments put by Burns's counsel were of no avail. The ruling came June 2, and President Pierce had seen to it that a United Sates warship was in port to transport Burns back to Virginia.

That day an entire brigade of Massachusetts soldiers, twenty-two companies, were on hand to guard against disturbance, together with a large body of Boston police, and a battery of artillery. The soldiers had guns loaded and capped, with fixed bayonets, with officers carrying side arms, while the soldiers forming a hollow square around the prisoner were armed with Roman swords, each with a revolver hanging from his belt. When the procession began a company of cavalry went ahead to clear the streets, which were then lined with bayonet-carrying soldiers all the way to the wharf. Windows along the march were draped in mourning, streams of crepe crisscrossing the street, when at the corner of Washington and State streets a coffin was suspended from a window with the words "The Funeral of Liberty," and a few paces farther an American flag edged in black was hung, the Union down. The object of all this—Anthony Burns—was to remark in the following year when a free man, "There was lots of folks to see a colored man walk down the street."[73]

Estimates are that as many as fifty thousand thronged the streets to watch the rendition of Anthony Burns, amidst groans and hisses. A shower of cayenne pepper, together with other irritants, wafted in a cloud from the Commonwealth building as the procession passed State Street. When the crowd surged forward, lancers charged into them, as people were struck with the flat of sabers, as a company with fixed bayonets ran into the mass. Some people were trampled, others pushed up stairs or into basements, many pressed against walls.

As the troops passed the Custom House a military band struck up the tune "Carry Me Back to Old Virginia," which was sung by soldiers down the length of Long Wharf. There the fugitive boarded the United States revenue cutter *Morris*. The *Liberator*'s headline cried: "Triumph of the Slave Power—THE KIDNAPPING LAW ENFORCED AT THE POINT OF BAYONET—Massachusetts in Disgraceful Vassalage."

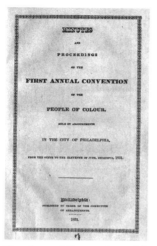

The First Annual Convention of the People of Colour met in Philadelphia in June 1831. This meeting led to the organization of the American Anti-Slavery Society. (*Library Company of Philadelphia*)

William Lloyd Garrison (1805–1879) in an 1833 portrait. Garrison cofounded the *Liberator* in 1831, an important weekly abolitionist newspaper. Garrison continued publication until the eradication of American slavery in 1865. (*National Portrait Gallery*)

The *Anti-Slavery Almanac* was an annual compendium of the degradations of forced human labor. The almanac for 1839 featured the case of Peter John Lee, a free black living in Westchester County, New York, who was lured from his family, bound, and sold into slavery. (*Library of Congress*)

The February 28, 1844, explosion aboard the U.S.S. *Princeton* during a trial of the longest naval cannon at the time, killed six people, including the secretary of the navy Thomas Gilmer and secretary of state Abel Upshur. President Tyler narrowly escaped being killed. Proslavery leader John C. Calhoun of South Carolina succeeded Upshur as secretary of state. In that capacity he urged the annexation of the Republic of Texas, which allowed slavery. (*Library of Congress*)

Wendell Phillips (1811–1884), a Boston lawyer, was an influential speaker for the American Anti-Slavery Society. He supported Southern secession as a means of removing slave holders' influence on government. (*Library of Congress*)

Gerrit Smith (1797–1874) was a social activist from New York state. He supported abolitionism, women's rights, and was a financial contributor to John Brown's efforts. (*Library of Congress*)

Frederick Douglass (1818–1895) escaped from slavery in 1838 and became one of the most important figures in the history of the anti-slavery movement. He was one of John Brown's earliest supporters. (*Library of Congress*)

Jermain Wesley Loguen (1813–1872), son of a slave woman and white "owner," escaped from slavery in 1834. A staunch abolitionist, he became bishop of the AME Zion Church in Syracuse, New York. (*Library of Congress*)

Lucretia Mott (1793–1880) was a Quaker abolitionist whose opposition to slavery forced activists to reconsider the role of women in society, politics, and government. (*Library of Congress*)

Elizabeth Cady Stanton (1815–1902), cousin of Gerrit Smith, helped transform part of the American abolitionist movement into one that also supported women's rights. (*Library of Congress*)

In September 1851, at Christiana, Pennsylvania, Edward Gorsuch, a Maryland slave owner, was killed attempting to repossess four slaves that had fled his farm. The Fugitive Slave Act allowed for such a process, but William Parker and other locals resisted any attempt to reclaim runaways. (*Library of Congress*)

CAUTION!!
COLORED PEOPLE
OF BOSTON, ONE & ALL,

You are hereby respectfully CAUTIONED and advised, to avoid conversing with the

Watchmen and Police Officers of Boston,

For since the recent ORDER OF THE MAYOR & ALDERMEN, they are empowered to act as

KIDNAPPERS
AND
Slave Catchers,

And they have already been actually employed in KIDNAPPING, CATCHING, AND KEEPING SLAVES. Therefore, if you value your LIBERTY, and the *Welfare of the Fugitives* among you, *Shun* them in every possible manner, as so many *HOUNDS* on the track of the most unfortunate of your race.

Keep a Sharp Look Out for KIDNAPPERS, and have TOP EYE open.
APRIL 24, 1851.

An 1851 broadsheet warned people of color that the Fugitive Slave Act was being abused in Boston. (*Library of Congress*)

Harriet Beecher Stowe's (1811–1896) 1852 novel, *Uncle Tom's Cabin*, had a profound effect on the abolitionist movement in the United States and Great Britain. (*Library of Congress*)

Anthony Burns (1834–1862) escaped slavery in 1853, but was captured in Boston in 1854 under the Fugitive Slave Act. He was tried, and returned to bondage despite violent protests. His freedom was eventually secured through payment. (*Library of Congress*)

Martin Delany (1812–1885) was one of the most dynamic abolitionists. He was a proponent of black nationalism and self-sufficiency, and became the first African American army officer in United States history.
(*West Virginia University Library*)

John Brown (1800–1859) was a zealous anti-slavery activist who believed slavery could only be eradicated by forcing slave owners to abdicate in the face of force. (*Library of Congress*)

Harriet Tubman (c. 1822–1913) escaped slavery, yet fearlessly returned to the South conducting numerous missions to lead slaves to freedom. She was unshaken in her support of John Brown. (*Library of Congress*)

President Franklin Pierce (1804–1869), a Northern anti-abolitionist, presided over the passing of the Kansas-Nebraska Act and the vigorous enforcement of the Fugitive Slave Act. (*Library of Congress*)

James H. Lane (1814–1866) was a leading Free Soil militant who allied himself with John Brown's efforts to keep Kansas from becoming a slave state. (*Library of Congress*)

Lawrence, Kansas, the main Free-State settlement in the territory, was attacked and severely damaged by proslavery forces on May 21, 1856. Their first act of violence was to destroy the two antislavery newspaper presses. (*Library of Congress*)

A Federal military prison in Alexandria, Virginia, in 1861. Prior to its capture by Union forces, the pen was used by the Price, Birch & Company slave dealership to hold their slaves before they were auctioned. (*Library of Congress*)

A large group of recently freed slaves processing cotton on an unidentified plantation in South Carolina in 1863. (*Library of Congress*)

Henry Highland Garnet (1814–1882) escaped from slavery with family members in 1824. An ordained minister, he advocated—as did John Brown—militant abolitionism, and for blacks to determine their own destinies. (*frontis*, A Memorial Discourse)

Karl Marx (1818–1883) was a European correspondent for the *New York Tribune* from 1852 to 1863. He identified John Brown's raid as a pivotal moment in the war against slavery. (*Bundesarchiv*)

William Wells Brown (1814–1884) escaped from slavery in 1835, and became an important American writer. He lectured extensively in the United States and Europe against slavery. (*frontis*, Three Years in Europe)

Frederick Law Olmsted (1822–1903), landscape architect, recorded his travels through the South prior to the Civil War. Like many others, he provided funds to help finance John Brown's activities. (*National Park Service*)

A Line of Living Fire

As the Kansas-Nebraska bill was enacted, and as the movement of settlers from New England sponsored by the Emigrant Aid Company began, Missouri residents passed over the line to register claims on the books of some "Squatter Association." Kansas's first territorial governor, Andrew Reeder, arrived in October 1854; a lawyer from Easton, Pennsylvania, he had no previous political experience. Elections for territorial delegate to Congress were held November 29 and carried by J. W. Whitfield, a proslavery man who'd been appointed Indian agent for Kansas by David Rice Atchison. His victory was helped by an inundation of an estimated 1,700 votes cast by Missouri residents. Atchison, acting vice president of the United States, in a speech published in the *Platte Argus* on the day of the election foretold what was to come:

> The people of Kansas in their first elections will decide the question whether or not slaveholders are to be excluded. Now if a set of fanatics

and demagogues a thousand miles off can afford to advance their money and exert every nerve to abolitionize Kansas and exclude the slaveholder, what is your duty when you reside within one day's journey of the Territory, and when your peace, quiet, and property depend on your action? You can, without an exertion, send five hundred of your young men who will vote in favor of your institutions. Should each county in the state of Missouri only do its duty, the question will be decided quietly and peaceably at the ballot-box.[1]

Despite the irregularity of the balloting Reeder ordered elections for a territorial legislature held March 30, 1855; when again men by the hundreds poured over the border, an estimated four to five thousand—rough, unkempt, brutal-looking men. They swaggered in with music playing and banners flying, armed with Bowie knives and revolvers, pistols and rifles. With many wearing the proslavery badge—a white or blue ribbon—they pitched tents, camping near polling places and intimidating the free-state voters. "Border Ruffians" James Redpath called them, in an apt expression coined in the *Tribune*; and they easily succeeded in electing an overwhelmingly proslavery legislature.

When it began its sessions this legislature met within a mile or two of the Missouri border at a place called Shawnee Mission, just beyond Weston. When Reeder notified both houses he would not recognize their legality or approve their legislation, he became the first of the territorial governors to vacate the platform, succeeded in that office by Wilson Shannon. Shannon was a former congressman from Ohio and minister to Mexico; tall, rough-featured, gray-headed, he shared the ruffians' taste for spirits. From August to September this "bogus" legislature proceeded to enact the most stringent slave codes seen anywhere in the South, designed to thoroughly protect slave property. These provided that anyone holding office in the territory—judges, sheriffs, justices of the peace, or whatever—must swear to uphold slavery. Dr. J. H. Stringfellow, a pillar of Weston, Missouri, and editor of the *Squatter Sovereign*, when elected speaker of the house, offered the following resolution: "Be it resolved by the House of Representatives, the Council concerning therein, That it is the duty of the proslavery party, the Union-loving men of Kansas Territory, to know but one issue, Slavery; and that any party making, or attempting to make, any other is and should be held as an ally of Abolitionism and Disunion."[2]

Prompted by poor prospects that year on farms in Ohio, and influenced by the surge of emigration from the North to the Kansas Territory, while envisioning opportunities opening to them and the prospect of making it a free land—five of John Brown's sons were considering becoming settlers in the untried region. In a letter of August 21, 1854, from Akron, Ohio, to John Jr., their father wrote, "If you or any of my family are disposed to go to Kansas or Nebraska, with a view to help defeat *Satan* and his legions in that direction, I have not a word to say; but I feel committed to operate in another part of the field. If I were not so committed, I would be on my way this fall."[3]

In October 1854, John Jr., Jason, Owen, Frederick, and Salmon began making preparations to emigrate in two parties. Owen, Frederick, and Salmon went first, driving their animals with them, arriving in spring 1855, followed by Jason and John Jr., and their families, traveling by rail to St. Louis, and continuing by steamboat up the Missouri River, also arriving in spring. The boat was crowded with men from the South, also journeying to Kansas. John Jr. wrote:

> That they were from the South was plainly indicated by their language and dress; while their drinking, profanity, and display of revolvers and Bowie-knives—openly worn as an essential part of their make-up clearly showed the class to which they belonged, and that their mission was to aid in establishing slavery in Kansas.
>
> A box of fruit-trees and grape vines which my brother Jason had brought from Ohio, our plough, and the few agricultural implements we had on the deck of that steamer looked lonesome; for these were all we could see which were adapted to the occupations of peace. Then for the first time arose in our minds the query: Must the fertile prairies of Kansas through a struggle of arms, be first secured to freedom before free men can sow and reap?[4]

The "brush fire" that would fret the undulating long grasses and wooded streams of the plains of eastern Kansas would likewise loom ominously over the political panorama of the North. Shortly after the Kansas-Nebraska bill was introduced, a group of anxious "anti-Nebraska" politicians—Conscience Whigs, Democrats, and American and Free-Soil members—first came together on February 28, 1854, in a schoolhouse in Ripon, Wisconsin, solely on the issue of opposing the extension of slavery. The same began holding meetings in Illinois, drawing among them Abraham Lincoln, showing him to be one of the principal politicians of the emerging movement. This was followed in Jackson, Michigan, on June 6 by a meeting of nearly 10,000 people held "under the oaks." Then on July 13, on the anniversary of the Northwest Ordinance of 1787, conventions under the banner of a new party would be held in Ohio, Indiana, Wisconsin, and Vermont; editorializing in the *Tribune* on the appropriate moniker to encompass these,

Horace Greeley had written in June: "We should not care much whether those thus united were designated 'Whig,' 'Free Democrat' or something else; though we think some simple name like 'Republican' would more fitly designate those who had united to restore the Union to its true mission of champion and promulgator of Liberty rather than propagandist of slavery."[5]

Hard pressed by Kansas matters himself, and pondering whether he should join his children there, John Brown wrote his eldest daughter, Ruth, and her husband, Henry Thompson, in a letter dated September 30, 1854. Would a commitment to Kansas be "more likely to benefit the colored people *on the whole* than to return with them to North Elba," he queried. Asking his children's advice, he was anxious to learn the opinion, too, of "Mr. Epps & all the colored people. . . . As I volunteered in their service (or the service of the colored people); they have a right to vote, as to course I take." He also had written to Gerrit Smith, Douglass, and Dr. McCune Smith for their advice.

As the first of his sons set out, after a month had passed Brown informed Ruth and Henry he was "pretty much determined to go back to North Elba. . . . Gerrit Smith wishes me to go back to North Elba; from Douglass and Dr. McCune Smith I have not yet heard."[6] But after John Jr.'s arrival, he wrote his father a letter dated May 20, 1855, giving a harrowing description of the situation of the free-state settlers, and John Brown began to perceive where his "duty" lay. Kansas men were deficient in arms and intimidated by the "ruffians," his son had written, with the result being "that the people here exhibit the most abject and cowardly spirit, whenever their dearest rights are invaded and trampled down by the lawless bands of Miscreants which Missouri has ready at a moment's call to pour in upon them." Could not his father obtain and send arms and ammunition, as war of "some magnitude" seemed inevitable? "We need them more than we do bread," he wrote.

Seeing the deficiencies of the Republican movement—that it was opposed to slavery's extension but willing to let it remain where it was—that spring Gerrit Smith and a handful of Liberty Party members began discussing holding a national convention which would call for "a clean sweep of slavery everywhere." Douglass was enthusiastic and endorsed the proposal, issuing a call in his paper April 20 and expressing the opinion that as the Republican Party grew in numbers, it would "also grow 'in the knowledge of the Truth.'"[7] After three months' preparation the convention convened in Syracuse June 26, holding three days of meetings under the newly adopted title of the Radical Abolition Party. With James McCune Smith elected chairman and Douglass serving on the business committee, an "Exposition of the Constitutional Duty of the Federal Government to Abolish Slavery" and an "Address to the Public" were drawn up and adopted, on a program calling for the use of the political power of the nation "to overthrow every part and parcel of American Slavery." These would be published and distributed in the form of pamphlets to the wider public. John Brown was among those arriving on the first day of the convention, and was invited to speak on its final day.

When he rose to speak Brown announced it was his intention to go out to Kansas, but would not go unless he could go armed. He had four sons in the Territory now, with three others expected to join them, and he wished to arm these as well. His poverty, however, prevented him from obtaining these; he must, therefore, appeal to the convention for aid.[8] Gerrit Smith then read two of John Jr.'s letters with "such effect . . . as to draw tears from numerous eyes." Some of those present, including two retired military men from Europe, contributed on the spot, "amounting," as Brown reported to his wife, "to a little over sixty dollars." Exalting, he also informed his wife in a letter dated June 28 from Syracuse, "The convention has been one of the most interesting meetings I ever attended in my life; and I made a great addition to the number of warm-hearted and honest friends."[9]

Brown's determination to import arms into Kansas had just been perceived as a necessity there as well. In April Charles Robinson, as the agent of the Emigrant Aid Company, sent G. W. Deitzler to Massachusetts to obtain weapons; and, with the financial aid of Amos Lawrence, the treasurer of the company, he did so. Then in July another agent was sent on a similar mission, and he also obtained weapons. In both cases these were the famous Sharp's rifles, a new breach-loading carbine with an effective range of 1700 yards. The arms were obtained also with help from Frederick Law Olmsted and the Rev. Henry Ward Beecher, and shipped in crates marked "Books"; these became the so-called "Beecher's Bibles." Brown went to Springfield, Massachusetts, to purchase his arms, and would make a successful appeal for arms while in Akron before setting out. When in Springfield, he had met again with Thomas Thomas, the Maryland free black whom he'd employed and shared his plans with in previous years. Attempting to enlist Thomas in his Kansas expedition, his confidant had instead determined on immigration to California, whence he went.

By spring 1855 the Kansas population had doubled, as the free-state settlements were coming into predominance. Meeting in convention at Big Spring on September 5, 1855, after a series of meetings held in

Lawrence, the free-state settlers repudiated the fraudulently elected legislature and vowed not to obey its "bogus enactments." That territorial
legislature in its first session had selected Lecompton as its capital, lying
about eight miles west of Lawrence, named after Judge S. D. Lecompte,
a proslavery jurist accommodating to the Atchison-Stringfellow clique.
To even the growing imbalance in settlement, appeals and meetings
were now convened across the South, but principally in South
Carolina, Georgia, and Alabama, to send men to Kansas; these went
under various names, but usually "Sons of the South" or, in Missouri
the "Blue Lodge," organized specifically to secure slavery in the Kansas
Territory. Stringfellow published an appeal in the *Montgomery
Advertiser*: "Not only is it profitable for slaveholders to go to Kansas,
but politically it is all-important."[10] Senator Robert Toombs, of
Georgia, heard the call, and urged a meeting in Columbus to organize
and send settlers. In Eufaula, Alabama, a slaveholder named Jefferson
Buford began campaigning for recruits, opening offices to support this
southern "Kansas emigration," from the Carolinas to Louisiana.[11]

In the succeeding months, the free-state movement began organizing
a state government, selecting Topeka as their capital, and sent an appeal
to the Congress and the nation. When a free-state man was brutally
murdered, the sheriff of Douglas County, Samuel Jones, to demonstrate the weakness of the free-state position, arrested not the suspect,
but the only free-state witness to the crime. With all the territorial officials and the United States government arrayed against them, Jones was
determined to ride the arrested man through Lawrence, hoping to pro-
voke a rescue, having a pretext to destroy the town. But before reaching
the free-state stronghold, Sheriff Jones—a man living in Weston,
Missouri—and his posse were met by eight men carrying Sharp's rifles.
Freeing the prisoner, the men carried the witness to safety in Lawrence,
where he gave a full recital of the episode.

Governor Shannon, to enforce territorial law, now called out the
militia, with Missouri's Platte County Rifles among those answering
the summons. As he appealed for federal troops at Fort Leavenworth,
these were refused by the commander, Colonel Edwin Sumner, unless
so ordered by the president. Before receiving this answer however, fifteen hundred amply armed men with cannon in tow, coming from as
far away as Jefferson City, and from Lexington and Waverly, wrangled
over the border toward Lawrence, where Jim Lane, elected "major general," began drilling five hundred men in that town, as details labored
on its defenses. When rumor of this reached the Brown settlement near
Osawatomie, Brown began making preparations for Lawrence's relief.

To authenticate the report, John Jr. started on horseback just as word reached them that their help "was immediately wanted." "[It] was at once agreed," Brown wrote soon after to his wife, "to break up at John's camp . . . and that all the men but Henry, Jason, and Oliver should at once set off for Lawrence under arms; those three being wholly unfit for duty. . . . The five set off in the afternoon, and after a short rest in the night (which was quite dark), continued our march until after daylight; next morning, when we got our breakfast, started again, and reached Lawrence in the forenoon, all of us more or less lamed by our tramp."[12]

Drawn by a lean horse, a rough-hewn wagon lumbered into town, led by a tall slim-faced man of fifty-five. Dark-complexioned, with blue-gray eyes, he had a bristle of gray hair growing low on his forehead. With spare arms lying in the bed of the wagon, four stalwart men stood at each corner, armed with a pike and sword; each with a rifle, and two revolvers tucked into a belt, each with a pistol in a pocket—all loaded and ready to discharge in aggregate a hundred rounds. This was John Brown and his son's first appearance in Lawrence, and the elder Brown at once became a conspicuous figure.[13] One of the two free-state papers published in Lawrence, the *Herald of Freedom* reported December 7, 1855:

> About noon, Mr. John Brown, an aged gentleman from Essex County, N.Y., who has been a resident of the Territory for several months, arrived with four of his sons—leaving several others at home sick— bringing a quantity of arms with him, which were placed in his hands by Eastern friends for the defense of the cause of freedom. Having more than he could use to advantage, a portion of them were placed in the hands of those more destitute. A company was organized and the command given to Mr. Brown for the zeal he had exhibited in the cause of freedom both before and since his arrival in the territory.

With 1500 border ruffians encamping in nearby Franklin opposing 500 men in Lawrence, a stand-off was unbroken for several days— Friday to Sunday—when "negotiations" were begun between the free-state leaders, Robinson and Lane, and Governor Shannon. Held in the uncompleted Free State Hotel, or Eldridge House—a well-made structure of three floors with two-feet-thick stone walls, and firing portals below the roof along each wall—as the talks proceeded the appearance of an agreement was reached, as the governor was assuaged with brandy. The invading force was to be withdrawn; in exchange the free-state leaders agreed not to resist the execution of any *legal* process of the elected legislature—a stay in hostilities in exchange for a concession. When Brown heard of this he was livid. E. A. Coleman was to write he came "into our council room, the maddest man I ever saw. He told Robinson that what he had done was all a farce; that in less than six months the Missourians would find out the deception, and things would be worse than they were that day (and so it was); that he came up to help them fight, but if that was the way Robinson meant to do, not send for him again."[14]

As Robinson and Shannon came out on the street to address the crowd, Brown continued his harangue. In his *Reminiscences of Old John Brown*, G. W. Brown (no relation) wrote:

> If he [John Brown] understood Governor Shannon's speech, something had been conceded, and he conveyed the idea that the territorial laws were to be observed. Those laws he denounced and spit upon, and would never obey—no! The crowd was fired by his earnestness and a great echoing shout arose: "No! No! Down with the bogus laws. Lead us out to fight first!" For a moment matters looked serious to the free state leaders who had so ingeniously engineered the compromise, and they hastened to assure Brown that he was mistaken; that there had been no surrendering of principles on their side.[15]

No doubt men with Sharp's rifles firing in on their campfires, as Brown evidently proposed, would have strongly persuaded the border ruffians that they were sitting on a hornets' nest—but he had not enough takers. Asked later about the two principal free-state leaders, Brown said, "They are both men without principle, but when worst came to worst, Lane will fight,—and there is *no fight in Robinson*."[16]

James H. Lane, a lawyer, had been a congressman in the United States House of Representatives for Indiana, a Democrat and supporter of Franklin Pierce; he had helped to pass the Kansas bill. Coming out to the territory himself and seeing the state of things, he switched sides, becoming a figure as large as any in Kansas's history, both before and during the war of 1861–1865. Ending his life in a suicide on the Kansas plains in 1866, he could be a gifted orator when giving a stump speech, but the leadership Lane assumed suffered from a temperamental and mercurial disposition. Robinson was a Massachusetts man who'd been out to California in '49, crossing the Nebraska Territory on his way. Returning by ship, he studied medicine and became a doctor; writing a few anti-Nebraska articles for the *Worcester Spy*, he came to the attention of Thayer and Amos Lawrence, and seemed to them just the man for their Emigrant Aid Company. Austere, with a Calvinist's constitution, he would increasingly be seen as the conservative, to Lane's radicalism.

On December 15, 1855, a vote was held on a "Topeka" constitution which passed among the free-state voters, with proslavery voters abstaining. In January, election for the legislature of this "illegal" free-state government was held, entirely carrying the legislative body, with Robinson elected as "governor." Denouncing this plebiscite, Stringfellow's *Squatter Sovereign* recommended that every "black and poisonous" abolitionist in Kansas be hung or shot. In Washington, pre-occupied with his renomination for president the following spring, Pierce summoned Governor Shannon, on leave in Ohio, for consultations. Giving a thorough report on the "Wakarusa war," as the stand-down in Lawrence at the end of the year was called, Brown wrote a letter to Akron's *Summit Beacon*, dated December 20, 1855, but published early in January 1856. He wrote optimistically; the result was the Missouri invaders left the territory "entirely in the power of the Free State men, with an organized militia, armed, equipped, and in full force for its protection." The northern people in the territory, he forecast, must now only hold the ground, and Kansas was free.

Of the "strong, hardy farmers and mechanics" assembled in Lawrence's defense, Brown noted warmly: "Here were developed such a set of determined men as I had no idea this Territory could boast of, in any such numbers. They now know their own members, and their condition for self-government and self-defense. They have now become acquainted, and in their feelings, strongly knit together, the result of having shared together some of the conditions of war in actual service."[17]

The Topeka legislature met on March 4, 1856, approving a memorial addressed to Congress seeking admission as a state under the just approved constitution. Two emissaries, Lane and Robinson, then set out for Washington to shepherd the initiative. The House of Representatives, with its anti-Nebraska majority, voted in favor; while in the Senate, Lewis Cass introduced an enabling act. On April 6, New York's Republican senator, William H. Seward, spoke for its immediate acceptance, and Illinois' Democratic senator, Stephen Douglas, against. There was as yet insufficient population for statehood, Douglas maintained, let the much-publicized southern aid societies send their emigrants, and then follow the will of the "squatters." But he had another objection; the document summited was partially forged by Lane, he said. A vote was taken, and the memorial was denied. Thwarted, the House resolved to send a committee of three, complete with clerks and secretaries, to the territory to learn the true condition of affairs.

The House committee arrived at Kansas City the week before Jefferson Buford came with the first large contingent of Southern men "to see Kansas through." The House committee would open its sessions in Lecompton April 18, scheduling its session in Lawrence to begin April 21. The first of the Buford "emigrants" came on a single boat, four hundred in all, waving state flags as they disembarked and carrying a banner that read KANSAS THE OUTPOST and SUPREMACY OF THE WHITE RACE. Henry Clay Pate, a rising newspaperman at the *Border Star* in Westport, originally from Virginia, welcomed them in his paper, describing the motley assemblage as valiant men of the South. From April to October no less than one thousand and as many as fifteen hundred of these proslavery stalwarts were in the Kansas Territory, gripping the entire eastern border, while blockading the Missouri River to northern emigration.[18]

The principal pro-southern towns in Kansas were Leavenworth and Lecompton, along with Atchison to the north, with an arc of border ruffian settlements in Paola, Franklin, Indianola, Ozawkee, Hickory Point, and Kickapoo; flanking and embracing the principal free-state towns, Osawatomie, Lawrence, and Topeka and the scattering of settlements and farms surrounding these. "The line thus indicated," wrote Richard Hinton regarding the conditions in summer 1856, "was almost completed and held by fortified camps occupied by Buford's Alabamians and Georgians; Atchison's, Stringfellow's, and Reid's Missourians."[19] In the south Fort Scott became the rendezvous of several smaller bodies coming in from Arkansas, Texas, and Louisiana, "not as well known and conspicuous as their confreres in the central and northern sections," Hinton wrote.[20]

About this time, too, John Brown, his sons, and other free-state settlers met in public assembly at Osawatomie, agreeing not to pay taxes to the "usurping" Lecompton legislature, and in a resolution they repudiated that body as one "forced upon us by a foreign vote." In the previous fall and winter, to aid their mutual protection and assist in gathering rapidly for defense, free-state men had formed a secret "League of Freedom," with Robinson its first commander or chief. Designed to enable each free-state man to know the other, and constituted in units or councils of ten, the League's badge of recognition was a little piece of black tape or ribbon worn in a buttonhole or at the throat.[21] Meanwhile military companies had been formed bearing names such as the Stubbs Rifles and Pottawatomie Rifles.

On April 7 the elder Brown addressed a letter to "wife and children": "John has just returned from Topeka, not having met with any difficulty; but we hear that preparations are making in the United States Court for numerous arrests of Free-State men. For one, I have no desire (all things considered) to have the slave-power cease from its acts of aggression." Only days before, on his way back John Jr. had passed through Lawrence and shared his observations in a letter dated April 4, published in *Frederick Douglass' Paper* May 2, 1856. Lawrence, he wrote, was flourishing with new arrivals all "full of earnest purpose to secure to Freedom this land of their adoption," people coming from Ohio, Massachusetts, Vermont, and New Hampshire. He noted "on Friday last" he saw forty settlers pass through the Osawatomie and Meridezine (Marais des Cygnes) rivers from Iowa, and on the day of writing he met "a characteristic emigrant train; a fine prairie plow projected from the rear of one of the wagons, and five Sharp's Rifles hung up in the fore part, indicating that where these men stop, the land may require to be *cleared* before it is ready for the plow."[22]

John Brown had anticipated the conditions then prevailing, as his "close study of current American history taught him the existence of a deliberate design to work the overthrow of the Federal Union"; and in resisting this he believed he was "obeying the highest obligations of citizenship, and fulfilling . . . the obligation due from a man to his God, his fellows, and to his country."[23] That others recognized this inconvenience, too, and were ready to fight was a revelation and great encouragement to him. Earlier that winter he had written: "We are very anxious to know what Congress is doing. We hear that Frank Pierce means to crush the men of Kansas. I do not know how well he may succeed; but I think he may find his hands full before it is over."[24] In ending his letter to Douglass's paper, John Jr. gave his readers a portent of this program: "From recent developments, it is now evident that our enemies are determined of prosecuting a series of oppressive measures in the form of vexatious suits in conformity with the Border Legislature, and to either compel us into slavish submission to the execution of those hated enactments—into acknowledgment in word or deed of the binding authority from which they emanate, or *drive us into forcible resistance*, and there by involve us in a quarrel with the general government. This . . . is to be the machinery at present to be employed for *crushing us out*."

To show that the territorial laws would be enforced, the next endeavor of Sheriff Jones was to execute an arrest of a man who'd allegedly participated in releasing the free-state prisoner in December, precipitating the Wakarusa War. That man was himself rescued by youths in Lawrence. The next day, a Sunday, Jones attempted an arrest with a ten-man posse that was again thwarted, this time by parishioners leaving church, and the man remained free. Appealing to Governor Shannon, who gave the sheriff a detail of United States dragoons, he returned to Lawrence to find the culprit had absconded. Encamped in a vacant lot near the Free State Hotel that night, Jones was pelted with eggs. As he stood sponging himself at a barrel, a shot splashed into the water. Later that evening another round was fired into his tent, tearing his outer clothing and leaving a superficial wound.

A name coming up in connection to these incidents was that of a young printer at the *Herald of Freedom*, Charles Lenhart. He had tossed eggs at Jones, Lenhart admitted, and shot into the barrel; but it was not he that fired into Jones's tent. As Shannon reported to President Pierce about a "plan of resistance" by a "dangerous, secret, oath-bound organization, unscrupulous as to the use of means to accomplish their objects," the president's determination was under strain as his party's convention was preparing to assemble in Cincinnati to name a nominee. The trend in Kansas did not look reassuring. Sterling Cato, a territorial judge, now opened court at a proslavery settlement on Pottawatomie Creek called Dutch Henry's Crossing, ten miles from the Brown settlement. As rumors began to circulate that indictments would be offered, John Brown sent his son Salmon and his son-in-law, Henry Thompson, into the court without arms, tempting arrest. With no action forthcoming, John Jr., as commander of the Pottawatomie Rifles, announced the company would meet later at parade grounds. Cato abandoned the court that evening, leaving for the safety afforded by proslavery Lecompton.

But already a more potent threat was on the ground, as Jefferson Buford had established his camp in the same precincts. When he wanted to gather information that spring Brown had already been circulating with his wagon laid out with his surveying instruments; as only proslavery men could hold title, the "old man" was thought to be "sound on the goose." Taking four of his sons, as chain carriers, axman, and marker, he found a section line that ran through the Alabamans' camp. This incident of Kansas lore was first narrated by Brown to E. A. Coleman, and appeared in Sanborn's book published in 1884. The men in the camp "indulged in the utmost freedom of expression" with him, Brown related, as he noted everything down in his jotter. One of them said, apparently Buford himself: "We've come here to stay. We won't make no war on them as minds their own business; but all the Abolitionists, such as them damned Browns over there, we're going to whip, drive out, or kill,—any way to get shut of them, by God!"[25]

On May 14 Judge S. D. Lecompte in United States Court charged a grand jury to issue subpoenas to free-state leaders instrumental in forming the Topeka government. The territory, he said in his charge, was organized by an act of Congress, and the legislature being an instrument of Congress had enacted laws that were therefore of United States authority, and all who resisted those laws were guilty of high treason. This tactic had been employed, free-state interests thought, not to get indictments but to frighten these men out of the territory before they could testify before the House committee. The committee's chairman, John Sherman, meeting with Robinson, urged him to flee, but to take with him a copy of the committee's findings thus far gathered to deliver to the House speaker, Nathaniel Banks. Robinson did flee with his wife, but was arrested as his boat docked in Lexington, on charges of escaping from an indictment for treason, although none had yet been issued. He was brought back to Lecompton and jailed, as his wife continued eastward carrying the incriminating evidence. Ex-governor Reeder, also leaving the territory, resisted arrest peaceably by side-stepping a deputy marshal in Leavenworth, and continued east on a steamboat disguised as a woodsman to evade a threatening mob. Robinson's wife would become an effective witness for the free-state cause that summer and during the presidential election. The grand jury, meanwhile, ordered the abatement of the Free State Hotel because it "had been used as a fortress," and for the two newspapers in Lawrence, the *Herald of Freedom* and the *Kansas Free State*, because "they had urged people to resist the enactments passed." The arrest of "the treason prisoners" would continue, amounting to a hundred and seven in all.

As the congressional investigating committee moved on to Leavenworth, Sheriff Jones called on the United States marshal in Lecompton, Israel Donaldson, for help, and the marshal issued a call for "law-abiding citizens" to muster and enforce the charge of the grand jury. Answering the call were Missouri militia companies, the Platte County Riflemen and the Kickapoo Rangers, along with three hundred Buford men. As these began crossing the border and drifting in the direction of Lawrence, and the congressional committee was in Westport, ready to begin its eastward journey, James Redpath, in Leavenworth, notified the readers of the *Chicago Tribune*: "There will in all probability be a battle in a day or two between the men of the North and the minions of the Slave Power in Kansas."[26]

As a proslavery "army" prepared to girdle Lawrence, and as the Cincinnati convention prepared to convene on June 2, on May 19, 1856, Massachusetts's Charles Sumner, who had replaced Webster as senator, rose to deliver an address titled "The Crime Against Kansas" in the Senate chamber. In the Senate the day before South Carolina's Andrew Butler had called those denouncing the "usurpation" in Kansas "an uncalculating fanaticism," while he and Stephen Douglas sought to shut down the debate on the enactment bill before that body. It was too late to dam up or divert the tide, said Sumner: "The muster has begun. The strife is no longer local, but national. Even now, while I speak, portents lower in the horizon, threatening to darken the land, which already palpitates with the mutterings of civil war." His colleague from Illinois, in their repartee after the conclusion of his two-day speech, he would characterize as a "noise-some, squat, and nameless animal . . . not a proper model for an American senator"; to his colleague from South Carolina, he dealt this counter-blow in his speech: "The senator from South Carolina has read many books of chivalry, and believes himself a chivalrous knight, with sentiments of honor and courage. Of course he has chosen a mistress to whom he has made vows, and who, through ugly to others, is always lovely to him; though polluted in the sight of the world, is chaste in his sight. I mean the harlot, Slavery. For her, his tongue is always profuse in words."

On the morning of May 21 Lawrence awoke to see a military array under banners overlooking the town from Mount Oread; while to the south along the California Road, others were marching to join those on the hill—eight hundred men in all. At mid-morning the deputy marshal rode into Lawrence with his entourage, deputizing six Lawrence citizens, and making arrests on charges of treason, among them the "procurer of Sharp's rifles," G. W. Deitzler. Invited to lunch by the proprietors of the Free State Hotel, the officers did so. In the afternoon Sheriff Jones clambered in with his posse, holding a sheaf of writs in his hand. Soon he had bagged the man who had thus far eluded him. Then he called upon Samuel Pomeroy, agent of the Emigrant Aid Company, to collect and surrender all arms. Two cannon were wheeled out and given up, but the Sharps rifles were private property, said Pomeroy, over which the agency had no jurisdiction.

Jones deemed this unacceptable. On the hill, among those leading the proslavery horde were George W. Clarke, Indian agent, A. G. Boone, a Westport merchant and descendant in that fabled pioneer family, and ex-senator Atchison and Dr. J. H. Stringfellow. Henry Clay Pate was also part of this backup, as was Jefferson Buford, who rode together with Harry Titus, a large grandiose man and slaveholder from Florida, who would be one of the most ruthless of the proslavery partisans in the subsequent fighting. As the men under them prepared to carry out the order of the grand jury, they set bayonets. Now Atchison addressed the throng: "Boys, this day I am a Kickapoo Ranger, by God! We have entered the damned town and taught the damned Abolitionists a Southern lesson they will remember until the day they die. And now, boys, we will go in again with our highly honorable Jones and test the strength of the damned Free State Hotel and teach the Emigrant Aid Company that Kansas will be ours. If man or woman dare stand before you, blow them to hell with a chunk of cold lead."[27]

The two newspapers' offices were entered and their type thrown into the river, with books and other items tossed into the streets. Atchison lit the fuse for the first shell aimed at the "nuisance" structure. It sailed cleanly over it, and more shots being fired had little effect; finally it was decided to blow the building up with kegs of powder. When this was done the resulting fire rendered it a smoldering ruin. Charles Robinson's home was burned, too, with other homes plundered and possessions ransacked. When this bravura show ended, Sheriff Jones stood in his stirrups, exalting: "Gentlemen, this is the happiest day of my life. I determined to make the fanatics bow before me in the dust and kiss the territorial laws. I have done it, by God. You are now dismissed."[28]

The next day, as John Jr. worked in his cornfield, startling news of the attack on Lawrence reached the Brown settlement near Osawatomie. Without delay he hurried to rally the men of the Pottawatomie Rifles. Joined by his father and brothers, they were ready to march for the relief of the beleaguered town at 6 P.M. Soon, however, word reached them that Lawrence had been razed by border ruffians and that there had been no resistance on the part of free-state men under explicit orders of Amos Lawrence and of Robinson of the Emigrant Aid Company. John Brown, an observer wrote, became "indignant that there had been no resistance; that Lawrence was not defended; and denounced the . . . leading free state men as cowards, or worse."[29]

Camping that night near Prairie City, the company was joined the next day by the Pomeroy Guards and a smaller company under the command of Samuel Shore. They had marched twenty-five miles, with Lawrence still twelve miles before them; here they held council. A blow must be struck and in such a way as to have a restraining fear, John Brown told the men. "Something must be done to show these barbarians that we too have rights."[30] Who was willing to go with him and act under his command, he asked? Calling his sons Watson, Frederick, Owen, and Oliver, he was joined by Henry Thompson, and an Austrian-Jewish immigrant named Theodore Weiner whose house smoldered in ashes along Pottawatomie Creek. James Townsley, a member of John Jr.'s company, offered his wagon and would act as guide to the neighborhood where the intended retaliation would fall. John Brown now took these accomplices to the act aside, talking earnestly with them. For the remainder of the morning and into the day this troop were busy sharpening the doubled-edged broad swords Brown had been given while in Akron the previous year. About two that afternoon as they drove off in the wagon, with Weiner jogging beside them on a pony, the free-state men remaining gave a rousing cheer.

Two days after Sumner's speech in the Senate and one day after the sack of Lawrence, Representative Preston Brooks of South Carolina and the nephew of the man "maligned" by Sumner, Andrew Butler, entered the Senate chamber after adjournment. He brought with him a fellow South Carolinian, Representative Lawrence Keitt, to stand guard lest anyone try to come to Sumner's aid. Brooks had broached challenging the Massachusetts senator to a duel as a gentleman; but Keitt counseled he merited beating like a rabid dog. Accordingly Brooks stepped up to the desk where Sumner was writing, and announcing his relation to his offended relative, savagely struck the top of Sumner's skull with his gutta-percha, a gold-handled cane. He repeatedly hit Sumner, who tried to rise but found his legs wedged under the desk. Bleeding profusely and unconscious, Sumner slumped into the aisle.

As the ill-omened tidings of the sack of Lawrence and Sumner's caning pulsed simultaneously through an anguished North, "one shout of exultation went up from the slaveholding States."[31] Back in Kansas John Brown's son Salmon would recount a rider galloping rapidly over the plains to report on Sumner's condition, remarking that for his father and the others that was the "decisive touch." Another suggests that since the telegraph only reached as far as Leavenworth, the report could not have reached Brown before the retaliation of the so-called Pottawatomie Massacre. While that may be uncertain, another son, Jason, was to recount: "On the afternoon of Monday, May 26th, a man came to us at Liberty Hill, . . . his horse reeking with sweat, and said, 'Five men have been killed on the Pottawatomie, horribly cut and mangled; and they say old John Brown did it.'"[32] On the previous night five men had been called out of their cabins and cut down by men calling themselves "the Northern army" wielding broad swords. Those killed had not been among the leading men or those encouraging violence by the proslavery partisans; they had only been their enablers and abettors, men who allowed the "terror" against the free-state settlers to occur in the first place. But with this joust came recognition, as John

Brown's son Salmon put it, that "there was as much room to give blows as to take them."[33]

Although disagreement and controversy generated by this shocking attack never waned, there is no doubt that it was perpetrated as an act of war. When he was in the Kansas Territory on a fact-finding tour for the Massachusetts Kansas Committee in September and October of that year, Thomas Wentworth Higginson wrote, "there appeared to be but one way of thinking among the Kansas Free State men, this being precisely the fact pointed out by Colonel William A. Phillips, in his 'Conquest of Kansas'. . . . I heard of no one who did not approve of the act, and its beneficial effects were universally asserted." Charles Robinson himself endorsed it to Higginson, "maintaining, like the rest, that it had given an immediate check of the armed aggressions of the Missourians."[34]

Assessing the deed's enduring significance, Sanborn was to write in his treatment, "Upon the swift and secret vengeance of John Brown in that midnight raid hinged the future of Kansas, as we can now see; and on that future again hinged the destinies of the whole country."[35] Although criticism of Brown's signal retaliation had not lain completely fallow in its immediate aftermath, there was to be a concerted effort led by Robinson thirty years after to downgrade Brown's importance to the free-state cause during "Bleeding Kansas," while highlighting his role in the Pottawatomie killing. While Higginson, who became one of Brown's intimates in 1857–58, provided his personal testimony in his book published in 1907, he himself offered as no more than an aside, that he did not hold Brown's act a completely balanced one.

Kansas and the extension of slavery were to be paramount issues in the summer of 1856. As the Republicans met in Bloomfield, Illinois, on May 29, those in assembly were in such an uproar over recent events in Kansas and in the capital city in Washington and over the perceived usurpations of the slave power, that when no less a political figure than Abraham Lincoln was to deliver his speech, so compelling it was to those present and so mesmerizing had its effect been that even reporters on hand failed to record it. Kansas' ex-governor Reeder was there, as was the wife of Charles Robinson, to add their testimony. The Democratic National Convention in Cincinnati was to follow on June 2, and the delegates there could see ample evidence of the threatening growth of a rival party. Dismissing the sack of Lawrence as the propaganda of partisans, they had telegrams telling of a terrible massacre of proslavery settlers on Pottawatomie Creek—evidence again of the fanaticism of the abolition movement. This burgeoning political party was a "sectional" party, the Democratic platform held, and was culpable for "treason and armed resistance."

When the nominating began Franklin Pierce was to be denied another run at the presidency, which he desired, on the seventeenth ballot. That title was to go to his minister in the Court of St. James, James Buchanan, with John C. Breckinridge of Kentucky for vice president. Buchanan was a sixty-five-year-old bachelor from Pennsylvania, where he'd been a congressman and senator, then Secretary of State for Polk, and then minister to Russia and Great Britain. He had been fortunate to have been out of the country during the tribulations of the Kansas-Nebraska bill, something on which Pierce had staked his leadership and failed. Now a more seasoned candidate could come in to manage the rollback of the rising antislavery sentiment in the North and mollify the South, in the hope of achieving national consensus and pacification of the slavery issue. One Virginia newspaper editor murmured approvingly that Buchanan "never uttered a word which could pain the most sensitive Southern heart."[36]

When news of the ghastly deed along Pottawatomie Creek spread through eastern Kansas, Henry Clay Pate at the head of the Westport (Missouri) Sharpshooters was breaking camp at Franklin. In the capacity of deputy marshal, Pate distinguished himself at the sack of Lawrence by riding about on a fine horse decorated with ribbons, and now this "man-butterfly," as Redpath christened him, who had aspired to a literary career, vowed he would capture John Brown. As he started out on this mission with forty proslavery men, his only fear, he boasted, was in not finding the elder man.

"Requisitioning" supplies at a free-state store at Prairie City, this "posse" pillaged the cabins of settlers as they headed south toward Osawatomie. Meanwhile Pate arrested two of John Brown's sons on Judge Lecompte's "constructive treason" warrants, turning them over to United States dragoons. Learning of their peril, their father sent a terse note that likely saved their lives: "I am aware that you hold my two sons, John and Jason, prisoners—John Brown."[37] Coming on the Brown settlement, Pate's company fired its buildings, destroying among other things the four-hundred-volume library of John Brown Jr., robbing and plundering residents while taking prisoners.

Visited in his camp on the night of May 31 by Samuel Shore and Orellius Carpenter, Brown was offered details of Pate's depredations, and this council decided to hold a meeting of free-state settlers the next day at Prairie City. When the meeting was held and some of the men declined to join in the resistance, Brown threatened withdrawal: "Why did you send Carpenter after us? I am not willing to sacrifice my men without having some hope of accomplishing something." Brown then suggested, in an interjection recorded later by one of his company, a course he evidently was considering: "If the cowardice and indifference of the free state people compel us to leave Kansas, what do you say, men, if we start south, for instance to Louisiana, and get up a Negro insurrection, and thereby compel them to let go their grip on Kansas, and so bring relief to our friends here?"[38] Only days before John Jr., in vehement disagreement with other free-state men over two slaves he had freed, resigned his command of the Pottawatomie Rifles. The Browns gave no truck to free-state men who supported the "Black Law," which a majority did at this time, and this undoubtedly was the impetus behind Brown's imprecation.

After learning Pate's whereabouts, Brown followed him with his small troop joined by Shore's company. Classing it as the best fight he'd seen in Kansas, Brown ascribed his defeating Pate to his selection of ground. Detailing the particulars in a letter to "wife and family," he wrote:

> On learning that this party was in pursuit of us, my little company, now increased to ten in all, started after them in company of a Captain Shore, with eighteen men, he included (June 1st). We were all mounted as we traveled. We did not meet them on that day, but took five prisoners, four of whom were of their scouts, and well armed. We were out all night, but could find nothing of them until about six o'clock next morning, when we prepared to attack them at once, on foot. . . . We got to within about a mile of their camp before being discovered by their scouts, and then moved at a brisk pace.[39]

With Pate's tents and wagons drawn up near a spring at a place called Black Jack, the direction of the fight devolved on Brown when on the day the Democratic Party convened in Cincinnati, he led the first of the stand-up engagements of the Kansas war. Sending Shore and his company to the left, to the bottom of a ravine before which the Missourians were encamped, Brown and his company moved to gain the top of the gorge. As this terrain turned Pate's company found they were in a cross-fire and were compelled to break from their wagons, seeking shelter themselves in the defile. Brown continued his exposition:

> Captain Shore, after getting one man wounded, and exhausting his ammunition, came with part of his men to the right of my position, much discouraged. The balance of his men, including the one wounded, had left

the ground. Five of Captain Shore's men came boldly down and joined
my company, and all but one man, wounded, helped to maintain the fight
until it was over. . . . After the firing had continued for some two to three
hours, Captain Pate with twenty-three men, two badly wounded, laid
down their arms to nine men, myself included.[40]

The Virginian's surrender and capture came about in this way:
Finding he could neither fight nor run, Pate sent his lieutenant out
under a flag of truce, albeit behind a free-state man held as prisoner.
Inquiring whether he was leader of the company, as he said he was not,
Brown told him to stay with him while his prisoner went and brought
the commander out. When Pate came up he began saying he was a
deputy United States marshal; dismissing him, Brown said, "I understand exactly what you are and do not want to hear more about it. Have
you a proposition to make to me?" As the twenty-four-year-old stum-
bled for a rejoinder, the elder man cut in, "Very well, Captain, I have
one to make of you, your unconditional surrender." Pate was later to
report in the *Missouri Republican*, the paper for which he acted as correspondent, "I went to take Old Brown, and Old Brown took me." So
that this turn in events might get wider notice, as he closed his letter
detailing the episode, Brown asked his wife to make a copy and send it
to Gerrit Smith: "I know of no other way to get these facts and our situation before the world, nor when I can write you again."[41]

This incident received wide publicity, reaching even the eastern
papers, as a cry for vengeance went up in Missouri. In his widely distributed and much read *The Conquest of Kansas by Missouri and Her
Allies* published in the fall of 1856, William Addison Phillips wrote: "It
was at this time that the Free State guerrilla companies sprang up.
Finding that armed bands of pro-slavery men were prowling about the
Territory, a handful of persons, chiefly youths, took the field. One company, under a young printer named Lenhart, was particularly active
and bold. Capt. John Brown, senior, who lived near Osawatomie,
immediately on the sacking of Lawrence concluded that the war was
begun, and that it ought not to terminate."

As the cry for war was heard, at Westport and Independence, and in
Lexington in Missouri men rallied under the leadership of the territo-
rial delegate of Kansas, J. W. Whitfield, with militia companies muster-
ing in a half dozen of the state's counties. While one hundred and fifty
Kansas men began marching toward the border to rally with John
Brown after his signal resistance—men enrolled in the Lawrence
Stubbs, the Bloomington Rifles, the Blue Mound Boys, Wakarusa Boys,
and the Prairie City Company.[42] On June 4, prompted by President

Pierce, a desperate Governor Shannon issued a proclamation ordering all illegal military organizations to disperse. The next day pursuant to the governor's proclamation, Col. Edwin Sumner and his adjunct, Lieutenant J. E. B. Stuart, with a company of fifty United States dragoons, approached John Brown's fortified encampment on an island in Middle Creek. Stepping out to meet the federal officers as they approached, Brown was intent on carrying out an agreement he'd already written up with Pate. He was proposing an exchange of prisoners, he said—the Missourians he held for the free-state prisoners held in Lecompton, and he especially had in mind exchanging a certain H. Clay Pate and his lieutenant for the liberty of his two sons.

He was not there to discuss terms, declared the officer, but to compel all illegally constituted armed bodies to disperse. Having too few men then on hand to prescribe another outcome, although Sumner supposed there were hundreds of men concealed in the brush, Brown led the officers into his camp. When Pate and his company were released, Pate began a harangue on a stump. Sumner snapped, "I don't want to hear a word from you, sir. You have no business here. The governor told me so." Turning to the deputy United States marshal, who'd accompanied him with a warrant for Brown's arrest for murder, the man inexplicably found he'd misplaced it, as the officer fumed that he'd seen it in his hand the previous night. Sumner was later to relate that Brown's bivouac even by only a small contingent "could have held against a thousand men, as, from the peculiar nature of the ground, artillery could not be brought to bear on it."[43] With both the free-state companies and the Missourians depleted of their provender, and the United States interceding militarily, the fighting would dwindle, becoming desultory for weeks, as Buford posted his men on the border and the Missouri River was blockaded to northern emigration, with cannon placed on both sides of the river above Lexington, and mobs of armed men bent upon "lynching" boarded steamers searching for northern emigrants and turning them back.

In the letter by Brown cited above, he reported Pate and his company when freed "did not go more than two or three miles before they began to rob and injure free state people. . . . Since then we have, like David of old, had our dwellings with the serpents of the rocks and wild beasts of the wilderness."[44] One of the extraordinary aspects of John Brown's mission, and the one circumstance that gave him the potency uniformly discerned, was the thorough organization of his company. This is certainly attributable to his decades-long study of the military arts and his reading on guerrilla war, but also due to the fact that he had given it his full attention in the preceding months. Although it is regarded as having sprung into existence in the space of a week between Pottawatomie and Black Jack, this was certainly not the case. James Redpath was the first journalist to stumble into Brown's encampment on May 31, 1856, just as he sought to confront Pate, and wrote in *The Public Life of Captain John Brown*, published in January 1860: "I shall not soon forget the scene that here opened to my view. Near the edge of the creek a dozen horses were tied, all ready saddled for a ride for life, or a hunt after Southern invaders. A dozen rifles and sabers were stacked against the trees."[45] Brown himself stood near the fire, wrote Redpath, his shirt sleeves rolled up, with a large piece of pork in his hand, as he cooked a pig. He had given just as careful a study too to the art of subsistence in the field as he had to commanding his men, and it was he who fed the company. One item of his research was a flour biscuit cooked on ashes or in a skillet, and mixed with ginger and molasses. Sanborn writes of seeing a copy of Brown's orderly book titled *Articles of Enlistment and By-Laws of the Kansas Regulars, made and established by the commander, A.D. 1856*, when he first met him in April 1857. Thirty-five names are found in its pages, noting the date of enlistment, the engagements fought by each, wounds if any, and the death of a few. This covenant began:

> We whose names are found on these and the next following pages, do hereby enlist ourselves to serve in the free state cause under John Brown as commander, during the full period of time affixed to our names respectively and we severally pledge our word and our sacred honor to said commander, and to each other, that during the time for which we have enlisted, we will faithfully and punctually perform our duty (in such capacity or place as may be assigned to us by a majority of all the votes of those associated with us, or of the companies to which we may belong as the case may be) as a regular volunteer force for the maintenance of the rights and liberties of the free state citizens of Kansas.[46]

This was followed by a score of by-laws, providing for the election of officers, for deportment and conduct under arms, for trial by jury for infractions, and the treatment and trial of prisoners, and the receipt and disposal of captured property. Among those enlisted were three German immigrants with experience in the revolutionary upheaval across continental Europe in 1848, August Bondi, an engineer and a Viennese Jew, an ethnic description also given to Theodore Wiener, and Charles Kaiser. Kaiser is often referred to as "Charley the Hungarian," but he was a German from Bavaria, settling in Hungry in his youth, and serving in the Hungarian revolutionary army in 1849 as a hussar.[47] His face, said Bondi, was marked with lance and saber-cuts; and he had a taste for war. He would be killed on August 26 of that year at Osawatomie. The most extensive description of life in Brown's camp and of the enlistees is from Bondi, who would write articles for Kansas papers in 1879 published in both German and English, and whose testimony is recorded in *Transactions* of the Kansas State Historical Society. Roughing it in the bush, Bondi recalled, "We had come down to wearing ideas, suspicions, and memories of what had once been boots and hats."[48] Bondi related, "Many and various were the instructions [Brown] gave."

> He expressed himself to us that we should never allow ourselves to be tempted by any consideration to acknowledge laws and institutions to exist as of right, if our conscience and reason condemned them. He admonished us not to care whether a majority, no matter how large, opposed our principles and opinions. The largest majorities were sometimes only organized mobs, whose howlings never changed black into white, or night into day. A minority conscious of its rights, based on moral principles, would, under a republican government, sooner or later become the majority. Regarding the curse and crimes of the institution of slavery, he declared that the outrages committed in Kansas to further its extension had directed the attention of all intelligent citizens of the United States and of the world to the necessity of its abolishment . . . that while it was true that the pro-slavery people . . . had the upper hand at present . . . we ought to be of good cheer, and start the ball rolling at the first opportunity.[49]

Redpath reported Brown saying in his meeting with him on May 31, "I would rather have the smallpox, yellow fever, and cholera all together in my camp, than a man without principles. It's a mistake, sir, that our people make, when they think that bullies are the best fighters, or that they are the men fit to oppose those Southerners. Give me men of good principles; god-fearing men, men who respect themselves; and, with a dozen of them, I will oppose any hundred such men as those Buford ruffians."[50]

Redpath was also told by one of the company that their commander would often "retire to the densest solitudes, to wrestle with his God in secret prayer." Concluding his letter to "wife and children," Brown wrote: "God, who has not given us over to the will of our enemies, but has moreover delivered them into our hand, will, we humbly trust, still keep and deliver us. We feel assured that He who sees not as men see, does not lay the guilt of innocent blood to our charge."[51]

Upon his arrest by a marshal's posse accompanied by United States dragoons, John Brown Jr. had his arms and wrists tightly bound behind his back, and he was driven at a brisk trot before the horses at the end of an extended rope. Compelled at this pace for nine miles to Paola, where Judge Cato was supposed to hold court, he was suffering from lack of sleep and anxiety when he became quite disoriented mentally and would not recover for many weeks. He remained tied in this way for twenty-seven hours, the circulation of blood in his arms becoming constricted, and causing his back to turn black with mortification; the binding on his upper right arms was especially severe, sinking into his flesh and leaving a permanent mark he would call his "slavery bracelet."[52] From Paola, he was chained at the ankle to his brother Jason, and they were now driven, tormented and thirsting, for forty-five miles over the sweltering plain to Lecompton, to be jailed with the other "treason prisoners." Jason would be freed after ten days; though a Brown, he was a pacifist and considered a thoroughly nonoffending individual. John Jr. would be held till September, when all of the prisoners would be released.

As the two manacled brothers were moved from Paola to Lecompton, their father followed for a time on a parallel course hoping to effect their rescue. William Addison Phillips in his *Conquest of Kansas by Missouri and Her Allies*, wrote: "Like a wolf robbed of its young, he stealthily but resolutely watched for his foes, while he skirted through the thickets of the Marais des Cygnes and Ottawa Creeks."[53] It was just after these scenes concluded that the first Republican National Convention convened in Philadelphia on June 17. On the first ballot the nomination went to a candidate with no political record, John C. Frémont, attractive to the public, and to free-state Democrats, as well as the new political grouping for the denationalizing of slavery. He was known as the "Pathfinder," an appellation bestowed for his mapping of routes to California in the previous decade. His wife was the socially prominent Jessie Benton, daughter of Thomas Benton, an enemy of the Atchison faction in Missouri; that he promoted a free California in 1849 and supported a free Kansas in 1856 completed his credentials. Abraham Lincoln made a good showing for the vice presidency of the ticket, but that went finally to New Jersey's William L. Dayton. Of the more prominent politicians of the party, Seward and his advisor Thurlow Weed thought their opportunity would be enhanced by the 1860 election cycle, as did Salmon P. Chase, and both had considerable numbers of opponents to contend with. The campaign slogan for the emergent coalition would be "Free Soil, Free Speech, Freemen,

Frémont." Kansas had been the major topic in Philadelphia, and the Democratic administration's failure there was sure to be exploited in the coming presidential canvas.

Concomitant with this, Pierce's secretary of war, Jefferson Davis, wrote to Brigadier-General Persifor Smith, commanding the department of the west at Fort Leavenworth, Kansas Territory: "The position of the insurgents is that of open rebellion against the Laws and Constitutional authorities, with such manifestation of purpose to spread devastation over the land as no longer justifies further hesitation or indulgence."[54] The Topeka legislature, scheduled to meet July 4, 1856, must not be allowed to convene, and Col. Sumner was ordered by proclamation of the president and of the governor of Kansas to be on hand to prevent their meeting. Dutifully five companies of dragoons with two pieces of artillery were encamped on the edge of town by July 3, while an even larger force under Col. Philip St. George Cooke moved in from Fort Riley, and camped northwest of Topeka. In the camp "clustered" with the federal troops were numerous territorial officials, marshals, and deputy-marshals; Governor Shannon, on the advice of the Pierce administration, boarded a steamboat in Leavenworth for St. Louis, so that he would be discreetly out of the territory when the edict was enforced. The original intent of the Atchison-Stringfellow faction in Kansas had been to lead a border ruffian army to break up the legislature, but with the fighting that spring that program now looked daunting. The border was seventy-five miles away, and it would be difficult to get an army over there, and even more difficult to get it back; hence a proclamation and the federal troops.

Leaving his company then numbering twenty-two mounted men camped on the bank of the Wakarusa a few miles from Lawrence, on July 2 John Brown sent word to William Addison Phillips that he'd like to see him at the Eastern House. There was a supply of arms and ammunition in Topeka and it was expected that a thousand free-state men would be on hand to protect their government; John Brown's movement was part of this general plan.

Phillips was a Scotsman who had immigrated to the United States with his parents in 1838. Admitted to the bar in 1855, he began his practice in Illinois and then went to Kansas as special correspondent for the *New York Tribune*. His book detailing events in Kansas was soon to be compiled from his dispatches, which Higginson would call "altogether the best and fairest book upon the confused history of that time and place." Not yet completed however—the denouement with the suppression of the free-state legislature had not yet occurred—it would become, along with Sara Robinson's testimony and authentication, an important item that fall among the Republican Party's campaign literature. Phillips was himself a significant figure in Kansas' history, and would publish his *Three Interviews with Old John Brown* in the *Atlantic Monthly* in December 1879.

That day spent in conversation with Brown, Phillips wrote, was his first "good opportunity to judge the old man's character." He continued: "I had seen him in his camp, had seen him in the field, and he was always an enigma, a strange compound of enthusiasm and cold, methodic stolidity,—a volcano beneath a mountain of snow. He told me of his experiences as a wool merchant and manufacturer in Ohio, and of his travels in Europe. I soon discovered that his tastes ran in a military rather than a commercial channel."[55]

Phillips was expected, in Topeka, to report on the situation for the *Tribune* the next day, and when Brown invited him to travel with him he consented to do so. Riding down Massachusetts Street, as one of Brown's men fell in behind them, the trio rode up Mount Oread and waited there for the rest of the company. Climbing the hill by twos, without giving any overt recognition, they fell in behind Brown and Phillips, moving up the California road as darkness settled. Passing Lecompton four miles in the distance, they were beyond Big Spring before they halted. They stripped the saddles and other articles from their horses, and set them out to graze. Phillips wrote: "The men ate of what provision they had with them, and I received a portion from the captain. I was not at all hungry, and if I had been I doubt if I could have eaten it. It was dry beef, which was not so bad; but the bread had been made from corn bruised between stones, and then rolled in balls and cooked in the coal and ashes of the camp fire. These ashes served for saleratus. Captain Brown observed that I nibbled it very gingerly."[56]

Placing their saddles together so that their heads were only a few feet apart, the two spread their blankets and commenced talking. "I soon found that he was a very thorough astronomer," recalled Phillips. Pointing out the different constellations and their movements, Brown said, "Now it is midnight," indicating the hands in the celestial mechanism. "In his ordinary moods," Phillips advised, "the man seemed so rigid, stern, and unimpressible when I first knew him that I never thought a poetic and impulsive nature lay behind that cold exterior. The whispering of the wind on the prairie was full of voices to him, and the stars as they shone in the firmament of God seemed to inspire him."[57]

Phillips wrote years afterward he could never forget this conversation. In discussing the men of Kansas, Brown was not wont to criticize both parties. The proslavery men he censured bitterly: slavery besotted everything, making men coarse and brutal. And while there were many among the free-state men that were admirable and sincere, there were too many broken-down politicians who would rather pass resolutions than act, said Brown: these men would always be found to sacrifice their principles for their advantage. "One of the most interesting things in his conversation that night," Phillips wrote—"and one that marked him as a theorist (and perhaps to some extent he might be styled a visionary), was his treatment of our forms of social and political life. He thought society ought to be organized on a less selfish basis; for while material interests gained something by the deification of pure selfishness, men and women lost much by it. He said that all great reforms, like the Christian religion, were based on broad, generous, self-sacrificing principles. He condemned the sale of land as a chattel, and thought that there was an infinite number of wrongs to right before society would be what it should be, but that in our country slavery was the 'sum of all villainies,' and its abolition the first essential work. If the American people did not take courage and end it speedily, human freedom and republican liberty would soon be empty names in these United States."58

Phillips thought he had fallen asleep; but suddenly pointing his index fingers to the sky, Brown said: "It is nearly two o'clock, and as it must be nine or ten miles to Topeka it is time we were marching." In less than ten minutes the company was saddled, mounted, and again on the march.

On the morning of the 4th, to the sound of fifes and marching men, a crowd clogged the streets of Topeka before Constitution Hall as members of the free-state legislature filed into the building. Marshal Donaldson too walked up its steps, reported by James Redpath in the *Chicago Tribune* as having "imbecile looking eyes."59 He was there to hand the proclamation of the president of the United States and the governor of Kansas to the presiding officer. At noon as a free-state battalion was receiving a banner inscribed OUR LIVES FOR OUR RIGHTS, standing in martial order before the hall, Col. Sumner appeared with his troop and cannon. When this ceremony concluded, the dragoons occupied the square, unlimbering their cannon and lighting slow matches.

Entering the hall with his sword sheathed at his side, Sumner strode to the desk of the clerk where the roll was being counted. "No quorum," the clerk announced. The speaker ordered the sergeant-at-arms to go out and bring in the other members. Sumner would wait no longer, announcing, "Gentlemen, this is the most disagreeable duty of my whole life. My orders are to disperse the legislature, and I am here to tell you that it cannot meet. God knows I have no partisan feelings in the matter. I have just returned from the border where I have been driving out bands of Missourians. You must disperse. This body cannot be permitted to meet. Disperse."[60] Redpath wrote in his dispatch, "On the day when, everywhere, Americans were celebrating their liberty, the free-state legislature was broken up by force. This was the last drop of bitterness in the free-state cup and the culmination of Southern success, the date at once the death and resurrection of Freedom in Kansas." As Col. Sumner turned and walked out of the building, the brogue of W. A. Phillips trailed after him—"Colonel, you have robbed Oliver Cromwell of his Laurels."[61]

Deeming the Emigrant Aid Company insufficient to raise the requisite flow of settlers to the Kansas Territory, in spring 1856 Eli Thayer proposed creation of a National Kansas Committee for the support and relief of free-state settlers, announcing a meeting on June 20, in Cleveland, Ohio. His plan called for an outfitting depot to be located at Chicago, with officers and directors also located there. A national committee would see to it that state, city, and district committees would be formed to allow that the work was carried out; while ex-governor Reeder proposed five thousand armed settlers be sent to Kansas, that they be provisioned for a year, supported from a $2 million fund to be raised, with emigration conducted through Iowa and Nebraska.

This initial effort was followed by a meeting at Buffalo, New York, on July 11, 1856, where the National Kansas Committee was formed, with Thaddeus Hyatt as president. An executive committee began its sessions on July 19, and had the necessary organizational work completed in twelve of the fifteen northern states by the middle of the following month. One of the most energetic states for this activity was Massachusetts, where the Emigrant Aid Company folded its work, becoming the Massachusetts State Kansas Committee, whose outstanding members were George Luther Stearns, Dr. Samuel Gridley Howe, Theodore Parker, and Thomas Wentworth Higginson, with Franklin Sanborn as its secretary. It would be Higginson's steadfast friend, Martin Stowell, of the Anthony Burns attempted rescue, who would lead the first contingent organized from the state.

In Chicago, James H. Lane (still a fugitive from indictment in Kansas) addressed an anti-Nebraska rally from the steps of the courthouse. Eulogizing the new territory, it was not the home of derided "Massachusetts Yankees" he pronounced, as the border ruffians claimed, but of Midwesterners like themselves, people from Illinois, Indiana, and Ohio—who now were shackled under the tyranny of slavocrats. Recalling his service at Buena Vista in the Mexican War, he had sat on his horse next to Illinois' own General J. J. Hardin, and its current candidate for governor, nominated at the Bloomington convention, William H. Bissell. "It did not occur to me that I should be indicted for treason because I loved liberty better than slavery." Brandishing the "bogus enactments" like a handful of sheaves, Lane pithily summarized their penalties: "To kidnap a white child into slavery, six months in jail—to kidnap a nigger into freedom, death!" These laws and all other outrages in Kansas were chargeable to the incumbent sitting in the presidential chair, Lane's oratory imputed. "Now before God, and his people, I arraign Frank Pierce as a murderer."[62] When he had finished, the audience stormed forward to donate hard-earned cash—working men, sailors, boys, widows, seamstresses. Lane would now make his appeal before audiences throughout the Middle West, calling for armed settlers to go to Kansas to help overthrow its southern "usurpation." With newspapermen reporting on his progress this became known as Lane's "Army of the North," and this agitation had a notable success in Chicago where a saloonkeeper and property owner, ward politician James Harvey, wholeheartedly joined Brigadier-General Lane, whom he commissioned colonel. Of the wider emigration that summer, which would see as many as a thousand armed northerners introduced into Kansas in July through September, Higginson would write, "it was all really a rehearsal in advance of the great enlistments of the Civil War."[63]

The agitation flared just as the presidential canvass was getting under way, lighting up the North. The various Kansas aid societies under the umbrella of the National Committee would raise $200,000 to defray the overland expenses of emigrants, with the Massachusetts Kansas aid committee alone raising $80,000. Finding he could no longer raise money from among the wealthy and the business class, Stearns turned to common workers, and it was they who made this sum with their earnings. The response was so widespread and astonishing that national committee members were given the gratis use of telegraph wires by telegraph companies, and the Burlington and Missouri Railroad donated one thousand free fares to settlers traveling from Burlington, Vermont, to Mt. Pleasant, Iowa; and the fare from Chicago to Mt. Pleasant was set at three dollars, with other railroads responding with the same. Of this contagion, Ralph Waldo Emerson said, "It is like setting a fire in the woods, no one can tell what will be the end of it."[64]

A great obstacle had been thrown before northern emigration to Kansas by the closing of the Missouri River. Now those making the trek, after disembarking from the nearest railhead at Iowa City, needed to toil week after week over three hundred miles of seemingly endless prairie. Fully exposed but for tents and wagons to the weather and the sun, they passed days on end without seeing a single dwelling, often camping with no wood, scarce water, and carrying every edible thing. Trains of various sizes came, but an emigrant colony of one hundred forty men was not unusual, with perhaps twenty women with children, in twenty-eight wagons. The nightly camp with tents exhibited a hectic scene. Some men would feed and water the stock, others brought in firewood, as others prepared bedding for sleeping. With men cleaning and reloading their arms, a watch was set out, while the cooking was done—bread baked, pork fried, coffee made, as women with babies tended and sat around the fire. The first attempt to cross the Missouri River by the new route was made toward the end of July by the Massachusetts party under the charge of Martin Stowell. Richard Hinton, another of the Scotsmen coming out to the territory and an enterprising journalist who became a noted partisan figure in Kansas affairs, was one of the company. Also coming out with them, after joining them in Buffalo, New York, was another of John Brown's sons-in-law, William Thompson.

Sitting idly in camp just over the Nebraska-Kansas line in the hottest hours of a late July day, Hinton had been watching a wagon and a single horse toiling northward along the trail stretching to Topeka opened by Aaron Dwight Stevens, then known under the *nom de guerre* Colonel Whipple. Stevens had been a sergeant in the United States Dragoons who'd been court-martialed for striking an officer who had abused a soldier; imprisoned, he escaped and became one of the fighting free-state leaders in Topeka. He was "engaged in opening a road from the Kaw River (at Topeka due north to the Nebraska line)," wrote Richard Hinton. "It was only by this flanking movement that the free-state settlements, then blockaded and surrounded, could be succored."[65]

As the wagon lumbered into camp, Hinton could see a wounded man lying on a bed and beside it an elderly man was riding a gaunt gray horse. Addressing him, the man said, "Have you a man in your camp named William Thompson? You are from Massachusetts, young man, I believe, and Mr. Thompson joined you at Buffalo." Aware of John Brown's reputation, and having had a description of him, Hinton wrote, "as I heard the question, I looked up and met the full, strong gaze of a pair of luminous, questioning eyes. Somehow I instinctively knew this was John Brown, and with that name I replied, saying Thompson was in our company."[66]

Riding up with Brown was Samuel Walker, a small man from the Midwest with a hip impediment, who had been one of the commanders of the free-state companies in the Wakarusa War. He'd brought fifteen of "his boys" up with him to meet Lane at the border and warn him he was liable to arrest if he entered the territory. Lane had been issuing high-sounding titles under his own authority, but had no standing with the National Kansas Committee whose leading members, Thaddeus Hyatt and Dr. Howe, were in Nebraska City. Meeting Lane at Nebraska City, Walker handed him a letter requesting he leave his "army" at the border. "The Grim Chieftain," as Lane came to be called, became disconsolate; he "could never go back to the states and look the people in the face and tell them that as soon as I had got these Kansas friends of mine fairly into danger I had to abandon them." He couldn't do it and would rather end the whole thing by blowing his brains out.[67] Walker now changed from being an emissary of political interest to a partisan. "General," Walker told him, "the people of Kansas would rather have you than all the party at Nebraska City. I have fifteen good boys that are my own. If you will put yourself under my orders, I'll take you through all right." An attempt was now made to disguise Lane by applying silver nitrate to his facial hair and giving him a set of old clothes in exchange for those he'd been wearing while delivering his northern oratory. But these could not hide the character already giving him distinction.

Also in Nebraska City, a glimpse of John Brown is given by Redpath: "The Captain was riding a splendid horse, and was dressed in plain white summer clothing. He wore a large straw hat, and was closely shaven: everything about him was scrupulously clean." Some youths, without knowing who he was, the journalists added, thought he must be a "'distinguished' man."[68] This triumvir of Lane, Walker, and Brown, together with Walker's boys, would now ride back into Kansas with the intention of reigniting the flames of civil war, covering the 160 miles to Lawrence in thirty hours.

At that time six fortified entrenched camps were maintained by the Southern partisans in Kansas, well provisioned, and with ample arms and munitions. On several of these block-houses had been constructed, some provided with other defenses, where up to thirty Missourians would make their headquarters for marauding, sallying out on free-state settlements and farms, plundering livestock and crops, and making it difficult for these communities to sustain themselves. Three of these, one at Franklin, another near Lawrence called Fort Saunders, and Fort Titus near Lecompton, where Henry Titus had built a pillared mansion complete with slave quarters, were used to maintain an embargo on the free-state stronghold at Lawrence. In a furious campaign in the third week of August all were to be carried in the space of a few days. The first attack came at Franklin where a cannon called "old Sacramento," captured in the Mexican War by a Missouri volunteer militia company, was seized. A well-known photograph of the weapon being manned by a free-state battery was undoubtedly taken at that time, since it would be returned to the proslavery side in Lecompton as a truce was arranged and prisoners exchanged after the campaign succeeded. Appearing from left to right in that image are James Redpath, Richard Realf, Augustus Wattles, John T. "Ottawa" Jones, George Gill, and John Brown's son Owen.[69] Several of these individuals are already known to this narrative, and some of the others will soon enter. Augustus Wattles was a noted abolitionist and friend of John Brown who had studied at Lane Seminary in Cincinnati, and "Ottawa" Jones, also an ally and confidant of Brown, was a farmer and Christianized and literate Indian, whose hospitality he often enjoyed.

After the assault at Franklin, in which Lane had not participated, he summoned the "old man" with his company to join him in the assault on Fort Saunders, Sanborn reporting: "General Lane drew his forces up in front of the fort while Captain Brown occupied the right wing with his cavalry."[70] A charge was ordered and the fort taken, Brown with his men first to reach the redoubt, which consisted of a high rail fence inside which were heavy earthworks. This attack was reported on by Atchison in the Missouri papers, he commenting August 17 on the so-called "Treadwell Settlement," where "They planted the old cannon 'Sacramento' towards the colony, and surrounded them."[71] Balls fired in the assault were made from the melted newspaper type destroyed in Lawrence in May and rammed down the gun's barrel, the canonries yelling, "Here comes another addition of the *Herald of Freedom*."[72]

Hinton says that Lane was the chief leader in these nine or ten weeks (August through September) "of marvelous activity, which saw a sufficient force of earnest men gathered, armed, and marched into Kansas from all parts of the North."[73] John Jr., receiving reports as they circulated through the grapevine into the jail at Lecompton, wrote of their father, to "Brother Jason and others" August 16, that he was in the fight at Franklin, and also "aided in routing the gang on Washington Creek [Fort Saunders], as well as in the capture of Titus and his crew." "He is an omnipresent dread to the ruffians," he wrote.[74] To their sister, Ruth, Jason wrote on August 13 a similar assessment, "Old Capt. Brown can now be raised from every prairie and thicket." Notwithstanding, it has often been difficult for historians to find John Brown's agency in the fighting because he typically took a "step back," and thus did not always appear prominently. Although he surely and effectually put his hand to the work, he kept his own counsel, consenting to assist in the general result while maintaining independence of action, for himself and of his own small company. He never sought overall command, as did Lane.

After the capture of Titus's blockhouse, Walker brought the prisoner into Lawrence, and would relate a vivid portrayal of Brown's presence.

> Our arrival at Lawrence created intense excitement. The citizens swarmed around us, clamoring for the blood of our prisoner. The committee of safety had a meeting and decided that Titus should be hanged, John Brown and other distinguished men urging the measure strongly. At four o'clock in the evening I went before the committee and said that Titus had surrendered to me, that I had promised him his life and that I would defend it with my own. Captain Brown and Doctor Avery were outside haranguing the mob to hang Titus despite my objections. They said I had resisted the committee of safety and was, myself, therefore a public enemy. The crowd was terribly excited, but the sight of my three hundred solid bayonets held them in check.[75]

On August 17 as his last act in the territory Governor Shannon would arrange for the release of Titus and the other prisoners held on both sides of the fighting. Brown delivered an address to the Missouri prisoners, who evidently were eager to see their vanquisher, and it is recorded in Johnathan Winkely's *John Brown the Hero*. Shannon returned to Lecompton to report on the condition of affairs to General Smith and to write out his resignation letter to the president, as gangs of proslavery vigilantes sought to even the score. In two days seven free-state cabins were burned, including that of Samuel Walker. Before Shannon's letter could reach Washington, Pierce's letter removing him from office arrived in Kansas. With proslavery Daniel Woodson temporarily standing in as acting governor as he had after Reeder's firing, Atchison and Stringfellow called for a meeting in Kansas City "to rally instantly to the rescue," as a mass meeting convened at Lexington, Missouri. With the *Weston Argus* trumpeting "Civil War has begun," Woodson called out the militia, accepting Missourians as had been the practice, while his proclamation bid: "Let the watchword be 'extermination total and complete.'"[76] Newspapers in the Southern states drew a harrowing rendition of Kansas—Lane and his marauders were in the territory, while another two thousand Northerners waited to enter the fray on the border. To the North the *Chicago Tribune* counseled: "Kansas is now in a state of open war. . . . It is not a war in which the interests of Kansas are alone at stake, but the cause of freedom in the whole country."[77] In Massachusetts, acting through the Massachusetts State Kansas Committee, George Stearns purchased two hundred Sharps Rifles, shipping them to the Iowa border to be distributed in Kansas.

Brown was back in Osawatomie August 20, Bondi related, "with a spic and span four-mule team, the wagon loaded with provisions; besides he was well supplied with money and all contributed by the Northern friends of Free State Kansas, men like Thaddeus Hyatt."[78] Joining in were the war-making parties of Captains James B. Cline and James H. Holmes; on August 25 Cline swept into Linn County to the south, capturing twelve prisoners and some military equipment, while the next day Brown led a raid on a proslavery settlement to the east, returning two nights later with a hundred and fifty cattle. This was the prelude to the last mass invasion from Missouri to engage in battle led by Atchison and Stringfellow.

Their first column—intending to wipe out Osawatomie—was commanded by a burly veteran of the Mexican War, John W. Reid, with two hundred and fifty men and one cannon. A second column of a hundred and fifty men was led by ex-Indian agent George Washington Clarke marching over the border with Reid's men, then heading toward Fort Scott. The main column under Atchison nearing a thousand marched in the direction of Lawrence, vowing to destroy the "Boston abolition town." Clarke's column fled precipitously after a light brush eight miles south of Osawatomie with free-state men led by James Montgomery, a diminutive, black-bearded "Campbellite" preacher. He had come out to Kansas by way of Kentucky and Missouri, hating slavery, and he made his name by destroying ballot boxes during the "fraudulent elections" in spring 1855 and winter 1856. Atchison's column would likewise flounder after a brief skirmish with Lane twelve miles north of Osawatomie. The deciding blow of the campaign occurred August 30 at Osawatomie, where Brown, although outnumbered nine to one, directed a withering fire into Reid's line as they approached along a ridge on the northwest of the town. After Brown's scourge of fire, withdrawing across the Osage River he was seen, the tails of his white linen duster floating behind him, wearing his large straw hat, holding two pistols up in his outstretched hands, as Reid's troops discharged their cannon and charged after the free-state men. Higginson, arriving in Lawrence on a fact-finding mission for the National Kansas Committee several weeks after this, would write, "Osawatomie was sacrificed, after one of the most heroic defences in history. . . . Brown and twenty-seven others resisted two hundred, killing thirty-three and wounding forty-nine." The free-state men had five killed, including Brown's son Frederick, slain unarmed by an advance scout, and Charles Kaiser, who was captured, pushed into a ravine, and executed. (This account of casualties among the Missourians, the largest by far in any engagement during "Bleeding Kansas," was dated October 4, 1856, and undoubtedly attributable to witnesses at the time of writing and accurate. Higginson reported in letters to the *New York Tribune* under the signature "Worcester," and published these soon after, appearing as a pamphlet under the title *A Ride Through Kansas*.)

In Lawrence the moment was seen as an auspicious one by the free-state fighters to attack Lecompton, ending the proslavery government there and freeing the "treason prisoners." Accordingly a plan was arrived at and the action set. Harvey, the Chicagoan, was to march up the north bank of the Kaw River with his men to the ferry to prevent retreat from the capital, while Lane was to lead a column and attack from the south. Harvey and his contingent were in position, and after waiting twelve hours they withdrew. Only then did Lane's column advance to be met by Lieutenant Colonel Philip St. George Cooke and the United States Army. Recognizing Walker, the federal officer called out, "What in hell are you doing here?"

"We are after our prisoners and our rights," answered Walker.

"How many men have you?"

"About four hundred foot and two hundred horseback."

"Well, I have six hundred men and six cannon, and you can't fight here—except with me."

"I don't care a damn how many men you have. We are going to have our prisoners, or a big fight!"

Dismissing this contention, Cooke insisted upon seeing General Lane. Lane was not in command, said Walker, if he wanted to parley he would call a council of war. Soon a half-dozen free-state officers drew their horses around the lieutenant colonel.

"You have made a most unfortunate move for yourselves," said Cooke. "The Missourians, you know, have gone and the militia have nearly gone, having commenced crossing yesterday to my knowledge. As to the prisoners, whilst I will make no terms with you, I can inform you that they were promised to be released yesterday morning." As a United States deputy marshal rode up demanding the arrest of Lane and Walker, Cooke ordered him back to his camp. He dared not go, the marshal replied, as men were now surely waiting with a bead drawn on him. In that case he would escort him, said Cooke, and as they rode off Sheriff Jones rode in demanding the arrest of Lane. Cooke replied, "If you want him arrested, write your requisition, but I think, on reflection, you will hardly make it."[79]

Four days later the new governor of Kansas, John W. Geary, steamed up the Missouri as Shannon's boat passed him headed east. At Lexington, a large crowd was waiting on the dock as an even bigger crowd awaited him at Kansas City. Striding down the gangplank at Leavenworth, Geary was an impressive sight: balding and bearded with a resemblance to John Knox, he was powerfully built at six-foot-six and two hundred and sixty pounds. A Pennsylvanian and a Democrat, he had led troops in the Mexican War where he was lionized; having employed slaves in Virginia mines he owned, he had also helped bring California into the Union as a free state, serving in 1850 as San Francisco's first mayor. He was not thought a good choice in the South, but he was Pierce's man, sent to grapple with a seemingly intractable quandary before the presidential election. The governor found Leavenworth overrun with a menagerie of outlandish fellows—men wearing weather-beaten hats pinned up in the front or on one side "with a cockade, star, or eagle," some with feathers adorning their crowns. With pistols hanging from every belt, and with knife handles protruding over the tops of rough boots, they sauntered or loitered in Leavenworth's streets, or drank in its saloons. In a letter to Pierce's secretary of state, William Marcy, Geary described the chaos he saw on entering the territory: "Desolation and ruin reigned on every hand; homes and firesides were deserted; the smoke of burning dwellings darkened the atmosphere; women and children, driven from their habitations, wandered over the prairies; the highways were infested with numerous predatory bands and the towns were fortified and garrisoned by armies of conflicting partisans, each excited almost to frenzy, and determined upon mutual extermination."[80]

Lane, who had disappeared into the ranks at Lecompton, grabbing a private's rifle as Walker faced down Cooke, headed for the Iowa border to avoid arrest the day Geary landed in Leavenworth. He would be escorted out at a rapid pace by Colonel Whipple (Stevens) and his company. Finding haven at Nebraska City, Higginson would see him in late September and wrote about it in his *Cheerful Yesterdays*:[81]

Some thirty rough-riders came cantering up to the hostelry. They might have been border raiders for all appearance of cavalry order: some rode horses, some mules; some had bridles, others had lariats of rope; one man had on a slight semblance of uniform, and seemed a sort of lieutenant. The leader was a thin man of middle age, in a gray woolen shirt, with keen eyes, smooth tongue, and a suggestion of courteous and even fascinating manners; a sort of Prince Rupert of humbler grade. This was the then celebrated Jim Lane . . . . He made a speech to the citizens of the town,—they being then half balanced between anti-slavery and pro-slavery sympathies,—and I have seldom heard eloquence more thrilling, more tactful, better adjusted to the occasion.

On September 10, 1856, Geary arrived in Lecompton, meeting the same rowdies in the streets he'd seen in Missouri and in Leavenworth. Establishing his headquarters, as he sought the dismissal of three hated federal officials—Judge Lecompte, Marshal Donaldson, and "General" Clarke—he rebuffed the proffered services of Henry Clay Pate and ordered the militia and all other armed bands to disperse, while the "treason prisoners" were released on bail. He would serve no faction, Geary announced, and would rely on United States troops to maintain order.

Teaming with people whom he had not known before his arrest, Charles Robinson was back in Lawrence on the evening of September 10, 1856, where a celebration was given in honor of all the released prisoners. John Brown was there for a joyous reunion with his son, and would be included among those giving addresses that night. The prisoners had marked only four days out of captivity when word came that Atchison was again leading his horde to administer a decisive retribution on Lawrence. He would demonstrate to the new governor the permanence of the proslavery reign. In Atchison's entourage were Reid, Whitfield, and Stringfellow, together with an army of twenty-five hundred, infantry and cavalry combined, with a howitzer and a six-pounder battery.

In Lawrence couriers were dispatched by three different routes summoning Geary from Lecompton, but he and Lieutenant Colonel Cooke would not set out in the town's relief till two o'clock that morning. The number of fighting men in Lawrence that day was small; Lane and his contingent were on the northern border, Harvey's Chicagoans and others were out conducting raids, as many fighters had gone home to their farms. As the several redoubts and defensive barricades prepared in previous fighting were manned, some merchants distributed pitchforks because of a dearth of rifles. Only about two hundred men were on hand, while a few women too bore arms, as others ran cartridges. But among them was John Brown, to whom an appeal was made to assume leadership in the fight. That he declined, proposing instead he act as advisor. Again, because of this "step back" it has been difficult to account the importance of his presence. In his dispatch to the *Tribune* of October 4, 1856, Higginson described his activity among the defenders of Lawrence: "They had no regular commander, any more than at Bunker Hill, but the famous 'Old Captain Brown,' moved about among them saying 'Fire low boys; be sure to bring down your eye to the hinder sight of your rifle, and aim at the feet rather than the head.'" In his letter of the same date, Higginson remarked: "Ever since the rendition of Anthony Burns, in Boston, I have been looking for *men*. I have found them in Kanzas." Giving further testimony in an earlier letter dated September 28, he wrote: "Never have I been in such a community as this; never seen such courage, such patience, such mutual generosity, such perfect buoyancy of spirit."[82]

In the afternoon that Sunday on September 13, 1856, Brown mounted a dry-goods box in the center of town, offering this: "Gentlemen— It is said there are twenty-five hundred Missourians down at Franklin, and that they will be here in two hours. You can see for yourselves the smoke they are making by setting fire to the houses in that town. Now is probably the last opportunity you will have of seeing a fight, so that you had better do your best." The tendency of the Sharps rifle bullet was to travel high; he advised, "You had better aim at their legs, than at their heads." He ended his words with a characteristically wry note: "It is from this reason that I myself have so many times escaped; for if all the bullets which have ever been aimed at me had hit me, I would have been as full of holes as a riddle."[83] Hinton remarks the rendition of Brown's words usually cited undoubtedly gave the "gist of the speech," but there probably was more to it given his thinking and concerns that did not survive in the record. James Redpath, who was in Lawrence, wrote:

> About five o'clock in the afternoon, their advance-guard, consisting of four hundred horsemen, crossed the Wakarusa, and presented themselves in sight of the town, about two miles off, when they halted, and arrayed themselves for battle, fearing, perhaps to come within too close range of Sharps rifle balls. Brown's movement now was a little on the offensive order; for he ordered out all the Sharps riflemen from every part of the town—in all not more than forty or fifty—marched them a half mile into the prairie, and arranged them three paces apart, in a line parallel with that of the enemy; and then they lay down upon their faces in the grass, awaiting the order to fire.[84]

Undoubtedly the most accomplished bard of "Bleeding Kansas" was the young Englishman and journalist Richard Realf, a protégé of Lady Byron, who wrote in his *Defence of Lawrence*:

> We were but thirty-nine who lay
> Beside our rifles then;
> We were but thirty-nine, and they
> Were twenty hundred men.
> Our lean limbs shook and reeled about,
> Our feet were gashed and bare,
> And all the breeze shredded out
> Our garments in the air.

As a scout for the Missouri horsemen dashed forward, a shot raised the sod before his horse. Now Brown changed the position of the riflemen to a rising ground about a quarter of a mile to the left, stationing them as before three paces apart with their faces to the ground.

> And when three hundred of the foe
> Rode up in scorn and pride,
> Who so had watched us then might know
> That God was on our side;
> For all at once, a mighty thrill
> Of grandeur through us swept,
> And strong and swiftly down the hill
> Like Gideons we leapt.[85]

With the attack repulsed by a line "of living fire," the following morning Geary arrived with his escort of four hundred dragoons with four cannon. At dawn an outdoor conference, with Robinson, the governor, Brown and a few others attending, was held amid the ash and ruin of May and the various redoubts and barricades that had gone up. Robinson excused the warlike display as being necessary for the protection of the town, while Geary acknowledged Americans of spirit would protect their property. In this conference, satisfied that the new governor sincerely intended to protect the free-state settlers from attack, Brown agreed that in exchange for a promise of immunity he would leave the territory. As the conference terminated, word came that Atchison's army had decamped and were returning to Missouri. Addressing a mass meeting, Geary reminded everyone of his proclamation commanding armed partisans of both sides to lay down their arms; he would make sure he emphasized Missouri obeyed it too. Urging everyone to return "to peaceful fields and benches in this fair and blooming land of opportunity," the governor mounted his carriage and headed for Lecompton with his military escort.[86]

As word came the next day that the Missourians had wheeled about and were again headed for Lawrence, Geary ordered Lieutenant Colonel Joseph E. Johnston to occupy Mount Oread with his troops, and whipped his horses around, driving his carriage straight toward Atchison's lines. Kansas's fledgling territorial governor and the former Democratic senator and one of the most important politicians in the country would meet in a room in a small clapboard house in Franklin. "Though held in a board house," Geary said to the gathered entourage of proslavery leaders, "the present is the most important council since the days of the Revolution, as its issues involve the fate of the Union now formed."[87] He was appealing to them as a member of the Democratic Party; another attack on Lawrence would injure their chances in the coming election, possibly throwing it to the Republican candidate. Atchison explained they were only there to apprehend an "organized band of murderers and robbers said to be under the command of Lane, who have plundered and butchered large numbers of our fellow-citizens."[88] Lane was not in Lawrence, countered Geary; he knew because he had just been there. A new Democratic administration would sort things out, he assured; meanwhile, he would deal with the abolitionists. Satisfied with Geary's declarations, Atchison could report to his confederates, "He [Geary] promised us all we wanted."[89]

The next day John Brown left Lawrence, but would remain nearby at the home of Augustus Wattles with his sons John Jr. and Jason and their wives, and Owen. On October 1 he was in Osawatomie, bidding farewell to his company, placing them under command of James H. Holmes, enjoining they uphold the highest standard in the fight against slavery. With the blockade of the Missouri River ended, the wives could take a steamboat, while the men, loading their arms and ammunition and other supplies into a wagon drawn by a four-mule team, with another one horse wagon, would take the overland route.

Traveling through Topeka, Brown would take into the smaller wagon a fugitive slave they found there, riding with the man in the bed hidden under a blanket when necessary. Brown drove this wagon with his son Owen, his surveying instruments hanging on the outside boards, as Aaron D. Stevens and his company, and Brown's other sons rode north on a parallel course as a protective escort, but keeping out of sight. There were no incidents before reaching Nebraska City, but Lieutenant Colonel Cooke would report October 7: "I arrived here yesterday at noon. I just missed the arrest of the notorious Osawatomie outlaw,

John Brown. The night before, having ascertained that after dark he had stopped for the night at a house six miles from the camp, I sent a party who found at 12 o'clock that he had gone."[90]

Such was the closing of John Brown's tumultuous first sojourn in Kansas. Higginson, who would be in Topeka at the time Brown was preparing to depart, would wonder years later in his *Cheerful Yesterdays* whether he might have seen him there. He would recollect being shown into a room where a fugitive slave was sheltered, and that sitting in a corner was an elderly-looking white man who had not spoken while he was there. Could that unassuming presence have been the legendary "Osawatomie Brown"? Corresponding with Higginson in February 1858, Brown would answer a query concerning his intentions by writing: "I have just read your kind letter of the 8th instant, & will now say that Rail Road business on a *somewhat extended scale*, is the *identical* object for which I am trying to get means. I have been connected with that business as commonly conducted from my boyhood & never let an opportunity slip." Was this his way of intimating they had met before, Higginson wondered.[91]

On March 4, 1857, with the new Democratic administration of James Buchanan coming into office, Geary would resign as Kansas territorial governor, effective March 20. Sam Walker, afterward to become sheriff in Jones's stead, had boldly told Geary as he assumed the office, "Mark my word, you'll take the underground railroad out of Kansas in six months."[92]

6

The Panic of 1857

Preceded by the moniker "Osawatomie" Brown, and with a letter of introduction from Charles Robinson dated September 15, 1857, John Brown appeared on October 25 at the headquarters of the National Kansas Committee in Chicago with a proposal and to consult about financial support, wishing to claim some of the benefit to which he and his destitute company had heretofore needed. He wanted to arm and equip as many as one hundred "regular volunteers" to operate under his command in furtherance of the free-state cause, and for this he calculated he needed a minimum of $30,000. Not delegated to consult with him on his request, the committee referred it to a national meeting to convene in January at the Astor House in New York City; meanwhile, Horace White, assistant secretary of the National Committee, gave Brown a letter of referral providing him free fare as their agent on three northern railroads, and fitted him too with a new suit of clothes. White also handed Brown a note: "Rev. Theodore

Parker, of Boston, is at the Briggs House, and wishes very much to see you."¹ Although there seems to be no evidence of the Brown and Parker meeting at this time, and Sanborn doubts that it occurred, the Chicago committee had a request for Brown: a wagon train was headed for Kansas with arms and other supplies that they wished to provide with an escort, as a previous train had been hijacked by border ruffians. Brown consented, intending to head off two of his sons, Watson and Salmon, who had left North Elba after hearing of the murder of their brother Frederick. On the train to Chicago the two had had a chance meeting with Frederick Douglass, who gave them twenty-five dollars from his own pocket; Watson reported at bit later he and his brother were "in the company of a train of Kansas teams loaded with Sharpe's rifles and cannon . . . on our way we saw Gerrit Smith, F. Douglass, and other old friends."² Brown would intercept Watson in Tabor when he reached that Iowa way station, while Salmon had gone on to Topeka. Two hundred Sharps rifles carried in the train of wagons would be stored in the cellar of the Reverend John Todd's home, where Brown would later retrieve them.

On his way now to Ohio for a reunion with his sons, Brown again was in Chicago where he learned that George Luther Stearns of the Massachusetts State Kansas Committee had invited him to visit Boston "to consult with the friends of freedom," offering to pay his expenses. On his way to Ashtabula, Ohio, Brown stopped to see Governor Chase in Columbus, soliciting a letter of introduction from him with the aid of Joshua Giddings. The governor also handed Brown a twenty-five dollar contribution. In Columbus, Brown also explored the possibility of obtaining aid from the state legislature to arm men for the free-state cause in Kansas, reported on at the time by the *Cleveland Leader*, whose reporter regarded it as provocative and incendiary. Next Brown was in Peterboro conferring with Gerrit Smith, before traveling on to Rochester where undoubtedly he updated his ongoing collaboration with Frederick Douglass, and then on to Albany to see William Barnes. Douglass gives an indication of his interactions with Brown during 1857–59 in his autobiography: "In his repeated visits to the East to obtain necessary arms and supplies, he often did me the honor of spending hours and days with me at Rochester."³ There is also a letter of uncertain year, yet dated December 7 from Douglass's hand addressing Brown: "I am very busy at home. Will you please come up with my son Fred and take a mouthful with me?"⁴

When welcoming him at his estate, Smith said: "Captain John Brown,—you did not need to show me letters from Governor Chase and Governor Robinson to let me know who and what you are. I have known you for many years, and have highly esteemed you as long as I have known you."[5] Brown's final stop before reaching Boston was Springfield, Massachusetts, where he met with George Walker, agent of the Kansas Committee in that city, and brother-in-law through Walker's marriage to his now deceased wife, who was sister to Franklin B. Sanborn, secretary of the Massachusetts State Kansas Committee.

On an early January morning in 1857, together with his son Owen, and preceded by his reputation and with four letters of introduction, Brown walked into the office of the Kansas committee in Boston on School Street. He was greeted by the committee's secretary and sole occupant of the sparsely furnished office, Franklin Sanborn; he was twenty-five years old, having graduated from Harvard only a year and a half before. Six-foot-three with his hair reaching his shoulders, he had delicate features said to resemble "an early portrait of Raphael." A protégé of Emerson, he'd gone to Concord at the philosopher's behest to run a school for the children of that community's better-placed families. He was to become an important chronicler of the lives of his friends in Concord as well as of John Brown, to whom he also averred a friendship. Sanborn provided the following summary in an article published in the *Atlantic Monthly* in April 1872 of Brown's intentions as they were soon to be understood by all of the committee members:

> His theory required fighting in Kansas; it was the only sure way, he thought, to keep that region free from the curse of slavery. His mission now as to levy war on it, and for that to raise and equip a company of a hundred well-armed men who should resist aggression in Kansas, or occasionally carry the war into Missouri. Behind that purpose, but not yet disclosed, was his intention to use the men thus put into the field for incursions into Virginia or other slave states. Our State Kansas Committee, of which I was secretary, had a stock of arms that Brown wished to use for this company, and these we voted to him. They had been put in the custody of the National Committee at Chicago, and it was needful to follow up our vote by similar action in the National Committee. For this purpose I was sent to a meeting of that committee at the Astor House, in New York, as the proxy of Dr. Howe and Dr. Samuel Cabot—both members of the National Committee.[6]

The members of the Massachusetts committee were George L. Stearns of Medford, chairman; Franklin B. Sanborn of Concord, secretary; and Patrick T. Jackson of Boston, treasurer. Other executive committee members were Dr. Samuel G. Howe, Dr. Samuel Cabot, Dr. William R. Lawrence, and Judge Thomas Russell. Of these, Stearns,

Sanborn, and Howe, together with Higginson in Worcester, Theodore Parker in Boston, and Gerrit Smith in Peterboro, would be the men most prominently behind Brown's Harpers Ferry campaign; reported in the press at that time under the designation "the secret six."

It has been asked, what would John Brown have been without them? That it was an association of paramount, even historic, significance, there can be no doubt. But which side of the transaction was stronger, when, as George L. Stearns's son, Frank Preston Stearns, suggests, it was as a magnet catches iron. Sanborn supposes there were a thousand men who knew Brown meant to harass the slaveholders in some part of the South with an armed force; but of these the number at any time who knew with any fullness of detail of the Virginian enterprise did not exceed a hundred. And these "were scattered over the whole country, from Boston to Kansas, from Maryland to Canada."[7]

Foremost among these was the preacher of American Transcendentalism, Theodore Parker, minister of the Unitarian Church. He was above all a reformer and abolitionist, of that generation who still traced their linage to the period of the Revolution, and he was fluent in half a dozen languages, specializing in German theology and thought. Drawn to the ideas of Carlyle and Coleridge, and of Ralph Waldo Emerson, he saw his career as an orthodox preacher culminate early as he began attending meetings of the Transcendental Club in 1837. Breaking with supernatural realism in 1838, he laid out his position in the next year in a sermon titled *A Discourse on the Transient and Permanent in Christianity*. Ostracized from the pulpits of Boston, he was invited by supporters to become minister of the 28th Congregational Society of Boston in December 1845—a congregation including Louisa May Alcott, William Lloyd Garrison, Julia Ward Howe, and Elizabeth Cady Stanton, which would grow with his influence to seven thousand parishioners. Gradually shifting his emphasis after the Compromise of 1850, Parker would devote his time to combating the Fugitive Slave Law, and would head the Vigilance Committee in Boston. He was also one of those in the forefront of the Kansas movement, contributing money to buy weapons for the free-state militias in Kansas.

Another of these was Dr. Samuel Gridley Howe, a noted humanitarian, founder of the Asylum for the Blind and of the Sanitary Commission during the Civil War. Shortly after obtaining his medical degree, inspired by the example of Lord Byron, he sailed for Greece, joining the Greek army as a surgeon on the side of the revolution. Bestowed the title "the Lafayette of the Greek Revolution" for his serv-

ices, he returned to the United States in 1827; raising funds and supplies to alleviate suffering in Greece, his appeals raised $60,000, and he
published a *Historical Sketch of the Greek Revolution* in 1828.
Continuing his medical studies in Paris, he investigated the prospect of
establishing an Asylum for the Blind; he took part in the July
Revolution in France in 1830, and lent a hand, too, to the Polish revolt,
becoming chairman of the American-Polish Committee at Paris. When
in Berlin to distribute supplies he was imprisoned for five weeks by the
Prussian government. In 1843 he married Julia Ward, a suffragist and
poet who would compose "The Battle Hymn of the Republic" on the
basis of the slower moving melody of the John Brown song; the couple
would found the antislavery newspaper the Boston *Daily
Commonwealth*.

Thomas Wentworth Higginson, who has already appeared numerous
times in this narrative, was also a Unitarian minister as active as Parker
in the abolitionist movement. Following the lead of Parker on theological matters, he began his preaching at the First Religious Society of
Newburyport, Massachusetts. Giving prominence to abolition and
criticizing the degrading conditions for workers in the cotton mills, he
invited Parker and Emerson as well as the fugitive slave William Wells
Brown to speak from his pulpit. When his church's pews began to
empty, leading to his forced resignation, he became in 1852 minister to
the Free Church in Worcester. A key member of the Boston Vigilance
Committee, he would join the Boston group too in its Kansas work,
undertaking an important fact-finding tour to the territory for the
National Committee. Identifying with disunion, he was preparing a
convention to convene in Worcester that January 15. With a rare combination of literary acumen and commitment to the cause of abolition,
he was one of the outstanding figures in American letters in the nineteenth century.

The most crucial member in this group was George Luther Stearns.
Without his support, those who know the record agree, John Brown
would not have been able to proceed. An industrialist and merchant, he
specialized in ship-chandlery, branching into the manufacture of sheet
and pipe lead, and became the supplier for plumbers and tinsmiths
throughout New England. Identifying with the abolitionist cause after
1848 when he supported the Free-Soilers, he established a branch of
the Underground Railroad in Medford, making a vow after the assault
on Sumner "to devote the rest of his life and fortune to the liberation
of the slave."[8] With passage of the Kansas-Nebraska bill he became one
of the chief financiers of Thayer's Emigrant Aid Company, while

becoming in spring of 1856 the chairman of the Massachusetts State Kansas Committee. A prodigious fund-raiser and tireless worker, he also was a founder of *Commonwealth* with the Howes and of the *Nation* and an intimate of the Concord Transcendentalists, as he was of Charles Sumner and Frederick Douglass. His wife, Mary Stearns, herself an intimate of John Brown, wrote that her husband and Brown were first introduced by a Kansas man who chanced to be with her husband on the street where the committee kept its office. "Captain Brown made a profound impression on all who came within the sphere of his moral magnetism," she wrote in her valuable retrospective.[9] On his death Whittier honored George Stearns with a poem:

> No duty could overtask him;
> No need his will out run;
> Or ever our lips could ask him;
> His hands the work had done.
> A man who asked not to be great
> But as he served and saved the state.[10]

Theodore Parker first met Brown at his Sunday congregation in the Boston Music Hall that January, although Sanborn notes Brown had come to hear him preach for the first time in 1853.[11] Higginson first met Brown for an interview on January 9 at the United States Hotel in Boston. Trying to ascertain the best date to assemble "the friends of freedom" to consult with Brown, Stearns found that Sunday, January 11, optimal. Inquiring if it would be consistent with his religious conviction to attend, Brown replied, "Mr. Stearns, I have a poor little ewe that has fallen into a ditch, and I think the Sabbath is as good a day as any to help her out. I will come." Among those invited to the Stearns residence were Doctors Howe and Cabot, Judge Russell and his wife, Pastors Higginson and Parker, John Andrew, and Sanborn. Mary Stearns was to write in her reminiscences, "It may not be out of place to describe the impression he made upon the writer on this first visit. When I entered the parlor, he was sitting near the hearth, where glowed a bright, open fire. He rose to greet me, stepping forward with such an erect, military bearing, such fine courtesy of demeanor and grave earnestness, that he seemed to my instant thought some old Cromwellian hero suddenly dropped down before me."[12]

Dressed in a brown coat of broadcloth, with wide brown trousers, he had the look of a farmer in his Sunday dress or a deacon of a church, and with his patent leather stock, gray surtout, and fur cap, his figure took on a military air. Then destitute of the full beard, he was cleanly shaven and scrupulous in his appearance; "His mien was serious and patient rather than cheerful," Sanborn wrote, "it betokened the 'sad, wise valor' which Herbert praises."[13] Finding she had interrupted the conversation when she entered, Mary Stearns's initial impression was strengthened, as Brown turned, continuing his remarks: "Gentlemen, I consider the Golden Rule and the Declaration of Independence one and inseparable; and it is better that a whole generation of men, women children should be swept away than that this crime of slavery should exist one day longer." These words were uttered in such an emphatic way, she wrote, her youngest boy, Carl, then only three, standing in the center of the room with his eyes fully absorbing the speaker, remembered it as one of his earliest recollections into manhood. Coaxing the boy to his knee, Carl remained there with a look of wonder until dinner was served.

Continuing in the parlor after dinner, when George Stearns asked Brown what sort of noise a Sharps rifle made, he replied: "It makes a very ugly noise, Mr. Stearns." Another attendee, Augusta King, then said: "We read a good deal in the newspapers about General Pomeroy, who seems to be an important man in Kansas. Is he a very good general?" Laughing silently to himself, as was his way, Brown replied: "I wish the ladies of Massachusetts would make a large military cocked hat, about three feet in length, and a foot and a half in height; and put the tail feathers of three roosters in it, and send it with their compliments to General Pomeroy." Then Brown added: "As a rule, Miss King, the higher the officer the less of a soldier. Now I am but a plain captain, and I am always ready to fight the enemy. Jim Lane is a colonel, but I have no doubt he would fight if Governor Robinson would let him. Pomeroy is a general, and there is no fight in him at all."[14] Half in jest George Stearns asked during this conversation, "I suppose, Captain Brown, that if Judge Lecompte had fallen into your hands, he would have fared rather hard." Brown turned around in his chair and uttered these words as a pistol shot: "If the Lord had delivered Judge Lecompte into my hands, I think it would have required the Lord to have taken him out again."[15]

Impressed with Brown's wit and sagacity, everyone laughed as twelve-year-old Henry Stearns approached him, saying, "Captain Brown, I wish you would tell me about your boyhood." For this innocence Brown had only the kindest manner. "My son, I cannot do that now, for I fear it would weary the ladies, but when I have time I will try to write something for you on the subject." Henry handed Brown some pocket change of a few dollars he'd been saving. "Will you please buy something with this for some poor little boy in Kansas?" About six months later Henry received Brown's autobiographical sketch written in Red Rock, Iowa, and addressed to "My Dear Young Friend."[16] Emerson would call Brown's colloquial rendition of his boyhood experiences "a positive contribution to literature."[17]

Shortly afterward a reception for John Brown was held at Theodore Parker's house, attended by William Lloyd Garrison and Wendell Phillips, among others. While Phillips was warmly cordial, in contrast, Frank Preston Stearns observed in his *The Life and Public Service of George Luther Stearns*, though Brown had sincere respect for Garrison, he did not get "an overfriendly reception" from him. Stearns wrote: "Garrison greatly regretted the course that the antislavery movement had taken, and considered the Free-soilers chiefly responsible for it. He thought Sumner's oration on the 'Crime Against Kansas' was very injudicious; and that it would be better to give Kansas to the slaveholders than to offer armed resistance to them. John Brown said afterward, that it was difficult to see the difference between Garrison's position, and that of a pro-slavery Democrat."[18]

On February 16, 1857, Brown wrote "Dear Brother and Sister Adair" back in Kansas, "I have been continually shifting about since my return to the States." Frequently staying at the Massasoit House, in Springfield, Massachusetts, Brown made fund-raising appeals to support his "hundred volunteers" in Hartford, Collinsville, Canton, and New Haven, in Connecticut, and at Worcester, Springfield, Concord, and Boston, in Massachusetts. He was voted possession by the Boston Kansas Committee of the two hundred Sharps rifles he had transported to Tabor the previous year, yet this vote had to be followed up with a similar vote at the National Kansas Committee meeting on January 23 at the Astor House in New York City. Accompanied by Sanborn, Brown was sharply questioned by H. B. Hurd, secretary of the committee. Hurd asked, "If you get the arms and money you desire, will you invade Missouri or any slave territory?" Brown replied, equally sharply, "I am no adventurer. You are acquainted with my history. You know what I have done in Kansas. I do not expose my plans. No one knows them but myself, except perhaps one. I will not be interrogated. If you wish to give me anything, I want you to give it freely." The committee voted $5,000 "in aid of Captain John Brown in any defensive measure that may become necessary," stipulating that it could be drawn in no more than $500 allotments.[19]

Sanborn again accompanied Brown as he appeared on February 18 before the Joint Committee on Federal Relations before the

Massachusetts legislature. Brown gave a lengthy recital of the property and financial losses to free-state families in Kansas, estimating the cost in money terms for his family alone at $7,500. Further he said: "It cost the U.S. more than half a million for a year past to harass poor Free State settlers in Kansas, & to violate all law & all right, moral and Constitutional. I challenge this whole nation to prove before God or mankind to the contrary." The committee concluded, however, that this was not the responsibility of the state. A similar effort spurred by Stearns in New York also had a similar outcome. On his own behalf Brown spoke in a number of cities; in Hartford he said: "I was told that the newspapers in a certain city were dressed in mourning on hearing that I was killed and scalped in Kansas, but I did not know of it until I reached the place. Much good it did me. In the same place I met a more cool reception than in any other place where I have stopped. If my friends will hold up my hands while I live, I will freely absolve them from any expense over me when I am dead."[20]

The morning after Brown gave his lecture at Collinsville he was in the village drug store where he chanced to meet the blacksmith, Charles Blair. Displaying the eight-inch dirk with a two-edged blade, Brown remarked that if he had a number of these attached to a six-foot pole "they would be a capital weapon of defense for the settlers of Kansas to keep in their log cabins to defend themselves against any sudden attack." Asked what it would cost to make them up, Blair supposed it could be done at $1.25 apiece for five hundred and $1 apiece for a thousand. Later that day showing up at Blair's shop, Brown said he wanted to draw up a contract with the forge-master for one thousand weapons at $1 apiece. Receiving a dozen samples, on March 31 Brown came again, giving Blair $350 as down payment, and mailing an additional $200 from Springfield on April 25.

The *New York Tribune* published Brown's appeal "To the Friends Of Freedom" on March 4, 1857, asking "all honest lovers of *Liberty and Human Rights, both male and female*, to hold up my hands by contributions of pecuniary aid, either as counties, cities, towns, villages, societies, churches or individuals."[21] This appeal, a reader may notice, was made on the day President Buchanan was inaugurated, and two days before the United States Supreme Court handed down its Dred Scott decision. A few days later in Worcester, a guest in the home of Eli Thayer, Brown was entertaining the children of the house on his knee when Dr. Wayland called. He was organizing a Frederick Douglass meeting for that evening, and had gotten agreement from the mayor that he would be on the platform, the first time in any American city that this had been done, and he had come to induce Thayer to do the same. "I was then introduced to John Brown of Osawatomie," Wayland wrote. "How little one imagined then that in less than three years the name of this plain homespun man would fill America and Europe! Mr. Brown consented to occupy a place on the platform, and at the urgent request of the audience, spoke briefly."[22]

On March 11 Brown spoke at the town hall in Concord, arranged by Franklin Sanborn with Emerson, Thoreau, A. Bronson Alcott, Judge Hoar, and many others in attendance. During his talk, speaking of the suffering of his sons, Brown exhibited the chains used to bind John Jr. as he was driven by United States dragoons to be jailed at Lecompton, saying, "Here is the chain with which one of them was confined, after the cruelty, sufferings and anxiety he underwent had rendered him a maniac—yes, a maniac." His words, Sanborn remarked, "rose to thrilling eloquence, and made a wonderful impression on his audience."[23] During his stay in Concord, Brown was conveyed to the Thoreau family house for lunch. The following can be found in Henry David Thoreau's journals of the period about his guest:

> He is a man of Spartan habits, and at sixty was scrupulous about his diet at your table, excusing himself by saying that he must eat sparingly and fare hard, as became a soldier, or one who was fitting himself for difficult enterprises, a life of exposure. A man of rare common-sense and directness of speech as of action, a transcendentalist, above all a man of ideas and principles—that is what distinguishes him. Not yielding to a whim or transient impulse, but carrying out the purpose of a life. I noticed that he did not overstate anything, but spoke within bounds.[24]

After lunch Sanborn excused himself as he returned to his school just across the street, leaving Brown and Thoreau wrapped in deeply mutual examination. A bit later Emerson dropped in, as he often did; Sanborn wrote, "Thus the three men, so celebrated each in his own way, first met under the same roof, and found that they held the same opinion of what was uppermost in the mind of Brown." Emerson was to record this in his journal of the time:

> For himself, Brown is so transparent that all men see him through. . . . He believes in two articles—two instruments, shall I say?—the Golden Rule and the Declaration of Independence; and he used this expression in a conversation here concerning them: "Better that a whole generation of men, women, and children should pass away by a violent death, than one word of either should be violated in this country." There is a strict constructionist for you. He believes in the Union of the States, and he con-

ceives that the only obstruction to the Union is slavery; and for that reason, as a patriot, he works for its abolition.[25]

Later that month, Sanborn would accompany Brown on another
mission together with Martin Conway, a man who had figured prominently in Kansas free-state affairs, to Easton, Pennsylvania, to the home
of Kansas ex-governor Reeder. The three tried to convince Reeder to
return to Kansas to lead the free-state interests, for which they deemed
Robinson inadequate owing to his propensity to temporize and his
growing involvement in land speculations. But Reeder, much to their
disappointment, felt he would serve himself and his family better by
remaining at home.

At about this time, Brown was introduced to an Englishman living in
New York who had been involved with Garibaldi and his campaigns in
Italy. He'd been a silk merchant in Siena and had identified himself
with the "Young Italy" party, becoming a trusted agent of both Mazzini
and Garibaldi. The man had notable military experience and had written a multivolume book detailing the European campaigns of 1848.
With defeat he'd gone to Paris where he married and started a family;
after being in London alone, he immigrated to New York in 1855. Eking
out an existence as a translator and sometime editor, he wrote an occa-
sional article for the *Tribune* and had given a series of lectures "On
Recent Events in Italy" at New York University. Also engaged in giving
fencing lessons, Brown hired him as drill instructor and master-at-
arms for his projected company at $100 per month, and paid him $600
out of his pocket to translate and prepare for publication a compendium of his book on the partisan fighting titled *A Manual for the Patriotic
Volunteer*. The author and military strategist's name was Hugh Forbes.

On April 16 from Springfield Brown addressed a letter to Eli Thayer:
"One of the US Hounds is on my track; & I have kept myself hid for a
few days to let my track get cold." He had just left the West Newtown
home of Judge Russell and his wife, where he had been placed by
Theodore Parker after telling Parker of his imminent peril. Parker had
counseled that if he were in a similar position, he would shoot any man
dead who should try to arrest him for any alleged crimes: "Then I
should be tried by a Massachusetts jury and be acquitted." Brown
stayed at the Russell home from April 6 to 15, barricaded in his room
with a supply of ammunition and two well-tended pistols, telling his
hostess, as she related, he would hate to "spoil her carpets." Passing the
time without incident as a blustering storm loomed over the
Massachusetts seacoast, Brown remained in his room composing his
plaintive leave-taking: "Old Browns *Farewell*: to the Plymouth Rocks;

Bunker Hill, Monuments; Charter Oaks; and Uncle Toms Cabbins."
Suffering from his periodic ague and feeling it was too cold for him to
travel, when he'd finished the composition he asked Mrs. Russell if she
might summon Mary Stearns from Medford. When she arrived, Brown
brought the paper down from his room, saying he'd written it to send
to Theodore Parker that he might use it in his next morning's sermon,
and wanted to know what the women thought. In April 1885, Mary
Stearns wrote Sanborn that "the emphasis of his tone and manner I
shall never forget, and wish I could picture him as he sat and read, lift-
ing his eyes to mine now and then to see how it impressed me."26
Delighted with his work, the women thought it should indeed be sent
to Parker, but as for his parishioners, they might not understand its
context. She wrote, further:

> This matter being settled, Brown began talking upon the subject always
> uppermost in his thought, and I may add, action also. Those who remem-
> ber the power of his moral magnetism will understand how surely and
> readily he lifted his listener to the level of his own devotion; so that it sud-
> denly seemed mean and unworthy—not to say wicked—to be living in
> luxury while such a man was struggling for a few thousands to carry out
> his cherished plan. "Oh," said he, "if I could have the money that is *smoked
> away* during a single day in Boston, I could strike a blow which would
> make slavery totter from its foundation." As he said these words, his look
> and manner left no doubt in my mind that he was quite capable of
> accomplishing his purpose.27

When Mary Stearns awoke that Sunday morning radiant sunshine
had replaced the bleak skies of the previous days, a change with which
the birds were heartily in accordance. Shouldn't she and her family be
the ones to aid Captain John Brown to his consummation, she asked
herself? Would it be just to the children if they sold their house? This
was the impetus for her letter to Sanborn in later decades, as the story
began to be told she'd suggested selling their "carriage and teams."
Mary Stearns concluded: "When Mr. Stearns awoke I told him my
morning thoughts. Reflecting a while, he said: 'Perhaps it would not be
just right to the children to do what you suggest; but I will do all I can
in justice to them and you.'"28

When he had breakfasted, George Stearns drove to Judge Russell's
residence and placed a letter authorizing him to draw $7,000 in
Brown's hand. After weeks of unrelenting fund-raising and some dejec-
tion, on April 15 John Brown wrote John Jr.: "My collections I may
safely put down at $13,000. I think I have got matters so much in train

that it will soon reach $30,000. I have had a good deal of discouragement & have often felt quite depressed; but hitherto God hath helped me." The lion behind Brown's apparent success was George Luther Stearns. Answering a query from Frank Preston Stearns, Gerrit Smith, the man next in financial importance in support of Brown, wrote on January 3, 1874: "I frequently gave John Brown money to promote his slave-delivering and other benevolent purposes,—in the aggregate, however, only about a thousand dollars. This would have been none too much to compensate him for the self-sacrificing interest in my colony. His dependence for means to execute his Southern undertaking was, as he informed me, mainly on the good and generous Mr. Stearns of Boston."[29]

Others on the committee contributed some amount to the fund as well, Sanborn contributing a great deal of his time and interest, and Theodore Parker his great moral attention. But no accounts were kept, and the members of "the secret six" generally destroyed their communications to one another after Brown's imprisonment, so that none would be implicated by what had been written.[30]

The Pierce administration, led by Secretary of War Jefferson Davis, along with proslavery leaders in Missouri and in Congress, had tried their hand in the contest for the Kansas Territory and been turned back largely by the scourging violence led by Lane and Brown in the summer of 1856, to be stayed finally in the following year by the predominance of northern emigration. That fall, as these paramount free-state military leaders retired, seeing that his usefulness in Kansas for the *southern cause* had waned, Colonel Henry Titus, too, after being feted at the Planters House in Leavenworth and the Gillis House in Kansas City, began another embarkation, to lead a filibuster army in Nicaragua, where Pierce in the last months of his presidency had recognized William Walker as dictator.[31] The expectation now was that the incoming Buchanan administration, with an older president with diplomatic experience, might straighten out the muddle that Kansas had become.

Throughout the year in 1857 over 100,000 immigrants would move into Kansas. Largely from Ohio and Missouri, this influx sparked an unprecedented rise in land values—lots that had cost $8 in Leavenworth shot up to $2,000—making that former proslavery bastion a free-state harbor. With Leavenworth and other Kansas towns booming, the overland transportation company Russell, Major, and

Waddell now employed 20,000 work cattle and 2,000 wagons, together with teamsters, wagon masters, and blacksmiths, as a macadam road was built from Kansas City Landing to Westport. What remained of the Atchison machine was thoroughly ensconced in the Lecompton legislature, but might easily be turned out in the next election by free-state votes. In its last session, instead of bowing out, the legislature passed a bill for a convention to draft a new constitution, specifying it be sent to Congress without ratification by the voters of Kansas, and that county sheriffs be entrusted with the registration of voters and county commissioners choose the judges of the election, in both instances assuring a proslavery vote. When Governor Geary vetoed this convention bill, the legislature promptly overrode his veto.

With his life threatened, a be-pistoled Geary told Samuel Walker he was going to Washington; once there he learned that it had been decreed that the Atchison machine must control Kansas, and his resignation became effective the day James Buchanan was inaugurated. As Buchanan took his oath of office he stood in the shadow of men who believed the Northwest Ordinance and the Missouri Compromise were void, that the Congress had no power to prohibit slavery in the territories, and that "Cuffee" (the term used by slaveholders in the South to designate an African) should remain in his normal condition. Moments before the new president declared in his inaugural address that the slavery question was to "be speedily and finally settled by the Supreme Court," eighty-year-old chief justice Roger B. Taney, frail and in ill health, was seen to whisper in Buchanan's ear. Hoping a decision on Dred Scott would contribute to dampening the rising tide against slavery, he had used his back-channel influence to assure the court would issue a ruling placing slavery beyond the realm of political debate.

To help govern Kansas, Buchanan would now call upon Robert J. Walker, a man with experience on the southern frontier, but originally, like himself, from Pennsylvania. A trusted entity in the South, Walker had served with Buchanan in the cabinet of the Polk administration as secretary of the treasury, won and lost a fortune in Mississippi, and had been a senator for that state during the nullification crisis. On Kansas's eastern border, too, two new proslavery Democrats had just been elected to the Senate opposed to the Thomas Hart Benton group, so despite the recent turmoil, the situation in the West did not appear dire. But Walker was doubtful he could settle the strife in Kansas and refused to accept the appointment unless the president and the leader in the Senate, Stephen Douglas, assured him that majority rule would prevail. With the promise that Buchanan would back a referendum on the constitution, Walker went out to Kansas. Taney's Dred Scott decision, too, had just set out a sweeping counterattack on the antislavery movement that Buchanan hoped might allay the controversy.

Dred Scott was born a slave in Virginia in 1795. Taken in 1820 to Missouri by his owner, Scott was later purchased by Dr. John Emerson, a U.S. Army surgeon. Emerson took him to Fort Armstrong in Illinois, which was part of the Northwest Ordinance when it became a state in 1819, and therefore an act of Congress had prohibited slavery there. Then in 1836 Emerson moved with his slave to Fort Snelling in the Wisconsin Territory, located in what would become Minnesota, part of the Louisiana Purchase. With the Missouri Compromise in 1820 Congress had likewise prohibited slavery there.

While at Fort Snelling, Scott married Harriet Robinson, a slave acquired by Scott's owner at the fort. In the following year Emerson was transferred to Jefferson Barracks, south of St. Louis, Missouri, leaving his slaves for hire at Fort Snelling, an act effectively in violation of both the Missouri Compromise and the Northwest Ordinance. When he was transferred again, this time to Fort Jesup in Louisiana, Emerson now married, sent for his slaves to serve himself and his new wife. On the way on a steamboat on the Mississippi River as it traversed the waters marking the boundary of two free states, Iowa and Illinois, Harriet gave birth to a girl, Eliza. Under both federal and state law, the child was technically a free person.

By the end of 1838 Emerson was reassigned again, serving in the Seminole War, while his wife and their human property took up residence in St. Louis. When Emerson died in 1843, his wife inherited his estate, leasing the Scotts out as hired labor. When Scott sought to purchase his and his family's freedom, Mrs. Emerson refused. In 1846 with legal advice from abolitionists, Scott sued for his freedom in Missouri Court.

The basis for Scott's suit was that his residence in free territories required his emancipation, and the same applied to his wife and child. Although his supporters expected he would win his suit, it was instead dismissed in June 1847 on grounds that he had failed to provide a witness of his ownership. Granted a new trial, Scott appealed the decision to the Supreme Court of Missouri. With trial delayed till 1850, the Scotts were placed in the custody of the St. Louis County sheriff, who continued to lease out their labor, placing their wages in escrow.

Producing a witness to confirm his ownership, the court ruled in favor of Scott and his family. Unwilling to accept the loss—although she had moved to Massachusetts and transferred title to her brother,

John Sanford—Mrs. Emerson appealed. In November 1852 the trial court's ruling was overturned. The Missouri Supreme Court ruled the Scotts should have brought suit while they were living in a free state; they were now still legally slaves. Giving the reasoning behind the ruling, Chief Justice William Scott declared that "a dark and fell spirit in relation to slavery" now possessed the country, and that "under such circumstances it does not behoove the State of Missouri the least countenance to any measure which might gratify this spirit."[32]

Scott then took his case to federal court, where at trial in 1854 the judge directed the jury to rely on Missouri law to settle the suit. Finding in favor of Sanford, the case was now before the United States Supreme Court for its consideration.

Did Dred Scott have a right to sue? Chief Justice Roger Taney's opinion asked. Was Dred Scott a citizen? Taney responded in a majority opinion that when the Constitution was ratified, Africans "had for more than a century before been regarded as beings of an inferior order, and unfit associates for the white race, either socially or politically, that they had no rights a white man was bound to respect." Having established this, Taney's lengthy opinion went on to argue that Congress did not have the right to prohibit slavery in the territories, as it had with the Missouri Compromise; a ban on slavery was an unconstitutional deprivation of property. "And if Congress itself cannot do this," Taney wrote in a swipe at popular sovereignty, "it could not authorize a territorial government to exercise" such a power.[33]

This "Taney settlement," as Frederick Douglass called it, had come after a long succession of "settlements" also meant to put the slavery question to rest. The nearest in time to it was the Kansas-Nebraska bill which itself had now been seen to have "unsettled all former settlements." Next in the progression had been that posed as the "final settlement," the Compromise of 1850 in which it was conceded slavery and liberty were co-equals. Prior to this the question had been "settled again" with the annexation of Texas and war with Mexico; as only a decade before it had been settled with the gag rule and voting down the right of petition. The earliest of these settlements had been the Missouri Compromise, admitting Missouri with a slave-holding constitution while prohibiting slavery in all territory north of thirty-six degrees north latitude.

This "Taney settlement" maintained that slaves within the purview of the Constitution of the United States were property, that the slaveholder's right was secured wherever the Constitution extended, that Congress had no right to prohibit slavery anywhere, and that persons of African descent were not and could not be citizens of the United States. "The fact is," said Douglass in a speech on the Dred Scott decision before the American Anti-Slavery Society in New York, May 11, 1857:

> The more the question has been settled, the more it has needed settling. The space between the different settlements has been strikingly on the decrease. The first stood longer than any of its successors.
> There is a lesson in these decreasing spaces. The first stood fifteen years—the second, ten years—the third, five years—the fourth stood four years—and the fifth has stood the brief space of two years. . . . You will readily ask me how I am affected by this devilish decision—this judicial incarnation of wolfishness? My answer is, and no thanks to the slaveholding wing of the Supreme Court, my hopes were never brighter than now.[34]

Said Douglass, by the laws of nature and of nature's God this decision could not stand. The very attempt to stamp out the hopes of an enslaved people was but a necessary link in the string of events leading to the complete defeat and overthrown of the whole slave system. The slogan "no union with slaveholders" uttered by abolitionists defied common sense; there was no efficacy to disunion—it was fighting a dead form and not a living reality. In a sharp retort—"I shall follow neither"—Douglass sparred with both Judge Taney and William Lloyd Garrison, for they held the view that the Constitution supported slavery. "To dissolve the Union would be to withdraw the emancipating power from the field," said Douglass. In his speech too he had thrown out there were two remarkable occurrences since the presidential election: "one was the unaccountable sickness traced to the National Hotel at Washington, and the other was the discovery of a plan among the slaves in different localities, to slay their oppressors."[35] These insurrectionary movements had been put down, but they could break out at any time. Then referring to demonstrations in St. Louis against the Taney decision, Douglass saw in them a ray of light cast from the southwest: "Dred Scott, of Missouri, goes into slavery, but St. Louis declares for freedom."

That winter Douglass had gone on record that peaceful annihilation of slavery was now almost hopeless, announcing that henceforth he would stand by the doctrine "that the slave's right to revolt is perfect, and only wants the occurrence of favorable circumstances to become a duty."[36] Other notables embraced this perception as well; Douglass was under the regard of Smith in his antislavery interpretation of the U.S.

Constitution as of the efficacy and necessity of political action; and of John Brown who had swayed each in regard to despairing of slavery's overthrow without resort to violence. As Douglass observed his remarks had became more and more "tinged" by his friend's "strong impressions," so too Smith's conversion to antislavery principles "edged with steel" had come from his association with Brown. Harvey B. Hurd, secretary of the executive committee of the National Kansas Committee and afterward a professor at the Chicago Law School, wrote in a letter to Richard Hinton dated October 1, 1892: "Gerrit Smith had said in the Buffalo Convention "that slavery would never be peacefully abolished, but must be washed out with blood," and he advocated such a course as would bring on open hostilities between the North and the South. It was my opinion at the time that John Brown and Gerrit Smith were in full accord, and Mr. Brown believed that that was the only way to abolish slavery. One of his purposes was to bring on that contest."[37]

In May Brown added to his war-making weaponry, obtaining from the Massachusetts Arms Company of Chicopee Falls at a 50 percent discount for "aiding in your project of protect the free state settlers of Kansas," two hundred revolvers for $1,300. "Now if Rev. T. Parker & other good people of Boston would make up that amount I might at least be well armed," Brown wrote Stearns, who paid the amount himself. In his own conception, and in that of his backers, John Brown was now operating wholly in the public service: a solitary man, he was moving toward the consummation of a design to which he had devoted twenty years of "silent study, observation, and planning."[38] But after the death of their brother, Frederick, and because of their own sufferings in Kansas, particularly that of John Jr., Brown's wife informed him that spring, "The boys have all determined both to practice and learn war no more."[39] Responding from Springfield, Massachusetts, Brown wrote his wife on March 31: "I have only to say as regards the resolution of the boys . . . that it was not at my solicitation that they engaged in it at first & that while I feel no more love of the business than they do, still I think there may be possibly in their day what is more to be dreaded, if such things do not now exist." Yet from Hudson, Ohio, on May 27 he would write, "There is some prospect that Owen will go on with me." Then he remarked concerning his memorial to posterity in the same letter: "If I should never return, it is my particular request that no other monument be used to keep me in remembrance than the same plain one that records the death of my grandfather and son; and that a short story, like those already on it, be told of John Brown the fifth, under that of grandfather. I think I have several good reasons for this. I would be glad that my posterity should not only remember their parentage, but also the cause they labored in."⁴⁰

While Brown would draw no salary, to allay his need and that of his family Gerrit Smith had proposed a subscription be raised to afford additional land and improvements on the house at North Elba that might serve as his retreat "if too hard pressed by his enemies."⁴¹ In a letter dated April 29, 1857, Stearns informed Brown that he and Amos Lawrence had agreed to contribute toward making such an arrangement, $1,000 being proposed to which Stearns contributed one fourth and Lawrence nearly a third, with Wendell Phillips and others making up the balance.⁴² This was intended to pay off Brown's previous agreement with Smith, and for construction expenses payable to William and Henry Thompson who had built the home, with Henry married to Brown's daughter, Ruth. This arrangement, like so many others made during Brown's painstaking canvas in the winter and spring of 1857, was to remain unfulfilled. In a letter dated April 3, 1857, from Boston to William Barnes of Albany, New York, before Stearns was to show his largesse, Brown wrote, "I am prepared to expect nothing but bad faith from the National Kansas Committee at Chicago."⁴³

Smith and Brown would both be in Chicago in July, Brown on his way back to Kansas, and Smith to speak in Illinois and Wisconsin in the wake of Dred Scott. Handing Brown $250 for horses and wagons to carry his sundry supplies and munitions, Smith also accompanied him to the offices of the National Committee, which had not honored his drafts. Harvey B. Hurd noted the meeting in his correspondence decades later with Hinton: "In consequence of the Committee's failure to pay Mr. Brown's drafts on account of the $5000 appropriation, Gerrit Smith came to Chicago to see me. He was very much offended because the Committee did not pay the drafts, but he was told that they had not the means with which to meet them, and there was no other way but to let them be protested."⁴⁴

In September Stearns wrote Martin Conway in Lawrence, Kansas, commenting on the reality then impinging on all their monetary transactions: "Our world in now engrossed with the impending financial crash. If it would snap the South as well as the North I would welcome it, so much do I hate the present state of affairs."⁴⁵

John Brown and his son Owen arrived in Tabor, Iowa, on August 7, 1857. In a letter dated the 13th he deposed Franklin Sanborn in a communication intended for Stearns and the other "stockholders" as well: "I find the arms and ammunition voted me by the Massachusetts State Committee nearly all here, and in middling good order,—some a little rusted. Have overhauled and cleaned up the worst of them, and am now waiting to know what is best to do next, or for a little escort from Kansas, should I and the supplies be needed. I am now at last within a kind of hailing distance of our Free-State friends in Kansas."[46]

When he left New England, in addition to a visit to his wife and younger children in North Elba, Brown's itinerary had included a stop in Cleveland on May 22, Milwaukee on June 16, Chicago on June 22, and a trip back to Tallmadge, Ohio, on June 24.[47] From May 27 to June 12 he was in Hudson, Ohio, in ill health. Hinton wrote that throughout these months John Brown "was kept faithfully advised . . . of the various phases of the Kansas strife. Among the more active of the radical section of the free-state party were several of the young men who afterwards followed him to Iowa, Canada, and Virginia. Kagi, Realf, and Cook especially were active as correspondents for the Eastern and Northern press."[48] Using the alias Nelson Hawkins in his correspondence while traveling under the pseudonym Jonas Jones, he wrote and received communications from Augustus Wattles, James Holmes, W. A. Phillips, Edmund Whitman, and his cousin, the Rev. Samuel Adair, in Kansas. Brown wrote to Wattles from Hudson, June 3: "There are some half-dozen men I want a visit from at Tabor, Iowa, to come off in the most QUIET way."[49] Wattles replied June 18, "We talked over matters here, and concluded to say, come as quietly as possible, or not come at present, as you may please."[50] Whitman, who was the agent of the National Committee in Kansas, sent Richard Realf to Tabor with $150 to cover Brown's expenses, but as Brown had not yet arrived, Realf deducted $40 for his travel expenses and returned to Kansas. Whitman added: "Your friends are desirous of seeing you. The dangers that threatened the Territory and individuals have been removed, in the shape of quashed indictments. Your furniture can be brought and safely stored while you are seeking a location."[51] A letter from Phillips dated June 24 awaited Brown on his arrival:

I fear I shall not be able to meet you at Tabor. I have just received the task of superintending and taking the census for the State election. As means are limited, those who can must do this. . . . Holmes I have seen; he is busy, and will not be able to come up. Several of those you mentioned are gone, and others cannot go to Tabor. I sent a message to Osawatomie, and enclosed your letter to Mr. Adair; told him that Holmes and the others could not go, and urged that some go from Osawatomie if possible. I have not yet heard from him. I start to Osawatomie when I finish this. . . . Two young men from this place have promised me that they will go if possible; but they have no horses, and horses cannot be hired for such a journey. I still hope to have a few friends at Tabor to meet you in a week.[52]

From James Holmes, the following reached Brown dated August 16, 1857: "I do not know what you would have me infer by 'business.' I presume, though, by the word being emphasized, that you refer to the business for which I learn you have a stock of material with you. If you mean this, I think quite strongly of a good (?) opening for this business about the first Monday in October next. If you wish other employments, I presume you will find just as profitable ones."[53]

In the months since he had engaged Forbes, Brown checked through a proxy on his progress translating and printing his *Manual for the Patriotic Volunteer.* On June 1 he was informed, "The colonel says he is getting along well in getting the printing done." On June 16 Forbes was reported "getting along . . . as fast as possible with his book; and will have it ready in about ten days."[54] A few days after Brown's arrival Hugh Forbes was on hand in Tabor. In a letter of August 17 to "Dear Wife and Children," he reported: "We are beginning to take lessons, and have (we think) a very capable teacher."[55] The pupils were of course Brown and his son Owen, there being no others on hand. In the same letter just referenced there is a curious intimation of what was to come, as Brown wrote, "Should no disturbance occur, we may possibly think best to work back eastward; cannot determine yet," even as he was also meditating on a proposed attack on slavery in Missouri.[56]

Brown's later biographers have dealt with the Forbes/Brown relationship as a cursory affair, one in which the two were quickly at odds. This being ultimately the case, it still merits further scrutiny. Hinton wrote: "At Tabor, in all probability, as to their disagreement, John Brown must have given Colonel Forbes his entire confidence, so far as naming to him, as he had done to Frederick Douglass, in 1847, and a few others of his race before and after that date, the place or region in and from which he designed to attack slavery. It is very evident that this was not at all the idea which Hugh Forbes had associated with the expected movement."[57]

Brown initiated an engagement with the drillmaster and tactician, Hinton suggests, because he perceived, after his twelve months' experience of partisan warfare and from his own theorizing, the need for competent men to train and direct the force he projected. He had "a system of his own as to field defenses, drill, and discipline. . . . Such matters would have been at once discussed," Hinton conjectures. "Then all that followed is simple enough. Forbes was familiar with the plans of the European revolutionary organizations and leaders. Among their instrumentalities were plans of street-fighting, guerilla and irregular warfare. . . . This system he embodied in a bulky 'Manual.'"[58] Forbes knew very well too who Brown's backers were, and on his way out to Iowa stopped at Peterboro to confer with Gerrit Smith, soliciting money from him. In Chicago, Forbes had gone to the office of the National Committee, as he had conferred, too, with Horace Greeley and others on the *Tribune* staff before leaving New York. Later in 1858, when Forbes made his disclosures in regard to Brown's plans to the Republican senators Wilson and Seward in Washington, with his demands that Brown be removed as commander of the expedition, it is evident that his difficulties with Brown arose in part from his misapprehension of the American political scene. Hinton wrote:

> He mistook the ferment and sympathetic excitement in favor of Kansas for a deep-seated revolutionary sentiment in favor of freeing the slave by force of arms, if necessary. The arming of Northern emigrants en route to Kansas, he accepted as a counterpart to the probable arming of the negroes, and evidently, as his letters of complaint against John Brown show he regarded the bold antagonism . . . of Republicans to the proslavery Democracy and its actions, an undoubted proof of the drift of the North towards open and armed resistance to the aggressions of the slave-power.[59]

In a letter to Dr. Howe, published in the *New York Herald*, October 27, 1859, Forbes divulged a somewhat peripheral understanding indicating the source of their disagreement. While he argued for the propriety of getting up "slave stampedes," Brown gave his to an elaboration of a plan along lines he would disclose to Douglass in the winter of 1858. Forbes wrote: "No preparatory notice having been given to the slaves (no notice could go or with prudence be given them) the invitation to rise might, unless they were already in a state of agitation, meet with no response, or a feeble one. To this Brown replied that he was sure of a response."[60]

The explanation for Brown's supposed inactivity during this period—when an invasion from Missouri was expected before the Kansas elections on October 5—as Frank Preston Stearns was to write in the biography of his father, "is strongly supported . . . as to Hugh Forbes conception of Brown's plan."[61] And in his testimony before the Mason Committee investigating Harpers Ferry, Senator Seward remarked, "In the course of their conversation as to the plan by which they should more effectually counteract this invasion . . . he (Forbes) suggested the getting up of a stampede of slaves secretly on the borders of Kansas, in Missouri, which Brown disapproved, and on his part suggested an attack upon the border states, with a view to induce slaves to rise and so keep the invaders at home to take care of themselves. He said that in their conversations Brown gave up and abandoned his own project as impracticable."[62]

In a letter dated August 10, Brown had written Stearns urgently as follows: "I am now waiting further advice from Free-state friends in Kansas, with whom I have speedy *private* communication lately started. . . . I am in *immediate* want of from five hundred to one thousand dollars for *secret service* and no questions asked."[63] What this matter referred to has never been ascertained, but in a letter dated October 1, 1857, over a month later, in regards to any disagreement with Forbes, Brown would write Sanborn that he and Forbes were still working together: "While waiting here I and my son have been trying to learn a little of the arts of *peace* from Colonel F., who is still with us. That is the school I alluded to."[64] This was how Frank P. Stearns appraised the matter:

> On September 16 General Lane wrote [Brown] an urgent letter to come to Kansas and assist in the preparations they were making against an expected invasion of the Missourians; but Brown answered in a dilatory manner and did not come until nearly a month later. It is evident that he also intended to act upon it in his own way. Tabor is on the northwest border of Missouri, and would have been a fine strategic position for him. In case of an invasion he could have made a descent into Missouri, and have easily stirred up a slave insurrection while the masters were absent. Brown might have been overpowered by the returning forces of the enemy, but the effect in any case would have been tremendous.[65]

That Buchanan had expected a special pleader and an adroit rationalizer for the Lecompton proslavery legislature from his appointment of Walker, none can deny. But with his assurances from the president and the majority leader, Walker tried to appear even-handed, urging the free-state party to run delegates in the election to the constitutional convention. Any resistance would be met by the United States Army, he cautioned in his inaugural address. The election for the constitutional convention was held on June 15, boycotted by free-state voters who had their own convention on July 15 presided over by Lane. This gathering set elections for officers of a free-state government for August 9. These competing elections were to demonstrate a clear preponderance of support for the free-state settlers, with 2,200 votes cast in the first balloting and 7,200 in the latter. In September Stearns wrote Judge Conway on the propriety of voting or not voting in the pending October legislative election, "I am inclined to think you had better vote rather than divide the party."⁶⁶ But the more radical of the free-state partisans were against it. In the letter to Sanborn already cited above, dated October 1, Brown wrote, "As to the policy of voting on Monday next, I think Lane hit his mark at the Convention of Grasshopper's, if never before; I mean 'An escape into the filthy sluice of a prison.'"⁶⁷

In correspondence dated October 2 the Rev. Adair wrote Brown that his own health and that of his family prevented him from coming to Tabor for a personal interview as he desired; but in his opinion, "An invasion such as we had in '54 and '55 I do not expect; but doubtless many voters from slave states will be smuggled in. . . . What course things will take if the Free-State men fail, I do not know. Some prophesy trouble right along. This would not surprise me were it to occur. But I would deplore a renewal of war. If it is to be commenced again, the boil had better be probed in the centre, at Washington, where the corruption is the worst. The proslavery men in the Territory are but petty tools."⁶⁸

Under these precarious conditions free-state voters would participate in the October election, where there was ballot-box stuffing by Missouri but no invasion. With a preponderance of free-state votes and a new majority set to come into the Lecompton legislature it now seemed the free-state movement might come to power. But the Atchison machine had one last line of defense: that the delegates sitting in the constitutional convention would draft a proslavery constitution and ask Congress's approval without a referendum.

The growing economic activity in all sections of the country after the United States acquired its western territories in the war with Mexico and the discovery of gold in California came to a stuttering standstill as the first global financial crisis debuted in the Panic of 1857. The first cracks in the new prosperity were detected just after the Supreme Court's Dred Scott decision, as the prices of land warrants in Kansas and of western railroad securities declined, signaling the political struggle between slavery and free-soil would now be reprised in western markets.

The basis for the economic boom had been railroads, when, aided by state land grants, government-financed bonds, Wall Street stocks, and foreign investment, particularly British capital, over 20,000 miles of track were laid, a three-fold increase; while between 1850 and 1857 the number of banks doubled, as did the total of notes, loans, and deposits, with reserve funds deposited in New York City branches. As railroads redounded to the benefit of commerce and industry, land speculators sought to capitalize in lucrative real estate markets, just as with continuing emigration from Europe, farming surged in the West, bringing with it, too, speculation. As Russian grain was lost to Europe during the Crimean War, grain prices in the American West rose to $2.19 a bushel. These economic bounties began to reel as a glut in agricultural commodities brought lower prices for farmers, stressing repayment of loans. With European markets opening again to Russian exports, the United States began running a trade imbalance, and gold reserves were drawn out of the country. In the summer of 1857, as banks sought to compensate by raising interest rates, investments in railroads and land, based on speculative credit, became unmanageable.

The crisis came suddenly on August 27 when the Cincinnati-based Ohio Life Insurance and Trust Company, with $5 million in loans to railroad companies, discovered that the manager of its New York branch had embezzled millions. As the company was forced into bankruptcy, New York bankers tightened credit, fearing Ohio Life wouldn't be able to meet its loan obligations. With bankers now demanding immediate payment on matured loans and refusing promissory notes of merchants and industrialists, in mid-September depositors began withdrawing assets, and gold reserves fell by $20 million. In its September 12, 1857, edition *Harper's Weekly* reported, "prominent stocks fell eight or ten per cent in a day, and fortunes were made and lost between ten o' clock in the morning and four of the afternoon." That same day the steamer *Central America*, carrying 30,000 pounds or $1.6 million in gold from the San Francisco Mint, had foundered in a hurricane off the North Carolina coast; a loss, together with over four hundred passengers, that spread panic when it was reported: half of New York City's brokerages, unable to meet specie payments, went bankrupt. In New York, Philadelphia, and Baltimore, banks closed as there was a surge in withdrawals, only to quadruple in the following weeks.

Spreading rapidly on the wings of telegraphed messages, businesses were shuttered, and railroads, particularly east-west lines, were starved for cash. The Great Lakes region, affected most severely, quickly passed the contagion to the East, which was dependent on western sales. With hundreds of thousands of workers thrown out of employment, thousands of investors were ruined. Manhattan and Brooklyn together had an estimated 100,000 unemployed by late October. The Illinois Central, Erie, Pittsburgh, Fort Wayne and Chicago, and Reading Railroads were all forced to cease operation; the Delaware, Lackawanna and Fond du

Lac Railroad companies went bankrupt; the Boston and Worcester Railroad was left straining under its commitments.[69]

In London, as political reaction had settled back on the foundation of the *ancien régime* in Europe after the revolutions of 1848–49, a hard-pressed Karl Marx with his wife and family gave up all hope of a return to the continent, and of a revivification of revolution. Marx's only source of income came from articles he wrote for the *New York Tribune* and for the *New American Cyclopedia*, but his remuneration for his work was worse than a penny a line. The articles for the *Tribune*, appearing for nearly a decade, were on the European scene, mostly on economic issues, which compelled him to occupy seemingly interminably a seat at the British Museum, which had one of the best research libraries extant on political economy, as he sought to further his studies. Heightened by "the new stage of development which this society seemed to have entered with the discovery of gold in California and Australia," his reading induced him "to start again from the very beginning and to work carefully through the new material."[70]

When the panic of 1857 struck, it was to plunge this nearly solitary individual into " the birth of [the] first great political synthesis of [his] thought."[71] These were the notebooks composed between August 1857 and June 1858 called the *Grundrisse*, or *Introduction to the Critique of Political Economy*. When calamity hit, Marx seemed as if he had been crossed by a revenant in the night.[72] On November 13, 1857, he wrote to Engels, who was then working in his family's cotton-spinning factory in Manchester: "The American crisis—which we foresaw, in November 1850 of the review, would break out in New York—is fantastic, even though my financial situation is disastrous; I have never felt so 'cosy' since 1849 than with this outbreak." Then on December 12 he wrote his friend: "I am working like a madman for whole nights in order to coordinate my work on economics, and to get together the *Grundrisse* before the deluge."

Marx's breakthrough was to reveal the essence behind the phenomenon of capitalist market relations: of the social and class genesis of a society dominated by the pursuit of surplus value. His analysis was distinguished by its historical setting but with deep philosophical antecedents, notably in Hegelian philosophy. The notebooks were not available to the decipherment of scholars until well into the twentieth century, but the first distillation and summation of these studies appeared when Marx's *A Contribution to the Critique of Political Economy* was published in 1859. The opportunity afforded by the imminence of crisis, the occasioning of an historical forecast, the polemic against "true socialism," and the critical exploration of the categories of political economy, ensconced Hegel over Marx's revolutionary outlook. On January 14, 1858, Marx wrote to Engels: "For the rest, I am making great progress. For example, I have thrown overboard all the theory of profit that has existed until now. As far as the *method* goes, the fact of having leafed through, once again, by mere accident, Hegel's *Logic* rendered me a great service." For Hegel, however, dialectic development started from abstract being, for Marx it originated from nature—from man as an integral component of nature, as a conscious being capable of self-development. That the work undertaken by Marx with his *Grundrisse*, the *Tribune* articles, and the subsequent *Critique*, are linked is undoubtedly true—it was a practical/critical synthesis that grasped the "revolutionary subjectivity implicated in the crisis."[73] As unemployed workers marched in several American cities demanding "work or bread," and the crisis impacted Europe, South America, South Africa, and the Far East, Marx and others expected renewed strife along predominantly class lines. In New York on November 5, four thousand persons rallied at Tompkins Square to hear speakers whose demands included that the city government establish public works, guarantee a minimum wage, stop landlords from evicting the unemployed, and build housing for the poor. The next day five thousand protesters descended on the Merchants' Exchange demanding loans be given to businesses to rehire workers. An even larger crowd gathered on November 9 at City Hall demanding action.[74] The next day, seeking $20 million in its vaults, unruly protesters on Wall Street threatened to forcibly enter the nearby U.S. Customs House and were dispersed by soldiers and marines.

The southern economy, on the other hand—its crops and the value of slaves, its railroads, and its merchant class—had scarcely been affected by the turmoil. Reflecting on this in the debate in the Senate on the Lecompton Constitution, a leading spokesman for the slaveholders, South Carolina's James Hammond, delivered a clarion call on March 4, 1858:

> Cotton is king. Until lately the Bank of England was king; but she tried to put her screws as usual, the fall before last, upon the cotton crop, and was utterly vanquished. The last power has been conquered. Who can doubt, that has looked at recent events, that cotton is supreme? When the abuse of credit had destroyed credit and annihilated confidence; when thousands of the strongest commercial houses in the world were coming down, and hundreds of millions of dollars of supposed property evaporating in thin air; when you came to a dead lock, and revolutions were

threatened, what brought you up? Fortunately for you it was the commencement of the cotton season, and we have poured in upon you one million six hundred thousand bales of cotton just at the crisis to save you from destruction. That cotton, but for the bursting of your speculative bubbles in the North, which produced the whole of this convulsion, would have brought us $100,000,000. We have sold it for $65,000,000 and saved you. Thirty-five million dollars we, the slaveholders of the South, have put into the charity box for your magnificent financiers, your "cotton lords," your "merchant princes."

In October when another invasion from Missouri had not materialized and elections in Kansas had come off peacefully with an apparent gain for the free-state cause, Brown changed his orientation, quitting his meditations at Tabor. It has never been clear that his relationship with Hugh Forbes had at this point degenerated into the vituperation Forbes displayed in the following year. Indeed Brown accompanied the Garibaldian to Nebraska City, where he would depart for the East by stagecoach on November 3, 1857, their intention still apparently to begin a military school at West Andover, Ohio, in Ashtabula County where Brown's sons John Jr. and Jason lived. On November 5 Brown appeared at the home of E. B. Whitman in Lawrence, where he obtained money, tents, and bedding. In two days he was gone, as Whitman reported to Stearns: "Brown then left, declining to tell me or anyone where he was going or where he could be found, pledging himself, however, that if difficulties should occur he would be on hand and pledging his life to redeem Kansas from slavery. Since then nothing has been heard of him and I know of no one, not even his most intimate friends, who know where he is." But Stearns had his channels, and disposed the best course for Brown and others in a letter dated November 7 as follows: "In my opinion the Free State party should wait for Border-ruffian moves and checkmate them as they are developed. Don't attack them, but if they attack you, 'Give them Jessie' and Fremont besides." Brown's return letter read: "I find matters quite unsettled; but am decidedly of the opinion that there will be no use for the Arms or ammunition here before another Spring. I have them all safe & together unbroken & mean to keep them so until I can see how the matter will be finally terminated. I have many calls upon me for their distribution, but shall do no such thing until I am satisfied they are really needed."[75]

It was at this time the constitutional convention completed its work at Lecompton. That document declared that "the right of property is before and higher than any constitutional sanction, and the right of the owner of a slave to such slave and its increase is the same and as inviolable as the right of the owner of any property whatever."[76] Stipulating that no amendment could be made to the document for seven years, it decreed even after that "no alteration shall be made to affect the rights of property in the ownership of slaves." This constitution would be sent to the Congress with a petition for statehood without a referendum, as Stephen A. Douglas stormed into the presidential office to denounce the "trickery and juggling" of this Lecompton constitution.

It was while he was at Whitman's that Brown again saw John E. Cook, whom he'd met the previous summer. Cook was to relate their meeting in his so-called "confession" given while he awaited trial in jail at Charlestown, Virginia, and which was published in pamphlet soon afterward. Cook said:

> I was then told that he intended to organize a company for the purpose of putting a stop to the aggressions of the proslavery men. I agreed to join him, and was asked if I knew of any other young men, who were perfectly reliable, who I thought would join. I recommended Richard Realf, Luke F. Parsons, and R. J. Hinton. I received a note from Brown the next Sunday morning while at breakfast, in Lawrence, requesting me to come up that day and bring Realf, Parsons, and Hinton with me. Realf and Hinton were not in town. Parsons and myself went and had a long talk with Captain Brown. A few days afterward I received another note which read as follows:
>> Dear Sir,—You will get everything ready to join me at Topeka by Monday night next. Come to Mrs. Sheridan's, two miles south of Topeka, and bring your arms, ammunition, clothing, and other articles you may require. Bring Parsons with you if he can get ready in time. Please keep very quiet about the matter.[77]

Joined by Stevens (Whipple), Charles Moffat, and John Henry Kagi, the company left Topeka for Nebraska City, camping at night on the prairie. "Here for the first time," Cook recounted, "I learned that we were to leave Kansas to attend a military school during the winter in Ashtabula County, Ohio."[78] As the others continued up to the border, Cook, with an eighty-dollar draft from Brown, was sent back to Lawrence with instruction to get Parsons, Realf, and Hinton and take a boat to St. Joseph, Missouri, and then the stage from there to Tabor. Cook found Parson and Realf, but Hinton was still away, and had also just concluded a contract for twelve months' newspaper work.[79] Hinton gives the following account:

I met Realf just as he was leaving, and we talked without reserve, he assuring me that the purpose was just to prepare a fighting nucleus for resisting the enforcement of the Lecompton Constitution, which it was then expected Congress might try to impose upon us. Through this advantage was to be taken of the agitation to prepare for a movement against slavery in Missouri, Arkansas, the Indian Territory, and possibly Louisiana. At Kagi's request (with whom I maintained for nearly two years an important, if irregular correspondence), I began a systematic investigation of the conditions, roads and topography of the Southwest, visiting a good deal of the Indian Territory, with portions of southwest Missouri, west Arkansas, and northern Texas, also, under the guise of examining railroad routes.[80]

All united, they were Stevens, Kagi, C. W. Moffat Parsons, Realf, C. P. Tidd, William Leeman, and Richard Richardson, a fugitive slave from Lexington, Missouri, with John Brown and his son Owen.

Notable among these men was Aaron Stevens, the only trained soldier. He stood six feet two inches with well-proportioned chest and limbs. From Lisbon, Connecticut, he had run away from home in 1847 at age sixteen, enlisting in a Massachusetts volunteer regiment, in which he served during the Mexican War. He later enlisted in the United States Dragoons, rising to the rank of sergeant; his death sentence in May 1855 after being court-martialed for striking an officer was commuted by President Pierce to three years' hard labor at Leavenworth, from which he escaped, leading free-state forces in Kansas. His skill with a saber was remarkable, and he was a good drillmaster for cavalry and irregular warfare. He possessed as well a remarkable baritone voice, and had a fondness for singing. A photograph of him reveals a dark-haired and bearded man, with a large head, and high forehead; a face with good features, with clear sparkling eyes. He was not, however, unlike his commander, of the Christian faith, but a spiritualist, as Hinton described him in his volume, "believing in the immortality of life."

Owen Brown, John Brown's third-born son, was thirty-one at the time. Six feet in height, he had a fair but somewhat freckled complexion, with red hair and heavy whiskers of the same color. He was a spare man, and had deep blue eyes; like his father he was described as a "host" in battle, and like all the men of the family possessed good humor.

John Henry Kagi was of Swiss descent, born in Bristolville, Ohio. He trained as an attorney, although he was largely self-taught. "An agnostic of the most pronounced type," he was described by George Gill as being a "tower of strength for John Brown," who referred to his lieu-tenant as "our Horace Greeley" for his journalistic prowess. Teaching school for a time in the Shenandoah Valley, he came to despise slavery by what he saw of it and was forced to leave Virginia as his opinions became more outspoken. Admitted to the Nebraska bar in 1855, he joined the fighting in Bleeding Kansas, first under Lane, then enlisted under Colonel Whipple. Kagi was an exceptional debater and speaker, and expert stenographer. Gill wrote comparatively of Stevens and Kagi—"Stevens—how gloriously he sang! His was the noblest soul I ever knew. Though owing to his rash, hasty way, I often found occasion to quarrel with him so than with others, and though I liked Kagi better than any man I ever knew, our temperaments being adapted to each other, yet I can truly say that Stevens was the most noble that I ever knew."[81]

Kagi was captured by United States Dragoons after the battle at Hickory Point, together with Colonel Harvey and an hundred or so of his Chicago Irish contingent. Held at Lecompton under the watch of Titus, they all escaped with aid from outside. Assaulted by proslavery Judge Rush Elmore on January 31, 1857, for the tenor of articles he'd written about him, Kagi was struck over the head with a cane and fired at three times; one of the bullets struck Kagi in the chest. But a heavy memo pad he carried in his breast pocket saved him. It took some time for him to recover, but the "house of Elmore," it was reported, ended when Kagi, defending himself, shot the judge in the groin. His articles where published in the *New York Daily Tribune*, the *New York Evening Post*, and the *National Era*.

John E. Cook was from Haddam, Connecticut, of a wealthy family. He too had studied law, in Brooklyn and in New York. He was good-looking, with blond curling hair falling on his shoulders. Five feet seven inches in height, he was an incessant talker; bold, fiery, and quick thinking, he was reputed to be the best pistol shot anyone had seen. He had figured, as had Kagi, Realf, Hinton, and Redpath, as a journalist on Kansas affairs.

Richard Realf was born in East Sussex, England, from an impover-ished working family. He himself worked as a boy to pay for his educa-tion; astonishing "the village clergyman by his precocity," a chronicler writes.[82] Still in his teens he came to the attention of some of the local literati, which included Lady Byron, publishing *Guesses at the Beautiful*. His matron sent him as steward to one of her country estates, where he had a love affair with one of her relatives, causing a rupture with the eminent lady. Afterward he fell into debt and became a wanderer indulging in excesses, and was at last found "barefoot and in rags in the streets of Southampton, singing ballads for the pennies that passersby threw in his hat."[83] Coming to the United States in 1854, he became a Five Points missionary in New York City, assisting in establishing at a low cost a lecture course and self-improvement association. He became a radical abolitionist, and in 1856 he joined an emigrant train going to Kansas. Thoroughly embroiling himself in Kansas affairs, he was as well a journalist and correspondent. A brilliant talker and orator, his lyrics were well circulated and well received. He is still the nineteenth century's unknown poet, yet much loved and highly regarded by John Brown.

Richard Hinton, an important albeit peripheral member of this coterie, was a Scotsman who had been born in London, where he pursued the stone-cutter's trade as a boy. Crossing the Atlantic in 1851, he resided in New York City, learning the printing trade. He joined an emigrant party at Worcester, Massachusetts, arriving in Kansas in August 1856, as has been discussed.

At Tabor these men learned that "Captain Brown's ultimate destination was the state of Virginia."[84] Hinton and Sanborn record that there was heated discussion among them when this was revealed; Realf and Parsons, in particular, were against it. But as they were united together, and apart each had scarce means, all resolved they forge on. Two teams were procured for the transport of the arms and supplies, two hundred Sharps rifles and two hundred revolvers, with other stores consisting of blankets, clothing, boots, and ammunition. On December 8, four days after leaving Tabor, on a cold, snowy night, as prairie wolves howled around them, the troop had a "hot discussion upon the Bible and war . . . warm argument upon the effects of the abolition of slavery upon the Southern States, Northern States, commerce and manufacture, also upon the British provinces and the civilized world; whence came our civilization and origin."[85]

As this company forged through Iowa, in Kansas Governor Walker called a special session of the newly elected legislature with its free-state majority, asking them to pass an act for a plebiscite on the Lecompton constitution. Not able to brook this, Buchanan recalled Walker from office, appointing James W. Denver, his Indian commissioner, as the territory's fifth governor. On the opening day of the legislature, December 7, followed by nine hundred celebrants on foot, horseback, and carriage, Jim Lane marched into Lecompton at the head the Lawrence Cornet Band, as George Deitzler was elected speaker of the house.[86] On December 21, 1857, the vote on the Lecompton constitution was held. With free-state voters refusing to participate, a vote of 6,226 to 569 for the constitution "with slavery" was obtained. Meanwhile the new free-state majority in the legislature set its own referendum for January 4, 1858, where, with proslavery voters abstaining, a vote 138 for the constitution "with slavery" and 24 votes "with no slavery," was obtained, and 10,226 against the constitution altogether. On February 2, 1858, Buchanan sent the Lecompton constitution to Congress with a message recommending Kansas' admission as the sixteenth slave state.

The march across a windswept snowbound prairie was arduous and slow, where the men gathered nightly around camp fires wrapping themselves in blankets, and shielding themselves from the elements in tents. During this passage, "Brown's plan in regard to an incursion into Virginia gradually manifested itself," Realf would recall. "It was a matter of discussion between us as to the possibility of effecting a successful insurrection in the mountains, some arguing that it was, some that it was not; myself thinking, and still thinking, that a mountainous country is a very fine country for an insurrection, in which I am borne out by historic evidence."[87] On Christmas Day the troop passed through Marengo, Iowa, then Iowa City was reached, and finally, a day before New Year's Day, the small Quaker settlement known as the Pedes settlement. Some of the men took lodging at an inn known as Traveler's Rest in West Branch, while others moved into the house of William Maxton at Springdale. The trek had taken them through two hundred and fifty miles of wintry landscape, and indoor quarters were a relief. The Quakers were friendly to the man known as "Osawatomie Brown"—to a point. "Thou art welcome to tarry among us," an elder said, "but we have no use for thy guns." Brown's intention now was to sell the teams and wagons for rail passage through to Ohio, from a nearby railhead. But the financial panic was in full swing in the West and the money could not be raised. Then it was decided the men would winter in Iowa while Brown went east to develop his agencies.

A makeshift military academy would be established to occupy the men under the superintendence of Stevens. All would rise at five for breakfast, commence studies till ten, then drill from ten to twelve. In the afternoon there was physical training, with gymnastics and target shooting. On the evenings of two weekdays, Tuesday and Friday, a mock legislature was held, at one of the homes or in a nearby schoolhouse, where the oratory of Realf, Kagi, Cook, and others was heard, with the townspeople participating, and on other evenings informal discussions were held. "There was no attempt to make a secret of their drilling," Hinton wrote. "The neighborhood folks all understood that this band of earnest young men were preparing for something far out of the ordinary. Of course Kansas was presumed to be the objective point. But generally the impression prevailed that when the party moved again, it would be somewhere in the direction of the slave states. The atmosphere of those days was charged with disturbance."[88]

Before departing for the East, Brown sat up with his host, the father of George Gill, a doctor in Springdale. Dr. Henry C. Gill reported:

> He informed me that he wished to have some private talk with me; we went into the parlor. He then told me his plans for the future. He had not then decided to attack the armory at Harper's Ferry, but intended to take some fifty to one hundred men into the hills near the Ferry and remain there until he could get together quite a number of slaves, and then take what conveyances were needed to transport the Negroes and their families to Canada. And in a short time after the excitement had abated, to make a strike in some other Southern state; and to continue on making raids, as opportunity offered, until slavery ceased to exist. I did my best to convince him that the probabilities were that all would be killed. He said that as for himself, he was willing to give his life for the slaves. He told me repeatedly, while talking, that he believed he was an instrument in the hands of God through which slavery would be abolished. I said to him: "You and your handful of men cannot cope with the whole South." His reply was: "I tell you, Doctor, it will be the beginning of the end of slavery."[89]

George Gill was to join the company here, as would Stewart Taylor, a Canadian friend of his who was then in Springdale. Two other recruits were also to come from the town, two Quaker brothers, Barclay and Edwin Coppoc. Another of Brown's troop from Montour, Iowa, was Charles Moffat. He would observe the broader framework of Brown's design: "When Brown left he gave Whipple charge of the school, and I had sent Forbes round by water to Ohio. Forbes had been engaged as drill-master at a hundred dollars a month, and when we stopped in Iowa Brown said he would give Forbes the choice of schools: if Forbes would come back to Iowa, Whipple would take the school in Ohio or in Canada. But when he got to Ohio, Brown found that Forbes had gone away, and so gave up the Ohio school."[90]

In Washington Charles Sumner, who had retained his Senate seat for Massachusetts despite his severe debility following his beating by Preston Brooks, and not yet returned full-time to the Senate, found two letters in his mail from Colonel Hugh Forbes. He had been grossly defrauded by John Brown who had engaged him for Kansas work,

Forbes wrote, and now he was destitute and his family suffering privation in Paris; the letter also named well-placed persons in Boston.
Sumner forwarded these letters to Sanborn, who was among those
named. Sanborn himself had received a letter intimating that Forbes,
unless properly compensated, intended to disclose a plan Brown evidently was maturing but that Sanborn knew nothing about. Sanborn
replied: "You are at liberty to speak, write or publish what you please
about me, only be careful to keep within the limits of your knowledge."
Sending the plaintiff $10 for his trouble, Sanborn concluded, "I can
excuse much to one who has so much reason for anxiety as you have in
the distress of your family." Forbes had also been in Rochester to see
Frederick Douglass, who wrote in his autobiography: "I was not favorably impressed with Colonel Forbes, but I 'conquered my prejudice,'
took him to a hotel and paid his board while he remained. Just before
leaving, he spoke of his family in Europe as in destitute circumstances,
and of his desire to send them some money. I gave him a little . . . and
through Miss Assing, a German lady, deeply interested in the John
Brown scheme, he was introduced to several of my German friends in
New York."[91]

These disclosures had come over the Christmas week of 1857. Brown
left Springdale, Iowa, on January 15, 1858. Those in Boston who had
done so much to outfit and arm him for the support of a free Kansas
were perplexed by his movements. What did they portend?

American Mysteries

When John Brown left Springdale, Iowa, and headed east on January 15, 1858, he had been contemplating his purpose of "carrying the war into Africa," as he phrased it, for twenty years. His first great stride in bringing his plan to fruition had perhaps been his confidences in 1847 with Jermain Loguen, Henry Highland Garnet, and Frederick Douglass, and in 1848 with his porter in Springfield, Massachusetts, Thomas Thomas. The only extended intimation of this early plan is found in *The Life and Times of Frederick Douglass*, when it was committed to pen and paper thirty years after it was laid out in private conversation. No one has maintained that Brown's oft-expressed belief that he was an instrument in the hands of God to destroy slavery in America was solely the product of rational thought, but the way he fitted himself to become this instrument was fully coherent. John Brown, as Sanborn remarked, "knew what he wanted to do," and now he'd set a timetable of sixty days in which to bring it off.

There is reason to suppose that the months of his sojourn at Tabor, Iowa—from August 7 to the beginning of November—had been an important period of meditation and study, and of preparation for him. It has been pointed out that there was a noticeable concurrence between the methods commended by Hugh Forbes in his book, which Brown had been reading and discussing with him, and those applied by him in his description at this time of his own project, and when juxtaposed to that rendered in Douglass's autobiography the similarity is striking. Forbes had written at paragraph thirty of the Manual: "A single band, whether large or small, would have but a poor chance of success—it would be speedily surrounded; but a multiplicity of little bands, some three to ten miles distant from each other, yet in connection and communication, cannot be surrounded, especially in a chain of well wooded mountains, such as the Apennines."[1] (The complete title of Forbes's book is: *Manual for the Patriotic Volunteer on Active Service in Regular and Irregular War, being the Art and Science of obtaining and maintaining Liberty and Independence.*) And to complement his military strategizing Brown would now write a *Provisional Constitution and Ordinances for the People of the United States*, which would be adopted at the Chatham Convention in Ontario on May 10, 1858. This document received its first notice again in Douglass's autobiography, where he writes Brown spent much of his three weeks as a guest in his home in February 1858 in "writing and revising" it. But that composition too—a substantial compendium requiring many months of thought— undoubtedly was begun at Tabor. Passing through Chicago, Brown met with Harvey B. Hurd of the National Kansas Committee, which was then wrapping up its affairs. Hurd wrote in his letter to Hinton dated October 1, 1892: "I saw [Brown] while he was then in Chicago, at that time, and talked with him to some extent about his operations in Kansas and his future purposes. He had a paper about which he wished to consult me, some parts of which he read to me. I afterwards found that it was a draft of the constitution which he intended to have adopted if it became necessary to form a government, as the result of his prospective operations in Virginia."[2]

At the beginning of February John Brown knocked at the door of Frederick Douglass in Rochester. Traveling incognito—he now had adopted the disguise of a long beard giving him a patriarchal appearance, and there is no suggestion Brown had written previous to his arrival—he announced he was in need of lodging for several weeks, but would not stay, he said, unless allowed to pay board. "Knowing that he was no trifler and meant all he said, and desirous of retaining him under my roof, " Douglass wrote, "I charged three dollars a week."[3]

In the Douglass home Brown was to be a model guest, occupied most of the time in his room, writing letters and putting the finishing touches on his "constitution." He wrote to Franklin Sanborn and George Luther Stearns, to Thomas Wentworth Higginson, Theodore Parker, and Samuel Howe, and to Gerrit Smith. Respondents were to direct posts to "N. Hawkins" care of his host, or put a sealed letter inside another addressed to Frederick Douglass. Remittances were to be made out to Douglass, while Charles, Douglass' youngest son, was engaged in carrying outbound and picking up inbound mail. Correspondence was in regard to an undisclosed plan Brown wanted to discuss with his addressees; to obtain from them further cooperation and commitment as he had obtained from them in the previous year, and requesting their attendance at a meeting at Smith's estate in Peterboro. But "his object was not simply to further his campaign for funds," DuBois writes, "but more especially definitely to organize the Negroes for his work. . . . [He] particularly had in mind the Negroes of New York and Philadelphia, and those in Canada."[4] The scholars among his communicants were the black leaders Henry Highland Garnet and James N. Gloucester in New York; John Jones and Henry O. Wagoner in Chicago, and J. W. Loguen of Syracuse; with his address book noting Downing of Rhode Island, Delany of Chatham, Ontario, William Still of Philadelphia, and James McCune Smith of New York, as well as others. Undoubtedly giving each something of the general tenor of his intent, he was requesting of his addressees they meet at an early date in March for consultation on his project.

To Theodore Parker, Brown wrote on February 2: "I am again out of Kansas, and am at this time concealing my whereabouts. . . . I have nearly perfected arrangements for carrying out an important measure in which the world has a deep interest, as well as Kansas; and only lack from five to eight hundred dollars to enable me to do so."[5] On the same day he addressed Thomas Wentworth Higginson about money for "secret service": "Can you be induced to operate at Worcester, & elsewhere during that time to raise from *Antislavery men & women*, (or any other parties) some part of that amount?"[6] Sanborn sent a query to Higginson on February 11: "I have received two letters from J. B. in which he speaks of a plan but does not say what it is. Still I have confidence enough in him to trust him with the moderate sum he asks for—if I had it."[7] On the 8th Higginson responded to "N. Hawkins": "I am always ready to invest money in treason, but at present have none to invest. As for my friends, those who are able are not quite willing, and those who are willing are at present bankrupt."[8] To Higginson, Brown then offered this tantalizing hint: "I have just read your kind letter of the 8th instant, & will now say that Rail Road business on a somewhat extended scale, is the identical object for which I am trying to get means. . . . I have been operating to some purpose the past season: but now have a measure on foot that I feel *sure* would awaken in you something more than a common interest; if you could understand it." To further this understanding Brown informed Higginson he'd written his "friends G. L. Stearns, & F. B. Sanborn," requesting they meet him "for consultation at Gerrit Smiths, Peterboro," adding, "I am very anxious to have you come along; certain as I feel; that you will never regret having been one of the council."[9]

After only a few days in Douglass's household Brown addressed the following remark in a letter to John Jr. at West Andover, Ohio, dated February 4: "He [Douglass] has promised me $50, and what I value vastly more he seems to appreciate my theories & my labours."[10] James Gloucester offered this endorsement of the project on February 18: "I wish you Godspeed in your glorious work," but in a letter on the next day cautioned Brown about being overly sanguine: "You speak of the people. I fear there is little to be done in the masses. The masses suffer for want of intelligence and it is difficult to reach them in a matter like you propose as far as it is necessary to secure their cooperation. The colored people are impulsive, but they need sagacity, sagacity to distinguish the proper course. They are like a bark at sea without a commander or rudder."[11]

Before he was to leave Rochester it was determined that a meeting between the black leaders contacted, including Frederick Douglass and Brown, would convene in Philadelphia on March 5 at the home of Stephen Smith. In the meanwhile the interest and imagination of all the correspondents had been aroused. Edwin Morton, a classmate of Sanborn's who was then employed at the Smith estate as tutor of his son, had written February 7 to his associate about what he'd gathered from Brown's suggestive messages: "This is news,—he 'expects to overthrow slavery' in a large part of the country." In short, Brown's plan called for an incursion to be made into Virginia in the mountainous region of the Blue Ridge, a country admirably adaptable and situated to carrying on guerilla warfare. The men he would bring with him were to act as officers of the different bands that would be formed; these bands were to act separately or in a concerted way starting on a line of twenty-five miles under John Brown's general command. The first movement would have the appearance of a slave stampede, or at most a local outbreak. The planters would give pursuit to their fleeing chattels and be defeated; as the militia was called out, they would also be defeated. Gaining a gradually increasing magnitude, the campaign would "strike terror into the heart of the slave States by the amount of organization it would exhibit, and the strength it gathered."[12] The slaves would be armed with weapons they could most effectively use— pikes, scythes, muskets, and shot-guns. They would procure provisions by forage and by impressing the property of slaveholders, including arms, horses and wagons, and ammunition. As regards the aforementioned constitution, Douglass wrote, "He said that, to avoid anarchy and confusion, there should be a regularly constituted government, which each man who came with him should be sworn to honor and support."[13]

Douglass also related:

> Soon after his coming to me, he asked me to get for him two smoothly planed boards, upon which he could illustrate with a pair of dividers, by a drawing, the plan of fortification which he meant to adopt in the mountains.
>
> These forts were to be so arranged as to connect one with the other, by secret passages, so that if one was carried another could easily be fallen back upon, and be the means of dealing death to the enemy at the very moment when he might think himself victorious.[14]

Douglass concludes, no doubt signaling an ambivalence he felt, that his children were more interested in these drawings than he was. "Once in a while," he added, "he would say he could, with a few resolute men, capture Harper's Ferry, and supply himself with arms belonging to the government at that place, but he never announced his intention to do so."[15]

That a successful incursion could be made and that it could be maintained, Brown held to be a certainty. One of his followers, Richard Realf, was to remark his commander believed "that the several slave States could be forced (from the position in which they found themselves) to recognize the freedom of those who had been slaves within the respective limits of those States."[16]

On February 20 in a letter addressed to John Jr., his father wrote, "I am here with our good friends Gerrit Smith and wife, who, I am most happy to tell you, are ready to go in for a share in the whole trade."[17] With none of his Massachusetts friends able to make the journey to Smith's estate, Sanborn was delegated to go as their representative, arriving on the evening of February 22. Sanborn related:

> After dinner, and after a few minutes spent with our guests in the parlor, I went with Mr. Smith, John Brown, and my classmate Morton, to the room of Mr. Morton in the third story. Here, in the long winter evening

which followed, the whole outline of Brown's campaign in Virginia was laid before our little council, to the astonishment and almost the dismay of those present. The constitution which he had drawn for the government of his men, and of such territory as they might occupy, was exhibited and explained, the proposed movements of his men indicated, and the middle of May was named as the time of the attack.[18]

Brown laid before them also his methods of organization in detail and fortification; of settlement on the conquered lands if possible, and retreat through the North if advisable; and the way such a campaign would be received in the country at large.[19] All he was asking was they raise collectively $800, and would think it bountiful if he collected a thousand.

"We listened until after midnight," Sanborn wrote of that evening, "proposing objections and raising difficulties; but nothing could shake the purpose of the old Puritan. Every difficulty had been foreseen and provided against in some manner; the grand difficulty of all,—the manifest hopelessness of undertaking anything so vast with such slender means,—was met with the text of Scripture: 'If God be for us, who can be against us?'"[20]

On the 23rd the discussion was continued, with Brown's meticulously wrought reasoning prevailing over all doubts. At the end of the day as Brown was left by the fire discussing points of theology with Charles Stewart, an old officer under Wellington who happened to be visiting the estate, Smith and Sanborn walked for an hour in the snow-covered woods. Restating Brown's propositions which he fully understood, finally Smith said, "You see how it is; our dear old friend has made up his mind to this course, and cannot be turned from it. We cannot give him up to die alone; we must support him. I will raise ($500) for him; you must lay the case before your friends in Massachusetts and perhaps they will do the same."[21]

Sanborn returned to Boston on the 25th and on the same day communicated the enterprise to Theodore Parker and Wentworth Higginson. The day before Edwin Morton had confided to Brown that his classmate had told him he felt tempted to make "common cause" with him. While still at Smith's Brown wrote to Sanborn, "I greatly rejoice at this; for I believe when you come to look at the ample field I labor in, and the rich harvest which not only this entire country but the whole world during the present and future generations may reap from its successful cultivation, you will feel that you are out of your element until you find you are in it, an entire unit."[22] In after years he was never able to read this letter without emotion, Sanborn would write. While most of Brown's letters to his coterie of supporters did not survive the aftermath of Harpers Ferry, when most were destroyed to prevent incriminating evidence from falling into the hands of Virginia prosecutors or federal marshals, this letter did. Sanborn had given it to Theodore Parker, who would die in 1860 in Florence, Italy, of tuberculosis, and Sanborn was able to retrieve it from Parker's papers two years later.

When Brown left Peterboro in late February he did so in order to confer with his friends among the black leaders in Brooklyn and New York. After arriving at the home of Rev. James Gloucester and his wife on Bridge Street in the Bedford-Stuyvesant neighborhood of Brooklyn, he received the following note from Douglass, dated February 27, 1858: "My Dear Friend,—When we parted, we were to meet in Philadelphia on Friday, March 5. I write now to postpone going to Philadelphia until Wednesday, March 10. Please write me at Rochester if this will do, and if you wish me to come at that time. You can, I hope, find work enough in and about New York up to that date. Please make my warmest regards to Mrs. and Mr. Gloucester, and accept that and more for yourself."[23]

James Newton Gloucester had been a founding member of the Siloam Presbyterian Church in Brooklyn in 1848, a noted station on the Underground Railroad, and at which he was then pastor. Both having come to Brooklyn from Richmond, Virginia, Gloucester and his wife, Elizabeth, had acquired some property, and she operated a furniture store. Brown entered their home at their invitation, and theirs was a decade-long relationship. Despite having been cautioned by his friend about his expectation of finding recruits among the city's young black men, Brown's zeal was not dimmed, as he wrote his wife in a letter dated March 2: "I find a much more earnest feeling among the colored people than ever before; but that is by no means unusual. On the whole, the language of Providence to me would certainly seem to say, 'Try on.'"[24] Among those Brown would have met with at this time, most significantly would have been Henry Highland Garnet, who in 1856 had become the pastor of the Shiloh Presbyterian Church in New York City, following the death of its former divine and his close friend the Rev. Theodore Wright. In 1850 Garnet went abroad, traveling on the Continent in Europe with his wife and family, then to England where they remained for several years. Becoming a sought-after lecturer among the antislavery societies in England and Scotland, he joined the Free Labor Movement and became active in the West India Committee, both organizations rejecting the use of the products of slave labor. In

1851 he was the official American delegate to the World Anti-Slavery Convention held in London, where he gave an address. In 1852 Garnet was sent to Jamaica as a missionary for the United Presbyterian Church of Scotland, presiding in a church near Kingston. Lecturing on the American scene, he gave talks that probed the origins and implications of the Fugitive Slave Act, which was designed, in his view, to assure that markets in Europe, and particularly in England, be maintained as an outlet for the products of the southern American economy. Contracting a fever that lingered for many months, Garnet returned to the United States in 1855, to Boston, where he proposed to become a "missionary for liberty," but when the pulpit in New York became available, he went hither. Contacted by John Brown in February 1858 about his help in "forming societies" to aid in the recruitment of blacks for his Virginia campaign, it was on Garnet's initiative that the Philadelphia meeting had been arranged, attesting to Brown's long-standing reputation among a select but important group of black leaders. John Brown, Garnet had said, was "the only white man who really understands slavery."[25]

While in Brooklyn, Brown received an invitation from Theodore Parker to visit Boston, and he did so, arriving on March 4, having been reluctant to travel there previously as it required passing through Springfield. Taking lodging through March 8 at the America House, he remained for the most part in his room, where the entire Massachusetts circle came to see him, and held long conferences where Brown disclosed his Virginia plan. Parker was reportedly deeply interested, but not very sanguine about its success; he wished to see it tried, however, believing it would do good even if it failed. Dr. Howe was reported as accepting "the idea with earnestness; within the lines to be worked upon, he saw real military possibilities." George Stearns was reported accepting it "with an utterly loyal belief in the old covenanter."[26] Holding the same view, Higginson believed that "with decent temporary success, [it] would do more than anything else to explode our present political platforms."[27] Sanborn, who nearly decided to take a personal stake in the project, was strongly enthusiastic.

As Douglass had, Sanborn related he thought it was probable Brown had not at that time definitively resolved on the seizure of Harpers Ferry; "yet," he wrote, "he spoke of it to me beside his coal-fire in the America House, putting it as a question, rather, without expressing his own purpose."[28]

Unlike the year before, Brown did not think it prudent to appear at Parker's Sunday evening reception held on March 7, but took time that day to write the preacher asking him to help with an important assignment:

> I want you to undertake to provide a substitute for an address you saw last season, directed to the officers and soldiers of the United States Army. The ideas contained in that address I of course like, for I furnished the skeleton. . . . In the first place it must be short, or it will not be generally read. It must be in the simplest or plainest language, without the least affectation of the scholar about it, and yet be worded with great clearness and power. The anonymous writer must (in the language of the Paddy) be "afther others," and not "afther himself at all, at all." If the spirit that communicated Franklin's Poor Richard (or some other good spirit) would dictate, I think it would be quite as well employed as the "dear sister spirits" have been for some years past. The address should be appropriate, and particularly adapted to the peculiar circumstances we anticipate, and should look to the actual change of service from that of Satan to the service of God. It should be, in short, a most earnest and powerful appeal to men's sense of right and to their feelings of humanity. Soldiers are men, and no man can certainly calculate the value and importance of getting a single "nail into old Captain Kidd's chest." It should be provided beforehand, and be ready in advance to distribute by all persons, male and female, who may be disposed to favor the right.[29]

Brown possessed among his qualities a refinement, even a literary subtlety as his writing often showed. A man of literary merit himself, Higginson wrote of Brown (with whom he had been in close contact that March) that he was "a man whom Sir Walter Scott might have drawn but whom such writers as Nicolay and Hay have utterly failed to delineate." While in Boston, as possibly his only excursion, Brown visited Charles Sumner in his home, accompanied by Reverend James Freeman Clarke and James Redpath, who narrated its incidents in his book on Brown in 1860. With Sumner lying on his bed recuperating from his wounds of nearly two years, after some conversation Brown asked, "Do you have the coat you were wearing when you were attacked by Brooks?" Sumner replied, "Yes, it is in the closet. Do you want to see it?" Redpath wrote: "I recall the scene vividly, Sumner standing slightly bent, supporting himself by keeping his hand on the bed, Brown, erect as a pillar, holding up the blood-besmirched coat in his right hand and examining it intently. The old man said nothing, I believe, but I remember that his lips compressed, and his eyes shone like polished steel."[30]

On March 6 Brown had written his eldest son: "My call has met with a most hearty response so that I feel assured of at least tolerable success." Again with the major contribution coming from Stearns, with lesser amounts coming from the others, Brown had been certain of an additional $500—enough, he'd calculated, for a tolerable beginning. "Hawkins goes to prepare agencies for his business," Sanborn reported, which all would now euphemistically allude to as "a speculation in wool."[31]

On March 10 Brown and his oldest son arrived in Philadelphia at the home of Stephen Smith on Lombard Street, making Smith's well-appointed domicile their headquarters during their stay in that city. DuBois remarks, "Brown seems to have stayed nearly a week . . . and probably had long conferences with all the chief Philadelphia Negro leaders."[32] These would have included Smith, William Still, Henry Highland Garnet, Frederick Douglass, as well as the two Browns, and others who are unnamed. J. W. Loguen, who was intending to travel with Brown from New York, reported ill, and James Gloucester was detained by other business, but sent a letter expressing his regret at not attending and pledging "$25 more" toward the fund-raising.[33] Brown of course continued his appeal for funds with these men, but his paramount purpose was that of procuring men, and facilitating their recruitment through organization. Those gathered on Lombard Street were all eminently qualified to give their influence toward this, and none were likely to have agreed to being summoned out of mere deferential regard for John Brown.

Stephen Smith, at whose home the conference took place, was the owner, together with his associate William Whipper, of Smith, Whipper & Co., a lumber and coal concern in Columbia, Pennsylvania. Born near Harrisburg, circa 1795 to a slave woman, Smith became indentured to a lumber mill merchant, who allowed him, as he grew into manhood, to manage his entire concern. In 1816 Smith borrowed $50 to gain release from his indenture and to purchase his freedom. Operating his lumber business, and becoming involved in real estate operations, he became wealthy, but raised the ire of his white competitors who thought a black in the business lowered the value of transactions. Moving to Philadelphia, his wife, Harriet, ran an oyster and refreshment house, as Smith became agent of the *Freedom's Journal*, delegate of the Colored Convention in 1830 and those held thereafter, and founding member of the Pennsylvania Anti-Slavery Society. He was as well an associate of Robert Purvis, buying his house on Lombard Street, and enduring with him the "anti-black" riots at the hands of the Irish in abutting neighborhoods in 1844.

At this time William Still was chairman of the Vigilance Committee of the Pennsylvania Anti-Slavery Society, and perhaps, along with

Douglass, is the most recognizable of these men today. His parents were both escaped slaves from Maryland's Eastern Shore, coming to New Jersey at the turn of the century. Still was the youngest of their fourteen children. Moving from New Jersey to Philadelphia in 1844, Still began working as a clerk for the Pennsylvania Anti-Slavery Society in 1847. After the Vigilance Committee was organized he was credited with helping as many as eight hundred escaping slaves, an average of sixty a month during the operation of the committee. Interviewing each fugitive he aided, and keeping detailed records, including a brief biography and destination of each, he self-published his chronicles as *The Underground Railroad Records* in 1872. Still had detailed knowledge of agents operating in the South, particularly in Delaware, Maryland, and Virginia, and in the counties of southern Pennsylvania; his network including agents in New Jersey, New York, New England, and Canada, as well—all information valuable to John Brown.

While only drawing cursory attention, these meetings need be brought more fully within Brown's activity of the first five months in 1858. Certainly no records were taken of these sessions, but there is nonetheless evidence that they took place. In a letter sent from Rochester dated February 4, Brown wrote his eldest son: "I have been thinking that I would like to have you make a trip to Bedford, Chambersburg, Gettysburg, and Uniontown, in Pennsylvania, traveling slowly along, and inquiring of every man on the way, or every family of the right stripe, and getting acquainted with them as much as you could. When you look at the location of those places you will readily perceive the advantage of getting up some acquaintance in those parts."[34]

The suggestion being to find out the Underground Railroad routes and stations, wrote Richard Hinton, and "to ascertain the persons who were actually to be relied upon, places to stop, means of conveyance, and especially to learn of the colored who could be trusted. The Philadelphia conference must have gone over this ground with the two Browns."[35] It can be supposed that Still supplied detailed knowledge of the operations in his preview, and given the timely notice he gave to William Parker and his associates in 1851 at Christiana, this is likely the kind of cooperation Brown was seeking. He had slated his operations to begin that May, and so the entire region would be on alert. Brown's primary concern however was to bring together these forces into larger cooperation, as implied in his *Provisional Constitution and Ordinances*. This required, he deemed, a legitimating convention, and for this Brown wanted to bring together black men like those to be found in Philadelphia, New York, and elsewhere throughout the North, and those in Canada, together with those men he had left in Iowa in January. That he sketched out the rudiments of his campaign is undoubtedly the case, but he would only have done so as it induced their further cooperation.

There is reason to suppose that William Still, and perhaps others, had reservations along the line that Gloucester suggested: that the "masses" were not sufficiently prepared, nor did their condition in America permit them the bold response to their oppression Brown was proposing. But of even greater concern, it would throw an unwelcome light on ongoing operations and bring a strong reaction against them. It would not be prudent to draw men to such proceedings, not in New York nor in Philadelphia, let alone in any other northern state. The thing to do was to remove it from under the jurisdiction of United States law and of America's withering prohibition on "color;" he must go to Canada, there he would find his likely coadjutors. He must see Dr. Martin Delany, it was suggested, about getting his meeting.

Delany had moved to Chatham, Ontario, together with his family in February 1856, as Harriet Tubman, too, was living in St. Catharines, Ontario, just then; these two would have been mentioned along with others. Tubman was well known to William Still; by 1858 she had made more than a dozen of her trips to Maryland's Eastern Shore, the site of most of her rescue missions, and had collaborated with him, and with Thomas Garnett, the station master at Wilmington, Delaware—an association well documented by correspondence in Still's *Underground Railroad Record*. Although she did not yet have the fame she would achieve by 1860, she was recognized in the Maryland and Delaware, Pennsylvania and New York routes, but had not yet been to Boston and was unknown in the West. She was however known to John Brown and he was eager to meet her. Brown had intended to visit Canada from the first anyway, but now that journey was doubly necessary.

Brown's opinion about acceding to the proscriptions placed upon blacks in the United States, and the reluctance on the part of black leaders in the northern states to overtly challenge them, would be bluntly expressed to Martin Delany when they met in April 1858. In Brown's view—respect was only won by compelling it; a blow for freedom was always a victory.[36]

After leaving Philadelphia, Brown was again in New York City, then in New Haven, hunting up possible donors. From New Haven he sent notice to Syracuse to Loguen, who would accompany him to Canada: "I expect to be on the way by the 28th or 30th inst." He now took the time to take leave of his wife and family in North Elba. Previously that spring he had written his daughter Ruth: "The anxiety I feel to see my wife and children once more I am unable to describe. I want exceedingly to see my big baby Ruth's baby, and to see how that little company of sheep look about this time. The cries of my poor sorrow-stricken, despairing children, whose 'tears on their cheeks' are ever in my eyes, and whose sighs are ever in my ears, may however prevent my enjoying the happiness I so much desire. But, courage, courage, courage!—the great work of my life (the unseen hand that 'guided me, and who had indeed holden my right hand, may hold it still,' though I have not known Him at all as I ought) I may yet see accomplished (God helping), and be permitted to return, and 'rest at evening.'"[37]

O n April 2, 1858, John Brown arrived at Gerrit Smith's estate at Peterboro, joined there by his eldest son. John Jr. would remark that he, Smith and his wife, and his father joined together in a thorough-going colloquy on the Virginia campaign, in which the philanthropist was not only fully conversant but an enthusiast. Before he left, Smith gave Brown a draft for $25 to give to Harriet Tubman, whom he commended. On the next day father and son traveled to Rochester, staying at the home of Frederick Douglass. As soon as J. W. Loguen came on, Brown and his friend crossed over to the province of Ontario, or Canada West as it was called. Their first stop, Hamilton, was where William Howard Day, a black printer, then resided. Day was an 1847 graduate of Oberlin College who moved to Canada in 1857; it was he who would arrange Brown's meeting with Tubman. "Among the slaves she is better known than the Bible, for she circulates more freely," Loguen remarked of her to Higginson, reported by him in the *Liberator* on May 28, 1858.[38]

When John Brown and Harriet Tubman were introduced at her home in nearby St. Catharines, he said: "The first I see is General Tubman, the second is General Tubman and the third is General Tubman."[39] He seems to have stayed three or four days a guest in her home, when she became completely conversant with his plans, and would subsequently do, as Sanborn wrote, "what she could in her wild sibylline way to further them."[40] Brown would give Tubman $15 out of his own purse to defray traveling expenses on his behalf and would later hand her a $25 gold piece, once he had exchanged Smith's draft. On April 8 he wrote of his Canadian sojourn thus far to John Jr., now back in West Andover; so impressed had he been, he felt compelled to masculinize the woman: "I came on here direct with J. W. Loguen the day after you left Rochester. I am succeeding, to all appearance, beyond my expectations. Harriet Tubman hooked on his whole team at once. He is the most of a man, naturally, that I ever met with. There is the most abundant material, and of the right quality, in this quarter, beyond all doubt."[41] Brown then returned to business first broached with his son that February: "Do not forget to write Mr. Case (near Rochester) at once about hunting up every person and family of the reliable kind about, at, or near Bedford, Chambersburg, Gettysburg, and Carlisle, in Pennsylvania, and also Hagerstown and vicinity, Maryland, and Harper's Ferry, Va. The names and residences of all, I want to have sent me at Lindenville."[42]

As Brown continued on his rounds, there is no further indication of Loguen's disposition; perhaps after giving Brown a sufficient start he returned to the States and to other business. On April 8 Brown left his handwritten copy of his "Provisional Constitution" in the care of William Howard Day for printing. After making calls in Ingersoll, he next visited Chatham, for twenty years a major terminus of the Underground Railroad. Calling at the home of Martin Delany, Brown found the doctor away and expected to be so for several more days. He declined to leave his name with Delany's wife, who could only report on her husband's return that an elderly white man had called who had the appearance of one of the Hebrew prophets.

Among those whom Brown sought out in Chatham was an influential group at the *Provincial Freeman*, an abolitionist and emigrationist organ whose editor at that time was Israel D. Shadd. These included Shadd's sister, Mary Shadd Cary, and her husband, Thomas Cary, Thomas Stringer, and the young printer's devil Osborne Perry Anderson. In the edition of the *Weekly Anglo African*, dated October 26, 1861, Mary Shadd Cary noted the tenor of John Brown's reception among them: "Some of us who knew dear old John Brown . . . well enough to know his plans, and who were thought 'sound' enough to be entrusted with them by him . . . have the greatest opinion of fighting anti-slavery—give us 'plucky' abolitionism." In a talk she was preparing several years later on Brown's relation to Chatham, her succinct sketch contains these expressions: "He taught something—He acted. Lessons of endurance, of Charity—of humanity, of zeal in a good cause. He wanted pure politics. Pure religion." It was clear to her Brown's stroke at Harpers Ferry when it came was aimed not only against the strategic vulnerabilities of American slavery, but was aimed equally in defiance of an entire nation; he was seeking to create a break that could become the starting point in revolutionizing its politics.

In September 1861 William Wells Brown would write, "In my walk from the railroad station to the hotel I was at once impressed that I was in Chatham, for every other person whom I met was colored"[43]—a town whose population of 4,466 in 1863 was fully one third black. Among its residents, with a sizable majority being fugitive slaves, were farmers and mechanics, merchants and professionals, with a black-run newspaper, the *Provincial Freeman*, a graded school, Wilberforce Institute, several churches, and a fire-engine company. Making it especially cohesive, DuBois would remark, was an organization called the True Band, an active self-improvement organization with 400 members, men and women. Most of Ontario's 40,000, and perhaps many more, black residents lived within a fifty-mile radius of Chatham. St. Catharines had a thousand; Dresden was an important center, as were Hamilton and London; and on the western extremity, across the water from Detroit, there were settlements in Amhurstburg, Colchester, and Malden, with Toronto at that time counting 1,200 black residents within its precincts.

After his first visit at Chatham, Brown ventured on, as there is indication of a meeting in nearby Buxton. William Parker of the Christiana Resistance lived in the country near there, and John Brown would seem to have met with him. The evidence for this would be that in the next year Kagi would direct John Jr. to him, and the son reported in a letter dated August 27, 1859: "At ("B-n") I found *the* man, the *leading spirit* in that 'affair,' which you, Henrie, *referred* to. On Thursday night last, I went with him on foot 12 miles; much of the way through new paths, and sought out in 'the bush' some of the *choicest*. Had a meeting after 1 o'clock at night at his home."[44] Then Brown went on to Toronto, where he knew Dr. Alexander M. Ross, a radical abolitionist and distinguished naturalist. Meetings were held for Brown in Toronto's Temperance Hall, and he stayed "in the home of Mr. Holland," notes DuBois.[45] Of Brown's presence, Osborne Anderson was to write, as he circulated around "although an entire stranger, he made a profound impression upon those who saw or became acquainted with him. Some supposed him to be a staid but modernized Quaker; others, a solid business man, from 'somewhere,' and without question a philanthropist."[46]

The only extended treatment of John Brown in Canada from that period, outside what is contained in Anderson's *A Voice from Harper's Ferry*, came in a monograph under that title published in the 1890s by James Cleland Hamilton, when only one of the participants in John Brown's convention was still extant. Hamilton wrote: "Mr. Brown did

not overestimate the state of education of the colored people. He knew
that they would need leaders, and require training. His great hope was
that the struggle would be supported by volunteers from Canada, educated and accustomed to self-government. He looked on our fugitives
as picked men of sufficient intelligence, which combined with a hatred
for the South, would make them willing abettors of any enterprise destined to free their race."[47]

Hamilton gives a prominent place in his account to Dr. A. M. Ross,
having met and interviewed him. In his *Recollections and Experiences of
an Abolitionist* Ross recounts two meetings with Brown, which others
have disputed. The first encounter was in the summer of 1857 at a hotel
in Cleveland, where Brown approached him and introduced himself
just after Ross's involvement in a significant fugitive slave rescue. The
second reputed encounter was on a train departing Springfield,
Massachusetts, as both men traveled to Boston in March 1858, where,
Ross claimed, the two had extensive discussion of Brown's plan, both
on the train and subsequently in Boston. In his account Ross says
Brown proposed he be in place in Richmond, Virginia, before Brown
and his men went into its mountains that year in May. While this is
considered dubious by some scholars, Richard Hinton included it in
his book. Perhaps, as Ross had been honored with titles and decora-
tions throughout his career, and Emerson would call him "The
Canadian Knight," the doctor was disposed to burnish his feathers as
he'd observed in the habits of birds in his ornithological studies. Yet his
understanding of Brown's intentions was exceptional, and lends some
credence to his assertions: Ross stated of his second interview with
Brown, that "[Brown] felt confident that the negroes would flock to
him in large numbers and that the slaveholders would soon be glad to
let the oppressed go free; that the dread of a negro insurrection would
produce fear and trembling in all the Slave States; that the presence in
the mountains of an armed body of Liberators would produce a general insurrection among the slaves, which would end in their freedom."[48]

Appearing again at Delany's residence in Chatham and finding he
was still away, Brown left a message that he would call again in two
weeks' time. Satisfied with the progress he'd been making toward his
convention, Brown now returned to Iowa to retrieve his men. Traveling
through Chicago and Detroit, this party of twelve whites and one fugitive slave, Richard Richardson, reached Chatham, taking lodging at the
Villa Mansion Hotel, under black proprietorship, in the first week of
May. Meanwhile Brown presented himself and his letter of introduction from William Howard Day at the house of James Madison Bell,

with whom he would stay for several days, before taking lodging with the others at the hotel. Bell was from Cincinnati, and had come to Canada in 1854; part of the circle around the *Provincial Freeman*, he was a poet who worked as a plasterer. Through his hands would pass all John Brown's Canadian mail for the next several weeks, and he was constantly at "the old man's" side during the preparatory meetings to the convention and at the convention.

John Brown now called again on Martin Delany whom he found within. As they met Brown said: "I came to Chatham expressly to see you, this being my third visit on the errand. I must see you at once, sir, and that, too, in private, as I have much to do and but little time before me. If I am to do nothing here, I want to know it at once." Delany's account of this encounter was furnished to his biographer, Frances Rollin Whipper, using the pseudonym Frank A. Rollin, for her *Life and Public Service of Martin R. Delany*, a book published in 1868. Delany continues:

> Going directly to the private parlor of a hotel near by, he at once revealed to me that he desired to carry out a great project in his scheme of Kansas emigration, which, to be successful, must be aided and countenanced by the influence of a general convention or council. That he was unable to effect in the United States, but had been advised by distinguished friends of his and mine, that, if he could but see me, his object could be attained at once. On my expressing astonishment at the conclusion to which my friends and himself had arrived, with a nervous impatience, he exclaimed, "Why should you be surprised? Sir, the people of the Northern states are cowards; slavery has made cowards of them all. The whites are afraid of each other, and the blacks are afraid of the whites. You can effect nothing among such people," he added, with decided emphasis. On assuring him if a council was all that was desired, he could readily obtain it, he replied, "That is all; but that is a great deal to me. It is men I want, and not money; money can come without being seen but men are afraid of identification with me, though they favor my measures. They are cowards, Sir! Cowards," he reiterated. He then fully revealed his designs. With these I found no fault, but fully favored and aided in getting up the convention.[49]

Notwithstanding this statement, Delany was under no misapprehension that Brown's intention was to make an incursion into the mountains of Virginia. That he referenced it as a "scheme of Kansas emigration" ten years later only suggests that it may have been an idea considered in one of the preliminary meetings to the convention. In both instances, Virginia or Kansas, the pertinent idea was that of defending and maintaining the human rights and rights of citizenship of blacks on United States soil. Some sixty to seventy persons were said to have come out to meet with John Brown after his initial round of introduction, many of them now induced by the active participation of Delany. The first of these preliminary meetings, James Hamilton reports in his *John Brown in Canada*, was held in a frame cottage on Princess Street, south of King Street, then known as the King Street School. A second was in the First Baptist Church; both meetings so large that the pretense had to be given out that they were assembling for the purpose of "organizing a Masonic Lodge of colored people." But the party of young white men joining them tended to undermine this cover. "The 'boys' of the party of 'Surveyors,' as they were called," Anderson wrote, "were the admired of those who knew them, and the subject of curious remark and inquiry by strangers." Anderson continues:

> So many intellectual looking men are seldom seen in one party, and at the same time, such utter disregard of prevailing custom, or style, in dress and other little conventionalities. Hour after hour they would sit in council, thoughtful, ready; some of them eloquent, all fearless, patient of the fatigues of business; anon, here and there over the "track," and again in the assembly; when the time for relaxation came, sallying forth arm in arm, unshaven, unshorn, and altogether indifferent about it; or one, it may be impressed with the coming responsibility, sauntering alone, in earnest thought, apparently indifferent to all outward objects, but ready at a word or sign from the chief to undertake any task.[50]

Hamilton in his monograph bases his account largely on the reminiscences of James Monroe Jones, a gunsmith and engraver who had come to Canada from his native Raleigh, North Carolina, then the only surviving member of the convention living in Chatham. "Mr. Brown," said Jones, "called almost daily at my gun shop, and spoke freely of the great subject that lay uppermost in his mind. He submitted his plans, and only asked for their approval by the Convention."[51] John Cook also was a good deal in the gun shop of Jones, repairing the revolvers of the company. During one of the sittings, Hamilton wrote, Jones had the floor, and discussed the likelihood of the success or failure of Brown's expectation of the slaves rising to support his plan. "Jones expressed fear that he would be disappointed, because the slaves did not know enough to rally to his support. The American slaves, Jones argued, were different from those of the West India island of San Domingo, whose successful uprising is a matter of history, as they had there imbibed some of the impetuous character of their French masters, and were not so over-awed by white men. 'Mr. Brown, no doubt thought,' said Mr. Jones, 'that I was making an impression on some of the members, if not on him, for he arose suddenly and remarked, 'Friend Jones, you will please say no more on that side. There will be plenty to defend that side of the question.' A general laugh took place."[52]

At one of the settings Brown's constitution was examined, with Delany serving as chairman and Kagi and Anderson as secretaries. The proposition of the organization as a legal and political entity was considered, the point being raised that since blacks had no rights, they "could have no right to petition and none to sovereignty." Therefore it would be "a mockery to set up a claim as a fundamental right." Delany remarked, "To obviate this, and avoid the charge against them as lawless and unorganized, existing without government, it was proposed that an independent community be established, without the state sovereignty of the compact, similar to the Cherokee Nation of Indians, or the Mormons. To these last named, references were made, as parallel cases, at the time." Also raised was the question of the opportune time for making the attack, one speaker holding it would be folly to begin while the United States was at peace with other nations, and he advocated that they wait till the country was embroiled in a war with a "first class" foreign adversary. One participant wrote, "Mr. Brown listened to the argument for some time, then slowly arose to his full height, and said: 'I would be the last one to take the advantage of my country in the face of a foreign foe.' He seemed to regard it as a great insult."[53] Some of those in the meetings, as had Jones, expressed apprehension that Brown's plan would not succeed in effecting much in the South. Delany in particular seems to have strongly questioned some of Brown's views. According to Richard Realf, Delany, "having objected repeatedly to certain proposed measures, the old captain sprang suddenly to his feet, and exclaimed severely, 'Gentlemen, if Dr. Delany is afraid, don't let him make you all cowards!' Dr. Delany replied immediately to this, courteously, yet decidedly. Said he, 'Captain Brown does not know the man of whom he speaks. There exists no one in whose veins the blood of cowardice courses less freely, and it must not be said, even by John Brown of Osawatomie.' As he concluded, the old man bowed approvingly to him, then arose and made explanations."[54]

Among those joining in the preliminary meetings were Isaac Holden, a surveyor and civil engineer and a native of Louisiana, who with his friends had built Chatham's No. 3 Fire-Engine House; Israel D. Shadd, publisher of the *Provincial Freeman*; James M. Jones; James M. Bell; Osborne Anderson; Thomas W. Stringer of Buxton, who helped establish the Methodist Episcopal Church in Chatham; James W. Purnell, a twenty-five-year-old merchant in Chatham; and Martin Delany, who, said Realf, "was one of the prominent disputants, or debaters." The whole tenor of his speeches "was to convey to John Brown that he might rely upon all the colored people in Canada to assist him." Many of those attending were fugitive slaves whose identities are now unknown, all of whose decision to meet with John Brown "was a reflection of their feeling that the conventional methods of striking at slavery were simply not working well, the times calling for new approaches."[55] Jones remarked, "In his conversations during his stay here, [John Brown] appeared intensely American. He never for a moment thought of fighting the United States, as such, but simply the defenders of slavery in the States. Only the ulcer, slavery, he would cut from the body politic."[56]

On May 5, 1858, invitations were sent out to persons with whom Brown had been in correspondence: "My Dear Friend: I have called a quiet convention in this place of true friends of freedom. Your attendance is earnestly requested. Your friend, John Brown." Among the invitees who did not attend were Douglass, Loguen, and Charles Lenox Remond. In a letter to Remond dated April 29, and signed by Brown, Bell, and Delany, they specified his traveling expenses would be paid, but he declined to respond. Douglass did not respond either, although he was fully cognizant of the proceedings and had helped in starting them. Perhaps he felt it would have been awkward to share the platform with Martin Delany. Loguen regretted his inability to attend in his letter in response, but added he would "like very much to see you and your brave men before you go to the *Mountains*." Efforts to contact Harriet Tubman were apparently unavailing, although it is said she was responsible for the attendance of a number of fugitive slaves.[57]

When the convention assembled on Saturday, May 8, at 10 A.M., of the forty-six attendees, ten were black men who had come from the United States and thirteen were of Brown's party, twelve whites and the fugitive Richard Richardson, the balance of twenty-three men were predominately from Chatham, with one coming from Toronto, the Rev. Thomas M. Kinnard, with perhaps Buxton and St. Catharines being represented as well. William Charles Monroe, an Episcopal clergyman who had presided at the emigration convention in 1854 in Cleveland and its follow-up meeting in 1856, came from Detroit; he would also preside over John Brown's convention. Also arriving from Detroit was William Lambert, a native of Trenton, New Jersey, who had prospered as a tailor in Detroit and had been for many years the head of that city's Colored Vigilance Committee. Both men were active in the Michigan Anti-Slavery Society and Liberty party politics. James H. Harris traveled from Cleveland, and Alfred Whipper, a school teacher, came from Pennsylvania. One of the strongest of these individuals attending the Chatham Convention was George J. Reynolds, a copper-smith from Sandusky, Ohio, and an outstanding figure of the Underground Railroad and of a little-disclosed organization of the Lake States called variously the "League of Freedom," or "African Mysteries," and even "American Mysteries."

As those assembled convened in the schoolhouse on Princess Street without ceremony, on motion of John J. Jackson, William Monroe was chosen president, and on motion of John Brown, John Henry Kagi was named secretary. Hardly had Monroe taken the chair than it was sug-gested they seek another building as a large crowd of the curious had gathered outside. Removing to the No. 3 Fire-Engine House where they would be unobserved, newly situated, Delany called for John Brown. The general idea of Brown's speech was to be outlined by Richard Realf before the Senate Committee investigating Harpers Ferry in 1860. In later years, reviewing that testimony, Hinton suggested while it might be apt in some regards, Brown's speech undoubtedly contained elements not touched on by Realf, and certainly would have rendered a far more powerful effect on the convention than that reflected by the Englishman's rhetoric. Osborne Anderson wrote in his account of Brown's oratory: "Being a devout Bible Christian, he sustained his views and shaped his plans in conformity to the Bible; and when setting them forth, he quoted freely from the Scripture to sustain his position. He realized and enforced the doctrine of destroying the tree that bringeth forth corrupt fruit. Slavery was to him the corrupt tree, and the duty of every Christian man was to strike down slavery, and to commit its frag-ments to the flames. He was listened to with profound attention."[58]

Realf's summation is the following:

He stated that for twenty or thirty years the idea had possessed him like a passion of giving liberty to the slaves; that he made a journey to England, during which he made a tour upon the European continent, inspecting all fortifications, and especially all earthwork forts which he could find, with a view of applying the knowledge thus gained, with mod-ifications and inventions of his own, to a mountain warfare in the United States. He stated that he had read all the books upon insurrectionary war-fare, that he could lay his hands on: the Roman warfare, the successful opposition of the Spanish chieftains during the period when Spain was a Roman province,—how, with ten thousand men, divided and subdivided

into small companies, acting simultaneously, yet separately, they with-
stood the whole consolidated power of the Roman Empire through a
number of years. In addition to this he had become very familiar with the
successful warfare waged by Schamyl, the Circassian chief, against the
Russians; he had posted himself in relation to the wars of Toussaint
L'Ouverture; he had become thoroughly acquainted with the wars in
Hayti and the islands round about.[59]

After Brown's opening remarks the constitution was brought forward, and after a parole of honor, was read through. This document
was a structure of authority modeled on the national constitution, paralleling its branches and offices, but designed and adopted as an instrument for the government of isolated guerrilla bands, and of a people
fighting for liberty. After hearing the document it was read again article by article for consideration. There were forty-eight articles, with
only the forty-sixth provoking debate. That article should be seen as
providing "the keynote to John Brown's position," which is seldom
properly understood in commentary.[60] It reads: "The foregoing articles
shall not be so as in any way to encourage the overthrow of any state
government, or the general government of the United States, and look
to no dissolution of the Union, but simply to amendment and repeal,
and our flag shall be the same that our fathers fought for under the
Revolution."

Reynolds made a motion that the article be stricken. He felt no alle-
giance, he said, to the nation that had robbed and humiliated the
Africans in its midst; and that they already carried their emblem on
their backs. Delany, Brown, Kagi, and others advocated the article and
it passed. Brown in his statement saying the flag had represented the
patriots in the war of the revolution and now he wanted it to perform
the same duty for black men. He would not fight without the "stars and
stripes."

The aspiration of the organization adopted in Chatham is succinctly
set out in the preamble of the constitution:

> Whereas slavery, throughout its entire existence in the United States, is
> none other than a most barbarous, unprovoked, and unjustifiable war of
> one portion of its citizens upon another portion—the only conditions of
> which are perpetual imprisonment and hopeless servitude or absolute
> extermination—in utter disregard and violation of those eternal and self-
> evident truths set forth in our Declaration of Independence:
>
> Therefore we, citizens of the United States, and the oppressed people
> who, by a recent decision of the Supreme Court, are declared to have no
> rights which the white man is bound to respect, together with all other

people degraded by the laws thereof, do, for the time being, ordain and establish for ourselves the following Provisional Constitution and Ordinances, the better to protect our persons, property, lives, and liberties, and to govern our actions.

The constitution as a whole was unanimously adopted, and on the motion of Delany it was ordered that those approving the document stand and sign the same. John Jones, who had not attended all of the meetings, had been urged by John Brown to attend on this day. "As the paper was presented for signature," James Hamilton wrote, recounting Jones's terms, "Brown said 'Now, friend Jones, give us John Hancock, bold and strong.' I replied that I thought it would resemble Stephen Hopkins."[61] After congratulatory remarks by Thomas Kinnard and Martin Delany, the convention adjourned at a quarter to four in the afternoon.[62]

At six in the evening the convention reassembled for the purpose of electing officers named in the constitution. It was called to order by Delany, upon whose nomination Munroe was chosen president, and Kagi, secretary. A committee consisting of Stevens, Kagi, Bell, Cook, and Monroe was chosen to select candidates for the various offices. On reporting, and asking leave to sit again, the request was refused, and the committee discharged. On motion of Bell the Convention went into the election of officers. On motion of Stevens, John Brown was nominated for commander-in-chief, seconded by Delany, and elected by acclamation. Realf nominated Kagi for secretary of war, who was also elected by acclamation. The convention then adjourned until nine in the morning, on Monday, May 10.

That Sunday many of the conventiongoers joined with John Brown in worship at the First Baptist Church presided over by Rev. Monroe, a service no doubt conducted with due solemnity appropriate to the occasion. On Monday morning the business before the convention was the further election of officers. Stevens nominated Thomas M. Kinnard for president. In a speech of some length, Kinnard declined. Osborne Anderson then nominated J. W. Loguen for the same. Not being present, and it being announced that he would not serve if elected, the nomination was withdrawn. Brown then moved to postpone the election of president, which carried. The convention then went into the election of members of Congress, electing A. M. Ellsworth and Osborne Anderson, both of Chatham; after which Richard Realf was chosen as secretary of state.

Adjourning at a quarter past two in the afternoon, the convention immediately reconvened for the balloting for the election of treasurer and secretary of the treasury, electing Owen Brown to the former, and George Gill as the latter. Brown then introduced a resolution appointing a committee delegated to fill by election all the offices named in the Provisional Constitution left vacant. The convention then adjourned. Another and larger committee was also organized at this time; in his biography Delany set out its scope this way: "This organization was an extensive body, holding the same relation to his movements as a state or national executive committee holds to its party principles, directing their adherence to fundamental principles."[63]

On May 12 John Brown ended a brief letter to "wife and children" with this: "Had a good Abolition convention here, from different parts, on the 8th and 10th inst. Constitution slightly amended and adopted, and society organized. Great unanimity prevailed."[64]

By the close of the proceedings in Chatham, Brown had spent all the cash he had received from his supporters, and debts totaling three hundred dollars were still to be settled. But as he delayed in Canada awaiting money to cover his receipts, and much more damaging to him, new disclosures by Forbes were coming to his attention. Forbes had been in New York City since November 1857 spinning out his story to anyone who'd listen: he had been deceived by "a vicious man," he said, and that he'd given up work to travel to Iowa to drill men and that he had not been paid for this, and now his family was destitute and starving in Paris and he was unable to provide for them. Gaining some commiseration along with some cash, Forbes decided to travel to Washington to solicit Republican leaders, where he began denouncing Brown's Boston supporters, of whom he'd evidently learned while in the trust of Dr. James McCune Smith in New York. Coming up to Senator Henry Wilson at his desk on the Senate floor, Forbes unburdened himself, making referral to some well-placed persons in Massachusetts. Then he sought out Senator Seward at his home, who "found his story incoherent," concluding he was a confused man soliciting charity.[65]

Wilson then wrote to Dr. Howe, warning him confidentially that any arms given to Brown should be removed from his control, inferring that he intended to use them for some action in Missouri. Wilson wrote: "If they should be used for other purposes, as rumor says they may be, it might be of disadvantage to the men who were induced to contribute to that very foolish movement." In consultation with Stearns and others, Howe quickly reacted: "Prompt measures have been

and will resolutely be followed up to prevent any such monstrous per-
version of a trust." On May 14 Stearns wrote Brown at Chatham that as
chairman of the Massachusetts Kansas Aid Committee he must warn
him not to use the arms "for any other purpose and to hold them subject to my order as chairman of said committee." Brown replied: "None
of our friends need have any fears in relation to rash steps being taken
by us. As Knowledge is said to be Power, we propose to become possessed of more knowledge. We have many reasons for begging our eastern friends to keep clear of F. personally unless he throws himself upon
them. We have those who are thoroughly posted up to be put on his
track and we humbly beg to be allowed to do so."[66] Brown now sent
Realf to New York City, instructing him to gain his countryman's confidence, find out what he knew, and secure any documents that may
have fallen into his hands. Meanwhile, part of the company—including
Stevens, Cook, and Owen Brown—had left Canada and gone to
Cleveland, taking day jobs in the countryside.

In Boston, Brown's supporters were bedeviled by Forbes's disclosures. Sanborn wrote: "It looks as if the project must, for the present,
be deferred, for I find by reading Forbes' epistles to the doctor that he
knows (what very few do) that the doctor, Mr. Stearns, and myself are
informed of it. How he got this knowledge is a mystery." Only
Higginson remained firm, writing to Parker: "I regard any postponement as simply abandoning the project; for if we give up now at the
command or threat of H. F., it will be the same next year. The only way
is to circumvent the man somehow (if he cannot be restrained in his
malice). When the thing is well started, who cares what he says?"[67]

After two weeks' delay, Brown received money to settle accounts in
Canada and immediately went on to Cleveland, leaving only Kagi
behind in Hamilton to finish printing the documents at Day's printing
press, while Richard Richardson would take up residence in Chatham.
Five "committee" members, absent Higginson, now met in Boston's
Revere House on May 24 to deliberate the situation in regard to Brown.
Decisions requiring he postpone the attack and place the arms under
temporary interdict had already been made; the questions remaining
were whether he should be obliged to go to Kansas, where there had
been a new spasm of violence, and how much money should be raised
for him in the future. Resolving unanimously that Brown should go to
Kansas immediately both to reinforce the Free State cause and to blind
Forbes, they suggested his Virginia campaign could safely be brought
off in the next winter or spring and they severally pledged from two to
three thousand dollars. Further, they resolved henceforth they would
not know nor inquire about Brown's plans.

Soon after the meeting at the Revere House concluded, Brown arrived in Boston. Stating his objections in a conversation with Higginson to the decision reached by Stearns, Howe, Smith, Sanborn, and Parker, he said delay was very discouraging to his men and to those in Canada. The others of the committee were not men of action; they had been intimidated by Wilson's letter and magnified the obstacles. The knowledge Forbes could give of his plan was injurious, for he wished his opponents to underrate him; still, the increased terror might counterbalance this, and it would not make much difference. If he had the means he would not lose a day; it would cost him no more than twenty-five dollars apiece to get his men from Ohio. Still, it was essential his backers not think him reckless, and they held the purse. Faced with being cut off from his financial resources, Brown finally acknowledged that he had little choice but to acquiesce. With all in agreement, Stearns foreclosed on his title to the Sharps rifles and gave them to Brown as a gift with no conditions attached. Henceforth it was agreed—*action would be all.*

George Gill decided to use the time in the interval for a visit to Reynolds in Sandusky. He left a narrative included in Hinton's *John Brown and His Men*, which relates a matter of historical consequence that has been little explored. He wrote:

> My object in wishing to see Mr. Reynolds . . . was in regard to a military organization which, I had understood, was in existence among the colored people. He assured me that such was the fact, and that its ramifications extended through most, or nearly all, of the slave states. He himself, I think, had been through many of the slave states visiting and organizing. He referred me to many references in the Southern papers, telling of this and that favorite slave being killed or found dead. These, he asserted must be taken care of, being the most dangerous element they had to contend with. He also asserted that they were only waiting for Brown, or someone else, to make a successful initiative move when their forces would be put in motion. None but colored persons could be admitted to membership, and in part to corroborate his assertions, he took me to the room in which they held their meetings and used as their arsenal. He showed me a fine collection of arms. He gave me this under the pledge of secrecy which we gave to each other at the Chatham Convention.[68]

When Gill reached Cleveland he found Stevens and Cook in a hotel, where they had been joined by Richard Realf on his way east. With Cook talking loosely with strangers and making rash avowals, Gill confided the details of his visit to Sandusky. Disturbed by this lack of discretion, Realf wrote an uncle in England of his reservations, stating one of his comrades had "disclosed objects to the members of a Secret society (colored) calling itself the 'American Mysteries,' or some other confounded humbug. I suppose it is likely that these people are good men enough but to make a sort of wholesale divulgement of matters at hazard is too steep even for me, who are not by any means over-cautious."[69]

Underground operations culminating at Cleveland, Sandusky, and Detroit were fed by extensive and distinct pathways running through Ohio up from the border of Kentucky, one of the most active of the Underground Railroad networks. From Kentucky they crept through the heart of the Cumberland Mountains, reaching into northern Georgia, east Tennessee, and northern Alabama.[70] Hinton writes: "As one may naturally understand, looking at conditions then existing, there existed something of an organization to assist fugitives and of resistance to their masters. It was found all along the Lake borders from Syracuse, New York, to Detroit, Michigan. As none but colored men were admitted into direct and active membership with this 'League of Freedom,' it is quite difficult to trace its working, or know how far its ramifications extended." Hinton continued, "One of the most interesting phases of slave life was the extent and rapidity of communication among them."[71] The flourishing state of these routes "establishes conclusively," wrote James Redpath in *The Roving Editor*, "the existence of secret and rapid modes of communication among the slave population of the South." That book, published in 1859, was a compendium of the author's travels in the South starting in spring 1854, with additional trips that autumn, and in 1858, and was dedicated to John Brown. Redpath reported:

Many extraordinary stories are told by the Southrons themselves of the facility with which negroes learn of all events that transpire in the surrounding country. In spite of strict surveillance on the plantation, and careful watching abroad, by means of numerous and well mounted patrols, the slaves pass freely over large tracts of country. More especially does this state of things exist among the plantations of the cotton growing states. . . . It seems to me that here lies a power by means of which a formidable insurrection, directed by white men, can safely be formed and consummated. And the slaves know this fact. The Canadian fugitives understand it; and are thoroughly systematizing this Underground Telegraph.[72]

That Brown, too, was totally cognizant of these passageways and this force of resistance has never been fully appreciated. And just as there is clear indication once beginning his campaign he expected to call upon a broad area of south-central Pennsylvania, he as likely expected increased activity in the form of fleeing slaves along the entire line of the Kentucky border, calling into play the "League of Freedom" that, as is suggested, he expected to form consorted and ongoing arrangements to meet the emergency. That the interior of Ohio and the Lake region offered an obvious area to open a second front is indubitable. James Montgomery, it will be shown, would have made an obvious choice for leadership in the Cumberland region; but Brown did not think this at all feasible until he had first made a successful and ongoing demonstration in the Virginia mountains.

Nat Turner met his confederates in secret places, Gabriel promulgated his rebellion in the silence of a dense forest, "but John Brown reasoned of liberty and equality in broad daylight" wrote Osborne Anderson in *A Voice from Harper's Ferry*. His allies met

> in a modernized building, in conventions with closed doors, in meetings governed by the elaborate regulations laid down by Jefferson, and used as their guides by Congresses and Legislatures; or he made known the weighty theme, and his comprehensive plans resulting from it, by the cosy fireside, at familiar social gatherings of chosen ones, or better, in the carefully arranged junto of earnest, practical men. Vague hints, careful blinds, are Nat Turner's entire make-up to save detection; the telegraph, the post-office, the railway, all were made to aid the new outbreak. By this, it will be seen that Insurrection has its progressive side, and has been elevated by John Brown from the skulking, fearing cabal, when in the hands of a brave but despairing few, to the highly organized, formidable, and to very many, indispensable institution for the security of freedom, when guided by intelligence.[73]

By 1858 with northeastern Kansas thoroughly under the standard of "Free-Soil," southeast Kansas, with its center of power in an abandoned army outpost, fell under the grip of the proslavery party. The majority of settlers in Bourbon and Linn counties were from Missouri, having been driven off claims in the northern counties. As proslavery Democrats awaited the vote of Congress on the Lecompton Constitution, ex-Indian agent Clarke and ex-chief justice of the Iowa Supreme Court "Fiddling" Williams administered "justice" at Fort Scott. Living among them was a diminutive man with a refined manner, the black-haired and black-bearded Campbellite preacher named James Montgomery. He, along with his followers, had decided to ignore Judge Williams's decisions in land disputes in favor of proslavery claimants. When the United States marshal was ordered to break up Montgomery's so-called "Self-Protection Company," men from Lawrence led by W. A. Phillips, Preston Plumb, and Jim Lane came to their assistance, and the new governor ordered U.S. dragoons to disperse them along with Clarke's regulators.

Arriving among the proslavery settlers was the handsome son of a wealthy Georgia planter, Charles A. Hambleton. As a provocation he had built a substantial log house complete with slave quarters just across the Missouri border inside Kansas near the settlement called Trading Post, and from there commanded a company of proslavery partisans. Montgomery and his men rode into his haven, and breaking barrels of corn whiskey, ordered Hambleton and his men to leave Kansas. Rallying men in Missouri, on May 19 Hambleton rode back into Kansas seeking retribution. Seizing eleven men working in their fields, or in their homes and businesses, Hambleton drove the men to a ravine where they were lined up and summarily shot. Five were killed, five were severely wounded and thought to be dead, and one lay under the bodies unhurt but feigning death. The killers pillaged their victims' pockets, and then rode off in different directions to cover their tracks back to Missouri. This was the infamous Marais des Cygnes Massacre. (French explorers in the previous century seeing swans in the wetlands christened the area "The Swamp of the Swan.") This is what brought John Brown back to Kansas.

Arriving in Lawrence with Kagi on June 25, using the nom de guerre Captain Shubel Morgan, Brown took a room at a hotel down by the river. As he sat in the lobby the next morning he was regarded with curiosity by two men—James Redpath and Richard Hinton—who soon penetrated his disguise. Hinton left an interesting account of a brief interview with John Brown on that subsequent Sunday; along with another taking place that September. These interviews were published in 1860 in Redpath's *The Public Life of Captain John Brown* and later became part of Hinton's own *John Brown and His Men*, with only slight changes, appearing in 1894. When they met, Brown was principally interested in learning the particulars of "various public men in the Territory, and the condition of political affairs," particularly of those of antislavery reputation; as he was also keenly interested to hear of James Montgomery. During the course of the conversation, with Hinton giving vent to his detestation of slavery and its underlings, and tetchily wishing for some way of injuring it, Brown responded: "Young men must learn to wait. Patience is the hardest lesson to learn. I have waited for twenty years to accomplish my purpose." He then reminded

Hinton of a message he had sent to him in the fall of 1857, saying that his heart was with him and he would join him, but must decline at that time because of his newspaper commitments. Brown admonished, "I hope you meant what you said, for I shall ask the fulfillment of that promise, and that perhaps very soon," adding, "I caution you against rash promises. Young men are too apt to make them, and should be very careful. The promise given was of great importance, and you must be prepared to stand by it or disavow it now."[74]

By July 1 Brown was at the site of the murders of May 19, accompanied by ten of his men who had come back to Kansas, organized in the coming weeks under regulations similar to those he produced in 1856, but now designated as Captain Shubel Morgan's Company. Realf was not among these, having abandoned his assignment of diverting his countryman, and sailing for England where he would lecture on American affairs before returning to the states, to Texas in 1860, when he would be subpoenaed to appear before the Senate Committee investigating Harpers Ferry. John Cook had gone to Harpers Ferry, perhaps at his own behest, as is suggested, but with the acquiescence of his leader. Brown sent the following communication off to Boston:

> Deserted farms and dwellings lie in all directions for some miles along the line, and the remaining inhabitants watch every appearance of persons moving about, with anxious jealousy and vigilance. Four of the persons wounded or attacked on that occasion are staying with me. . . . A constant fear of new trouble seems to prevail on both sides of the line, and on both sides are companies of armed men. Any little affair may open the quarrel afresh. . . . I have concealed the fact of my presence pretty much; but it is getting leaked out, and will soon be known to all. As I am not here to seek or secure revenge, I do not mean to be the first to reopen the quarrel. How soon it may be raised against me, I cannot say; nor am I over anxious.[75]

It was during these weeks Brown gained a valuable ally in James Montgomery, the two often appearing in each other's camp as each sought the cooperation of the other. Montgomery was born in Ohio's Western Reserve in 1814, migrated to Kentucky, where he took an illiterate but brave wife, and they moved to Missouri in 1852, settling in Kansas in 1856. Like Brown he was of a religious nature; when Sanborn met him in 1860 he was surprised to find that "he had an air of elegance and distinction which I hardly expected. He was a slender, courteous, person with a gentle cultivated voice and the manner of a French chevalier."[76] Montgomery would famously, and to the South notoriously, command a black regiment in South Carolina during the Civil War.

Pursued in April by United States dragoons, Montgomery posted his men in good position, killing one soldier and wounding half a dozen, leaving a number of dead horses on the field. "When he learned the particulars of this engagement," Hinton wrote, "he (Brown) said the like had not happened before in the Territory, and that the skill with which he conducted the engagement, stamped him as one of the first commanders of the age."[77]

On August 2 Kansas voters went to the polls to vote on the Lecompton Constitution, with Buchanan offering a backhanded inducement with a block of public lands for new settlement, after the Senate had approved the constitution. All but two thousand of thirteen thousand votes were cast against it. "The Election of the 2nd Inst. passed off quietly on this part of the line," remarked Brown in a letter to John Jr. Meeting Robinson in Lawrence after the vote, Brown said to him, "You have succeeded in what you undertook. You aimed to make Kansas a free state and your plans were skillfully laid for that purpose. But I had another object in view. I meant to strike a blow at slavery."[78]

Soon after coming on the scene Brown arranged to buy land near Trading Post, and together with his company and some of Montgomery's men began to build a fortification, affording a commanding view across the border into Missouri and of the surrounding country. Undoubtedly he thought it was in his interest to occupy a strong position, but it is more likely he had in mind a practical demonstration in building a type of defensive work which, before this, he'd largely theorized. Said to be of a design that twenty men would be able to construct in a day without using implements or draft animals, the structure, of hewn logs twelve by fourteen feet, had two levels with portholes interspaced on each level for firing positions. Earth and stone were mounded around the perimeter to a height of four feet, making it a thorny problem to assault and impervious to artillery. Upon its completion Brown wrote his eldest son on August 9, "In Missouri . . . the idea of having such a neighbor improving a Claim (as was the case) right on a conspicuous space and in full view for miles around in Missouri produced a ferment there you can better imagine than I can describe. Which of the passions most predominated, fear or rage, I do not pretend to say."[79]

Brown was ill off and on much of that summer, and in the last weeks of August and early September was convalescing at the cabin of his wife's cousin, the Rev. Adair, near Osawatomie. He was thinking in these weeks of writing a biography and a history of the Browns, to be published serially with August Wattles acting as agent. The proposed title was "A Brief History of John Brown; otherwise (old B) and his family; as connected with Kansas; By one who knows." But illness, and other preoccupations, precluded his beginning its composition. It was during this time that Brown and Kagi met with Richard Hinton for a second interview. Arriving at ten in the morning one September day, they would remain in discussion till three in the afternoon.

Speaking of his treatment at the hands of "ambitious men" among the free-state leaders, Brown said: "They acted up to their instincts. As politicians, they thought every man wanted to lead, and therefore supposed I might be in the way of their schemes. While they had this feeling, of course they opposed me. Many men did not like the manner in which I conducted warfare, and they too opposed me. Committees and councils could not control my movements, therefore they did not like me. But politicians and leaders soon found that I had different purposes, and forgot their jealousy. They have all been kind to me since."[80]

Of Governor Robinson's actions, he spoke of their being of a "weather-cock character." Of Lane, alluding to his recent slaying of Gainius Jenkins in a claim dispute, Brown said, "I would not say one word against Lane in his misfortunes. I told General Lane myself he was his own worst enemy." Of Montgomery Brown said, "[He] is the only soldier I have met among the prominent Kansas men. He understands my system of warfare exactly. He is a natural chieftain, and knows how to lead." He was both "kind and gentlemanly . . . and what was infinitely more a lover of Freedom." The younger man criticized the management of the Free State struggle from an antislavery point of view, pronouncing it "an Abortion." "Captain Brown, looked at me with a peculiar expression in the eyes, as if struck by the word," Hinton wrote, "and in a musing manner remarked, 'Abortion!—yes, that's the word.'"

As he brought up his intention of embarking on a newspaper enterprise, Brown reminded him, referring to Hinton's letter in 1857, of his promise. He advised him not to enter into any "entangling engagements," saying, "I think all engagements should be considered sacred, and would like you to adhere to the one you were committed to. That is why I have not sent for you; but now I hope you will keep yourself free." Then Brown continued: "For twenty years I have never made any business arrangements which would prevent me at any time answering the call of the Lord. I have kept my business in such condition, that in two weeks I could always wind up my affairs, and be ready to obey the call. I have permitted nothing to be in the way of my duty, neither wife, children, nor worldly goods. Whenever the occasion offered, I was ready. The hour is very near at hand, and all who are willing to act should be ready." All through the conversation, Hinton wrote, he had the feeling that Brown's "blue eyes, mild yet inflexible, and beaming with the steady light of a holy purpose," were probing his inmost thoughts and that he was completely transparent to the older man. "I shall never forget the look," he wrote, "with which he said: 'Young men should have a purpose in life, and adhere to it through all trials. They would be sure to succeed if their purpose is such as to deserve the blessing of God.'"[81]

After dinner Brown and his lieutenant had some conversation apart; then saying he wanted to do some fishing, Kagi asked Hinton to accompany him to the river. Stopping half way, the two sat on a fence rail as the conversation turned to Brown's nearer object. In his account, Hinton states Kagi began by asking him what he supposed to be the plan of John Brown. Hinton responded that he understood that to be reference to an attack in Louisiana and retreat into the southwest states and the Indian Territory of Oklahoma. He was then given a full account of the meetings in Chatham, as well as of the organization effected there. The true location of their operations was to be in the mountains of Virginia, said Kagi; and he went on to describe their mode of operation, sketching a theory of how the campaign would develop and be received in the North and in the South. Given a country admirably adaptable to guerilla warfare, the freed slaves were to be armed and organized into companies, headed by the men Brown had selected and the Canadian recruits that would be sent down. The southern oligarchy, Kagi continued, would become alarmed by the discipline maintained and by the show of organization. At no point was the South more vulnerable, he emphasized, than in its fear of servile insurrection; they would imagine that the whole North was down upon them, as well as their slaves. "Kagi had marked out a chain of counties," Hinton related, "extending continuously through South Carolina, Georgia, Alabama, and Mississippi." These counties were ones that contained a predominance of black over white, "and with the assistance of Canadian negroes who had escaped from those States, they had arranged a general plan of attack." Their plan was to make a fight in the Virginia mountains, and to hold the egress into the free states as long as possible, in order to retreat when that was advisable. But their intent was to retreat southward, toward those regions with a predominance of slaves, "extending the fight into North Carolina, Tennessee, and also to the swamps of South Carolina, if possible."[82]

One of the reasons that induced him to go with the enterprise, Hinton wrote of Kagi, "was a full conviction that at no very distant day forcible efforts for freedom would break out among the slaves, and that slavery might be more speedily abolished by such efforts than by any other means. He knew by observation in the South, that in no point was the system so vulnerable as in its fear of a slave-rising. Believing that such a blow would soon be struck, he wanted to organize it so as to make it more effectual, and also, by directing and controlling the negroes, to prevent some of the atrocities that would necessarily arise from the sudden upheaval of such a mass as the Southern slaves."

Returning to the house the conversation continued, Hinton wrote, "mostly upon Brown's movements and the use of arms." Brown expressed his ideas of forcible emancipation tersely:

> "Give a slave a pike and you make him a man. Deprive him of the means of resistance, and you keep him down."
>
> "The land belongs to the bondman. He has enriched it, and been robbed of its fruits."
>
> "Any resistance, however bloody, is better than the system which makes every seventh woman a concubine."
>
> "I would not give Sharpe's rifles to more than ten men in a hundred, and then only when they have learned to use them. It is not every man who knows how to use a rifle. I had one man in my company who was the bravest man and worst marksman I ever knew."
>
> "A ravine is better than a plain. Woods and mountain sides can be held by resolute men against ten times their force."
>
> "A few men in the right, and knowing they are, can overturn a king. Twenty men in the Alleghenies could break Slavery to pieces in two years."
>
> "When the bondmen stand like men, the nation will respect them. *It is necessary to teach them this.*"

Brown ended with this evocation of the storied leader of the Southampton slave revolt in 1831, referring to the endemic fear it inspired among the whites: "Nat Turner, with fifty men, held Virginia five weeks. The same number, well organized and armed, can shake the system out of the state."[83]

By the Midnight Sky
and the Silent Stars

During the fall of 1858 John Brown's adjunct and constant companion was George Gill. More than thirty years after the death of his chief, in a letter dated July 7, 1893, Gill confided his private thoughts to Richard Hinton about the elder man's intolerance and single-mindedness in regard to the wishes of others. He wrote: "All great men have their foibles or what we in our difference from them call their weakness." Intimate acquaintance had shown him that John Brown was very human, with a love of command and adventure, together with firmness and combativeness, which sometimes was given vent in vindictiveness. Brown's "immense egotism coupled with love of approbation and his god idea begot in him a feeling that he was the Moses that was to lead the Exodus of the colored people from their southern taskmasters. Brooding on this, in time he believed that he was God's chosen instrument, and the only one, and that whatever methods he used, God would be his guard and shield." "And yet," Gill concluded, "this very concentration on self commanded the grand advance on American slavery."

One night in December as he "was scouting down the line," Gill got a striking demonstration of the extraordinary union of messianic belief and the antislavery fight in his leader, when he came across a black man ostensibly engaged in the earthly occupation of peddling brooms. After both resolved the propriety of making the other his confidant, Gill learned the man's name was Jim Daniels, and he had come across from Missouri looking for assistance. He, his wife, and his children belonged to an estate that was to be sold at an administrator's sale, and Daniels wished to avoid the likelihood of seeing his family separated and sold into the Deep South. They immediately hunted up Brown, who "hailed it as heaven sent," quickly devising a scheme to bring the needed assistance. On the night of December 20, seventeen heavily armed and mounted men crossed the border into Missouri; dividing into two parties, Brown's column, guided by Daniels, rode to the estate where he and his family belonged, while Stevens with his party rode toward neighboring farms. The house of Daniels's proprietor was surrounded, with several men entering with drawn revolvers, while others rounded up the animals in the corrals and barns. Less than a mile away Stevens did likewise, telling the startled slave owner at gunpoint: "We have come after your Negroes and their property. Will you surrender or fight?" In all, Brown's party freed ten slaves on two adjoining estates, while Stevens freed but one after killing his owner, who had resisted, taking with them two white men as hostages. Gill wrote of the property seized:

> All of the personal property belonging to the estate that he could find, Brown intended to take as being owned by the slaves, having surely been bought with their labor. In his view, they were entitled to all the proceeds of their labor. He would have taken the real estate as well if he had the facilities for moving it across the country to Canada. He reasoned that they, the slaves, were the creators of the whole, and were entitled to it, not only as their own, but from necessity, for they must have conveyance and also something to dispose of in order to raise funds to defray the expenses of the long overland trip.[1]

Brown's purpose in carrying the war into Missouri had long been contemplated by him, and was directed then so as to have a restraining effect on the internecine strife that had been on-going in southeast Kansas in the fall of 1858. But more especially it was designed to lessen the value of slave property in that section of Missouri in which it was executed, which several contemporary authors remarked it surely did. He also projected delivering a direct blow against slavery. All of these objectives were promoted by the raid, as it was, too, a signal to his supporters in the East of the vitality of his movement, for it was widely reported.

Once back in Kansas the hostages were released with the admonition that they could follow if they wished, while shelter was sought in a ravine from the wind and cold for the animals, the armed men, and the newly freed people. In anticipation of being hunted by Missourians, wrote Gill, "Captain Brown commenced a system of earthworks in a naturally inaccessible position on the Little Osage, close to Bain's house. The position properly defended, would have been well-nigh impregnable, and could have been held by a handful against a small army." Gill added, "To our contrabands, the conditions produced a genial warmth not endorsed by the thermometer."[2]

When night came the train resumed its travel, reaching the farm of Augustus Wattles at midnight a day later. Bedded in the loft in the house with a few of his men, and stirred by the commotion below, James Montgomery looked down as Brown ushered the fugitives into the parlor, exclaiming, "How is this Captain Brown? Whom have you here?" Waving his straw hat broadly, Brown replied, "Allow me to introduce to you a part of my family. Observe, I have carried the war into Africa." Three of the persons introduced were men, five were women—one of them, the wife of Jim Daniels, was pregnant—and three were children, two boys and a girl.

With calls for the arrest of both Brown and Montgomery, a five-hundred-man posse assembled to ride in from Missouri. But Brown's forcible expropriation of slaveholder property also met with severe condemnation in Kansas—one criticism circulating was that Brown intended to leave the territory, and a retaliatory attack would fall upon other, and not his head; another was that the Buchanan administration would now only redouble its effort to impose a proslavery constitution on Kansas. While news of the incursion spread and the Missouri press howled for retribution for "Old Brown's" infamy, Montgomery, Brown, and Kagi sat debating the situation at Wattle's home, as Brown wrote out his famous "Parallels," published on January 22, 1859, in the *New York Tribune*. Contrasting the reaction of the administration and the law enforcement agencies to the May Hambleton murders, about which nothing had been done, to his own exploit, where Missouri's governor offered $3000 for his capture dead or alive, to which President

Buchanan would personally add $250, and Kansas's territorial governor an equal amount.

On Christmas Eve a covered wagon into which the fugitives had been secreted, packed with provisions and tethered to oxen, with Brown and Gill occupying the driver's seat, lumbered up to the Adair cabin near Osawatomie. Remaining in the warmth of the kitchen through Christmas Day, in the early hours of the following morning all moved into a roughly hewn abandoned cabin on Pottawatomie Creek. As improvements were hastily made to the dwelling, in this setting was born the first of the John Brown namesakes, John Brown Daniels, attended by a physician of the neighborhood, Dr. J. G. Blunt, who was sympathetic to Brown.

"It was at this time," wrote Gill, "when Mr. Wattles and other friends urged upon the captain that Kansas was too greatly harassed, that the latter replied: "He would soon remove the seat of the trouble elsewhere."[3] "I have been at your abolition meetings," Brown further retorted to Wattles. "Your schemes are perfectly futile. You will not release five slaves in a century. Peaceful emancipation is impossible. The thing has gone beyond that point."[4]

The publication of "Old Brown's Parallels" in the *Tribune* and the keen interest of the paper in Kansas affairs assured that Brown's foray would be well reported. "Old Brown Invades Missouri" would be the caption of the lead story on January 6, 1859, while Horace Greeley editorialized: "Captain Brown, who had cooperated with Montgomery and whose property had been destroyed and his son murdered in the former wars, did not wait for invasion. He led a party into Bates County, who retorted on the slaveholders of the vicinity the same system of plunder which the Free State people of Kansas have suffered during the recent invasion." On January 10 Gerrit Smith noted in a letter to his wife: "Do you hear the news from Kansas? Our dear John Brown is invading Missouri and pursuing the policy which he intended to pursue elsewhere."[5] Would that the spur of the Allegheny's extended into Kansas, Smith would lament, in another missive on January 22 containing $25 forwarded to Brown.

But Brown's prescription for resolving the state of war with a more thorough war may have been too strong even for Montgomery. With his support waning among men who had sustained him in the past, he felt a need to distance himself from Brown, and walked into the territorial court in Lawrence on January 18 and turned himself in. Freed on $4,000 bail, Montgomery made an appearance at the territorial legislature then in session in Lecompton. The *New York Times* correspondent described the occasion: "Scores were pressing to grasp him by the hand while he 'looked down' upon the heads of those who but a few days before were branding him as the arch-robber. Firm, fearless, erect, he now stood in the same hall where his name had been traduced and vilified. This must have been to him one of the strange vicissitudes of human life."[6]

In this charged atmosphere, with Gill and eleven "contrabands" plus one newborn, on January 20 Brown's ox-drawn wagon lumbered northward inconspicuously toward Lawrence, over labyrinthine roads crisscrossing fields of dried cornstalks and dead sunflowers. Everywhere spies were on the lookout, as posses of armed men scoured in every direction. In parting Brown gave this assessment to Augustus Wattles: "I considered the matter well. You will probably have no more attacks from Missouri. I shall now leave Kansas and probably you will never see me again. I consider it my duty to draw the scene of the excitement to some other part of the country."[7]

Arriving in Lawrence, Brown took a room in the Whitney Hotel and sent Kagi to summon William A. Phillips for a private interview. Phillips was one of a select group of men among Kansas free-state political circles whom Brown had sought as allies, and he now wished to draw his engagement toward the broader object he had in view—the struggle between slavery and freedom that was harrying the nation toward the precipice of war. At first, showing his reticence, Phillips sent back word that he would not come as Brown never took his advice and he saw no reason to offer any now. On being summoned again, he relented, agreeing to an interview in the hotel where Brown was staying.

Phillips's feeling of ambivalence had perhaps been overcome by his journalistic curiosity; there was a fascination about the "old man" which he had clearly recognized. Although he was not in agreement with some of Brown's more strongly held convictions, Phillips was not of the view that would come to prevail in later decades—that Brown was "fanatical," or a "monomaniac," to cite two terms often circulating in American scholarship about him. In fact when they met in the previous year, Phillips had tried to placate Brown by recommending that he and his adherents stay in Kansas and take claims, suggesting Salina, one hundred and fifty miles from the border; they could keep their arms in self-defense, but otherwise would assure the territory entered upon statehood a prosperous and free country. Brown of course would not consider this, but Luke Parsons did—thus Brown would lose another of his highly esteemed recruits for Harpers Ferry.

Phillips wrote: "He had changed a little. There was in the expression of his face something even more dignified than usual; his eye brighter, and the absorbing and consuming thoughts that were within him seemed to be growing out all over him." This interview, the last of three conducted with Brown in Kansas, was reported by Phillips, together with the others, over twenty years later in the *Atlantic Monthly*, December 1879. "He sketched the history of American slavery from its beginnings in the colonies, and referred to the States that were able to shake it off. He recalled many circumstances that I had forgotten, or had never heard of," Phillips wrote of the beginning of their exchange. Brown then went on by reviewing the entire course of the previous decades: When the religious and moral sentiment of the country indicated a desire to check slavery's alarming growth, a threat of secession had been uttered; at length, the slaveholders had gradually been enabled to seize the reins of the government; now appeals were made not to risk the perpetuation of the republic by fanatical abolitionism, and men full of professions of love of country were willing, for peace, to sacrifice everything for which the republic was founded. Northern politicians had become "trimmers," while southern politicians became mere "propagandists" for slavery.

Calling this meeting his most important with Brown, and "one that has peculiar historical significance," Phillips endeavored to cite him verbatim, although he conceded it was "impossible to quote such a conversation accurately." Coming to his main argument, Brown said:

> And now we have reached a point where nothing but war can settle the question. Had they succeeded in Kansas, they would have gained a power that would have given them permanently the upper hand, and it would have been the death-knell of republicanism in America. They are checked, but not beaten. They never intend to relinquish the machinery of this government into the hands of the opponents of slavery. It has taken them more than half a century to get it, and they know its significance too well to give it up. If the [R]epublican party elects its president next year, there will be war. The moment they are unable to control they will go out, and as a rival nation along-side they will get the countenance and aid of the European nations, until American republicanism and freedom are overthrown.[8]

Astonished by the thrust of Brown's analysis, Phillips suggested that surely he was mistaken. The collision that occurred in Kansas would soon die down, and it was in the northern interest to let it do so. Now his interlocutor countered: "No, no, the war is not over. It is a treacherous lull before the storm. We are on the eve of one of the greatest wars in history, and I fear slavery will triumph and there will be an end of all aspirations for human freedom. For my part, I drew my sword in Kansas when they attacked us, and I will never sheathe it until this war is over. Our best people do not understand the danger. They are besotted. They have compromised so long that they think principles of right and wrong have no more any power on this earth."

"Let us suppose all you say is true," said Phillips. "If we keep companies on the one side, they will keep them on the other. Trouble will multiply; there will be collision, which will produce the very state of affairs you depreciate. That would lead to war, and to some extent we should be responsible for it. Better trust events. If there is virtue enough in this people to deserve a free government, they will maintain it."

Brown: "You forget the fearful wrongs that are carried on in the name of government and law."

Phillips: "I do not forget them—I regret them."

Brown: "I regret and will remedy then with all the power that God has given me."

Brown went on to parallel his argument with reference to the example of the Thracian gladiator and slave revolt leader Spartacus, who had defied Rome. Phillips pointed out that the Roman slaves were a warlike people, trained in arms and in combat, the American slaves were far more domestic and "in all their sufferings they seem to be incapable of resentment or reprisal."

"You have not studied them right; and you have not studied them long enough. Human nature is the same everywhere." Brown continued by pointing out the mistakes of that ancient insurrection, showing he had given it his best study. "Instead of wasting his time in Italy, the leader should have struck at Rome, or if not strong enough for that, escape to the northern provinces to build an army. But Rome's armies were able to swoop down on them to destroy them."

Hearing nothing but more talk of war, Phillips finally bridled, predicting Brown would end by bringing himself and his men into a desperate enterprise, where they would be imprisoned and disgraced.

Brown: "Well, I thought I could get you to understand this, I do not wonder at it. The world is very pleasant to you; but when your household gods are broken, as mine have been, you will see all this more clearly."

"Captain, if you thought this, why did you send for me?" As he rose to leave and reached for the door, Phillips felt a hand touch his shoulder. Turning, the old man took Phillips's hands in his, tears glistening his hard bronzed face, and he said: "No, we must not part thus. I wanted to see you and tell you how it appeared to me. With the help of God, I will do what I believe to be best." Holding his hands tightly in his own, Brown leaned forward and kissed him on the cheek and, Phillips wrote, "I never saw him again."[9]

On January 25 Brown and Stevens and their smuggled contraband—Gill stayed in Lawrence recovering from frostbite—pressed on through biting cold. He had very nearly a superstitious faith in his appointed mission (as John Brown replied to one who earlier foretold his doom: "Sir, the angel of the Lord will camp round about me");[10] but the route northward he had penciled out before hand, noting the names of safe stopping places that could be relied on. These he invariably followed: Sheridan's, Hill, Holton, Fuller's, Smith's, Plymouth, Indians, Little Nemaha, Dr. Blanchard's, Tabor.[11]

Reaching the outskirts of Topeka, Stevens went into town for provisions, while the wagon pulled up to the Sheridan cabin, a few miles away. Summoning Jacob Willetts from Topeka, Brown and Willetts rode into town together for food, raising some money, and obtaining shoes for the blacks, who till then had none. As they rode back in the wagon, Willetts noticed Brown shivering with cold. "Mr. Brown, have you no drawers?" he asked. He had none, Brown answered. "Well, there is no time to go to the store now, but I have on a pair that was new today and if you will take them you are welcome." The men duly switched the undergarment.

Three days later the party was some fifteen miles farther north, in Holton. The next day, six miles on, they sought refuge during a snowstorm at the cabin of Abram Fuller. By then it was well known they were passing through the country and an eighty-man posse led by a United States marshal rode up from Missouri to apprehend them, even as he wired Kansas's new territorial governor, Samuel Medary, premature affirmation of his success. As the marshal advanced, scouts approached Fuller's cabin, Stevens stepped out to meet them. "Gentlemen," he said, "you look as if you were looking for somebody or something." "Yes," one of them replied, "we think you have some slaves up in that house." "Is that so? Well, come on with me and see." As he reached the door, Stevens opened it just wide enough to grab a shotgun resting inside. Pointing it at the men, he said: "You want to see slaves, do you? Well, just look up those barrels and see if you can find them."

All three men ran, but as one had a bead drawn on him, he was captured. Samuel Harper, one of the fugitives, later recounted in

Hamilton's *John Brown in Canada*: "Captain Brown went to see the prisoner, and says to him, 'I'll show you what it is to look after slaves, my man.' That frightened the prisoner awful. He was a kind of old fellow and when he heard what the captain said, I suppose he thought he was going to be killed. He began to cry and beg to be let go. The captain only smiled a little bit, and talked some more to him, the next day he was let go." Meanwhile Brown had sent word back to Topeka that he needed help, and soon Kagi arrived with twenty well-armed men; leaving the odds still four to one against them. With the marshal and his posse waiting in a strong position of ambush at Fuller's Ford, and even as Governor Medary telegraphed President Buchanan of Brown's imminent capture, one of the men asked Brown what he was going to do. "Cross the creek and move north."

"But, Captain," he objected, "the water is high and I doubt if we can get through. There is a much better ford five miles up the creek."

Brown replied: "I intend to travel it straight through and there is no use to talk of turning aside. Those who are afraid may go back. The Lord has marked out a path for me and I intend to follow it. We are ready to move."

George Gill, who had come up with the Topeka men to rejoin the company, wrote, "The scene was ridiculous beyond description." Placing a double row of mounted men before the wagon, giving them sufficient room of maneuver, Brown gave the order to charge straight at the enemy. From waiting in ambush, they now found they were the ones under attack. Seeing horsemen bearing down on them, the entire posse along with the marshal jumped for their horses and fled in disarray. Samuel Harper's account of what became known as the Battle of the Spurs continues: "Captain Brown and Kagi and some others chased them, and captured five prisoners. There was a doctor and a lawyer amongst them. They all had nice horses. The captain made them get down, then he told five of us slaves to mount the beasts and we rode them while the white men had to walk. . . . The mud on the roads was away over their ankles. I just tell you it was mighty tough walking, and you can believe those fellows had enough of slave-hunting. The next day the captain let them all go."[12]

For eighty-one days Brown and his party doggedly trekked before reaching the "land of Canaan," as fugitive slaves called Canada. On February 1 they approached the Nebraska border. With the Nemaha River only partially frozen and too deep to cross, they waited through a bitterly cold night. By morning the ice was solid enough to bear the weight of a man, but not a team and wagon. Disassembling the wagon, it was pushed across in pieces, and a makeshift bridge of lumber, poles, and brush was laid for the horses. Three days later, eluding another posse, Brown and his troop crossed the Missouri River into Iowa.

As they entered Tabor on February 4, news of the exploit had preceded them. There the fugitives would be housed in the schoolhouse of a local church and provided for by member families; but there was controversy in regard to their benefactors. At Sunday service a clergyman refused to entertain Brown's petition to the pulpit asking for "public thanksgiving to Almighty God in behalf of himself, & company; and of their rescued captives," because they had killed a man and taken horses and other property. And the following evening, as Brown was giving a public recital, he interrupted his remarks when a slaveholder from St. Joseph, Missouri, entered. Brown requested the man withdraw, but the sense of the meeting was that he remain. As Brown walked out he remarked to Charles Plummer Tidd, one of his followers, and a headstrong mechanic from Maine, "There are some there who would give us a halter for our pains. We had best look to our arms and horses." The meeting then debated and passed a resolution of support for the fugitives, but stipulated, "We have no sympathy with those who go to slave states to entice away slaves and take property or life when necessary to attain that end."[13] Leaving Tabor on February 11, and traveling twenty-five miles a day, on the 18th Des Moines was reached. There Kagi would visit the office of the *Register*, giving its editor an account of Brown's Missouri feat, with Brown following up with a letter. Two days later they were in Grinnell, where Brown knocked at the door of Josiah Bushnell Grinnell, the abolitionist and founder of the town and college bearing his name. "This cannot be a social visit," he began. "I am that terrible Brown of whom you have heard." As he explained that he needed a place to stay for himself and his companions, Grinnell forthwith threw open the door to his parlor, henceforth called the Liberty Room, saying, "This room is at your service and you can occupy the stalls at the barn which are not taken. Our hotel will be as safe as any place for part of your company."[14]

On successive nights there were standing-room only meetings at which Brown and Kagi spoke where they "were loudly cheered; & fully indorsed," as Brown wrote. Contributions in clothing, food, and cash were raised for the fugitives, and J. B. Grinnell, now called "John Brown" Grinnell, arranged for rail conveyance to Chicago for them, from the railhead at West Liberty, Iowa. The contrast between the receptions in Tabor and in Grinnell was striking, and Brown exalted. In a letter dated February 26, 1859, written from Springdale, he emphasized the points of variance to some of those back in Tabor, under the title "Reception of Brown & Party at Grinnell, Iowa":

> Three Congregational Clergymen attended the meeting on Sabbath evening (notice of which was given out from the Pulpit). All of them took part in justifying our course & in urging contributions in our behalf & there was no dissenting speaker present at either meeting. Mr. Grinnell spoke at length & has since labored to procure us a free and safe conveyance to Chicago: & effected it. . . .
>
> As the action of Tabor friends has been published in the newspapers by some of her people (as I suppose), would not friend Gaston or some other friend give publicity to all the above.

By the 25th the party had moved on to Springdale, where Brown's Quaker friends extended their hospitality. George Gill would remain there with his family to recover from an inflammation in his joints and would never see his companions again. As they were enjoying their reunion, word would reach Springdale that a large posse of "Kansas men" was arriving in a nearby town proposing to apprehend them. Brown and his entourage were whisked off to West Liberty and on March 9 boarded an unbilled boxcar for Chicago. The car had been decoupled and pushed by a group of men to a side track for loading. Fresh straw was bought up and John Brown climbed into the boxcar, laying the material for bedding. Then he reached down taking each child and placing them on it. Then, extending a hand to each adult, he helped them clamber aboard.

The following morning the train reached Chicago, and drew up a half-mile from the depot where the car with the fugitives was detached and pushed to a side track where its occupants were discharged. Brown was soon in touch with the famed detective Allen Pinkerton, who showed no reserve whatever about escorting the fugitives to the mill owned by Henry O. Wagner, who put out a sign "closed for repairs," while Brown went to the home of his friend, John Jones. That afternoon Pinkerton sought $400 from C. G. Hammond, superintendent of the Michigan Central Railroad, for a freshly provisioned boxcar to Detroit. Meanwhile Brown had boarded an earlier train after telegraphing Frederick Douglass, whose whereabouts he'd learned from Jones, requesting that they meet in Detroit.

During the winter of 1858–59, Douglass, together with John Jones and H. Ford Douglass, had been making an intensive swing through Illinois, Wisconsin, and Michigan. Finding audiences that gave them a positive, even enthusiastic hearing, Douglass was to write of "Our Recent Western Tour" in his April *Monthly*: "A Negro lecturer [is] an excellent thermometer of the state of public opinion on the subject of slavery." He was much better than a white antislavery lecturer, Douglass argued, because "a hated opinion is not always in sight—a hated color is. . . . The Negro is the test of American civilization." It was while completing his tour of Michigan—where he visited Battle Creek, Marshall, Albion, Jackson, and Ann Arbor—that he received the telegram from John Brown, then with John Jones in Chicago, summoning him to a meeting in Detroit. For this reason an appearance at Detroit's City Hall was added to Douglass's itinerary, and he arrived in the city on March 12, a day of blizzard conditions. That same afternoon the fugitives arrived at the wharf in Detroit to await embarkation for Windsor. Shortly before they boarded the ferry, John Brown arrived to see them off; said he: "Lord, permit Thy servant to die in peace; for mine eyes have seen Thy salvation! I could not brook the thought that any ill should befall you—least of all, that you should be taken back to slavery. The arm of Jehovah protected us."[15]

There was now to be a closed-door meeting of a small group of select persons at the home of William Webb. Those included were William Lambert and William C. Munroe, together with George DeBaptista, who had taken over leadership of the Detroit Vigilance Committee from Lambert, and at least three other black Detroiters, along with William Webb and John Brown. While there are few details available one can be sure the gathering had an earnest, if congratulatory air, as undoubtedly Brown's recent exploit was discussed, its implications and incidents narrated. As far as Brown's Virginia campaign was of concern, the fact that several of the participants had been at the Chatham convention the previous year suggests it too was up for discussion. It is known that DeBaptista questioned the efficacy of Brown's plan, and in its stead suggested a program of bombings across the South as a way to throw the slave oligarchy off guard and to raise a national outcry against slavery. Whatever the resolution on the issue, Brown surely would have demurred from being connected with it on humanitarian grounds. There has been the suggestion too that there was sharp disagreement between Douglass and Brown, some supposing Brown challenged Douglass's courage when he opposed certain measures. After interviewing Douglass about the matter in subsequent years as well as discussing other pertinent issues of his relationship with Brown, Richard Hinton was to write in his book, "Mr. Douglass assures me that nothing of the sort occurred."[16] The two would be seen working together in the coming months, and any friction displayed at Webb's home likely had more to do with Brown's aversion to merely talking abolitionism, than any reservations Douglass may have had. While he was by no means a mere talker, Douglass was among the best of them. "Talk, talk, talk," Brown said to another at another time; "Talk is a national institution, but it does no manner of good for the slave."[17]

In the columns of his April *Monthly* Douglass would avow his confidence in John Brown, writing the basis of his idea was that "the enslavement of the humblest human being is an act of injustice and wrong, for which Almighty God will hold all mankind responsible; that a case of the kind is one in which every human being is solemnly bound to interfere; and that he who had the power to do so, and fails to improve it, is involved in the guilt of the original crime. He takes this to be sound morality, and sound Christianity, and we think him not far from the right."

Uppermost on Brown's mind then—and this is another subject likely discussed at William Webb's—was not only the organizing of black recruits, but the need to find a recognized leader of demonstrated ability who would not shrink from the dangers his Virginia campaign would entail. After the plan was postponed, the setback in regard to the Canadian refugees had to be addressed, and Brown must have thought to rely on Harriet Tubman and Martin Delany for this. But there had been no contact with either of them, and Delany—who had corresponded with Kagi in Kansas, assuring him, in a letter dated August 16, 1858, of his and other Chathamites' continued support—had other priorities. He was making arrangements just then to embark for Africa on his Niger Valley expedition, commissioned by the 1856 follow-up to the emigration convention in Cleveland in 1854. Others, who had been at the Chatham convention or had knowledge of it had also turned their attention elsewhere. William Howard Day would be sailing for Dublin, Ireland, and Isaac Holden and James Monroe Jones would be traveling to the Canadian and U.S. Pacific coasts. Reverend Munroe was to set sail for Africa on the same vessel with Delany in May, going under church auspices to Liberia.

Others to whom Brown may have looked were Gloucester, Loguen, and Garnet. But Garnet had founded his African Civilization Society in 1858 and was thoroughly engaged in controversy. He and Gloucester, moreover, had been skeptical, counseling that they did not think the time was ripe, that slaves were not sufficiently aware of their rights to respond in the way Brown predicted, nor were northern blacks duly prepared. Perhaps none of these either, excepting Delany and Tubman (whose commitment remained unshaken), had the necessary military aptitude for Brown's enterprise.

A well-publicized event happening at the same time was a significant slave auction taking place on March 2 and 3 in 1859 in Savannah, Georgia. An advertisement for the sale of "Long Cotton and Rice Negroes" appeared in ten of the leading southern newspapers—from Richmond to New Orleans, from Macon to Memphis—indicating "where the purchasers were expected to come from and the slaves to go."[18] *New York Tribune* correspondent Mortimer Thomson, writing under the pen name Q. K. Philander Doesticks, was to report on the sale in an article published March 9, 1859, under the title "What Became of the Slaves on a Georgia Plantation," made available subsequently as a twenty-eight-page pamphlet by the American Anti-Slavery Society. The reporter appeared at the auction incognito, joining in the bidding to cover his identity; as the name of the owner of the slaves too was withheld. But as he appeared during the transaction and was seen saying farewell to his slaves after their sale, there was no doubt as to his identity. The largest sale of human beings in the history of the United States was from the estate of Pierce Mease Butler involving 436 of his chattel. The auction was so large it had to take place at the race course, and occurred on a succession of rainy days—as if heaven itself were weeping for those distraught and shaken by the proceedings—that was known as "the Weeping Time."

Pierce Butler and his brother John had inherited their wealth from their grandfather, Major Pierce Butler, the wealthiest planter and slave owner in the new republic. He was the man, as a delegate from his state to the constitutional convention in Philadelphia, who would insist that slavery be codified in the founding document, overseeing the placement of the "fugitive slave clause" as part of article IV section 2. The Butlers owned two plantations on Georgia's seacoast, planting rice and long cotton, Butler Island (present-day Darien) and St. Simon's Island. The young Pierce Butler owned the island of his namesake, but had established residence in Philadelphia; with a love of cards and stock market speculation, he led a profligate's life, marrying the English actress Fanny Kemble. Visiting the plantation after their marriage for several months in the winter of 1838–39, Kemble kept journals that would be published only in 1863, long after her divorce from Butler, as *Journal of a Residence on a Georgian Plantation*; this antislavery testament became instrumental in staying the hand of the British upper classes and parliamentary leaders eager to recognize the Confederate States of America. In 1856 the management of Pierce Butler's finances was handed over to three trustees to satisfy his debt. After selling his Philadelphia mansion and liquidating other properties, he was hit hard in the Panic of 1857. In February 1859 the trustees traveled to Georgia to appraise Butler's share of slaves.

After the slaves began arriving for the sale and were unloaded from boxcars, they had to be accommodated in the horse stables at the race course, three miles outside of Savannah. Two hundred planters and slave traders came from all parts of the South, and all the hotels were filled, the taverns bustling with men clinking glasses and blowing cigar smoke. The talk, the historian Frederic Bancroft bitingly noted, "was, of course, almost entirely about 'niggrahs' or 'niggers'"—what prices some had brought recently; whose had made large crops or been especially prolific, had run away or been recovered; whether the successful trip of the "Wander" meant that a reopening of the foreign slave-trade was possible, and if so, what effect this would have on the value of "home-raised niggers."[19]

Without benches or tables the slaves sat on the bare floor, or used what baggage they had for their accommodation. Special correspondent Mortimer Thomson depicted the haunting scene for his reading public: "On the faces of all was an expression of heavy grief; some appeared to be resigned to the hard stroke of Fortune that had torn them from their homes, and were sadly trying to make the best of it; some sat brooding moodily over their sorrows, their chins resting on their hands, their eyes staring vacantly, and their bodies rocking to and fro, with restless motion that was never stilled; few wept, the place was too public and the drivers too near, though some occasionally turned aside to give way to a few quiet tears."[20]

Despite the continuing rain the attendance at the auction was large. Before 10 o'clock March 2, the slaves with their hand baggage were crowded into the grandstand, a room one hundred feet by twenty. The auction was held in an adjoining space open to the storm on one side. The platform where the slaves were exhibited was two and a half feet high, with desks on either side for the clerks. With spectators and bidders crowding around the platform, the *Tribune's* reporter noted that the slaves who were not high on the list "gathered into sad groups in the background to watch the progress of the selling in which they were so sorrowfully interested. The wind howled outside, and through the open side of the building the driving rain came pouring in; the bar downstairs ceased for a short time its brisk trade; the buyers lit fresh cigars, got ready their catalogues and pencils, and the first lot of human chattels was led upon the stand, not by a white man, but by a sleek mulatto, himself a slave, and who seems to regard the selling of his brethren, in which he so glibly assists, as a capital joke."

A sixteen-page catalogue was printed for the auction with meager information of the people concerned, describing but barren existences. Each slave bore a number:

> 99—Kate's John, 30; rice, prime man.
> 118—Pompey, 31; rice—lame in one foot.
> 345—Dorcas, 17; cotton, prime woman.
> 346—Joe [Dorcas's baby and the only member of her "family" present] 3 months.[21]

One of the families sold consisted of a carpenter and his wife, with a baby and a three-year-old daughter. The wife, Daphney, kept a large shawl wrapped securely around herself and her baby. With this poignant scene drawing attention, some of the bidders saw it as an attempt at deception, and commented: "'What do you keep your nigger covered up for? Pull off her blanket.' 'What's the matter with the gal? Has she got the headache?' 'What's the fault of the gal? Ain't she sound? Pull off her rags and let us see her.'" At last the auctioneer obtained a hearing: he had no intention or desire to palm off an inferior article, he explained, but the fact of the matter was only days ago Daphney had left confinement, and must be allowed this "slight indulgence of a blanket, to keep from herself and child the chill air and the driving rain."[22]

The aggregate received from the sale was over $300,000, enough to restore Butler's fortune. The auction completed, baskets of champagne were brought forth and a generous popping of corks ensued. As the weather cleared it was noticed that there was a swarming of the newly sold people around the man known as Pierce Butler. "He had come to the sale," wrote Bancroft, "bringing from the United States Mint bags of bright new quarters, and was giving each adult Negro four shining pieces of silver as a farewell consolation."[23] Now the property of new masters, for a week scarcely a boat or a train left Savannah without taking some of these to their new homes across many parts of the South.

The entire front page of *Frederick Douglass' Paper* of March 25, 1859, was taken by Pierce M. Butler's slave auction. Pass the account around, Douglass urged his readers, "circulate it largely among your neighbors"; "it is an admirable anti-slavery document, and the N.Y. *Tribune* is entitled to much credit for furnishing the public with it."[24] A remarkable detail about "this grand vendue," said Douglass, was that the owner of the slaves was a citizen of a free state, a resident of Philadelphia, and a gentleman—"aye, a gentleman, if one can be such, who can breed men for the market, and drag a woman from a bed of confinement with a baby six days old in her arms to the auction, and there sell her and her baby to pay debts which this prodigal gentleman had contracted by riotous living."25 Doubtless other Pierce Butlers were in the city of Philadelphia—and this, Douglass maintained, was the reason for the slow growth of antislavery opinion in the great cities of the North. But it was wise for them to come north to defend slavery, "for here its fate is to be decided"; and nothing furnished a better barricade against assault than money and social position. With tart irony of pen Douglass then asked, who knew that Butler was not suffering patriotically; that he may have spent the earnings of his slaves too lavishly, but still at the call of his country? "If this be the case, his brother slaveholders have dealt ungratefully with him in allowing him thus to fall beneath the weight of his debts. They should have made common cause with him in this bitter hour of his need," Douglass concluded caustically.

In the same issue of his paper Frederick Douglass was to draw attention on one of his coadjutors on his "western tour," H. Ford Douglass. "He has that quality without which," he gave notice, "all speech is vain—earnestness. He throws his whole soul into what he says. His person is fine, his voice musical, and his gestures natural and graceful." This recognition, however, was advanced, "not as incense offered to vanity," but that he might better serve the cause. "We call upon H. Ford Douglass to put himself unreservedly into the lecturing field, not upon the platform of an African Civilization Society." That society had been organized in the previous summer, among whose principals was Henry Highland Garnet, who was chosen president. As with Martin Delany as its most prominent spokesman, along with an increasing number of influential leaders, this movement began promoting emigration, with a growing number of target areas. With Central America and South America, the Caribbean Islands—with Jamaica, Haiti, Santo Domingo, and Cuba—and various places in Africa, including Liberia being considered. The thrust was that American blacks should immigrate to a region in which the ruling element was African; in Garnet's phrase, "to establish a grand center of negro nationality." Commercial relations would flourish, and there would be growing intellectual and cultural exchanges. Invariably a component of this was to establish a rival to southern cotton production for the British and European and even northern markets, thereby undermining American slavery. The problem of course was from where would the capital come; and obviously for the project to become effective would require considerable time.

In the meantime, Douglass and others pointed out, such identifications ran too far afield; when the fight to be fought and won was within the United States. "Emigrationists" too were vulnerable to the criticism that their aim closely paralleled that of the American

Colonization Society. Indeed, one of the principals of the African Civilization Society, whose membership was open to all, was Benjamin Coates, the Quaker merchant from Philadelphia and a longtime colonizationist; but then, Garnet countered, Joshua Giddings was also a member.

Frederick Douglass rejected the idea of seeking a "nationality" far from the shores where the struggle must take place. He retorted: "We have an African nation on our bodies. . . . We are contending not for the rights of color, but for the rights of men." Therefore he was calling upon H. Ford Douglass to "stand upon the platform of Radical Abolitionism and go to the people of the country with a tangible issue." What better issue could be made, he advised, than to return to the state of Illinois and agitate for the repeal of its Black Law, a fight being led there by John Jones. "All that is malignant and slaveholding in that state, clings around and supports these atrocious laws. The immediate repeal of these cruel enactments, (which the white [Stephen A.] Douglas is endeavoring to sustain) should be the demand of the black Douglass of Chicago."

There was, too, an air of fatalism in Garnet's views that was not found in Douglass; Garnet said more than once he did not expect to live to see the end of slavery, and as he thundered defiance he might at times seem impetuous. The *Wanderer* with its forbidden cargo of four hundred slaves from the Congo, brought directly from a port on the Angolan coast, landed at Jekyll Island in Georgia on November 28, 1858. The slaves were quickly sold, but the vessel was seized by the United States Navy and the Buchanan administration would put the owner and officers on trial for piracy, only to have them acquitted at court. Garnet was asked at a meeting in Boston at the Joy Street Baptist Church to promote discussion of the African Civilization Society that September, where should a "negro nationality" be established, in the United States or in a far-off clime? He answered: "I hope in the United States, especially if they reopen the African slave trade. Then, if we do not establish a nationality in the South, I am mistaken in the spirit of my people. Let them bring in a hundred thousand a year! We do not say it is not a great crime, but we know that from the wickedness of man God brings forth good; and if they do it, before half a century shall pass over us we shall have a negro nationality in the United States. In Jamaica there are forty colored men to one white; Hayti is ours; Cuba will be ours soon, and we shall have every island in the Caribbean Sea."26

John Brown now arrived in Cleveland where the Oberlin-Wellington rescue trial was just getting under way. An outraged Buchanan admin-

istration had decided to make a signal example in this fugitive slave rescue, and thirty-seven warrants were issued against residents of Oberlin
and Wellington, including professors, clergy, students, free blacks, and
fugitive slaves alike. Twenty-three of those charged refused bail and
were confined en masse in Cleveland to await trial. When he arrived on
March 20 Brown took a room at a hotel only four blocks from the U.S.
marshal's office, making no effort to conceal his identity. Several days
later he stood before an auction to raise money by the sale of two horses and a mule, despite their "questionable title," even as posters were
being displayed calling for his arrest. A short time after this, drawing an
audience of fifty at a quarter-dollar admission, both Brown and Kagi
spoke. In his remarks, noted by the reporter for the *Cleveland Leader*,
Brown called attention to the fact that he was "an outlaw, the governor
of Missouri having offered a reward of $3000, and James Buchanan
$250, for him. He quietly remarked, parenthetically, that 'John Brown'
would give two dollars and fifty cents for the safe delivery of the body
of James Buchanan in any jail of the free states. He would never submit
to an arrest, as he had nothing to gain from submission; but he should
settle all question on the spot if any attempt was made to take him. The
liberation of those slaves was meant as a direct blow to slavery, and he
laid down his platform that he had considered it his duty to break the
fetters from any slave when he had an opportunity."[27]

In the audience that evening was a young man from Oberlin named
Lewis Sheridan Leary, the uncle of John Copeland, who was being held
in the jail awaiting the beginning of the trials with the other rescuers of
the fugitive slave John Price. Leary was a saddle and harness maker by
trade, and like Copeland, who had come to Oberlin to enter its university's preparatory school, he was originally from North Carolina. They
were foremost among a community where blacks bore an attitude
toward whites, a contemporary remarked, that said "touch me if you
dare"; and both had a keen interest in John Brown. Copeland was the
man who accompanied the fugitive slave to Cleveland, along with
Simeon Bushnell, one of the principals in the trials, to await the ferry
to Canada. Another of those charged in the case was Charles H.
Langston—the younger brother of the prominent abolitionist John
Mercer Langston. It was Charles, the secretary of the Ohio Anti-Slavery
Society, who led the charge from a growing crowd to free Price.

The first defendant to be tried was Bushnell; he was adjudged guilty
and sentenced to sixty days in the county jail, with a fine of six hundred
dollars and ordered to pay the cost of his prosecution. Charles
Langston was the next up; his speech to the court—"Should Colored

Men Be Subjected to the Penalties of the Fugitive Slave Law?"—had a powerful effect, both on the court and in wider circulation. Printed in its entirety in the *Cleveland Leader* and in the *Columbus State Journal*, it again appeared in the *Anglo-African*, which had begun publication that January by two New York City printers, Thomas and Robert Hamilton, where it was printed together with his brother's account of the entire rescue episode, then circulated as a pamphlet. Langston too was adjudged guilty, but on the eloquence of his statement the judge pronounced a less stringent sentence, twenty days in the county jail with a fine of one hundred dollars plus the cost of prosecution.

Brown was in Cleveland for ten days only and certainly did not meet with Charles Langston, but he was surely familiar with his plea for justice in the court. Kagi and others of their party, however, did become Langston's intimate; Kagi reported on the trials as a correspondent to the *New York Tribune* and the *Cleveland Leader*. While in Cleveland Brown received an invitation from Joshua Giddings to speak at the Congregational Church in Jefferson where Giddings was a member; receiving donations from the congregation, including money from Giddings, and an invitation to his home for dinner, Brown undoubtedly considered this contact with the leader of antislavery opinion in the House of Representatives fortuitous. Together with the addition of Leary, Copeland, Langston, and others as adherents, it argued well for his coming campaign.

In the second week of April, traveling with Jeremiah Anderson, a recruit gained from among Montgomery's men on the recent visit to Kansas, who was acting as his adjunct, Brown was in Rochester. Biographers who note this meeting often infer it was a stop of several hours only, while in fact it was at this time that Douglass arranged for Brown's appearance at Rochester City Hall. He gave notice of it in his paper, coming out now as *Douglass' Monthly*, published April 15 under the heading "Old Brown in Rochester." Rebuking self-professed "Republicans" for staying away, Douglass wrote, "Even our newly appointed Republican janitor ran off with the key to the bell of the City Hall, and refused to ring it on the occasion! Shame upon his little soul, and upon the little souls who sustained him in his conduct."

During this visit Douglass introduced Brown to an individual he intended as a contribution to the recruiting for the Virginia campaign, who was then a boarder in his home. He was a fugitive slave from Charleston, South Carolina, who had come to Rochester after escaping aboard a ship in 1856. Leaving a son in slavery after the death of his wife, he had been in St. Catharines for several years where he was engaged as a house servant and waiter. Returning to Rochester in 1858, he proposed to establish himself in business as a clothes cleaner. The man's name had been Esau Brown, which he exchanged for Shields Green; a full-blooded African, he was twenty-four years old, of slight stature but well built, possessing a self-confident bearing. Styling himself in dress and action a "Zouave," he was reputedly in the lineage of an African prince and referred to himself as "Emperor." His host described him as "a man of few words," with speech that was singularly broken, "but his courage and self-respect made him quite a dignified character." The bond between the elderly white man and the young black could not have been greater, Douglass concluded: "John Brown saw at once what 'stuff' Green was made of, and confided to him his plans and purposes. Green easily believed in Brown, and promised to go with him whenever he should be ready to move."[28]

Just how far was Douglass himself willing to go in support of John Brown? For several decades he had participated in any number of platforms for antislavery action; he had been ever ready to publish, to speak, to combine or to conspire with any individual, society, or party, as he would say, "to head off, hem in, and dam up the desolating tide of slavery." But the sad fact was, Douglass wrote later that summer, "that in the hands of all these societies and committees, nearly all our antislavery instrumentalities have disappeared. . . . The Radical Abolition Society . . . was built on a faultless plan, but where is that society to-day? Where is its committee? Where its paper, its lecturers and patrons? All gone!" He was therefore opting, he wrote, "to work for the present on the plan of individualism, uttering our word for freedom and justice, wherever we may find ears to hear, and writing our thoughts for whosoever will read them."[29] It is on this ground one must look for complementarity between Brown and Douglass, noting that the latter supplied the former with a recruit, convened meetings, and collected money for him, and had facilitated his contact with Harriet Tubman—all for an attack on slavery "with the weapons precisely adapted to bring it to the death." The orientation of Douglass and his solidarity with Brown's mission was strongly exhibited in a letter of Jeremiah Anderson dated June 17, 1859. Writing to his brother, Dr. John B. Anderson, as he and his leader prepared to travel to Chambersburg, Pennsylvania, and were again in Rochester, Anderson divulged: "Our theory is new, but undoubtedly good, practicable, and perfectly safe and simple, but I judge when we put it into practice, it will astonish the world and mankind in general. We called on Fred. Douglass again as we passed through Rochester; he is to be one of us."[30]

Brown and Anderson next traveled to Peterboro to the estate of Gerrit Smith. In the evening Brown addressed a small gathering including Smith and his wife, and Edwin Morton, then employed by Smith as tutor for his son. Morton left an interesting record, giving an intimation that Harriet Tubman was also in attendance. She often traveled across New York from her home in Auburn, where her parents lived, to St. Catharines, and would assuredly have received word from Douglass that Brown would be at Smith's. Morton wrote to Sanborn that Brown had been "tremendous," and that he no longer had any doubts as to the soundness of his course, adding, "I suppose you know where this matter is to be adjudicated. Harriet Tubman suggested the 4th of July as a good time to 'raise the mill.'" After Brown spoke, with an eloquence that moved both Smith and his wife to tears, the philanthropist rose to hail Brown as "the man in all the world I think most truly Christian," and he wrote a pledge for a $400 contribution.

Harpers Ferry, Virginia (now West Virginia), is a town occupying a narrow spit of land at the confluence of the Shenandoah and Potomac rivers, situated between two towering ridges, Maryland and Loudoun Heights, and rising on a hill called Bolivar Heights. It is a natural bridge from Maryland into Virginia's Blue Ridge Mountains; and to the thinking of John Brown, it was indeed the Thermopylae of Virginia. By 1859 it was a bustling center of commerce and industry, with a population of three thousand persons, including three hundred free blacks and slaves among them. The Baltimore and Ohio Railroad, connecting Baltimore and Washington to Ohio west of the mountain ranges, and the Winchester and Harper's Ferry Railroad, running some thirty miles into Virginia's Shenandoah Valley, were routed through it. Converging in a Y-junction near the confluence of the rivers, the tracks crossed the Potomac River to Maryland on a single-truss iron suspension bridge, at the time the largest such on the continent. Three main streets traversed the town; Shenandoah and Potomac streets running parallel to the rivers, and High Street ascending Bolivar Heights.

The United States Congress, at the urging of the first president, had established a national arms manufactory and arsenal there, which had previously seen the development of Hall's Rifle Works by Eli Whitney and another Connecticut Yankee. By 1850 the United States Armory was a substantial works: divided by a single street, two orderly rows of multistoried buildings ran for two thousand feet along the Potomac; with shops for stocking and machining, smith and forging, annealing and carpentry, and mills for sawing and grinding, with ware and storehouses. Fronted by an open area known as the Ferry Lot, across from the armory were some of the commercial establishments, the train depot, and a hotel. Beside these on the Shenandoah River, with the Winchester and Harper's Ferry Depot behind it, was a walled enclosure called Arsenal Square, whose buildings housed at any given time between one and two hundred thousand stand of arms.

The ruling element in the South lived as an unassailable aristocracy in a population of five million whites and four million black slaves, as no more than fifty thousand of the three hundred thousand slaveholders were set up as planters. As a geographical entity their hegemony extended from the mid-Atlantic states down the seaboard through the Old South, pushing westward through the tier of states known as the Deep South; touching thence on the Gulf of Mexico, it ranged up the Mississippi River Valley, claiming all land to the northern borders of Kentucky and Missouri; extending thereafter, on the western bank of the Mississippi, into the rich cotton country in Arkansas, and claiming the river valleys of eastern Texas. The South drew in fully fifteen states; with an extensive shoreline, it encompassed the broad middle region called the border states, as well as a part of the Southwest. Each of these regions was as diverse from the other as they were from any of the northern states—in geography and latitude, in the admixture of the emigrant European stock, in resources and the various pursuits of industry. What gave this expanse its cohesion was the recognition by law and custom of the ownership of black-skinned human chattel.

Harpers Ferry came to figure prominently in Brown's mind because of the vast cordillera that broadens and rises reaching heights of three thousand feet and more that begins only twenty-five miles below Maryland's border. Within a thirty-mile radius of Harpers Ferry were twenty thousand slaves; and thereafter starting at the head of the Blue Ridge a continuous chain of counties extended clear to Virginia's southern border where black predominated over white. Together with the eastern counties of Maryland and its Eastern Shore, and the northern counties of North Carolina—this comprised one of American slavery's great cantons. Another, extending from the Atlantic shore islands through South Carolina and mid-Georgia, taking in a large swath of north-central Florida to its panhandle, thence ranging through mid-Alabama down to the gulf and embracing the whole of the southern Mississippi River Valley, found its western limit in the river valleys of the Brazos and Neches rivers of eastern Texas.

"The South . . . is neither a territory strictly detached from the North geographically, nor a moral unity," contended Marx in the second of two important articles written for Vienna's *Die Presse* on October 25 and November 8, 1861, respectively. "It is not a country at all, but a battle slogan." Citing the "decisive" importance of a strictly "numerical proportion" of black to white in the temperamental disposition of the South, in the article titled "The Civil War in the United States," Marx elaborated: "The soul of the whole secession movement is South Carolina. It has 402,541 slaves and 301,271 free men. Mississippi . . . comes second. It has 436,696 slaves and 354,699 free men. Alabama comes third, with 435,132 slaves and 529,164 free men." Brown and Kagi, as has been seen, devoted considerable study to this significant configuration, developing a series of seven large maps plotting out these "black belts" on a county-by-county basis; noting such details as census figures, indicating many of the large plantations where masses of slaves were held, as well as marking out the mountain ranges, rivers, and railroad lines and many of the swamps and places of refuge, and also designating some of the places to be attacked as their campaign took hold and developed. This campaign, as has been indicated, they projected to extend down the mountainous line in Virginia into North and South Carolina, and westward into Tennessee. These maps would be found by his captors after John Brown's defeat and commented on by editorialists throughout the South; the documents' importance was attested to by the fact that the Virginian authorities would destroy them to suppress the incendiary information they contained. Douglass was familiar with them and would also have been cognizant of their import.

Brown was continually reiterating that nowhere was the South more vulnerable than in its fear of servile insurrection. With a successful issue at Harpers Ferry, the slaveholders would imagine the whole of the North and all of their slaves crashing down upon them pell-mell, and it would recoil remarkably throughout the region. If he could conquer Virginia, Brown would say, "the balance of the southern states would nearly conquer themselves, there being such a large number of slaves in them."[31]

On Maryland's Eastern Shore, where Harriet Tubman had been particularly active in the Bucktown-Cambridge region of Dorchester County in the period 1857 through 1859, culminating in 1860, the slaveholders were already on the point of taking armed action against the Underground Railroad.[32] A movement of Eastern Shore slaveholders, initiated in 1857, came to a head in the summer of 1859, as decades-old laws regulating and restricting free blacks and the movement of slaves were enforced with renewed vigor. In August 1858 the slaveholders had trumpeted their manifesto as reported in the Eastern

Shore newspapers: "Let us not only have a Convention here on the eastern shore, but let it be held in view of the holding hereafter of a great Slaveholding Convention of the slave states. . . . Not a convention of mere words, but one of action—an action which coming events will force upon the South and upon us of Maryland."[33]

A reward had been offered for the apprehension "of the Negro woman who was denuding the fields of their laborers, and cabins of their human livestock,"[34] but this "greatest heroine of the age," as Harriet Tubman was billed, was to all appearance an ordinary woman of the South. Wearing her hair closely cropped, she had a round and receding chin, ponderous eyelids, large protruding lips, with her upper front teeth missing. Commonly "attired in coarse, but neat apparel," as William Wells Brown described her, "with an old-fashioned reticule or bag suspended by her side," she always wore a bandana headdress. Adept at disguise, concealment, and maneuver, she conducted her charges through "middle passage"—as William Still called escape from bondage to freedom—as if it were a military campaign, enforcing strict discipline, always armed with a revolver.

Although her reputation was growing, and she had begun to address antislavery conventions, she had not yet gained the prominence she would have by 1860. To be sure she was well known to Douglass, Loguen, and Still, but she had been obliged to drop out of sight for periods of time, working and saving money for her rescue missions, and to support her aging parents, who lived in Auburn, New York, in a home provided on generous terms by William H. Seward.

From April 9 to May 5 Brown was with his wife and younger daughters in North Elba, where he would remain mostly convalescing from illness. May 7 to June 2 found him again in New England. Before arriving in Boston, where Harriet Tubman had also gone, Brown visited Sanborn in Concord, where he delivered an address. A. Bronson Alcott noted in his diary entry: "I have a few words with [Brown] after his speech, and find him superior to legal traditions, and a disciple of the right in ideality and the affairs of the state. He is Sanborn's guest, and stays a day only. A young man named Anderson accompanies him. They go armed, I am told and will defend themselves, if necessary."[35] While in Concord Brown brought up the subject with Sanborn that he undertake a journey for him, but because of his obligations the scholar demurred. In a letter to Higginson, Sanborn in turn wrote that Brown was "desirous of getting someone to go to Canada and collect recruits, with H. Tubman, or alone as the case may be & urged me to go. . . . Last year he engaged some persons and heard of others, but he does not want to lose time by going himself now. I suggested you to him. Now is the time to help the movement, if ever, for within the next two months the experiment will be made."[36] Sanborn added, "As a reward for what he had done, perhaps money might be raised for him." In his reply, apparently referring to Brown's raid in Missouri, Higginson wrote, "It is hard for me to solicit money for another retreat." His ardor evidently had cooled from the previous year as he would recall in his *Cheerful Yesterdays*: "It all began to seem rather dubious."[37]

The following day Brown was to call on Amos Lawrence, who had also turned decidedly cool to him. Lawrence wrote in his diary: "He has been stealing Negroes and running them off from Missouri. He has a monomania on that subject, I think, and would be hanged if he were taken in a slave state. . . . He and his companion both have the fever and ague, somewhat, probably, a righteous visitation for their fanaticism."[38] While in Boston, Samuel Gridley Howe and Stearns were to convey Brown as their guest to a dinner meeting of the Bird Club, of which they were members, where he met Senator Henry Wilson. When Brown remarked that he understood the senator did not approve of his course, Wilson replied that he did not, and that if he had gone into Missouri two years before there would have been a retaliatory invasion with great resultant bloodshed. Brown replied with a scathing look that he thought he had acted right and that it had exercised a salutary influence. Howe introduced Brown to John Murray Forbes, a wealthy clipper trader and railroad financier. Invited to his home in Milton, Brown held the businessman and a few of his friends up past midnight "with his glittering eye" and talk of the coming war between North and South. At another meeting, John A. Andrew (soon to be elected governor of Massachusetts) contributed $25 and noted, "The old gentleman in conversation scarcely regarded other people, was entirely self-possessed and appeared to have no emotion of any sort but was entirely absorbed in an idea which pre-occupied him and put him in a position transcending ordinary thought and ordinary reason."[39]

In the spring of 1859 Harriet Tubman came to Boston primarily to arrange for the security of her parents, so she could go on to do "practical work" with John Brown. Sanborn wrote: "Pains were taken to secure her the attention to which her great services to humanity entitled her, and she left New England with a handsome sum of money towards payment of her debt to Mr. Seward."[40] "Before she left, however," he continued, "she had several interviews with Captain Brown, then in Boston. . . . He always spoke of her with the greatest respect, and declared that 'General Tubman,' as he styled her, was a better officer than most whom he had seen, and could command an army as successfully as she had led her small parties of fugitives." Wendell Phillips wrote to Sarah Bradford of being called on by two distinguished visitors: "The last time I ever saw John Brown was under my own roof, as he brought Harriet Tubman to me, saying 'Mr. Phillips, I bring you one of the best and bravest persons on this continent— General Tubman as we call her.'"[41]

It was at this time that the woman whose activity, as Douglass would write, had been witnessed only "by the midnight sky and the silent stars," began to appear on the public stage, leaving deep impressions on abolitionist circles and forming lasting friendships with many persons. Higginson would write in a letter to his mother, dated June 17, 1859:

> We have had the greatest heroine of the age here, Harriet Tubman, a black woman, and a fugitive slave, who has been back eight times secretly and brought out in all sixty slaves with her, including all her own family, besides aiding many more in other ways to escape. Her tales of adventure are beyond anything in fiction and her ingenuity and generalship are extraordinary. I have known her for some time and mentioned her in speeches once or twice—the slaves call her Moses. She has had a reward of twelve thousand dollars offered for her in Maryland and will probably be burned alive whenever she is caught, which she probably will be, first or last, as she is going again. She has been in the habit of working in hotels all summer and laying up money for this crusade in the winter. She is jet black and cannot read or write, only talk, besides acting.[42]

Since February Brown had been preparing his financial backers about collecting the money promised him after the Chatham convention. That fund-raising, he would report to Kagi in Cleveland, "was a delicate and very difficult matter." It had been complicated by the departure of Theodore Parker, who, ill with consumption and no longer able to take New England's winters, had gone to Cuba in December 1858 accompanied by Dr. Howe. After two months he would sail for Rome and, at age fifty, die in Florence in 1860. Parker's interest in Brown's crusade was undiminished, however, as he wrote Sanborn from Rome: "Tell me how our little speculation in wool goes on, and what dividend accrues there from."[43] But he had to drop all active participation and could offer nothing in monetary aid. For his part, Howe began to take a more nuanced view in regard to a military attack on slavery after visiting Wade Hampton's plantation in South Carolina on his way home. His interest in Brown's sanguinary outlook lessened after partaking of his host's gracious hospitality; Howe himself explained he felt he had to relinquish his stake in the enterprise after imagining its consequences for Hampton and his family.

The amount finally raised for Brown at this time came to something over $2000; and all in all he probably marked it up as sufficing his purposes. Leaving his supporters in Boston "much in the dark concerning his destination and designs for the coming months,"[44] Brown next appeared on the evening of June 3 at the shop of Charles Blair in Collinsville, Connecticut. Reminding the blacksmith who he was, he said he had come to fulfill the contract they had made in the previous year. After some parleying Blair agreed, when paid the remaining $450 he would "find a man in the vicinity to do the work." (Blair was summoned to testify at the Senate Committee hearings into Harpers Ferry in 1860.) The following day Brown came again, handing Blair $50 in cash and a $100 check, mailing the balance in a check on June 7 from Troy, New York, for the manufacture of one thousand pikes.

On June 9 Brown was in North Elba for a week for a last reunion with his wife and daughters. Then traveling across New York he stopped in Rochester for a last conference with Douglass; and after a stop in Cleveland, on June 18 he was in West Andover, Ohio. His eldest son would be his indispensable liaison in the preparations for the Virginia campaign—shipping arms, collecting money, maintaining contacts with supporters, and gathering and forwarding recruits—and this would be his last consultation with him before setting up his "southern headquarters." Then, from Akron, with two of his sons, Owen and Oliver, and Jeremiah Anderson, Brown notified Kagi that he was on the way to the Ohio River.

They traveled by boat to Pittsburgh, then by rail through to Harrisburg, before arriving at Chambersburg, where lodgings were taken for the night by "Isaac Smith & Sons." Hagerstown, Maryland, was reached the next day, and they again took lodgings. At eight the next morning, July 3, the quartet reached Harpers Ferry; surveying the town and the surroundings, Brown and his party would have crossed the Potomac Bridge and begun making inquiries about renting a farm on the Maryland side of the river. Soon learning of a site owned by the heirs of a Dr. Kennedy a mile or two east of the river on the Boonesborough Pike, within a day or two Brown had rented the buildings and land for $35, until March 1, 1860. Once this preparatory work was done, Oliver was sent back to North Elba to bring his sixteen-year-old sister, Anne, and his seventeen-year-old wife, Martha, who was pregnant with their child, back to the Maryland farm. They would provide a setting of normality to outside curiosity, also providing sustenance and comforts for the men as they arrived.

Notified of these developments, John Jr. received $100 from his father for traveling expenses and was instructed to "hold back Whipple & Co" until the quarters were ready. The agent was also told to "be in readiness to make the journey through the country northward." Meanwhile Kagi, who would use the name "John Henrie," had arrived in Chambersburg, fifty miles north of Harpers Ferry, with instruction to take lodgings at an inn on East King Street, of which Mary Ritner was the proprietor. He was also instructed to make the acquaintance of Henry Watson "and his reliable friends," the effective Underground Railroad operatives in that Pennsylvania town, but he was in no way to appear "thick" with them.[45]

Into the Untried Future

S peaking at Storer College at Harpers Ferry, West Virginia, on May 30, 1881, Frederick Douglass addressed the subject of his relationship with John Brown and the enduring significance of that "raid" of which Brown was the commander, saying, "That startling cry of alarm on the banks of the Potomac was but the answering back of the avenging angel to the midnight invasions of Christian slave-traders on the sleeping hamlets of Africa." Before "this simple altar of human virtue," said Douglass, scholarship, poetry, and eloquence, story and song, retire dissatisfied with the thinness of their offerings, and as he expected, so too would his. Indicating that judgment toward which all commentary must aspire, Douglass continued: "Though more than twenty years have rolled between us and the Harper's Ferry raid, though since then the armies of the nation have found it necessary to do on a large scale what John Brown attempted to do on a small one, and the captain who fought his way through slavery has filled with honor the Presidential chair, we yet stand too near the days of slavery, and the life and times of John Brown, to see clearly the true martyr and hero that he was and rightly to estimate the value of the man and his works."[1]

The difficulty that American historiography and literature have encountered in assessing the man and the meaning of his actions results from the circumstance, and this was Douglass's contention, that the long shadow of slavery "yet falls broad and large over the face of the whole country"—and as those tendentious currents of this ongoing challenge impact how we perceive events, we are continually taken unaware as if by the uncanny.

The idea behind the selection of Harpers Ferry for an opening salvo was twofold. Foremost was to give Southern "firebrands" the pretext they sought to carry out their threat of secession; this "far more than any other" was the idea behind it, Brown's son, Salmon, was to relate—in Oswald Garrison Villard's *John Brown: Fifty Years After.* "All writers," Salmon Brown said, had "failed heretofore to bring out this far-reaching idea to the extent it merits."[2] Once a complete schism had taken place, the predicate was, the North would be compelled to whip the South back into the Union without slavery. And as its corollary, it was Brown's intention to anticipate this rebellion by using Harper's Ferry as "a trumpet to rally the slaves to his standard," as Douglass phrased it, as a signal to be heard across the South that "friends" in the North were prepared to intervene on their behalf and inspire them to rally. He had "unsheathed his sword," as he said, to forestall for the country the necessity of going through the war he had seen prefigured in the events of the day—a war issuing on the requirements of the collisions of great armies, over great distances. At one blow, the political platforms upon which the country tottered would come crashing down and a war begun for the liberation of the slaves.

One of the difficulties Brown sought to resolve by beginning at Harpers Ferry was that of introducing a significant body of men into Virginia's Blue Ridge Mountains; another was to give the movement sufficient momentum. These two purposes were co-determinate. Brown's plan called for a party to cross the Potomac Bridge at night, seizing and holding the bridge; the telegraph wire would be cut, with the telegraph wire on the Virginia side also being cut. Crossing the Ferry Lot to the United States Armory, the watchman would be called out and compelled to open the gate, or it would be broken open. The two buildings fronting the government works overlooking the Ferry Lot were to be seized—the fire engine house and the paymaster's office.

On Shenandoah Street, across the Lot, the arsenal would also be invested, and behind it the bridge to Loudoun Heights. Finally Hall's Rifle Works situated with a number of other fabrics, a half mile up the Shenandoah between the river and a canal, was to be invested. All the gaslights in the lower part of town were to be extinguished, and a roving picket and sentries established to assure unimpeded access and communication among the points seized. Trains arriving during the night would be stopped and prohibited from passing, and the tracks torn up on each side of the river to ensure it. Incendiary devices would be placed on the bridges so that they could be fired if that became advisable.

By beginning the operation at night, the possibility of encountering any resistance would be minimized and the town quickly secured before alarm could be given. As people awakened and the day began, unaware of what had happened, they would find the government works and their streets under the control of armed men, who would have, as well, a monopoly on all the best arms in the neighborhood. They would be dissuaded from opposing him and hold to their houses, or else flee the town. Those who did not, and who sought to interfere, would, for their own safety, be held prisoner for a time. At the outset "without the snapping of a gun," Brown said, they would have possession of the government property and the rifle factory, and the points of entrance and egress from the town.

When the Ferry was secure, and before daybreak, a second phase would have commenced. A party was to proceed up Bolivar Heights to selected slaveholding estates. Slaves would be freed and brought back to the government grounds along with their masters, together with other seized property, horses, and wagons. Another party would execute the same procedure on nearby farms in Maryland, seizing selected slaveholders and their property and bringing them to the Ferry. These prominent slaveholding citizens would be the very persons who could be expected to lead any resistance, and those who wanted to oppose them would be restrained so as not to harm them. In the worst case, too, they would be able to dictate the terms of their withdrawal by the influence and prominence of these men.

Brown's intention, moreover, was not to harm them, but to make a signal example of them by arranging with their "friends" for their exchange for able-bodied male slaves. The fact that Brown envisioned this exchange suggests a formal setting, where before a sizable assembly a thunderbolt would roll across the nation as emancipation was proclaimed in Maryland and Virginia. The seizure of the government armory and the capture of prominent hostages, while freeing and arming slaves, was the prelude to moving arms and supplies to the country beyond. Finally the bell in the cupola of the engine house would be rung, summoning slaves and others for the march into the mountains—a culmination implicit in the planning that has never appeared in any of the accounts of the Harpers Ferry invasion.

By early August the number of men taking residence at the Kennedy farm had grown considerably. Beside the leader and the two teenage girls, there were three of Brown's sons, a son-in-law, and two Quaker brothers from Springdale, in addition to half a dozen veterans who had seen service with either Brown or Montgomery in Kansas. Aaron Stevens had taken up station in Hagerstown to assist in the forwarding of men and in communications between Chambersburg and "headquarters." With matters progressing, Brown was distressed by the reluctance of some of the men to come forward. George Gill was one of these, prompting Brown to write Kagi, "I hope George G. will so far redeem himself as to try; & do his duty after all. I shall rejoice over 'one that repenteth.'"[3]

In his diary John Brown recorded making eight trips between the Kennedy farm and Chambersburg; riding either on a mule or in a wagon, sometimes taking overnight lodging at the Union Hotel in Greencastle. These trips were accomplished mostly at night, and while in the Pennsylvania town he would stay for several days. It was in mid-August during one of these journeys that Brown revealed to his son Owen, who rode with him in the wagon, what only Stevens and Kagi knew—that the initial objective of the company would be the seizure of the government works at Harpers Ferry. Having frequented the town and easily apprehending the dangers, Owen recoiled, and would later recall he told his father, "You know how it resulted with Napoleon when he rejected advice in regard to marching with his army to Moscow."[4] When they returned to the farm and a meeting was held to acquaint the rest of the company with the new plan, there was immediate dissension. The younger Browns, Oliver and Watson, and Charles Plummer Tidd, in particular, were opposed to it; put bluntly, it appeared to them they would be committing suicide. Brown answered that even in the event of their death it would be a gain: "We have only one life to live and once to die, and if we lose our lives, it will perhaps do more for the cause than any other way."[5] The quarrel was so great it threatened to break up the camp. Finally to calm the dissension, Brown relented, saying if that was the way they felt he would resign as commander and follow another proposal if they had one. Tidd was so upset he went to stay with Cook at Harpers Ferry for a few days. However since they were an oath-bound company they all finally agreed to follow the elder man's leadership on the stipulation that both bridges in Harpers Ferry be fired, and for this reason that was included in the preparation. Owen drafted the following note acknowledging their consent, dated August 18, 1859: "Dear Sir—We all agree to sustain your decisions until you have proved incompetent, and many of us will adhere to your decisions so long as you will."[6]

On August 1 a meeting of the New England Colored Citizens had convened in Boston and was addressed by the Rev. J. W. Loguen and, as reported in the *Liberator*, by one "Harriet Garrison." The temporary use of the cognomen of its editor, no doubt, signaled her acceptance into the antislavery family, but was also a precaution as Tubman was presented as "one of the most successful conductors on the Underground Railroad." Shortly after this she was to drop out of sight and her location was unknown for many weeks. Suffering from illness brought on by exposure, and from spells of unconsciousness caused by a head injury she received as a girl from an overseer, she had gone to recuperate at the home of a friend in New Bedford. Although few have looked beyond the simple assertion that there was a profound bond between Brown and Tubman, there has never been any doubt about her determination to join his campaign in the Virginia mountains.

The key to the full development of his plan, in Brown's opinion, now lay with the Canadian recruits and with Douglass and Tubman. Accordingly, the work undertaken by his son is crucial to an understanding of that action and of its outcome. After arranging the shipment of "mining tools," John Jr. awaited the order to begin his "Northern tour." At the beginning of the second week of August he arrived in Rochester at the home of Frederick Douglass; with Douglass away at Niagara Falls, the younger Brown awaited his return. The next day he did so, and John Jr. informed Kagi in a letter dated August 11: "I spent remainder of day and evening with him and Mr. E. Morton, with whom friend Isaac [Brown's assumed name] is acquainted." Of Morton he wrote, "He was much pleased to hear from you; was anxious for a copy of that letter of instructions to show your friend at 'Pr.,' who, Mr. M. says, has his whole soul absorbed in this matter." Said instructions, in part, were how to reach his father by mail; referring broadly to his discussion with Douglass, John Jr. wrote: "The friend at Rochester will set out to make you a visit in a few days. He will be accompanied by that 'other young man,' and also, if it can be brought around, by the woman that the Syracuse friend could tell me of. The son will probably remain back for a while." That Douglass's son Lewis was being considered for active service with John Brown indicates a level of involvement beyond what is usually acknowledged; Douglass had also volunteered that "'the woman' . . . whose services might prove invaluable, had better be helped on." John Jr.'s letter concluded: "If alive and well, you will see him ere long. I found him in rather low spirits; left him in high."[7]

From Syracuse, where he had gone to meet with Loguen and expected to find Harriet Tubman as well, John Jr. reported that said minister and "also said woman" were in Boston. Informed by Loguen's wife that he was expected to visit Canada soon, and would "contrive to go immediately," John Jr. resolved to go on to Boston. In his letter of August 11 he added to Kagi, "Morton says our particular friend Mr. Sanborn, in that city, is especially anxious to hear from you, has his heart and hand engaged in the cause. Shall try and find him. . . . I leave this evening on the 11:35 train from here; shall return as soon as possible to make my visit at Chatham."[8]

The next morning, a Friday, arriving in Boston the younger Brown soon found Loguen, who informed him that Harriet Tubman was not known to be in the city, nor was anyone there aware of her present circumstance. As to going to Canada, his schedule was such that he could not leave till the end of the following week. It was not until the next Tuesday that the younger Brown posted the letter informing Kagi of this, and that he had decided in the interim to improve the time by "making acquaintance of those staunch friends of our friend Isaac."[9]

He first called upon Dr. Howe, who, although he had no referral, received him cordially. In his letter John Jr. wrote: "[Howe] gave me a letter to the friend who does business on Mills Street. Went with him to his home in Medford, and took dinner. The last word he said to me was, 'Tell friend Isaac that we have the fullest confidence in his endeavor, whatever may be the result.' I have met no man in whom I think more implicit reliance may be placed. He views matters from the standpoint of reason and principle, and I think his firmness is unshakable."[10] Stearns was to introduce John Jr. to an individual who was to make a substantial contribution. This was Lewis Hayden; originally from Kentucky, he had seen all of his family separated and sold, and had twice stood on the auction block, while his mother descended into madness. At age thirty-three, with his wife and son, he quit Kentucky for Canada. Afterward moving to Detroit, he rose to prominence in that city's growing black community, building a church and a school. In the early 1850s he moved to Boston where he established a clothing store and assumed an outstanding role in Beacon Hill's African

American community, heading Boston's Vigilance Committee and its Underground Railroad operations. It was Hayden who would locate the elusive Harriet Tubman, as he as well would raise money and recruits to be sent to John Brown in Virginia.

Traveling next to Concord, John Jr. found Sanborn away in Springfield on business related to Brown's enterprise, and wrote Kagi: "The others here will, however, communicate with him. They are all, in short, very much gratified and have had their faith and hopes strengthened. Found a number of earnest and warm friends, whose sympathies and theories do not exactly harmonize; but in spite of them selves their hearts will lead their heads."[11]

On August 20 John Brown was back in Chambersburg to begin the transfer to the Kennedy farm of the crates of arms that had arrived from Ohio—his "mining tools"—and just as importantly to keep his appointment with Frederick Douglass. Joining Kagi at the boarding-house of Mary Ritner on East King Street, he would confide the details of the anticipated meeting with Henry Watson, information likely disclosed too to Joseph Winters, a known confidant of Brown and a leader in Chambersburg of Underground operations and prominent in its black community. An old stone quarry situated on the south side of town near a bend in the Conococheague Creek, only a short walk from the train station, had been selected for the rendezvous.

Why was Douglass willing to promptly answer his friend's summons, and what was he prepared to do in assuring his success? Although far from being the only antislavery action Douglass was prepared to embrace, in his view Brown's movement offered a more "zealous and laborious self-sacrificing spirit" lacking in other quarters. Not only was he remarkable in his stewardship of men; he also had heart enough to set his plan in motion while seeking to establish cooperation among abolitionists. But despite his deep respect for the project, Douglass was never disposed, as some were, to dedicate himself wholly to it. He would seem to have been prepared to offer his support, as he said, "in an individual way"; and while his commitment was substantive, he was also planning a trip for the fall and winter of 1859 to the British Isles and to France, and was contracting for a number of lectures in Philadelphia, Boston, and Rhode Island, to be delivered before his departure. Brown however, it must be stipulated, evinced a great deal of confidence in and respect for Douglass due to his past experiences and confidences with him that could only have served as the basis for summoning him to Chambersburg.

At the scheduled hour no doubt Brown and Kagi were close enough to hear the train from the east as it pulled into the depot, among whose passengers would be the famed abolitionist and his companion, a vigorous young man with sharply drawn African features. While it was not entirely unexpected that Douglass should come to south-central Pennsylvania, it was unusual that he would appear unannounced, and before he had left the platform several people recognized him. Receiving a cordial welcome, he resolved the propriety of his being there by saying he was on personal business, and when offered an invitation to speak that evening at a public meeting to be held in Chambersburg, agreed to make an appearance. The duo then made their way to the barbershop of Henry Watson, who, though busily engaged, pointed out the way to where Brown and Kagi waited.

Cautiously approaching the old quarry, "for John Brown was generally well armed, and regarded strangers with suspicion," Douglass and Green were soon recognized and cordially received. Brown, Douglass reported, looked in every way a man of the neighborhood, and was "much at home as any of the farmers around there." "He had in his hand when I met him a fishing-tackle, with which he had apparently been fishing in the stream hard by, but I saw no fish, and did not suppose that he cared much for his 'fisherman's luck.'" Propriety perhaps dictated Douglass first handed Brown a letter of which he was the recipient. He and Green had stopped the previous night in Brooklyn where they had been guests of the Gloucesters. That letter dated August 18, 1859, reads: "I gladly avail myself of the opportunity afforded by our friend Mr. F. Douglass, who has just called upon us previous to his visit to you to enclose to you for the cause in which you are such a zealous laborer a small amount, which please accept with my most ardent wishes for its and your benefit. The visit of our mutual friend Douglass has somewhat revived my rather drooping spirits in the cause; but seeing ambition and enterprise in him, I am again encouraged. With best wishes for your welfare and prosperity, and the good of your cause, I subscribe myself your sincere friend."[12]

Douglass's travel itinerary would appear to have included a stop in Philadelphia, as John Jr. would write Kagi on August 17 as he again passed through Rochester, "On my way up to our friend's house, I met his son Lewis, who informs me that his father left on Tuesday, August 16, *via* New York and Philadelphia, to make you a visit."[13] The time of that visit would certainly include Saturday and Sunday, August 20 and 21, which is as Douglass has it in his *Life and Times.* Sanborn surmises, however, that Douglass may have been in Chambersburg on Friday the 19th as well, since he and Green were in New York on Thursday night. Hence there is the possibility, as Lewis Douglass may have been privy, that his father also stopped and saw some persons in Philadelphia before traveling to Chambersburg the next morning, a trip requiring no more than a few hours.

The four men—John Brown, John Henry Kagi, Frederick Douglass, and Shields Green—now settled among the stones and castaways of the old quarry with the wagon loaded with Brown's "mining tools" close by, to discuss the enterprise soon to be undertaken. The two principals would spend many hours of two days in deliberation, with Kagi and Green remaining, on Douglass's telling, "for the most part silent listeners." While many elements making up the moments of this "council of war" can only be conjectured, it is known Douglass was familiar with Brown's plans, as he was aware he had something in mind concerning Harpers Ferry. Now he would be surprised to hear that Brown had renounced that old plan in favor of a bold new strategy of seizing the United States arsenal at the outset. But he had summoned Douglass to this August meeting, not to elicit his further understanding prior to beginning "his work," but because Brown wanted Douglass to join him in it as co-leader. His success, he now believed, was contingent upon it.

The bond between them clearly was an affiliation of more than friendship; and the issues they engaged must have come from the fullness of their hearts, as of their minds—surely one of the more poignant collaborations to be celebrated on the American scene. Douglass wrote: "He described the place as to its means of defense, and how impossible it would be to dislodge him if once in possession. Of course I was no match for him in such matters, but I told him, and these were my words, that all his arguments, and all his descriptions of the place, convinced me that he was going into a perfect steel trap, and once in he would never get out alive. . . . He was not to be shaken by anything I could say, but treated my views respectfully, replying that even if surrounded he would find means for cutting his way out."[14]

Douglass understood as well as anyone that the "sectional conflict" was ultimately one for dominion. He took the position espoused by Gerrit Smith and others—that the Congress had the right to legislate on slavery and, as John Quincy Adams had argued, by its war powers under the Constitution could abolish it. Certainly Douglass put considerable effort along this line to dissuade Brown, believing, contrary to his expectation, that his gambit was bound to misfire. It was an attack upon the federal government and would array the country against them. The battle for freedom must be fought within the Union; it would only be the power of the federal government after all, supported by its armed forces, that could deal with the issue on the scale proposed. Beginning on such a rousing blow would only sacrifice the lives of everyone engaged in it; it would not help their cause, and it would do nothing to help the slave. Brown would be discredited and the South given the excuse, not for secession, but for the complete suppression of all antislavery opinion throughout the northern states. Assuredly too, Douglass suggested, in attempting to mount such a scheme, however unlikely its success, an indiscriminate slaughter of the male portion of the slaves would commence.

Brown clearly shared none of Douglass's scruples. A resounding blow was just the thing to wake the northern people out of their torpor on the subject of slavery. In Brown's view it was too late to destroy and erase the South's peculiar institution by means less harmful than the evil itself. The slaveholders not only lived in the South, to the exclusion of all others they were "the South" itself; they were the only active power there. They could not be talked down, and would not consent to be hemmed in by political means alone. War was at that very moment being contemplated in the cabinet of President Buchanan. Out of his success at Harpers Ferry, Brown was convinced, would come freedom for the enslaved; and since slavery could only end in blood, there could be no better time to end it than now. In the sight of the American people and of the world, the slaveholders could proceed only to a limited extent in the shameless slaughter Douglass feared.

One of the chief difficulties Douglass foresaw was presented by the terrain around Harpers Ferry itself. Constricted by the natural setting and by the limited points of entrance and of exit, and by a relatively large population, however securely in control, Brown faced the obvious risk of being bottled up. They could easily become isolated one party from the other, and if any casualties were sustained it could be detrimental to them. There were, too, a number of towns within a very short radius, and the militia companies maintained in every community could be assembled against them. Then again, Harpers Ferry was served by two rail lines, one of them connecting to a major city, Baltimore, and beyond that to the nation's capital. On the first news of uprising, troops would be sent to deal with them. Brown was thrusting himself and his men, said Douglass, into dangers, and worse, that may be easy to get into, but impossible to get out of. He would be walking into a perfect cul-de-sac.

For his part Brown thought the militia companies would not be eager to converge on Harpers Ferry until they had looked to their own neighborhoods. The news that men were in possession of the armory and were freeing and arming slaves would alarm and disconcert them. The

militia companies weren't a serious military threat, either; they were
poorly armed and poorly trained. Even if they did manage to converge
on the Ferry they would only come with outdated arms, and would
quickly be dissuaded by the disproportion of force. Neither did Brown
think federal troops would immediately be a factor. The governor of
Virginia would have to call upon the president for them, and would
first want to see how the militia fared against him. In any event, since
he didn't intend to remain at Harpers Ferry, they would be delayed, as
all means of communication would be severed, the rail lines broken,
and the bridges burned.

Douglass places his various reminiscences with John Brown as principal within a curious template, which serves to obscure rather than
reveal the extent of his commitment prior to this meeting; a commitment which could only have been the basis for John Brown to ask him
to join with him at Harpers Ferry. "From 8 o'clock in the evening till 3
in the morning, Capt. Brown and I sat face to face, he arguing in favor
of his plan, and I finding all the objections I could against," Douglass
wrote of their first meeting in Springfield, Massachusetts, in 1847. And
of their last meeting in the old quarry outside Chambersburg,
Pennsylvania, he wrote, "Our talk was long and earnest; we spent the
most of Saturday and a part of Sunday in this debate . . . he for striking
a blow which should instantly rouse the country, and I for the policy of
gradually and unaccountably drawing off the slaves to the mountains,
as at first suggested and proposed by him." Douglass was also to recall
Brown saying to him at their first introduction that he "had been
watching and waiting" for the heads of collaborators such as he would
need from among his race to "pop-up," as it were, above the surface of
the water.[15] At the height of his pre–Civil War fame, Douglass was a
man of considerable bearing, a veritable Spartacus of his people as
evinced in his untiring oratorical combat and commitment to all
things pertaining to antislavery agitation. This is the aspect of the
drama passed over without remark by Douglass, hidden beneath the
wavering conceit of a rhetorical device. But this is *the* feature of the
American condition that is and has been paramount—its racial division—and was something that, in attempting to surmount it, both he
and Brown were profoundly aware of. If Douglass was seen to be for
him, who then could be against him?

Some observers have drawn attention to the happenstance that
Douglass conflated details of his first meeting with Brown with
Brown's stay in his home in February 1858. After that earlier meeting
Douglass significantly observed his remarks on the lecturing circuit

began to take on "a color more and more tinged" by his friend's "strong impressions."[16] Is it in order, then, to suggest it was after Harpers Ferry and John Brown's death that there can be found traces of those August hours, particularly in Douglass's speeches from 1860 and 1861?[17] And that it would not be wholly conjectural to suppose that Brown asked Douglass to prepare and publish a call upon the Negro in both the North and in the South? Brown had "no hesitation in saying that ten thousand black soldiers might be raised in the next thirty days to march upon the South."[18] Accordingly, Douglass spoke out with expressions that do not differ appreciably, as he also understood the crucial significance of drawing on the black manpower strung across the northern states and Canada: "There are men out there who only wait to be brought into this war. From Rochester and Auburn, from Syracuse and Ithaca, from Troy and Albany, could be drawn an hundred men. Philadelphia alone has a hundred, as do New York and Boston. In the west—in Buffalo and Cleveland and Chicago—could be added five hundred to the cause. Add to these the hundreds in Canada West and the thousands of the South. . . . One black regiment alone, in such a war, would be the full equal of two white ones. The very fact of color in this case would be more terrible than powder and balls"— these are words from Douglass's speeches in the winter of 1863.[19]

Other considerations arising in their encounter can be delineated more broadly still from several trenchant contemporaneous presentations: Wendell Phillips's speech "The Argument for Disunion," and Ralph Waldo Emerson's essay "American Civilization."[20]

Three elements comprised the irresistible strength, analogous to a three-stranded cable, of the so-called slave power, said Phillips. The first came in the omnipotence of money: with two thousand million dollars invested in slaves, the South acquired the ability to draw into its reach the support of all other large capital. A second substantiating strand came in the "three-fifths" clause in the Constitution, allowing three or four large planters of South Carolina "riding leisurely to the polls, and throwing in their visiting cards for ballots," to "blot out the entire influence of [a] New England town in the Federal government." A third strand was constituted in "the potent and baleful prejudice of color."

The South's aim really, Emerson contended in his essay, was not the dissolution of the national government, but its reorganization on the basis of slavery. The motive of its political leaders in threatening secession was clear—by withdrawing from the authority of the Union and uniting the seceded states in a Confederacy, they sought to secure the border states and then lay claim to the entire territory of the United States from the old line of the Missouri Compromise to the Pacific Ocean. They had set themselves on this course because their goals were no longer amenable under the Union. Since a large part of their claim was under the control of that Union and would have to be wrested from it, this necessitated on their part "a war of conquest." If they did anything other than wage war on these terms they would be relinquishing their capacity to continue with their dominion in the South and defeat the purpose of secession itself.

Peaceable secession was impossible, because the divided sentiment of the border states made it so, as well as the insatiable South. Once in possession of New Orleans and Charleston and Richmond, slaveholders would demand St. Louis and Baltimore. If they got these, they would insist on Washington. Once in Washington they would assume the army and navy, and, through these, Philadelphia, and New York, and Boston. This contest would force the North, which would fight for the survival of the Union, to adopt on its banner the formal internment of slavery.

The following words are Douglass's, but one is struck by how utterly they are owed to Brown: "Whether the slaveholder is in the cotton states, the slave breeding states or the border states, one is as bad as the other. In every state they held the reins of government they would take sides openly. They know that if the government was a miserable and contemptible failure—then that government must meet them in the field and put them down, or itself be put down. They were all traitors to the government and the constitution, and only waited to spring up by the heat of surrounding treason. This conspiracy must stand together or fall together; strike it at either extreme—either on the head or at the heel, and it dies."[21]

In the late afternoon when he and Green left the stone quarry, Douglass must have been overwhelmed by what he had heard; but he might also have been a little buoyed—something new needed to be tried. The prospect of a nearing contestation of the very ground of slavery's existence in the United States would have made him somber, and his remarks that night in Chambersburg's Franklin Hall might have taken the form of an exposition of the hour and a denunciation of the Slave Power. That night, after what he had heard, Douglass undoubtedly cast his thoughts on the war John Brown was about to commence, mindful of his own relation to that war. On that night, as he surveyed the situation, it was evident that the previous twenty years had brought a marked change in the condition of the antislavery lecturer. Once he and his colleagues had been met with mobs with rotten eggs and brickbats, but now the country had been rocked from end to end by the strength of the faithfulness of abolitionists to the freedom of the slave. Yet slaveholders still were coolly estimating the value of their victories and congratulating themselves upon their security. It was impossible to disguise the fact that slavery had made great progress and had riveted itself more firmly in the southern mind and heart, and the whole moral atmosphere of the South had undergone a decided change for the worse. (These were thoughts Douglass penned in his *Monthly* that appeared in August 1859, "Progress of Slavery.")

Douglass may not have acknowledged the man known as Isaac Smith; but John Brown was in Franklin Hall. He may have come in and departed alone, or sat near and conversed with his confidants. After the meeting, as Douglass took his leave and walked to his lodging at the home of Henry Watson, he could not have been cognizant that away in the night were dozens of names studded throughout the far-flung landscape of the American scene—names that in a few years would be lifted to immortality by a dignity only death could bestow upon them; names that would be pronounced like anthems on the lips of those touched by what was to happen in or near them.

Douglass sums up everything in a succinct paragraph concerning his meeting with Brown and the two younger men, one black and one white, on August 20 and 21 in 1859:

> Capt. Brown summoned me to meet him in an old stone quarry . . . near the town of Chambersburg. . . . His arms and ammunition were stored in that town and were to be moved on to Harper's Ferry. In company with Shields Green I obeyed the summons, and prompt to the hour we met the dear old man, with Kagi his secretary, at the appointed place. Our meeting was in some sense a council of war. We spent the Saturday and succeeding Sunday in conference on the question, whether the desperate step should then be taken, or the old plan as already described should be carried out. He was for boldly striking Harper's Ferry at once and running the risk of getting into the mountains afterwards. I was for avoiding Harper's Ferry altogether. Shields Green and Mr. Kagi remained silent listeners throughout. It is needless to repeat here what was said, after what has happened. Suffice it, that after all I could say, I saw that my old friend had resolved on his course and that it was idle to parley.[22]

But this summons to a council of war, the details of which it is needless to repeat, possesses an eloquence of its own. Through long hours Douglass tried to moderate Brown's course, seeking a return to an undertaking originally proposed by him, a plan to which Douglass had committed his support. Although their differences, as some have suggested, may not have devolved into acrimony, one can see Brown rising to his feet, exasperated at not winning his friend over. This was just the moment when decisive action was called for. One writer has heard Brown bitterly accusing Douglass of becoming "soft," of enjoying overmuch "the limelight" that his prominence had brought him. And when Douglass found he had exhausted his arguments, he too rose, declaring he could not countenance such an action. Expressing his "astonishment" that Brown "could rest on a reed so weak and broken," that he could think he would be able to guarantee his safety and that of his men by the fact he would retain a number of hostages from among Virginia's citizens, he warned flatly "that Virginia would blow him and his hostages sky-high rather than that he should hold Harper's Ferry an hour."[23]

After recounting the well-known dénouement of their meeting where Brown pleads—"Come with me, Douglass; I will defend you with my life. I want you for a special purpose. When I strike, the bees will begin to swarm, and I shall want you to help hive them"— Douglass offers this aside: "There has been some difference of opinion as to the propriety of my course in thus leaving my friend. Some have thought that I ought to have gone with him, but I have no reproaches for myself at this point, and since I have been assailed only by colored men who kept even farther from this brave and heroic man than I did, I shall not trouble myself much about their criticisms. They compliment me in assuming that I should perform greater deeds than themselves."[24]

Feeling he'd justified himself, Douglass turned to Green and said: "Now Shields, you have heard our discussion. If in view of it, you do not wish to stay, you have but to say so, and you can go back with me."

When he was about to leave, Douglass concluded, "I asked Green what he had decided to do, and was surprised by his coolly saying, in his broken way, 'I b'leave I'll go wid de ole man.' Here we separated— they to go to Harper's Ferry, I to Rochester." Surely in giving tribute to the singular courage and devotion of Shields Green with this rhetorical flourish, Douglass has shown his own mettle, and returns it.

In A. Bronson Alcott's diary entry for May 8, 1859, we find a record of John Brown's visit to Concord where he spoke to Emerson, Thoreau, Judge Hoar, as well as others, where we read:

> Our acts our angels are,—or good or ill,
> Our fatal shadows, that walk by us still.[25]

In *A Plea for Captain John Brown*, written in the weeks following Brown's defeat and capture at Harpers Ferry, Henry David Thoreau too spoke in Concord, October 30, 1859, saying, "He is not Old Brown any longer; he is an angel of light."

Alcott then continued in his diary, noting on Friday, November 4, 1859: "Thoreau has good right to speak on Brown. . . . The men have much in common. . . . Both are sons of Anak and dwellers in Nature,— Brown taking more to the human side, and driving straight at institutions, while Thoreau contents himself with railing at and letting them otherwise alone. He is the proper panegyrist of the virtues he owns himself so largely, and so comprehends in another."[26]

Although the networks put in motion in preparation for the Harpers Ferry raid have eluded almost all scrutiny, passing silhouettes are still discernible, and their movement made perceptible to a retrospective glance, brings out their deeper context and meaning.

With John Brown Jr. and J. W. Loguen on their way to Ontario by August 18 the prospects of organizing the Canadian recruits began to brighten. In the last weeks of August through the first week of September they visited St. Catharines, Hamilton, London, Chatham, Buxton, and Windsor, and on the state-side Detroit, Sandusky, and Cleveland. Forming an auxiliary named the League of Liberty in each of these locations, and certainly in alliance with existing black organizations throughout the Lakes region as previously delineated, they were to ensure a steady issue of recruits for Brown's campaign. Thomas Cary became its chairman, I. D. Shadd its corresponding secretary, James M. Bell its secretary, and William Lambert the treasurer. Once back in West Andover, the following letter dated September 8, 1859, was sent by John Jr. to John Henry Kagi: "I yesterday received yours of September 2, and I not only hasten to reply, but to lay its contents before those who are interested. . . . Through those associations which I formed in Canada, I am able to reach each individual member at the shortest notice by letter. . . . I hope we shall be able to get on in season some of those old miners of whom I wrote you. Shall strain every nerve to accomplish this. . . . You may be assured that what you say to me will reach those who may be benefited thereby, and those who would take stock in the shortest possible time, so don't fail to keep me posted."[27]

In a letter dated the previous week and posted from Sandusky, where he met with George J. Reynolds, whom he described as "one of those men who must be obtained if possible,"[28] John Jr. writes of meeting with William Parker. Parker was about five years younger than Frederick Douglass, and their lives had taken a parallel course. Both had escaped from slavery in Maryland—Parker when he was seventeen—and both were to make great efforts to throw off the mental shackles bred in them from servitude, both becoming leaders "among their people." And just as Douglass had become a confidant of John Brown, so had Parker. Referencing Parker in the letter dated August 27, John Jr. wrote: "After viewing him in all points which I am capable of, I have to say that I think him worth in our market as much as two or three hundred average men, and even at this rate I should rate him too low. For physical capacity, for practical judgement, for courage and moral tone, for energy and force of will, for experience that would not only enable him to meet difficulty, but give confidence to overcome it, I should have to go a long way to find his equal, and in my judgement, [he] would be a cheap acquisition at almost any price. I shall individually make a strenuous effort to raise the means to send him on."[29]

A few days after the meeting in the stone quarry, Owen Brown and Shields Green set out on foot for the Kennedy farm. Richard Hinton noted, "The section of Pennsylvania over which they passed was then more dangerous to them than the neighborhood of Harper's Ferry itself, 'hunting niggers' was a regular occupation at that date."[30] Four men intent on catching fugitives did spot them, whereupon they fled into a wood, while the slave-catchers returned whence they had come for more help. Coming to a river, Brown took Green, who could not swim, upon his back, and since they were headed south and not north, they escaped.

Green was the first black recruit arriving at "headquarters"; a second, Dangerfield Newby, was recruited several days later. He was a freeman living on the Pennsylvania line, born about 1825 in Virginia's Fauquier County to a slave mother, with a Scotsman as his father/owner. Together with his brothers, Gabriel and James, he was freed by his father and taken to Ohio. The three brothers later returned to Virginia where they lived and worked as freemen, Dangerfield as a blacksmith. He had married, and with his wife, a slave woman named Harriet, lived in Warrenton twenty miles farther south, where they had six children. It is often assumed that Brown had no contact with, nor had given advance notice of his intentions, to blacks in either Virginia or Maryland. While this was largely to avoid disclosure, Newby surely provided Brown with information about the feelings and conditions of blacks in the vicinity, and there is a suggestion that his brothers were in his confidence. The manner in which Newby came to this association may not now be discernible, although it wouldn't have been unlikely, given the unseen contacts that existed, that he was a referral of those "reliable friends" in Chambersburg.

Brown was so satisfied with how "the business" was progressing that he wrote exaltedly, "The fields whiten unto harvest," beckoning to a few choice correspondents suggestively, "Your friends at headquarters want you at their elbow." At the end of July, Sanborn apprised Brown of his activities in Springfield, including the following crucial information: "Harriet Tubman is probably in New Bedford sick. She has stayed in N.E. a long time, and been a kind of missionary."[31] In a letter dated August 27, 1859, published in the *Syracuse Herald*, Gerrit Smith announced he would not preside that year at the anniversary of the "Jerry rescue," a celebration at which he had heretofore been a constant presence. He now considered commemorative exercises of the kind "shameless" and "pernicious hypocrisy." He further wrote:

> It is, perhaps, too late to bring slavery to an end by peaceable means,— too late to vote it down. For many years I have feared and published my fears, that it must go out in blood. These fears have grown into belief. So debauched are the white people by slavery that there is not virtue enough left in them to put it down. If I do not misinterpret the words and looks of the most intelligent and noble of the black men who fall in my way, they have come to despair of the accomplishment of this work by the white people. The feeling among blacks that they must deliver themselves gains strength with fearful rapidity. No wonder, then, is it, that intelligent black men in the States and in Canada should see no hope for their race in the practice and policy of white men.[32]

Then in a speech in September he placed himself on the same foundation as John Brown, declaring "the movement to abolish slavery is a failure." To those who hoped to repeat the example of British emancipation in the West Indies in America, Smith pointed out the analogy was imperfect: "England was not debauched and ruled by her slavery— but American slavery has left scarcely one sound spot in American character; and it is, confessedly, the ruler of America." He warned, "For insurrection, we may look any year, any month, and day. A terrible remedy for a terrible wrong."

To redress the problem presented by Douglass's refusal to take a part in helping "to hive the bees," as Brown had expressed it, a meeting of select persons was arranged sometime during the third week of September at an undisclosed location, although near Chambersburg. Anne Brown would refer to this meeting as constituting the "missing link" in her father's movements in her correspondence years later with Richard Hinton, who utilized her reminiscences and observations throughout his book. While this meeting has eluded comprehensive notice in the historical record, it appears most likely to have taken place in the village of Mont Alto on the western slope of South Mountain, about twelve miles east of Chambersburg. This conjecture can be based upon Brown's purported connections there; he was sometimes a worshiper at the Emmanuel Chapel in Mont Alto, and is reported to have set up "Sunday school classes for Negro children," as well as it being supposed that he contracted some work in an iron mill near there for the South Mountain Railroad. One or more buildings in or near the village may have been at his disposal. Osborne Anderson indicates in *A Voice from Harper's Ferry* that some unspecified "friend" was sent down to the Kennedy farm to accompany Shields Green to the mysterious location, "whereupon a meeting of Capt. Brown, Kagi and other distinguished persons, convened for consultation." Who were the men, and how many were attending? Anderson represents them as "distinguished," suggesting they were known leaders, more than likely from Philadelphia, with others most likely coming from Chambersburg, and perhaps other locals as well. This meeting clearly, as Anne Brown suggests, was crucial to the maturation of her father's plan, having to do with that crucial sector from which "workmen" were expected—New York and Philadelphia—and although its impact on what ultimately transpired has never been weighted, it was undoubtedly great.[33]

That Green was attendant led John Jr. and Hinton in later years to speculate that he had acted as a "representative" for Douglass. But there was no indication of this from Douglass. In the letter summoning Douglass to the meeting signed by a number of "colored men," he only mentioned as an aside, "I never knew how they came to send it, but it now seems to have been prompted by Kagi who was with Brown when I told him I would not go to Harper's Ferry." The letter posted from Philadelphia and addressed to Douglass—found in Douglass's *Life and Times* and in Sanborn's *The Life and Letters of John Brown*—reads as follows, with all the signatories omitted in later publication:

> Dear Sir—The Undersigned feel it to be of utmost importance that our class be properly represented in a convention to come off right away [near] Chambersburg, in this state. We think you are the man of all others to represent us; and we severally pledge ourselves that in case you will come right on we will see your family well provided for during your absence, or until your safe return to them. Answer to us and John Henrie, Esq., Chambersburg, Penn, at once. We are ready to make you a remittance, if you go. We have now quite a number of good but not very intelligent representatives collected. Some of our members are ready to go with you.

Assessing his justification in refusing to accompany Brown to Harper's Ferry and on the rancor Douglass was to endure, Richard Hinton remarked: "Frederick Douglass's refusal to finally join the enterprise has never, to me, appeared to warrant adverse criticism. His position before the land justified, in 1859, a choice between both conditions, nor failed of endeavor. Certainly he was doing a large work, compelling, by his intellectual power and eloquence, a fast-growing recognition for the oppressed race, of which he was an able leader. He might well weigh, as he did, the question of casting this upon the 'hazard of a die.' The 'logic of events' at least has justified Frederick Douglass, and his faithful services must silence critics; those who also had the opportunity and did not follow John Brown."[34]

It was a profound disappointment to Brown when Douglass did not appear, as it appreciably lessened his chances of obtaining the recruits. Around the time of this meeting, Kagi received an important letter, showing both hope and the difficulties abounding, from James M. Bell in Chatham:

Dear Sir—Yours came to hand last night. One hand left here last night, and will be found an efficient hand. Richardson is anxious to be at work as a missionary to bring sinners to repentance. He will start in a few days. Another will follow immediately after, if not with him. More laborers may be looked for shortly. "Slow but sure." Alexander has received yours, so you see all communications have come to hand. Alexander is not coming up to the work as he agreed. I fear he will be found unreliable in the end. Dull times affect missionary matters here more than anything else, however, a few laborers may be looked for as certain. I would like to hear of your congregation numbering more than "15 and 2" to commence a good revival; still our few will be adding strength to the good work.[35]

The "hand" referred to was Osborne Anderson, arriving in Chambersburg on the eleven o'clock train on the morning of September 16. He had been sent under the auspices of the *Provincial Freeman*, whose editor, I. D. Shadd, thought it obligatory his office be represented. Accordingly lots had been drawn, the distinction falling to Anderson. He was the only one of those who accompanied Brown to write a firsthand account, and remarked on his arrival he was "surprised" to find that all but a small part of the arms had been removed from Chambersburg to the Kennedy farm. This would indicate that a date to begin operations had been selected, contingent upon the ill-omened meeting in Mont Alto. That date was October 25.

Hinton remarked in *John Brown and His Men* that for John Brown, Canada had proved to be "a broken reed indeed." Others who have remarked on this connection, who may not have been able to appreciate the true relation and its significance, have been even more dismissive. Hinton apprehended just how it foreshadowed the tragedy that would unfold at Harpers Ferry.

Quoting John Jr.'s enumeration of the reasons for delay of many of those expected to come on, in his letter to Kagi, Hinton adds these details excerpted from that letter: Robinson Alexander "Thinks he can now close out by 1st November, and in the meantime to prove his devotion will furnish means to help on two or three himself." Richard Richardson was "away harvesting." George J. Reynolds in Sandusky, Ohio, "had a job, which he cannot leave until finished."[36] On August 22, Kagi received a letter from Cleveland from James H. Harris with a similar sense of foreboding: "I wrote you immediately on receipt of your last letter; then went up to Oberlin to see Leary. I saw Smith, Davis, and Mitchell; they all promised, and that was all. Leary wants to provide for his family; Mitchell to lay his crops by; and all make such excuses, until I am disgusted with myself and the whole negro set. God dam em! . . . Charlie Langston says 'it is too bad,' but what he will do if anything, I don't know."[37]

Several days after Bell's letter from Chatham, a letter posted from Boston reached Kagi from Lewis Hayden: "My dear sir—I received your very kind letter, and would state that I have sent a note to Harriet requesting her to come to Boston, saying to her in the note that she must come right on, which I think she will do, and when she does come I think we will find some way to send her on. I have seen our friend at Concord; he is a true man. I have not yet said anything to any body except him. I do not think it is wise for me to do so. I shall, therefore, when Harriet comes send for our Concord friend, will attend to the matter. Have you all the hands you wish? Write soon./Yours, L. H."[38]

Sanborn wrote Thomas Wentworth Higginson on September 14 that Tubman was "to be sent forward soon," but then says later she still was not heard from. Meanwhile Lewis Hayden had been raising money and recruits, one of whom was to be on hand. In his article published in the *Atlantic Monthly*, December 1875, titled "The Virginia Campaign of John Brown," Franklin Sanborn wrote: "Mr. Hayden entered warmly into the work, and undertook to enlist a few colored men in Massachusetts. . . . According to his recollection he did enlist six such recruits." One of these he reported was named John Anderson who was purported to have reached Harpers Ferry during the fighting, but took no part in it, and later returned to Boston. Hinton writes he was never able to trace this individual, and his existence is usually discounted, although DuBois included him in his account. Since, however, he was part of Hayden's recollection, perhaps he can be attributed as one of those furtive beings in which this story abounds.

The "hand" sent by Hayden who did play a role in the tumult was Francis J. Merriam, a young white man of a New England aristocratic family turned abolitionist crusader. Hayden met him in Boston and after a few words said, "I want five hundred dollars and must have it." To which Merriam replied: "If you have a good cause, you shall have it." Hayden then told him what he had learned from John Brown Jr., that his father was preparing to lead men into the Virginia mountains and needed money. Merriam replied, "If you tell me John Brown is there, you can have my money and me along with it."39

Richard Hinton received the following from Kagi: "I have to-day written Redpath and Merriam respecting our Nicaragua Emigration, and wishing them to meet me in Boston at an early day. . . . I wrote them in care of Francis Jackson. I need not say that I would like to see you also at that time, which I am now unable to name."40 Hinton also received several letters of inquiry about Richard Realf and Charles W. Leonhardt. Of Polish extraction from Posen, Prussia, Leonhardt was educated as a Prussian soldier, and "in 1848 he joined the German and Polish revolutionists," wrote Hinton, "and soon found his way with Dembrowski and the Polish army to Hungary, where he served against Russia."41 When defeat came he escaped to Turkey and came to America when Kossuth did. Arriving in Kansas in the fall of 1856, he wrote for German and American newspapers, and was an enthusiastic free-state partisan, active in aiding fugitive slaves. He became a well-known and well-received speaker, associating with Montgomery in 1858 and 1859. Introduced to Kagi, through him he subsequently was introduced to John Brown. In early August, now in Cincinnati, Ohio, where he studied law, Leonhardt received letters from both "Isaac Smith," and "John Henri," while Hinton informed him the "mines" were ready and that "workmen" were needed.42

Hinton surmises it was Leonhardt who disclosed Brown's intentions to Edmund Babb, a correspondent of the *Cincinnati Gazette*, who had also figured in Kansas affairs. It was Babb who wrote John Floyd, Buchanan's secretary of war:

> I have discovered the existence of a secret association, having for its object the liberation of the slaves at the South and by a general insurrection. The leader of the movement is "old John Brown," late of Kansas. He has been in Canada during the winter, drilling the negroes there, and they are only waiting his word to start for the south to assist the slaves. They

have one of their leading men (a white man) in an armory in Maryland—where it is situated I have not been able to learn. As soon as everything is ready, those of their number who are in the Northern States and Canada are to come in small companies to their rendezvous, which is in the mountains in Virginia. They will pass down through Pennsylvania and Maryland, and enter Virginia at Harper's Ferry. Brown left the North about three or four weeks ago, and will arm the negroes and strike the blow in a few weeks; so whatever is done must be done at once. They have a large quantity of arms at their rendezvous, and are probably distributing them already.[43]

Floyd set the letter aside, having more important details related to the coming crisis in 1860 to attend, saying to the Mason Committee before which he testified "magniloquently," in DuBois's phrase, "I was satisfied in my own mind that a scheme of such wickedness and outrage could not be entertained by any citizens of the United States, I put the letter away, and thought no more of it until the raid broke out."[44]

Brown's efforts to have a recognized black leader on hand included attempts to enlist J. W. Loguen and a principal in the Oberlin-Wellington rescue trials, Charles Langston. In a letter dated the previous May, Brown had written suggestively to Loguen, "I will just whisper in your private ear that I have no doubt you will soon have a call from God to minister at a different location." But John Jr. was to confide to Kagi that Loguen's "heart was only passively in the cause" and that he was "too fat" for the arduous undertaking. Charles Langston, of slighter stature, had been ill, and moreover John Jr. reported he had become "discouraged about the mining business," believing there were too few hands. "Physical weakness is his fault," he concluded.[45]

On September 20 Osborne Anderson related, "Capt. Brown, Watson Brown, Kagi, myself, and several friends, held another meeting."[46] While it is likely these "several friends" were men from Chambersburg, it is also evident Anderson was to assume an increasingly prominent role, as Brown saw him as the most promising candidate then on hand to provide the leadership for the expected black conscripts. He was to be dubbed by those at the farm "Chatham Anderson," to distinguish him from Jeremiah Anderson. Toward the end of September, after his introduction to the preparations in Chambersburg, Osborne Anderson started out for the Kennedy farm. Walking alone at night, he reached the Maryland border and found John Brown waiting in his wagon. Riding the remainder of the journey, they reached the Kennedy farm about daybreak.

The house where they made their "headquarters" was rough-hewn, of log construction; on the first floor a kitchen, parlor, and dining room, and above that a spacious attic that served as bunk room, storehouse, and drill room. The men were under strict instruction to be as discreet as possible and not to be seen around the yard. Chores were delegated among the men, while Anne Brown was posted as the watch and Mary Thompson did the cooking and superintended. With the arrival of Anderson, as previously with Green, the comings and goings at the farm became even more problematic, as the presence of black men would raise suspicions that the premises were being used as a station on the Underground Railroad.

John Brown Jr. sent the following to "Friend Henri," dated September 27:

> Since I became aware that you intended opening the mines before spring, I have spared no pains, and have strained every nerve to get hands forward in season. I do not, therefore, feel blame for any error in respect to time. I had before never heard anything else than that the spring was the favorable time, unless uncontrollable circumstances should otherwise compel! At this distance I am not prepared to judge, but take for granted that wisdom, or perhaps necessity dictates the change of programme. Immediately on receipt of your urgent communications I have dispatched copies where they would be most likely to avail anything, and have devoted, and am still devoting my whole time to forming associations for the purpose of aiding. There will be a meeting of stockholders at my house this eve; a distinguished gentleman from New Hampshire, who is anxious to invest, will be present. Whether it is best for me to come to you now or not I cannot say; but suppose it will be impossible for me to remain here when you are actually realizing your brightest prospects. When in C., and in all other places, I have at all times urged all hands to go on at once, since necessity might render their presence an imperative want at any time.[47]

With issues of importance remaining, on October 6, Brown and Kagi journeyed to Philadelphia where they remained for three days. DuBois remarks, "[Thomas] Dorsey the caterer with whom he stayed, at 1221 Locust Street, is said to have given him $300." Upon their return they met Francis Merriam in Chambersburg, whom Lewis Hayden had forwarded to Sanborn. Sanborn in turn sent him on to Higginson with a note that included "Perhaps you will have a message for the Shepherd." Of slight frame and build, Merriam to all appearance was unfit for a soldier's life, and in the bargain had but one eye (the other was glass). Higginson had questions about him for Sanborn, who replied, "I consider him about as fit in this enterprise as the Devil is to keep a powder house, but everything has its use & must be put to it if possible." Merriam had withal a purse of six hundred dollars in gold pieces, and he was dispatched directly to Baltimore with instruction to buy a large quantity of percussion caps.

When they returned to the Kennedy farm, a meeting of those present was called where Brown acquainted all with what had transpired in Philadelphia. Anderson indicates the purposes touched upon, their significance, and the deep pathos felt by all, as during his recital Brown wept. Anderson wrote: "How affected by, and affecting the main features of the enterprise, we at the farm knew well after their return, as the old Captain, in the fullness of his overflowing, saddened heart, detailed point after point of interest. God bless the old veteran, who could and did chase a thousand in life, and defied more than ten thousand by the moral solemnity of his death!"[48]

Kagi expected to maintain correspondence so far as possible with three persons. One was John Brown Jr., as their general agent in the North; the others were Charles A. Dana of the *Tribune* and William A. Phillips of Lawrence, Kansas. In his last letter to John Jr., dated October 10, Kagi wrote:

> We shall not be able to receive any thing from you after to-day. It will not do for any one to try to find us now. You must by all means keep back the men you talked of sending and furnish them work to live upon until you receive further instructions. Any one arriving here after to-day and trying to join us, would be trying a very hazardous and foolish experiment. They must keep off the border until we open the way clear up to the line from the south. Until then, it will be just as dangerous here as on the other side, in fact more so; for, there will be protection also, but not here. It will not do to write to Harper's Ferry. It will never get there—would do no good if it did. . . . We will try to communicate with you as soon as possible after we strike, but it may not be possible for us to do so soon. If we succeed in getting news from outside our own district it will be quite satisfactory, but we have not the most distant hope that it will be possible for us to receive recruits for weeks, or quite likely months to come. We must first make a complete and undisputably open road to the free states. That will require both labor and time.[49]

It has been remarked that Brown's Provisional Army was to be led by whites, with blacks filling in the lower ranks, while in fact, as has been seen, he sought to establish a fully collaborative relationship with blacks taking positions of co-leadership. Anderson addressed this issue:

It has been a matter of inquiry, even among friends, why colored men were not commissioned by John Brown to act as captains, lieutenants, &c. I reply, with the knowledge that men in the movement now living will confirm it, that John Brown did offer the captaincy, and other military positions, to colored men equally with others, but a want of acquaintance with military tactics was the invariable excuse. Holding a civil position, as we termed it, I declined a captain's commission tendered by the brave old man, as better suited to those more experienced; and as I was willing to give my life to the cause, trusting to experience and fidelity to make me more worthy, my excuse was accepted. The same must be said of other colored men . . . who proved their worthiness by their able defense of freedom at the Ferry.[50]

Earlier that week Leary and Copeland had received word to come forward. "Without tools" of their own, they were helped along by two Oberlin professors, Ralph and Samuel Plumb. They were in Cleveland on October 10 at the home of the Sturtevants, supporters of John Brown, and while there met with Charles Langston and James H. Harris, who would not be coming with them, but in any event wished them Godspeed. Traveling via Pittsburgh and Harrisburg, the two men arrived in Chambersburg on October 12 and stayed in the home of Henry Watson.

Occupying the next day and part of the night traveling to Maryland, they reached the farm as the sun rose on the morning of the 14th. Meanwhile, George Stearns has been in consultation with Lewis Hayden and other black Bostonians. Harriet Tubman was feeling well enough and Hayden had written Gerrit Smith requesting and receiving money for her expenses. By October 15 she was in New York City in the company of four recruits headed for Chambersburg. That same day, Richard Hinton reached Hagerstown to be met with a letter and money instructing him to return to Chambersburg to hire a horse and wagon to carry a quantity of arms still in the town. Hinton arrived too late to effect this and lodged the night with Henry Watson. Elsewhere men were on the roads—George Gill among them. He was to write later regarding this, "I had been in correspondence with Kagi and knew the exact time to be on hand and was on my way to the cars when the thrilling news came that the blow had been struck. Of course, I went no further."[51]

Dr. A. M. Ross in his *Recollections and Experiences* has it that he received a letter from John Brown, dated October 6, 1859, stating, "I shall move about the last of this month. Can you help the cause in the way promised? Address your reply to Isaac Smith, Chambersburg,

Penn." Ross asserts in his interview with Brown in Springfield, Massachusetts, in 1858, that when Brown was ready to invade the slave states he wanted Ross in Richmond, Virginia, where he would be in position to watch the course of events, and with their success could seek to enlighten the slaves as to his purposes. As has been stated, some have doubted Ross's creditability; yet his understanding of what Brown was about is creditable and his description of the night of October 17 has the ring of authenticity. Writing of his friend's debacle, Ross recalled the scene: "Crowds of rough, excited men filled with whiskey and wickedness stood for hours together through the night in front of the offices of the *Enquirer* listening to reports as they were announced within. When news of Brown's defeat and capture was read from the window, the vast crowd sent up a demonic yell of delight, which to me sounded like a death-knell to all my hopes for the freedom of the enslaved."[52]

As John Brown labored through the summer and fall of 1859 to inaugurate his great work of emancipation, his expectation of a sizable number of black recruits, chiefly from New York and Philadelphia and from Canada, had been disappointed. The response by men in Cleveland and throughout the Lake states where recruits had been also expected had been desultory, and Harriet Tubman had been ill and unaccounted for through many weeks. But the "express packages" that did come through—the term used for the black recruits coming down—raised suspicions that the Kennedy farm was being used as a station on the Underground Railroad. Brown was informed of this by a trusted confidant, and a search of the premises was to be expected in the coming week. Letters had already gone out that all who were coming forward should be on hand on October 25, and the argument can be made that over a score of these, with perhaps more, including those "reliable friends" among black residents of Chambersburg, were expected. But it would not do to disband or to postpone the attack now. They had done too much and come too far; they must strike, or forever lose what might be gained.

On October 16, a Sunday, a cold and rainy night, after the usual religious services he always held in camp, and after giving some last-minute instruction to his men before they began their march into Harpers Ferry, John Brown said: "Come, boys, and remember that a long life is not of so much concern as one well ended."[53]

And so, as John Brown Jr. concluded after giving it years of consideration, it would appear that despite all the meticulous preparation and planning, and the far-flung vistas opened, John Brown had expected to die at Harpers Ferry, and went there with the intention of making no effort to escape. And suddenly before the nation, as Thoreau remarked, "he was more alive than ever."[54]

John Jr. would recall his father saying to him at their last meeting: "There is no seed that comes to so swift and abundant a harvest as the blood of martyrs spilled upon the ground."[55]

The war that would be fought in the years 1861–1865 was formida- ble and could not be avoided, said Emerson. Speaking on the place and significance of the Emancipation Proclamation for the American republic in January 1863, he said: "Every step in the history of political liberty is a sally of the human mind into the untried Future. . . . Liberty is a slow fruit. It comes like religion, for short periods, and in rare con- ditions, as if awaiting a culture of the race which shall make it organic and permanent. . . . At such times it appears as if a new public were cre- ated to greet the new event."[56]

And so the footfalls of an antislavery struggle over the tribulations of three decades had been set like stepping-stones in history's currents, and with these the crossing had been made.

Notes

CHAPTER I: THE MYSTIC SPELL OF AFRICA

1. Sherwin, *Prophet of Liberty*, 65.
2. Ibid., 67.
3. "In Defense of Lovejoy," in *Wendell Phillips on Civil Rights and Freedom*, Louis Filler, ed.
4. Sanborn, *The Life and Letters of John Brown*, "Owen Brown's Autobiography," 4–10.
5. Ruchames, ed., *John Brown*, 43–49.
6. Ibid.
7. Ibid.
8. Sanborn, *Life and Letters of John Brown*, 37–39.
9. Ibid.
10. Ibid., chapter III, "John Brown as a Businessman."
11. Ibid., 69.
12. Ibid., 139.
13. Ibid., 10–11.
14. Ruchames, *The Abolitionists: A Collection of Their Writings*, 78–83.
15. Sanborn, *The Life and Letters of John Brown*, 35.
16. Ibid., 40–41.
17. Ibid.
18. Ruchames, *John Brown*, 188.
19. Bancroft, *The Slave Trade in the Old South*, 2.
20. Ibid., 11.
21. Ibid., 134.
22. Ibid., 197.
23. T. S. Ashton, *The Industrial Revolution, 1760–1830*.
24. Marx, *The Poverty of Philosophy: A Reply to M. Proudon's Philosophy of Poverty*, 94.
25. Marx, *A Contribution to the Critique of Political Economy*, 33.
26. Marx, *Capital* III, 940.
27. Marx, *Theories of Surplus Value*, Part II, 225.
28. Grundrisse, 105.
29. Derrida, *Dissemination*, 31.
30. Bancroft, *Slave Trading in the Old South*, 67.
31. Excerpted in ibid., 72–73 from the *American Quarterly Review*, December 1832, 391–92.
32. "The Right of Petition," Phillips, in *Speeches, Lectures, and Letters*, Second Series, 1–6.
33. DuBois, *John Brown*, 92.
34. Sterling, *Martin Robison Delany*, 57–58.
35. Nelson ed., *Documents of Upheaval*, xiii–xiv.
36. Sherwin, *Prophet of Liberty*, 108–109.
37. Truman, *Documents of Upheaval*, 150–151.
38. Quarles, *Black Abolitionists*, 55.

39. Sanborn, *The Life and Letters of John Brown*, 134.
40. Sherwin, *Prophet of Liberty*, 112.
41. Ibid., 113.

CHAPTER 2: THE NORTH STAR

1. *The Century*, November 1881, 124–131.
2. Words taken from the narrative of Rev. James W. C. Pennington, *The Fugitive Blacksmith*, 1849, as read by this author.
3. W.E.B. DuBois, *The Negro*, 115.
4. Bayliss, *Black Slave Narratives*, 17.
5. DuBois, *The Negro*, 118.
6. Dumond, *Antislavery*, 313.
7. Ibid., 312.
8. Douglass, *Life and Times of Frederick Douglass*, 205.
9. Holland, *Frederick Douglass*, 363.
10. Douglass, *Life and Times*, 213–216.
11. Dumond, *Antislavery*, 291–296.
12. Ibid., 297.
13. Ibid.
14. Sherwin, *Prophet of Liberty*, 138, speech quoted from the *Liberator*, Nov. 11, 1842.
15. Quarles, *Black Abolitionists*, 193.
16. Sherwin, *Prophet of Liberty*, 140.
17. "The American Tract Society," in *The Complete Writings of James Russell Lowell*, Elmwood Edition, VI, 12.
18. Quarles, *Black Abolitionists*, 194.
19. Ofari, *"Let Your Motto Be Resistance,"* 34.
20. Ibid., 35.
21. Ibid., 38.
22. *Liberator*, September 8, 1843, quoted in ibid.
23. Redpath, *Public Life of Captain John Brown*, 65.
24. Ruchames, ed., *John Brown*, 58.
25. Ibid., 60.
26. *West Virginia Archives and History*, chapter two, online exhibit.
27. Sanborn, *Life and Letters of John Brown*, 95.
28. Quoted in ibid., 63.
29. Sanborn, *Life and Letters of John Brown*, 22.
30. Ables, *Man on Fire*, 22.
31. Sanborn, *Life and Letters of John Brown*, 143.
32. Ibid., 62.
33. Reports of Senate Committees, 36th Congress, 1st Session, No. 278, Testimony of Richard Realf, 96.
34. DuBois, *John Brown*, 101.
35. Ibid.
36. Ruchames, ed., *John Brown*, 70-72.
37. Douglass, *Life and Times*, 226.
38. Ibid., 228.
39. Ibid., 230.
40. Foner, ed., *The Life and Writings of Frederick Douglass*, vol. 5, 3.
41. Quarles, *Frederick Douglass*, 37.
42. Dunayevskaya, *Marxism and Freedom*, 42, 53.
43. *The Letters of Karl Marx*, trans. and ed. Padover, 273–74.
44. Douglass, *Life and Times*, 240–241.

45. Quarles, *Frederick Douglass*, 51.
46. *Life and Times*, 257.
47. Ibid., 260.
48. Sterling, *Martin Robison Delany*, 95.
49. Ibid., 90–91.
50. Ibid., 96.
51. Letter dated August, 20, 1847, cited in Quarles, *Frederick Douglass*, 66.
52. Quarles, *Allies for Freedom*, 21, see footnote 14.
53. *Life and Times*, 271–275. DuBois, *John Brown*, 110.
54. Foner, ed., *The Life and Writings of Frederick Douglass*, vol. 2, 86.
55. Douglass, *Life and Times*, 275.
56. Ruchames, *John Brown*, 278–299.

CHAPTER 3: FOR THE SAKE OF THE UNION

1. E. W. Emerson and W. E. Forbes, eds., *Journals of Ralph Waldo Emerson*, VII, 206.
2. Bancroft, *Slave Trading in the Old South*, 339.
3. Quoted by Aptheker, *American Negro Slave Revolts*, 15.
4. Marx, *The Civil War in the United States*, 67–68.
5. Aptheker, *American Negro Slave Revolts*, 325.
6. John Taylor, Wikipedia.
7. Cobbe, *Theodore Parker, Collected Works*, vol. V, 115.
8. Redpath, *The Public Life of Captain John Brown*, 55.
9. Sanborn, *Life and Letters of John Brown*, 24–25.
10. The Project Gutenberg EBook #2523, *The Memoirs of Victor Hugo*.
11. Sanborn, *Life and Letters of John Brown*, 68.
12. DuBois, *John Brown*, 61.
13. Sanborn, *Life and Letters of John Brown*, 85.
14. DuBois, *John Brown*, 110–11.
15. Sanborn, *Life and Letters of John Brown*, 97.
16. Statement of Ruth Brown, in ibid.,101.
17. Ibid., 100.
18. Ibid.
19. Foner, *The Life and Writings of Frederick Douglass*, vol. 2, 68–69.
20. McMillen, *Seneca Falls and the Origins of the Women's Rights Movement*, 93–94.
21. Douglass, *Life and Times*, 276.
22. Foner, *The Life and Writings of Frederick Douglass*, vol. 2, 26.
23. Ibid., 48.
24. Sanborn, *Memoirs of John Brown*, 23.
25. Redpath, *The Public Life of Captain John Brown*, 46.
26. Sanborn, *Memoirs of John Brown*, 23.
27. Sanborn, The Life and Letters of John Brown.
28. Ibid., 71.
29. Hinton, *John Brown and His Men*, 35.
30. Redpath, *The Public Life of Captain John Brown*, 47.
31. Sanborn, *The Life and Letters of John Brown*, 73.
32. Bradford, *Scenes from the Life of Harriet Tubman*, 19.
33. Ibid., 29.
34. Ibid., 20.
35. Sanborn, *The Life and Letters of John Brown*, 25.
36. Redpath, *The Public Life of Captain John Brown*, 44–45.
37. McPherson, *Battle Cry of Freedom*, 66.
38. Douglass, "Weekly Review of Congress," *North Star*, March 15, 1850.

39. Wiltse, *John C. Calhoun: Sectionalist, 1840–1850*, 465.
40. McPherson, *Battle Cry of Freedom*, 73.
41. *Frederick Douglass' Paper*, July 1, 1852.
42. Foner, *The Life and Writings of Frederick Douglass*, vol. 2, 134.
43. Campbell, *The Slave Catchers*, 15.
44. Ibid., 16.
45. Ibid., 17.
46. Foner, *The Life and Writings of Frederick Douglass*, vol. 2, 52.
47. Ibid., 155, 156.
48. For the split with the Garrisonians, see ibid., 52, footnote 4.
49. Sherwin, *Prophet of Liberty*, 211.
50. Nelson, ed., *Documents of Upheaval*, 215.
51. Quarles, *Frederick Douglass*, 87.

CHAPTER 4: AT THE POINT OF A BAYONET

1. Speech in *The Rev. J. W. Loguen, As a Slave and As a Freeman: A Narrative of Real Life.*
2. Weiss, *Life and Correspondence of Theodore Parker*, vol. 1, 102.
3. Dillon, *The Abolitionists*, 179.
4. Ibid., 178.
5. Sanborn, *The Life and Letters of John Brown*, 106–107.
6. Conrad, *Harriet Tubman*, 45.
7. Campbell, *The Slave Catchers*, 63.
8. Ibid., 62.
9. Ibid., appendix, table 1 Fugitive Slaves Cases, 1850.
10. Conrad, *Harriet Tubman*, 42.
11. Ibid.
12. Ibid., 49.
13. Ibid., 116–117.
14. Sanborn, *The Life and Letters of John Brown*, 132.
15. In Sanborn, *The Life and Letters of John Brown*, 124–127.
16. In ibid.
17. Ibid.
18. Foner, ed., *The Life and Times of Frederick Douglass*, 282.
19. Higginson, *Cheerful Yesterdays*, 136.
20. Dillon, *The Abolitionists*, 182.
21. Ibid., 183.
22. Ibid.
23. Bordewich, *Bound for Canaan*, 333.
24. Higginson, *Cheerful Yesterdays*, 139–140.
25. Campbell, *The Slave Catchers*, 99–100.
26. Parker, "The Freedman's Story," published in the *Atlantic Monthly*, February 1866.
27. Katz, *Resistance at Christiana*, 94.
28. Ibid., 100.
29. Ibid., 103.
30. *Life and Times of Frederick Douglass*, 281.
31. Ibid., 282.
32. Ibid., 157.
33. Syracuse University Libraries, online exhibit for the Jerry Rescue.
34. Sanborn, *The Life and Letters of John Brown*, 34.
35. *Life and Times of Frederick Douglass*, 279.
36. Sherwin, *Prophet of Liberty*, 212.
37. Foner, *The Voice of Black America*, vol. 1, 118.

38. Ruchames, ed., *John Brown*, 86–87.
39. Foner, *The Voice of Black America*, vol. 1, 124–126.
40. Marx, *The 18th Brumaire of Louis Bonaparte*, 18.
41. Sanborn, *The Life and Letters of John Brown*, 148.
42. To Gerrit Smith, May 21, 1851, in Foner, ed., *The Life and Writings of Frederick Douglass*, vol. 2, 156.
43. Foner, *The Life and Writings of Frederick Douglass*, vol. 2, 58–59.
44. Ibid., for entire speech see 243–254.
45. H.O. Wagoner, in ibid, 269–270.
46. Ibid., 227.
47. *Life and Times of Frederick Douglass*, 282.
48. Hedrick, *Harriet Beecher Stowe*, 208.
49. *Life and Times of Frederick Douglass*, 283.
50. Foner, *The Life and Writings of Frederick Douglass*, vol. 5, 274.
51. Ibid., 275.
52. Aptheker, *A Documentary History of the Negro People in the United States*, vol. 1, 329.
53. Foner, ed., *The Life and Writings of Frederick Douglass*, vol 5, 276.
54. Ibid., 279-280.
55. Speech in Foner, vol. 2, 254–268.
56. *Life and Times of Frederick Douglass*, 291.
57. Foner, *The Life and Writings of Frederick Douglass*, vol. 5, 289.
58. Ibid., 291.
59. Sterling, *The Making of an Afro-American*, 154.
60. Stuckey, *The Ideological Origins of Black Nationalism*, 197.
61. Aptheker, *A Documentary History of the Negro People in the United States*, vol. 1, 367.
62. Ruchames, ed., *John Brown*, 92–93.
63. Leddy, "The Fugitive Slave Case of Anthony Burns," *Civil War Times*, May 2007.
64. Monaghan, *Civil War on the Western Border*, 6.
65. Aptheker, *A Documentary History of the Negro People in the United States*, vol. 1, 369.
66. Maltz, "The Trial of Anthony Burns," in *Encyclopedia Virginia*, Nov. 11, 2013.
67. Redpath, *The Public Life of Captain John Brown*, 58.
68. Higginson, *Cheerful Yesterdays*, 149–150.
69. Speech reported in the *Liberator*, June 2, 1854.
70. Higginson, *Cheerful Yesterdays*, 158.
71. Campbell, *The Slave Catchers*, 127.
72. Ibid., 331.
73. Ibid., 322.

CHAPTER 5: A LINE OF LIVING FIRE

1. Quoted in Sanborn, *Life and Letters of John Brown*, 164.
2. Ibid., 176.
3. Ruchames, *John Brown*, 94.
4. Sanborn, *Life and Letters of John Brown*, 189.
5. Quoted in UShistory.org—*The Origins of the Republican Party*.
6. Ruchames, ed., *John Brown*, 94–95.
7. *Frederick Douglass' Paper*, July 27, 1855.
8. Redpath, *Public Life of Captain John Brown*, 81.
9. Sanborn, *Life and Letters of John Brown*, 193–194.
10. Ibid., 165.
11. Monaghan, *Civil War on the Western Border*, 35.
12. Sanborn, *Life and Letters of John Brown*, 217–221.
13. Hinton, *John Brown and His Men*, 45.

14. Quoted in Sanborn, *Life and Letters of John Brown*, 220.
15. Quoted in Redpath, *Public Life of Captain John Brown*, 90.
16. Quoted in Sanborn, *Life and Letters of John Brown*, 220.
17. Ruchames, ed., *John Brown*, 100–101.
18. Hinton, *John Brown and His Men*, 71.
19. Ibid., 55.
20. Ibid., 71.
21. Ibid., 88.
22. Boyd B. Stutler Collection, West Virginia State Archives, online exhibit.
23. Hinton, *John Brown and His Men*, 68.
24. Sanborn, *Life and Letters of John Brown*, 223, letter to wife and children, February 20, 1856.
25. Ibid., 260.
26. Monaghan, *Civil War on the Western Border*, 53.
27. Ibid., 58.
28. Ibid.
29. James Hanway in Hinton, *John Brown and His Men*, 695.
30. Bondi, *Transactions of the Kansas State Historical Society*, vol. 8, 279.
31. Sanborn, *Life and Letters of John Brown*, 249.
32. Ibid., 273.
33. Ibid., 262.
34. Higginson, *Cheerful Yesterdays*, 207.
35. Sanborn, *Life and Letters of John Brown*, 248.
36. USHistory.org, Democratic National Convention in 1856, the nomination of James Buchanan.
37. Sanborn, *Life and Letters of John Brown*, 278.
38. Bondi, *Transactions of the Kansas State Historical Society*, vol. 8, 285.
39. Letter in Sanborn, *Life and Letters of John Brown*, 236–241.
40. Ibid.
41. Ibid., 240.
42. Monaghan, *Civil War on the Western Border*, 64.
43. Redpath, *Public Life of Captain John Brown*, 138.
44. Sanborn, *Life and Letters of John Brown*, 236–241.
45. Ibid., 112–113.
46. Ibid., 288–290.
47. Ibid., 297.
48. In ibid., 298.
49. *Transactions*, vol. 8, 282–284.
50. Redpath, *Public Life of Captain John Brown*, 112–114.
51. Sanborn, *Life and Letters of John Brown*, 241.
52. Ibid., 279.
53. Quoted in Redpath, *Public Life of Captain John Brown*, 123.
54. Quoted in Sanborn, *Life and Letters of John Brown*, 284.
55. Ruchames, ed., *John Brown*, 218.
56. Ibid., 219.
57. Ibid., 220.
58. Ibid., 200.
59. Monaghan, *Civil War on the Western Border*, 67.
60. Quoted in Abels, *Man on Fire*, 94.
61. Monaghan, *Civil War on the Western Border*, 68.
62. Ibid., 69–70.
63. Higginson, *Cheerful Yesterdays*, 198.
64. Stearns, *The Life and Public Services of George Luther Stearns*, 108.
65. Hinton, *John Brown and His Men*, 53.

66. Ibid., 201.

67. Monaghan, *Civil War on the Western Border*, 73.

68. Redpath, *Public Life of Captain John Brown*, 145.

69. On-line source at Bleeding Kansas 1856–1857, Latinamericanstudies.org.

70. Sanborn, *Life and Letters of John Brown*, 309.

71. Ibid.

72. Monaghan, *Civil War on the Western Border*, 77.

73. Hinton, *John Brown and His Men*, 57.

74. Sanborn, *Life and Letters of John Brown*, 311.

75. Samuel Walker in *Transactions of the Kansas State Historical Society*, vol. 6, quoted in Abels, *Man on Fire*, 98–99.

76. Monaghan, *Civil War on the Western Border*, 78.

77. Ibid., 79.

78. Quoted in Abels, *Man on Fire*, 99.

79. Monaghan, *Civil War on the Western Border*, 83–84.

80. Ibid., 85; Abels, *Man on Fire*, 105.

81. Higginson, *Cheerful Yesterdays*, 203.

82. Higginson, *A Ride Through Kansas*.

83. Speech of John Brown in Redpath, *Public Life of Captain John Brown*, 163–164.

84. Ibid., 164–165.

85. Ibid., 168–170.

86. Monaghan, *Civil War on the Western Border*, 88.

87. Quoted in Abels, *Man on Fire*, 107.

88. Monaghan, *Civil War on the Western Border*, 88.

89. Ibid., 89.

90. Cited in Abels, *Man on Fire*,110.

91. Letter in Sanborn, *The Life and Letters* of *John Brown*, 434–435.

92. Monaghan, *Civil War on the Western Border*, 86.

CHAPTER 6: THE PANIC OF 1857

1. Sanborn, *The Life and Letters of John Brown*, 342.

2. Letter dated October 30, 1856, in ibid., 341.

3. *Life and Times of Frederick Douglass*, 302.

4. Foner, ed., *Life and Writings of Frederick Douglass*, vol. 2, 439.

5. Smith's remark included in his letter of introduction, in Sanborn, *The Life and Letters of John Brown*, 364.

6. Franklin Sanborn, "John Brown in Massachusetts," *Atlantic Monthly*/Digital Edition, April 1872.

7. Sanborn, *The Life and Letters of John Brown*, 496.

8. Frank Preston Stearns, *The Life and Public Services of George Luther Stearns*, 198.

9. Reminiscences of Mrs. Mary E. Stearns, in Hinton, *John Brown and His Men*, 719–727.

10. John Greenleaf Whittier quoted in Frank Preston Stearns, *The Life and Public Services of George Luther Stearns*.

11. Sanborn, *The Life and Letters of John Brown*, 511.

12. Webb, *The Life and Letters of Captain John Brown*, 91. Reminiscences of Mrs. Mary Stearns in Hinton, *John Brown and His Men*, 719–727.

13. Sanborn, "John Brown in Massachusetts."

14. Stearns, *The Life and Public Services of George Luther Stearns*, 133.

15. Webb, *The Life and Letters of Captain John Brown*, 91.

16. Stearns, *The Life and Public Services of George Luther Stearns*, 133.

17. Ralph Waldo Emerson, quoted in Hinton, *John Brown and His Men*, 29.

18. Stearns, *The Life and Public Services of George Luther Stearns*, 137.

19. Abels, *Man on Fire*, 132–133.

20. Ruchames, ed., *John Brown*, 109.

21. Ibid., 110.

22. Reminiscences of Dr. Wayland, Sanborn, *The Life and Letters of John Brown*, 381.

23. Sanborn, *The Life and Letters of John Brown*, 244.

24. Henry David Thoreau, in ibid., 503.

25. Emerson, in ibid., 501–502.

26. Sanborn, *The Life and Letters of John Brown*, 508–511.

27. Ibid.

28. Ibid., 508–509.

29. Stearns, *The Life and Public Services of George Luther Stearns*, 137.

30. Sanborn, *The Life and Letters of John Brown*, 514–515.

31. Monaghan, *Civil War on the Western Border*, 93.

32. *Scott v. Emerson*, 15 Mo. 576, 586, Mo. 1852, quoted Wikipedia.org/*Dred Scott v. Sanford*.

33. McPherson, *Battle Cry of Freedom*, 173–176.

34. Foner, ed., *Life and Writings of Frederick Douglass*, The Dred Scott Decision, 407–424.

35. Ibid.

36. Ibid., 406.

37. Hinton, *John Brown and His Men*, 123–124.

38. Ibid., 147.

39. Ruchames, ed. *John Brown*, Brown quoted in a letter to Sanborn, August 13, 1857, 116.

40. Ibid., 114–115.

41. Stearns, *The Life and Public Services of George Luther Stearns*, 136.

42. Ibid.

43. Ruchames, ed., *John Brown*, 112.

44. Hinton, *John Brown and His Men*, 125.

45. Stearns, *The Life and Public Services of George Luther Stearns*, 142.

46. Sanborn, *The Life and Letters of John Brown*, 412–413.

47. Abels, *Man on Fire*, 147.

48. Hinton, *John Brown and His Men*, 110.

49. Sanborn, *The Life and Letters of John Brown*, 391.

50. Ibid.

51. Ibid., 396–397.

52. Ibid., 397.

53. Ibid., 396.

54. Ibid., 390.

55. Ibid., 414.

56. Ibid., 391.

57. Hinton, *John Brown and His Men*, 149–150.

58. Ibid., 147.

59. Ibid.

60. Richard Warch and Jonathan Fanton, editors, *John Brown*, 50.

61. Stearns, *The Life and Public Services of George Luther Stearns*, 160.

62. Ibid., 172.

63. Ibid., 144.

64. Sanborn, *The Life and Letters of John Brown*, 399.

65. Ibid., 160.

66. Stearns, *The Life and Public Services of George Luther Stearns*, 141.

67. Sanborn, *The Life and Letters of John Brown*, 400.

68. Ibid., 416.

69. Ross, *Justice of Shattered Dreams*, 41.

70. Marx, preface to *A Contribution to the Critique of Political Economy*.

71. Negri, *Marx Beyond Marx*, 1.

72. See Derrida's *Specters of Marx*.

73. Negri, *Marx Beyond Marx*, 2.

74. *On This Day*, online collaboration of NYTimes/HarpWeek.

75. Abels, *Man on Fire*, 156.

76. McPherson, *Battle Cry of Freedom*, 164.

77. Quoted in Sanborn, *The Life and Letters of John Brown*, 423.

78. Ibid., 424.

79. Hinton, *John Brown and His Men*, 153.

80. Ibid., 157–158.

81. Ibid., 499.

82. Delay, "Richard Realf, Poet and Soldier," *Home Monthly*, May 1899.

83. Ibid.

84. Cook's "Confession."

85. Abels, *Man on Fire*, 162.

86. Monaghan, *Civil War on the Western Border*, 99.

87. Richman, *John Brown Among the Quakers*, 58.

88. Hinton, *John Brown and His Men*, 156.

89. Richman, *John Brown Among the Quakers*, 28–29.

90. Sanborn, *The Life and Letters of John Brown*, 425.

91. Douglass, *Life and Times of Frederick Douglass*, 317.

CHAPTER 7: AMERICAN MYSTERIES

1. Richman, *John Brown Among the Quakers*, 17–18.

2. Hinton, *John Brown and His Men*, 126.

3. *Life and Times of Frederick Douglass*, 315.

4. DuBois, *John Brown*, 247.

5. Sanborn, *Life and Letters of John Brown*, 434–435.

6. Watch and Fanton, ed. *John Brown*, 35.

7. Sanborn, *Life and Letters of John Brown*, 434–435.

8. Watch and Fanton, *John Brown*, 36.

9. Ibid, 37.

10. Quarles, *Frederick Douglass*, 39.

11. Ibid., 40; Ables, *Man on Fire*, 187–188.

12. Hinton, *John Brown and His Men*, 672–675.

13. *Life and Times of Frederick Douglass*, 316.

14. Ibid.

15. Ibid.

16. Senate Select Committee Report on the Harper's Ferry Invasion, Testimony of Richard Realf, 90–113.

17. Sanborn, *Life and Letters of John Brown*, 437.

18. Ibid., 438–440.

19. Ibid.

20. Ibid.

21. Ibid. 438–440.

22. Ibid., 444–445.

23. Ibid., 443.

24. Ibid.

25. Earl Ofari, "*Let Your Motto Be Resistance*," 106.

26. Hinton, *John Brown and His Men*, 168.

27. Quoted in Abels, *Man on Fire*, 176.

28. Sanborn, *Life and Letters of John Brown*, 450.

29. Ibid., 448.

30. Ables, *Man on Fire*, 178.

31. Abels, *Man on Fire*, 174.

32. DuBois, *John Brown*, 248.

33. Quarles, *Allies for Freedom*, 40.

34. Hinton, *John Brown and His Men*, 169.

35. Ibid., 170.

36. Ibid., 165.

37. Sanborn, *Life and Letters of John Brown*, 440–441.

38. Quarles, *Allies for Freedom*, 41.

39. Earl Conrad, *Harriet Tubman*, 115.

40. Sanborn, *Life and Letters of John Brown*, 453.

41. Ibid., 452.

42. Ibid.

43. Quarles, *Allies for Freedom*, 43.

44. Jonathan Katz, *Resistance at Christiana*, 281.

45. DuBois, *John Brown*, 251.

46. Anderson, *A Voice from Harper's Ferry*, chapter II.

47. Hamilton, *John Brown in Canada*, 16.

48. Ross, *Recollection and Experiences of an Abolitionist*, chapter III.

49. Rollin, *Life and Public Service of Major Martin R. Delany*, 85–90.

50. Anderson, *A Voice from Harper's Ferry*, chapter III.

51. Hamilton, *John Brown in Canada*, 14.

52. Ibid.

53. Ibid.

54. Reports of Senate Committees, 36th Congress, 1st Session, No. 278, Testimony of Richard Realf.

55. Quarles, *Allies for Freedom*, 46.

56. Hamilton, *John Brown in Canada*, 16.

57. Quarles, *Allies for Freedom*, 44.

58. Anderson, *A Voice from Harper's Ferry*, chapter II.

59. Reports of Senate Committees, 36th Congress, 1st Session, No. 278, Testimony of Richard Realf.

60. Hinton, *John Brown and His Men*, 180.

61. Hamilton, *John Brown in Canada*, 16.

62. Kagi's minutes are found in the appendix of Hinton, *John Brown and His Men*, and in Anderson, *A Voice from Harper's Ferry*, chapter II.

63. Rollin, *Life and Public Service of Major Martin R. Delany*, 85–90.

64. Sanborn, *Life and Letters of John Brown*, 455.

65. Ibid., 448–461.

66. Abels, *Man on Fire*, 197.

67. Sanborn, *Life and Letters of John Brown*, 463–464.

68. Reminiscences of George B. Gill in Hinton, *John Brown and His Men*, 732–733.

69. Ables, *Man on Fire*, 199.

70. Hinton, *John Brown and His Men*, 173.

71. Ibid., 171.

72. Redpath, "A Southern Underground Telegraph," in *The Roving Editor*, 284–287.

73. Anderson, *A Voice from Harper's Ferry*, chapter II.

74. Redpath, *Public Life of Captain John Brown*, 200.

75. Sanborn, *Life and Letters of John Brown*, 470–477.

76. Ables, *Man on Fire*, 203.

77. Redpath, *Public Life of Captain John Brown*, 199–206.

78. Abels, *Man on Fire*, 209.

79. Ibid., 209–210.

80. Redpath, *Public Life of Captain John Brown*, 199–206.

81. Redpath, *Public Life of Captain John Brown*, 203.

82. Ibid., 672–675.

83. Ibid.

CHAPTER EIGHT: BY THE MIDNIGHT SKY AND THE SILENT STARS

1. Hinton, *John Brown and His Men*, 218.

2. Ibid., 221.

3. Ibid., 222.

4. Abels, *Man on Fire*, 222.

5. Ibid., 226.

6. Mortimer Thomson, "The Kansas War. The Disturbances in Southern Kansas—Brown and Montgomery—Facts of the Case," *New York Times*, January 28, 1859.

7. Abels, *Man on Fire*, 78.

8. Ruchames, ed., *John Brown*, 224–225.

9. Ibid., 223–226, Phillips's interviews also in Hinton, *John Brown and His Men*, appendix.

10. Redpath, *Public Life of Captain John Brown*, 48.

11. Sanborn, *Life and Letters of John Brown*, 483.

12. Account of Samuel Harper in Hamilton, *John Brown in Canada*, 4–5.

13. Abels, *Man on Fire*, 228.

14. Ibid.

15. Sanborn, *Life and Letters of John Brown*, 491.

16. Hinton, *John Brown and His Men*, 227–228.

17. Hamilton, *John Brown in Canada*, 3.

18. Bancroft, *Slave Trading in the Old South*, 224.

19. Ibid., 225.

20. Mortimer Thomson, "A Great Slave Auction, 400 Men, Women and Children Sold," *New York Tribune*, March 9, 1859, cited in Bancroft, *Slave Trading in the Old South*.

21. Ibid., 227.

22. Ibid.

23. Ibid., 235.

24. Foner, ed., *The Life and Writings of Frederick Douglass*, vol. 5, 426.

25. Ibid., 425.

26. Garnet's speech in Sterling Stuckey, ed., *The Ideological Origins of Black Nationalism*, 183.

27. Report in the *Cleveland Leader*, March 22, 1859, in Redpath, *Public Life of Captain John Brown*, 239–240.

28. *The Life and Times of Frederick Douglass*, 317.

29. A Plan of Anti-Slavery Action, in *Life and Writings of Frederick Douglass*, Foner, ed., vol. 5, 453–454.

30. Hinton, *John Brown and His Men*, 238–239.

31. Abels, *Man on Fire*, 241.

32. Conrad, *Harriet Tubman*, 101.

33. Ibid., 103.

34. Quoted from *New York Herald*, September 22, 1907, in ibid., 101.

35. Diary of A. Bronson Alcott in Sanborn, *Life and Letters of John Brown*, 504–505.

36. Oswald Garrison Villard, *John Brown*, 396.

37. Higginson, *Cheerful Yesterdays*, 223.

38. Abels, *Man on Fire*, 238.

39. Ibid., 239–240.

40. Sanborn, writing in the *Commonwealth*, July 17, 1863, quoted in Conrad, *Harriet Tubman*, 120.

41. Conrad, *Harriet Tubman*, 120.

42. *Letters and Journals of Thomas Wentworth Higginson, 1846–1906*, 81.

43. Abels, *Man on Fire*, 259.

44. Alcott in his diary entry in Sanborn, *Life and Letters of John Brown*, 504–505.

45. Letter from Brown to Kagi, July 12, 1859, in Sanborn, *Life and Letters of John Brown*, 533.

CHAPTER NINE: INTO THE UNTRIED FUTURE

1. Ruchames, ed., *John Brown*, 283.

2. Villard, *John Brown*; Salmon Brown interviewed by Katherine Mayo.

3. Abels, *Man on Fire*, 256.

4. Sanborn, *Life and Letters of John Brown*, 541.

5. Ibid.

6. Letter in Hinton, *John Brown and His Men*, 259.

7. John Brown Jr. to Kagi, Aug. 11, 1859, in Sanborn, *Life and Letters of John Brown*, 536.

8. Ibid.

9. Ibid.

10. Ibid.

11. Ibid.

12. Sanborn, *Life and Letters of John Brown*, 538.

13. Ibid.

14. *The Life and Times of Frederick Douglass*, 319.

15. In Douglass's speech at Storer College in 1881; in Ruchames, ed., *John Brown*, 294.

16. *Life and Times of Frederick Douglass*, 275.

17. See "The Prospect for the Future," in *Douglass' Monthly*, Aug. 1860—"The Future of the Abolition Cause," April 1861—"Nemesis," June 1861—"Danger to the Abolition Cause," July 1861—"Notes of the War," etc., in Foner, ed., *The Life and Writings of Frederick Douglass*, vol. 3.

18. Douglass, "How to End the War," *Frederick Douglass' Monthly*, May 1861.

19. Letter to Hon. Gerrit Smith, March 6, 1863, in Foner, ed., *The Life and Writings of Frederick Douglass*, vol. 3, 320.

20. Filler, ed., *Wendell Phillips on Civil Rights and Freedom*, 114–136; Ralph Waldo Emerson, *Complete Works*, 1208–1213.

21. "The Proclamation and A Negro Army," February 1863; "Another Word to Colored Men," April 1863, in Foner, ed., *The Life and Writings of Frederick Douglass*, vol. 3, 321–344, 344–347.

22. Douglass speech at Storer College, Harpers Ferry, West Virginia, May 30, 1881.

23. *Life and Times of Frederick Douglass*, 319.

24. Ibid., 320.

25. Sanborn, *Life and Letters of John Brown*, 504–505.

26. Ibid., 506.

27. Ibid., 547–548.

28. Hinton, *John Brown and His Men*, 262.

29. Jonathan Katz, *Resistance at Christiana*, John Brown Jr.'s letter cited, 281.

30. Hinton, *John Brown and His Men*, 251.

31. Sanborn, *Life and Letters of John Brown*, 535.

32. Ibid., 544.

33. Anderson, *A Voice from Harper's Ferry*, chapter V.

34. Hinton, *John Brown and His Men*, 262–263.

35. Anderson, *A Voice from Harper's Ferry*, chapter V; letter dated September 14, 1859.

36. Hinton, *John Brown and His Men*, 262.

37. Sanborn, *Life and Letters of John Brown*, 541.

38. Conrad, *Harriet Tubman*, 124–125.

39. Hinton, *John Brown and His Men*, 570.

40. Ibid.

41. Hinton, *John Brown and His Men*, 253.

42. Ibid., 255.

43. Abels, *Man on Fire*, 265.

44. Reports of Senate Committees, 36th Congress, 1st Session, No. 278, Testimony of John B. Floyd, 250–252.

45. John Brown Jr. to Kagi, August 27, 1859, quoted in Quarles, *Allies for Freedom*, 75.

46. Anderson, *A Voice from Harper's Ferry.*

47. Cohen, *John Brown: A Pictorial Heritage*, 64; letter no. 8, dated September 27, 1859, facsimile of a sheet from the *Baltimore Sun.*

48. Anderson, *A Voice from Harper's Ferry*, chapter VII.

49. Villard, *John Brown*, 422–423.

50. Ibid., chapter III.

51. Abels, *Man on Fire*, 257.

52. Ross, *Memoirs of a Reformer*, 91–92.

53. Interview with John Brown Jr., by Eleanor Atkinson in "The Soul of John Brown," *American Magazine*, 640.

54. Ibid. Henry David Thoreau, *The Last Days of John Brown.*

55. Cited in Atkinson, "The Soul of John Brown."

56. Ralph Waldo Emerson, *Complete Writings*, "The Emancipation Proclamation," 1213–1214.

Bibliography

Abels, Jules. *Man on Fire: John Brown and the Cause of Liberty*. New York: Macmillan, 1971.

Anderson, Osborne Perry. *A Voice from Harper's Ferry: A Narrative of Events at Harper's Ferry; with Incidents Prior and Subsequent to Its Capture by Captain Brown and His Men*. Boston: Privately printed, 1861.

Aptheker, Herbert. *American Negro Slave Revolts*. New York: International Publishers, 1963.

———. *A Documentary History of the Negro People in the United States, Vol. 1: Colonial Times to the Civil War*. New York: Citadel Press, 1951.

Atkinson, Eleanor. "The Soul of John Brown." *American Magazine* (October 1909).

Bancroft, Frederic. *Slave Trading in the Old South*. 1931. Reprint. Columbia: University of South Carolina Press, 1995.

Bayliss, John F., ed. *Black Slave Narratives*. New York: Collier Books, 1970.

Bondi, August. "With John Brown in Kansas." *Transactions of the Kansas State Historical Society*, vol. 8.

Bordewich, Fergus M. *Bound for Canaan: The Underground Railroad and the War for the Soul of America*. New York: Amistad, 2005.

Campbell, Stanley. *The Slave Catchers: Enforcement of the Fugitive Slave Law, 1850–1860*. Chapel Hill: University of North Carolina Press, 1970.

Cobbe, Frances P., ed. *Theodore Parker, Collected Works*, vol. V. London: Truebner, 1863.

Cohen, Stan. *John Brown: A Pictorial Heritage*. Pictorial Histories, 1999.

Conrad, Earl. *Harriet Tubman: Negro Soldier and Abolitionist*. New York: International Publishers, 1942.

Derrida, Jacques. *Specters of Marx: The State of the Debt, the Work of Mourning, and the New International*. Trans. Peggy Kamuf; with an introduction by Bernd Magnus and Stephen Cullenberg. New York: Routledge, 1994.

Dillon, Merton Lynn. *The Abolitionists: The Growth of a Dissenting Minority*. New York: W. W. Norton, 1979.

Douglass, Frederick. *Life and Times of Frederick Douglass* (1881, revised 1892). Reprint. New York: Thomas Crowell, 1966.

DuBois, W. E. B. *John Brown: A Biography*. 1909. Reprint. Introduction by
    David R. Roediger. New York: Modern Library, 2001.
————. *The Negro*. New York: Holt, 1915. Reprint. Mineola, N.Y.: Dover,
    2001.
Dumond, Dwight Lowell. *AntiSlavery: The Crusade for Freedom in America*.
    Ann Arbor: University of Michigan Press, 1961.
Dunayevskaya, Raya. *Marxism and Freedom*, 4th ed. New York: Columbia
    University Press, 1988.
Emerson, E. W., and W. E. Forbes, eds. *Journals of Ralph Waldo Emerson*.
    Boston: Houghton Mifflin, 1909.
Emerson, Ralph Waldo. *The Complete Works of Ralph Waldo Emerson*. New
    York: William H. Wise & Co., 1929.
Foner, Philip S. *Frederick Douglass: Selected Speeches and Writings*. Chicago:
    Chicago Review Press, 2000.
————. *The Life and Writings of Frederick Douglass*. 5 vols. New York:
    International Publishers, 1950–1975.
————. *The Voices of Black America: Major Speeches by Negroes in the United
    States, 1797–1971*. New York: Simon and Schuster, 1972.
Garrison, William Lloyd. *A Letter to Louis Kossuth; Concerning Freedom and
    Slavery in the United States*. Boston: R. F. Wallcut, 1852.
Hamilton, James C. *John Brown in Canada*. 1894.
Hedrick, Joan D. *Harriet Beecher Stowe, A Life*. New York: Oxford University
    Press, 1994.
Higginson, Thomas Wentworth. *Cheerful Yesterdays*. 1899. Reprint. New
    York: Arno Press, 1968.
————. *A Ride Through Kansas*. New York, 1856.
Hinton, Richard J. *John Brown and His Men*. 1894. Reprint. New York: Ayer,
    1968.
Holland, *Frederick Douglass: The Colored Orator*. New York: Funk &
    Wagnalls, 1891.
Katz, Jonathan. *Resistance at Christiana: The Fugitive Slave Rebellion,
    Christiana, Pennsylvania, September 11, 1851, a Documentary Account*. New
    York: Crowell, 1974.
Loguen, J. W. *The Rev. J. W. Loguen, As a Slave and As a Freeman: A Narrative
    of Real Life*. Syracuse, N.Y.: J. G. K. Truair & Co., 1859.
Marx, Karl. *The 18th Brumaire of Louis Bonaparte*. Sterling, Va.: Pluto Press,
    2002.
————. *The Letters of Karl Marx*, trans. and ed. Saul K. Padover. Englewood
    Cliffs, N.J.: Prentice-Hall, 1979.
————. Preface to *A Contribution to the Critique of Political Economy*.
    Cambridge: Cambridge University Press, 1996.
Marx, Karl, and Frederick Engels. *The Civil War in the United States*. New
    York: International Publishers, 1961.

McMillen, Sally. *Seneca Falls and the Origins of the Women's Rights Movement.* New York: Oxford University Press, 2008.

McPherson, James M. *Battle Cry of Freedom: The Civil War Era.* New York: Oxford University Press, 1988.

Monaghan, Jay. *Civil War on the Western Border, 1854–1865.* Lincoln: University of Nebraska Press, 1985.

Negri, Antonio. *Marx Beyond Marx: Lessons on the Grundrisse.* South Hadley, Mass.: Bergin & Garvey, 1984.

Nelson, Truman, ed. *Documents of Upheaval: Selections from William Lloyd Garrison's The Liberator, 1831–1865.* New York: Hill and Wang, 1966.

Ofari, Earl. *"Let Your Motto Be Resistance": The Life and Thought of Henry Garnet Highland.* Boston: Beacon Press, 1972.

Phillips, Wendell. *Speeches, Lectures, and Letters.* Boston: Lee and Shepard, 1884.

———. *Wendell Phillips on Civil Rights and Freedom,* ed. Louis Filler. Lanham, Md.: University Press of America, 1982.

Phillips, William A. *The Conquest of Kansas by Missouri and Her Allies: A History of the Troubles in Kansas from the Passage of the Organic Act Until the Close of July 1856.* Boston: Phillips, Sampson and Co., 1856.

Quarles, Benjamin. *Allies for Freedom: Blacks and John Brown.* New York: Oxford University Press, 1974.

———. *Black Abolitionists.* New York: Oxford University Press, 1970.

———. *Frederick Douglass.* New York: Macmillan, 1968.

Redpath, James. *Public Life of Captain John Brown.* Boston: Thayer & Eldridge, 1860.

———. *The Roving Editor.* New York. 1859.

Richman, Irving Berdine. *John Brown Among the Quakers.* Des Moines: Historical Department of Iowa, 1894.

Rollin, Frank A. [Frances Rollin Whipper]. *Life and Public Service of Major Martin R. Delany.* Boston. 1868. Reprint. New York: Arno Press & New York Times, 1969.

Ross, Alexander M. *Memoirs of a Reformer.* Toronto. Hunter, Rose, 1893.

———. *Recollection and Experiences of an Abolitionist,* Toronto: Rowsell & Hutchison, 1876.

Ross, Michael A. *Justice of Shattered Dreams: Samuel Freeman Miller and the Supreme Court During the Civil War Era.* Baton Rouge: LSU Press, 2003.

Ruchames, Louis, ed. *John Brown: The Making of a Revolutionary.* New York: Grosset & Dunlap, 1969.

Sanborn, Franklin B. "John Brown in Massachusetts." *Atlantic Monthly,* April 1872.

———. *The Life and Letters of John Brown: Liberator of Kansas and Martyr of Virginia.* Reprint. Boston: Roberts, 1891.

Sherwin, Oscar. *Prophet of Liberty: The Life and Times of Wendell Phillips.* New York: Bookman Associates, 1958.

Stearns, Frank Preston. *The Life and Public Services of George Luther Stearns.* 1907. Reprint. New York, Arno Press, 1969.

Sterling, Dorothy. *The Making of an Afro-American: Martin Robison Delany.* Garden City, N.Y.: Doubleday, 1971.

Stuckey, Sterling. *The Ideological Origins of Black Nationalism.* Boston: Beacon Press, 1972.

Thoreau, Henry David. *A Plea for Captain John Brown: Read to the Citizens of Concord, Massachusetts on Sunday Evening, October Thirtieth, Eighteen Fifty-Nine.* 1859. Reprint. Boston: David R. Godine, 1969.

———. *The Portable Thoreau.* Carl Bode, ed. New York: Viking Press, 1947.

Villard, Oswald G. *John Brown, 1800–1859: A Biography Fifty Years After.* 1910. Reprint. New York: A. A. Knopf, 1943.

Watch, Richard, and Jonathan P. Fanton, eds. *John Brown.* Englewood Cliffs, N.J.: Prentice-Hall, 1973.

Webb, Richard D., ed. *The Life and Letters of Captain John Brown.* London: Smith, Elder & Co., 1861.

Weiss, John. *Life and Correspondence of Theodore Parker*, vol. 1. New York: D. Appleton, 1864.

Wiltse, Charles M. *John C. Calhoun: Sectionalist, 1840–1850.* Indianapolis: Bobbs-Merrill, 1951.

Index

War of 1812, 24
Washington, Madison, 83
Watson, Henry, 267, 274-275, 281
Wattles, Augustus, 160, 168, 189, 235, 241-
    243
Webb, William, 250-251
Webster, Daniel, 70-71, 83, 88-91, 104, 108-
    109, 142
Weed, Thurlow, 152
Weekly Anglo African, tenor of John Brown's
    reception and, 218
Weiner, Theodore, 144
Weitling, Wilhelm, 52
Weld, Theodore, 22-23, 25, 28, 57, 99
Wellington, 25
Wesleyan Methodist Chapel, 79
Western Anti-Slavery Society, 56, 59
Western New York Anti-Slavery Society, 48
West India, 12, 14-15, 57, 75, 117, 211, 222
West India Committee, 211
Weston Argus, Civil War headline and, 162
Westport (Missouri) Sharpshooters, 146
Wheaton, Charles, 109
Whipper, Frances Rollin, 221
Whipper, William, 35, 40, 214
White, Horace, 170
White, William A., 48
Whitfield, J. M., 119, 129, 148, 165
Whitman, Edmund, 189, 197-198
Whitney, Eli, 15-16, 260
Whittier, John Greenleaf, 12, 90, 175
Wiener, Theodore, 151
Wilberforce Institute, 219
Wilberforce, William, 55
Wilhelm IV, Friedrich, 74
Willetts, Jacob, 246
Wilmot, David, 65, 77, 87-89
Wilmot Proviso, 77, 87-89
Wilson, Henry, 96, 228, 264
Wilson, William J., 96
Winkely, Johnathan, 161
Winters, Joseph, 274
Wood, George, 101
Woodson, Daniel, 161-162
Woodson, Lewis, 40
Worcester Spy, anti-Nebraska articles and,
    136
Words of Advice (Brown), 102
World Anti-Slavery Convention, 38, 212
Wright, James N.S.T., 55
Wright, Martha, 78
Wright, Theodore S., 40, 48, 211

Young Hegelians, 50, 52

Zwanzinger, 51

Acknowledgments

M y first book's reader and publisher, Bruce H. Franklin of Westholme
Publishing, must have apprehended something of the mood dictating
that text, which I titled *To Raise Up a Nation*; distilled entirely through that
singular encounter of the two principals of my interest—Frederick Douglass
and John Brown, and their fated engagement outside Chambersburg,
Pennsylvania, in August 1859. A second was Oliver St. Clair Franklin of
Philadelphia, honorary chairman of that city's Civil War Museum, who later
told of how he'd seen the cover of that book in a book store with its depiction
of the 54th Regiment Massachusetts Volunteer Infantry assaulting Fort
Wagner—a point of memory for him that had adorned a wall at his grandpar-
ents' home. Another of the readers I must salute is John David Smith, the distinguished Civil War scholar and professor at the University of North Carolina
at Charlotte, who provided a generous assessment seen of the back cover of
the first book. Another was Rich Rosenthal, president of the Northern New
Jersey Civil War Round Table, who garnered other valued readers in the round
table's meeting acknowledging this author, a New Jersey resident.

Bruce initially broached the proposition—if I should want to write another
book on the subject he would publish it. Giving it consideration, I realized I
had the material and drive for a fresh approach, and consented: ten months
later I'd written *Till the Dark Angel Comes*. After discarding a previous title,
this was only designation I ever considered, a fragment found in Frank Preston
Stearns's biography of his father, in lines written by Rev. Edmund Sears,
Unitarian minister:

> John Brown shall tramp the quaking earth
> From Blue Ridge to the sea:
> Till the dark angel comes again,
> And opes each prison door;
> And God's great charter yet shall wave
> O'er all his humble poor.

There is, too, my family: My wife, *Patricia*, with an ear for the nuances of language, who consenting to hear passages I'd written, would softly encourage "go on, now," when, thinking I'd read too long, I'd break off. And our daughters: Cheryl, supremely patient with her father who ushered him falteringly toward these new writing machines; and Claudia, who fortifies me with the thought she is my fiercest partisan.

I am grateful, again, to those at Westholme who have assisted in bring *Till the Dark Angel Comes* to fruition—copy editor Noreen O'Connor-Abel, cover designer Trudi Gershenov, proofreader Mike Kopf, and indexer John Hulse.